# THE COMPETENT CHILD

# The Competent Child

## AN APPROACH TO PSYCHOTHERAPY
## AND PREVENTIVE MENTAL HEALTH

JOSEPH M. STRAYHORN
*University of Pittsburgh*

THE GUILFORD PRESS
*New York   London*

© 1988 The Guilford Press
A Division of Guilford Publications, Inc.
72 Spring Street, New York, NY 10012

Printed in the United States of America

Last digit is print number: 9   8   7   6   5   4   3   2   1


Library of Congress Cataloging-in-Publication Data
Strayhorn, Joseph M.
    The competent child.

    Includes bibliographies and index.
    1. Child psychotherapy.   2. Mental illness—
Prevention.   3. Parent and child.   4. School children—
Mental health.   I. Title.   [DNLM: 1. Mental Disorders—
prevention & control.   2. Mental Health—in infancy &
childhood.   3. Psychotherapy—in infancy & childhood.
WS 105.5.M3 S913c]
RJ504.S77   1988        618.92'8914        87-21086
ISBN 0-89862-710-9

# *Preface and Acknowledgments*

This book provides a conceptual framework that seems to make possible an integration of nearly all I have learned about psychotherapy and preventive mental health that seems useful and helpful. The premise is simple: There are certain competences we want to see children develop, and certain methods of promoting those competences; we can keep things straight more easily if we try to list those ends and those means, and decide systematically which to adopt at which times. Much of the vast and fascinating literature on psychotherapy consists of an in-depth elaboration on one or another competence, or one or another method of influence. In this book I attempt to climb up the "abstraction ladder" to a height where we may see the forest comprising those trees. On the other hand, I frequently climb down the abstraction ladder to focus in on limbs and leaves as well, presenting some of the exact words that I find useful in communicating with parents and children. I hope that the lives of some children and families may be enriched as a result of our climbing expedition.

I acknowledge with gratitude those who have helped me in this project, only some of whom are named here. The Pittsburgh Child Guidance Center Foundation funded a research venture and a clinic that exposed me in large doses to the issues discussed in this book. Two grants from the National Institute of Mental Health, one a New Investigator Research Award (MH39461) and the other a research project grant (MH41127), also partially funded this work. (This book is not a report of that research itself, but a summary of the clinical and theoretical background that guides it.) Sharon Panulla and Judith Grauman at The Guilford Press have been most helpful to me in bringing this work to publication. Staff members at the Matilda Theiss Center and the Pittsburgh Board of Education have provided access to children and parents. Pamela Bram, Frederic Hine, Richard

Martini, Alan Bedell, and Clair Cohen have given valuable feedback in refining this book. Carla Weidman, my colleague in the research endeavor, and the staff of the preschool research project have helped me gain insight into the uses of these methods in prevention; Ursula Schwartz, my colleague in the clinic, has also given quite valuable feedback and encouragement, while applying her talent to testing and using the methods described herein. Naomi Wenkert Strayhorn has provided useful comments on the manuscript and much support in the writing. The parents and children and other individuals I have known who have worked very hard at the task of psychological growth have taught me much, and have given me much that is valuable; they and others like them give us reason for hope that life can be made better. Finally, I would like to express great appreciation and gratitude to Catherine Strayhorn for her patient efforts on my behalf that began, but did not end, a long time ago when I was trying to be a competent child.

# Contents

1. THE NATURE OF THE SKILLS × METHODS MATRIX      1

*The Structure of the Theory, 2; Some Case Illustrations, 3;
Conceptual Uses of the Matrix, 10; The Place of Learning-Based
Treatment in the Total Armamentarium, 13; Alternatives to the
Competence Orientation, 14; The Matrix as an Emerging
Framework in the Field of Mental Health, 19*

2. THE SKILLS AXIS      21

*Symptom Clusters Should Not Determine Direction of Psychotherapy,
22; Skills Concepts and Their Advantages, 23; The Nine Major
Groups of Skills, 26; The Length of the Skills Axis, 41; Contracting
the Skills Axis, 42; The Central Vignette of Helping, 43*

3. MAKING DIAGNOSES ON THE SKILLS AXIS      45

*Thinking Scientifically about Skills-Oriented Diagnoses, 46;
Gathering Information for Skills-Oriented Diagnoses, 47; Ability
versus Motivation, and Self-Motivation as a Skill, 49; Inferences
Concerning the "Fantasy Repertoire," 50; Questionnaire
Information Regarding Psychological Skills, 51; Diagnosis of Skills
Sufficiencies, 54; Skills-Oriented Diagnosis with Families, 54;
Defining a Skillful Response, 56; Inferring Causal Relations
between Skill Deficiencies and Symptoms, 58*

4. SKILLS-ORIENTED CONTINGENCY PROGRAMS      60

*Choosing Target Skills for Treatment, 61; Keeping Records, 62;
Moving Down the Abstraction Ladder to Positive Examples, 62;
Baseline Observations, 64; Preparing to Reinforce Positive
Examples, 66; Helping Parents to Recognize "Trigger Situations,"
67; Establishing Routine Nightly Feedback and Review, 69; Rapid
Implementation of the Monitoring and Rewarding Procedure, 70;
Deciding How Many Demands to Make upon Parents, 70;
Nontraditional Aspects of the Procedure, 71; Dealing with
Undesirable Behaviors, 76; A Checklist for Contingency Programs,
78; Who Reinforces Parents?, 78; Fading versus Continuing
Contingency Programs, 80; When the Problems Exist at School and
Not at Home, 81*

5. THE METHODS AXIS                                                                  82

*Goal Setting, 83; Forming a Hierarchy, 86; Modeling, 87;
Providing Instruction, 92; Providing Practice Opportunities, 93;
Controlling Stimulus Situations, 95; Monitoring Progress, 97;
Controlling or Communicating Consequences, 98; Attribution, 103;
The Skills × Methods Matrix as a General Framework for Mental
Health Promotion, 104*

6. TECHNIQUES FOR SESSIONS WITH YOUNG
   CHILDREN                                                                           107

*Moving Down the Abstraction Ladder Using Fantasy, 108; The
Therapist's Sessions as Laying Groundwork for Parents' Sessions,
109; "Contaminating" the Child's Fantasies: Problem or Tool?,
110; The Concept of a "Versatile Vehicle," 110; The Techniques,
111; Literature on the Usefulness of Dramatic Play and Story
Reading, 136*

7. TECHNIQUES FOR SESSIONS WITH OLDER
   CHILDREN AND ADOLESCENTS                                                           141

*Techniques for Grade-School-Age Children, 143; Techniques for
Adolescents and Older Individuals, 157*

8. TRAINING PARENTS AND OTHERS TO HAVE
   SESSIONS WITH CHILDREN                                                             169

*The Centrality of Mutual Gratification in the Parent–Child
Relationship, 170; The Individual Parent–Child Session as a
Vehicle for Parent Training, 171; Steps in Training Parents to
Hold Sessions with Their Children, 172; Promoting Generalization
to Home Interaction, 184; Increasing Psychological Competences in
Parents, 186; When Parents Have Severe Skill Deficits or Lack
Motivation, 193; The Empirical Literature on Teaching Lay People
to Work with Children, 194*

9. DIFFICULTIES IN PRODUCING POSITIVE RESULTS:
   THE TWO DILUTION EFFECTS                                                           199

*Is It Difficult to Produce Positive Mental Health Outcomes?, 200;
The Question for This Chapter and the Nature of the Answer, 203;
Examples and Implications of the First Dilution Effect (Too Many
Skills), 204; Remedies for the First Dilution Effect, 206; Examples
and Implications of the Second Dilution Effect (Too Many
Influences), 208; Remedies for the Second Dilution Effect, 210*

10. APPLICATION OF THE MATRIX TO PREVENTIVE
    MENTAL HEALTH                                                                     213

*Rationales for Interventions in Community Settings, 214; Possible
Hazards of Generalizing Methods from Therapy to Prevention, 215;
Responses to Possible Objections, 215; Competence-Oriented*

*Prevention Programs in the Literature, 218; The Range of Possible
Prevention Programs, 222; Work in Progress, and Work That
Should Be in Progress, 225; Data Bases and Downloading of
Competent Patterns in the Information Age, 232*

11. RESEARCH QUESTONS                                                           236

*The Skills Axis: Measurement and Assessment Techniques, 238; The
Methods Axis: Measurement and Assessment Techniques, 245;
Studies Connected with Dilution Effects, 249; Outcome Studies of
Preventive Intervention, 250; Studies Relevant to the
Competence-Promoting Culture, 250; The Most Useful Applied
Study, 252*

APPENDICES                                                                      253

*Appendix 1. Summary Suggestions for Parents, 253; Appendix 2.
Stories That Model Psychological Skills, 255; Appendix 3. Modeling
Plays for Preschoolers or Young Grade-School Children, 268;
Appendix 4. Sample Situations for Fantasy Practice, 272; Appendix
5. Conceptual Sharpening Exercises: A Story Illustrating Cognitive
Responses, 277; Appendix 6. Exercises Using the Inner Guide, 280;
Appendix 7. Written Exercises for Psychological Skill Building, 283*

REFERENCES                                                                      287

INDEX                                                                           301

# CHAPTER 1

# The Nature of the Skills × Methods Matrix

## OVERVIEW

Two concepts central to this book are those of "psychological skills" and "methods of influence." "Psychological skills" are adaptive patterns of thought, feeling, and behavior, employed in ways appropriate for particular circumstances; each skill contributes to overall competence, which can be called "mental health." Examples of such skills are frustration tolerance, conflict resolution, relaxation, and trusting and depending. "Methods of influence" are the ways in which the learning of such skills is promoted; examples are insight-oriented goal setting, modeling, practice, and reinforcement contingencies. The central thesis of this book is that many of the useful strategies from seemingly disparate approaches to psychotherapy can be integrated in a construct I call the "skills × methods matrix."

The skills × methods matrix may serve as a guide to the conduct of child psychotherapy. We may conceive of the clinician's job as determining the highest-priority skills for the child or family to learn, and then determining and carrying out the most effective methods of promoting those skills. This matrix is a suitable framework for viewing therapy from a variety of orientations, including psychodynamic approaches, and not just those derived from social learning theory or cognitive–behavioral theory. The matrix may also be a conceptual model for predicting and explaining the learning-based component of the development of psychopathology: Maladaptive learned patterns in each of the skill areas may be promoted by the same mechanisms as may the adaptive patterns. Furthermore, the matrix may be a useful structure for theories of developmental psychology: Each of the skills may be thought of as a developmental line. And finally, the matrix serves as a guide to preventive mental health interventions: When mechanisms exist to deliver positive influences in psychological skill development to large numbers of the children, we have the wherewithal for primary prevention in mental health. The same skills combine to constitute mental health, whether we promote them after a disorder has arisen or in the absence of a disorder.

Despite its versatility, the matrix is directed only toward the "learning-based" fraction of the total variation in behavior; it complements rather than opposes conceptions of biological and situational influences. It applies to most, but not all, that is useful in psychotherapy. The general orientation of the matrix is much more complex than the often harmful orientation toward getting negative feelings "out." According to the theory embraced here, expressing negative feelings may be helpful at times to the extent that such expression is a step toward, or the actual accomplishment of, a pattern of thought, feeling, and behavior that is useful in living; we should not conceive of it as a way of expelling from oneself such negative feelings.

The skills × methods matrix is a construct whose implicit use seems to be growing in the mental health literature; this book attempts to make the use of that matrix more explicit and more fully elaborated.

---

A family brings a child to a clinician, complaining of any of a variety of symptoms: conduct problems, self-defeating behavior, academic problems, fears, unhappiness, psychosomatic symptoms, or interpersonal difficulties. Some time later, the family emerges from psychotherapeutic treatment with the child's symptoms drastically reduced or absent. What has happened? How has this result come about? Why doesn't it happen more often? And can the same good thing that happened to this hypothetical lucky child somehow also be made to happen to vast numbers of other children, before they develop symptoms in the first place, without having to come to a psychotherapist? This book takes on these questions. The answers all revolve around the notion of learning to do something better—the attainment of greater psychological competence.

In approaching these questions, this book presents a theory, a way of thinking about seemingly disparate ways of promoting mental health. In addition, it presents some of the concrete and specific techniques dictated by this theory.

## THE STRUCTURE OF THE THEORY

The theory set forward here integrates strategies that many effective psychotherapists are already using. These strategies are not entirely subsumed by any one school of therapy, but are more coherently organized than the vague word "eclectic" would suggest. The best descriptor for the orientation taken here is the "competence-based approach."

Let us define the competence-based approach by giving its general prescription. The job of the therapist or the preventive mental health specialist is *to choose and enact, for a given person or a given group, the most useful cells from a two-dimensional matrix formed by a set of competences (or skills) and a set of competence-promoting methods (or methods of influence).* In plainer language, the job of those who would promote mental health is (1) to decide what the target persons need to learn to do better, and (2) to pick the best ways to influence them toward such learning.

One of the tasks this book undertakes is actually to list both the competences and the influence methods felt to be most important in clinical psychotherapy and preventive mental health. I refer to these lists as the "skills axis" and the "methods axis," respectively.

Once these axes are delineated, however, the theory can do more than provide a way of describing what most competent therapists already do. The axes provide a systematic way of finding useful strategies for therapy and prevention, and constitute, in other words, a device for facilitating appropriate decision making. In this book, we examine some concrete and possibly innovative ways of working with children and families—ways that are suggested by examining the various possible combinations of skills and influence methods. In addition, the way of thinking about human behavior that is implied by the two axes and by the matrix they form generates a variety of hypotheses regarding both the possibilities and the limitations of mental health intervention.

## SOME CASE ILLUSTRATIONS

To avoid dealing too completely in abstractions, and to form a mental image of the matrix that is referred to throughout this book, let us examine some cases briefly and see how the interventions can be integrated into this orientation.

A 4-year-old boy was brought to the clinic by his mother. His former preschool teacher described him as "sadistic" and reported that he had no friends. His mother reported that he used profanity toward her daily and physically attacked her at least once a day. Each night, he refused to go to bed when directed to do so, and he and his mother engaged in a bedtime power struggle lasting several hours. On the first clinic visit, when he was ready to leave the session and his mother demurred, he literally slapped her in the face.

What skills or competences constituted the opposites of the negative patterns that the child exhibited? In this case, the therapist and the parent decided to emphasize the psychological skills of (1) taking pleasure in doing kind, considerate, cooperative things; (2) complying with reasonable authority; and (3) tolerating frustration calmly and without aggression or other maladaptive responses. We may think of these skills as listed vertically on the left, naming the rows of our matrix.

The mother was taught to enact a skill-oriented contingency program of the sort to be described in Chapter 4. She began to watch very closely for examples in his behavior of any of these skills, and to provide attention and approval whenever she noted an example; she used the mild punishment of "time out" when her child responded to frustration by aggression or defiantly refused to comply. This portion of the treatment was an example of the use of *consequences* as a competence-promoting method. In addition, the treatment invoked the principle that children tend to imitate what they see and hear. The therapist constructed stories for the mother to read to the child; these stories were written so as to model the skills on the priority list, giving the child concrete examples of the types of behavior, thought, and feeling that were desired from him. We may think of these two methods—the use of consequences, and modeling through stories—as heading the columns of the matrix.

The matrix for this case may be depicted as follows:

|  | Methods | |
| --- | --- | --- |
| Skills | Consequences: approval, time out | Modeling through fiction |
| Pleasure from kindness |  |  |
| Frustration tolerance |  |  |
| Compliance |  |  |

The results with this child were positive. One of the modeling stories his mother read to him contained an incident wherein a boy wanted something from his mother; he saw her resting and decided to wait until later and not disturb her. The character in the story felt good about helping his mother in this way. A couple of days after reading the child this story, the mother was actually lying on a couch with her eyes closed. She heard her son and his 3-year-old sister run into the room. Then she heard him say to his sister, "She's resting; let's not bother her." When the mother heard this comment she was astonished, because his behavior was so out of character with what she had seen until that time. She then realized that his behavior was an imitation of the modeling story that she had read to him. This event increased her enthusiasm for further use of "modeling stories." Over the course of the entire program (which involved more than I go into here), this child's behavior improved rapidly; within 3 or 4 months, all of the problems mentioned above had totally ceased. At that time, the mother began to turn her attention to other skills that demanded attention less urgently.

This book goes into some detail concerning the methods mentioned in this case: setting up consequences for behavior based on high-priority skills, and using stories and dramatic play to provide models of those skills. But I wish to emphasize that the competence-based approach does not confine itself to methods derived from social learning theory or from behavioral or cognitive–behavioral therapists. To illustrate this fact, let us look at some examples described by psychoanalytic therapists. With some inevitable allowance for incomplete communication of what actually took place, portions of these case histories can be translated into competence-oriented language. The following example is from Anna Freud (1946, p. 11):

> [A 10-year-old boy] had recently developed . . . noisy outbursts of rage and naughtiness, which broke out for no intelligible outward reason and were very strange in this other wise inhibited and timid child. . . . Of them he was unmistakably proud, regarding them as something which distinguished him from others . . . he enjoyed the worry they caused his parents. He thus felt himself in a certain sense at one with this symptom, and would probably at that time have resisted any attempt to rid him of it with analytical help. But here I ambushed him in a not very honest way. I resolved to embroil him with that part of his nature, I made him describe the outbreaks as often as they came and showed myself concerned and thoughtful. I enquired how far in such states he was yet master of his action at all, and compared his fits of rage to those of a madman who would be beyond my aid. At that he was startled and

rather frightened, for to be regarded as mad naturally did not chime with his ambitions. He now tried himself to master these outbreaks, began to resist them instead of as earlier to encourage them. . . . The symptom finally, as I had intended, turned from a treasured possession into a disturbing foreign body, to fight which he only too readily claimed my help.

Was Anna Freud attempting to help a child learn to do something better, and if so, what? She describes this child as "inhibited and timid"; this is fairly similar to saying that the child was not very skilled at obtaining attention and social contact in appropriate ways. To say that he "enjoyed the worry [his symptoms] caused his parents" is similar to saying that he was not doing a very good job of choosing appropriate ways of obtaining attention from his parents. Without too much distortion, then, we can say that the therapist was helping the child to obtain attention and social contact in more appropriate ways, or, at the least, to stop obtaining them in an inappropriate way.

What method of influence did Anna Freud use in order to promote this improved competence? The conversation she describes effected a change in one of the child's goals: He became persuaded that his outbursts were something to work at avoiding, whereas before treatment he would not have espoused this goal. In Chapter 5 I speak of several methods of "goal setting"—ways of helping children or parents decide to work toward certain goals. In this case, Anna Freud carried out her persuasion not by argument and exhortation, but by adroit labeling, sometimes referred to as "reframing." Much of the insight obtained in "insight-oriented" therapy is achieved in the service of setting appropriate goals for self-change.

The matrix for this vignette, then, may be pictured as follows:

|  | Methods |
| --- | --- |
| Skills | Goal setting (persuasion through relabeling) |
| Obtaining social contact and attention in appropriate ways |  |

A third case example is described by another analyst, Selma Fraiberg (1967, pp. 229–287). An 8-year-old girl presented with

symptoms of withdrawal, moodiness, irritability, and defiance toward
her mother, with the feeling that her mother was persecuting her; she
also had epilepsy manifested by absence seizures. Fraiberg states,
"The major work during the first year of analysis had to do with the
defenses against affect" (p. 234). The child gradually began to talk
about and experience feelings of sexuality, anger, and affection that
she had apparently not considered permissible before. After noting a
recovery in the child's ability to experience genital sensation, where
before she had been "anesthetic" in her genital region, Fraiberg
states, "I can only guess that 'permission to talk' and the neutrality of
the analyst on the subject of having sexual feelings may have been
taken by the child as permission to have the feelings once again" (p.
237). Later the therapist helped the child's mother to stop disapproving of certain of the child's actions; up to that point, the child had
seen her mother's attitudes as prohibitions or threats concerning
masturbation and sexual feeling. The therapist reported that with
recovery of the child's ability to experience such feelings, "the per-
secutory feelings in relation to [the] mother disappeared from the
picture and there was a marked diminution of seizures. At the same
time, spontaneity returned to her personality and, in all areas, affect
became freer" (p. 238).

How would we conceptualize such material in terms of our
matrix? According to Fraiberg, this child certainly seemed to learn
to do certain things better. She became more competent at recognizing her own feelings, tolerating her own feelings without fearing
them or prohibiting them, and specifically not fearing her sexual
impulses. What methods were used to promote these competences? Fraiberg reasonably attributes much of the child's progress to
her having much opportunity to talk about such feelings in the sessions (i.e., to practice such new patterns of thought and emotion)
with the therapist. In response to such practice, Fraiberg provided the consequences of "neutrality" (a term that, I suspect, de-
notes a rather non-neutral nurturing interest). Furthermore, consequences of approval and disapproval as delivered by the mother
were also marshaled in favor of the development of these skills.
Using the language that I develop in more detail later, we might say
that the child was given "practice opportunities" for the skills in
question, together with favorable "consequences" from the analyst
and the parent.

The matrix for this case, then, would be as follows:

|  | Methods | |
| --- | --- | --- |
| Skills | Practice opportunities | Consequences |
| Being aware of one's own feelings |  |  |
| Tolerating a wide range of feelings in oneself without fearing them |  |  |
| Tolerating one's sexual impulses without fear |  |  |

A fourth case illustration is provided by Richard Gardner (1975, pp. 134–140). A 10½-year-old girl came to therapy because of facial tics, nail biting, emotional inhibition, preoccupation with thoughts that she was inadequate, and impaired self-assertion. "She was easily teased by friends and would not fight back. She poorly communicated her thoughts and feelings and became withdrawn and somber in situations that would arouse emotions—especially anger" (p. 134). Gardner describes the use of his "mutual storytelling method" with this child. The child, when prompted to make up an original story, told one about a dragon who got water up his nose so that he couldn't breathe fire out his nose any more; the dragon was cured of this malady by a doctor and was happy. Gardner interpreted this story as follows:

> I considered the dragon to represent [the child] herself and its inability to breathe fire an expression of repressed hostility. The fire, with its potential for massive destruction, well lends itself to symbolizing anger. Similarly, water—as the most potent antagonist to fire—lends itself well to the symbolization of those forces that squelch anger. (p. 136)

Gardner then responded with a story of his own in which the main character was also a dragon who could no longer breathe fire; in his story, however, the recovery of this ability required the protagonist's active participation. The dragon did some thinking about whether it was wrong to use his flame, and gradually overcame some fear of using the flame. He eventually was able to use the flame judiciously to keep people from taking advantage of him.

Here the skill that Gardner was attempting to foster was the appropriate use of self-assertion, and the method he employed was modeling through a fantasy that was fashioned to be as close to a spontaneous fantasy of the child as it could be.

The matrix for this vignette would be as follows:

| Skill | Method |
|---|---|
|  | Modeling (through fiction) |
| Self-assertion |  |

For our final example, let us examine not a description of one case, but a therapy manual developed by Kendall, Padawer, Zupan, and Braswell (in Kendall & Braswell, 1985, pp. 179–209). This manual describes a session-by-session approach to a "cognitive–behavioral" intervention for use with impulsive children. The child is first introduced to the consequences used in the treatment: Reward chips are given or taken away according to the child's performance, and these may buy tangible reinforcers such as puzzle books. The child is taught five "steps" to go through when faced with a problem: identifying the goal; generating possible solutions; "focusing in" on the task at hand; picking a solution; and monitoring the correctness of the solution and congratulating oneself if one did a good job. The therapist models the use of these steps in a variety of contexts. The child practices using these steps in a variety of cognitive tasks and puzzles, such as a checkers-like game. Then there is a unit on identifying emotions that someone else might be feeling in a hypothetical situation supplied by the therapist; the child practices making such inferences. Next, the child practices using the five steps with hypothetical interpersonal situations, mostly situations involving some conflict. After that, the child practices with hypothetical situations, role-playing the decided-upon response, rather than just telling what the response would be. Finally, the child uses the steps and practices the response, role-playing situations from his or her real life, rather than hypothetical situations.

According to the language of the skills axis described in this book, Kendall *et al.*'s program covers several different competences: thinking before acting, making decisions systematically, generating

multiple alternatives, using self-reinforcement, recognizing and labeling emotions, and dealing with interpersonal conflict. The methods
employed to promote these skills include tangible and social
reinforcement or response cost as consequences; modeling of appropriate verbalizations; direct instruction (e.g., the listing of the steps);
and the provision of many practice opportunities through verbal or
role-played response to hypothetical or real situations. Each of these
methods applies to each of the skills. Kendall *et al.*'s method may be
depicted in terms of the matrix as follows:

| Skills | Methods | | | |
|---|---|---|---|---|
| | Consequences | Modeling | Instruction | Practice |
| Thinking before acting | | | | |
| Decision making; generating multiple alternatives | | | | |
| Using self-reinforcement | | | | |
| Recognizing and labeling emotions | | | | |
| Decision making in situations of interpersonal conflict | | | | |

## CONCEPTUAL USES OF THE MATRIX

### The Matrix as a Structure for Psychotherapy Strategies

In the cases above, a total of 13 competences and 5 competence-
promoting methods are mentioned. A major thesis of this book is that
if we were to go on examining case after case, we could subsume a
very large fraction of the useful strategies of psychotherapy and
mental health education in a matrix consisting of some 62 skills and 9
methods of influence. The conclusion we come to by inductive rea-

soning from the case presented here and many others is that the skills × methods matrix provides a general framework with which we may unify our thinking about psychotherapy. The matrix provides a structure for organizing our strategies of helping—a structure that transcends the somewhat arbitrary boundaries separating one therapeutic orientation from another.

A unifying structure within which to conceptualize psychotherapeutic strategies should be quite useful, for a number of reasons. Perhaps foremost among these is that the current boundaries of psychotherapy permit and even encourage the focus upon certain competences or the employment of certain methods of influence according to the training and experience of the practitioner, not according to what is best for the individual in treatment. A certain analyst may be very likely to focus upon skills of tolerating dependence and independence, whereas a certain behavior therapist may be very likely to focus upon skills of assertion and relaxation; an analyst may primarily use the method of goal setting through insight, whereas a behaviorist may primarily use the methods of providing practice and manipulating consequences. In order to best serve the patient, the therapist should have in his or her repertoire the ability to promote those competences the individual needs the most, and should employ the methods of influence most effective for that individual. In other words, the selection of the cells in the matrix should be governed by the needs of the patient and not by a narrow conceptual framework of the therapist.

The Matrix as a Structure for Hypotheses of Psychopathology

If a therapist can promote a child's learning of a given psychological competence through modeling, practice, reinforcement, or other methods to be detailed later, then so can a parent, a peer, a teacher, or anyone else in the child's social field. And if those influences can be favorable (facilitating increased competence), then they can also be unfavorable (facilitating maladaptive patterns and incompetence). The matrix thus provides a way of accounting for skill deficiencies. Has the child received many models of maladaptive strategies in the skill of conflict resolution? Has the child failed to receive positive models in the skill of celebrating his acts of accomplishment? Has the child been punished for positive examples of the skills of relaxing and playing? Has the child been rewarded for maladaptively responding to his own failures in a harshly self-punitive way? The use of the matrix can proceed in a forward-looking way as well as a backward-looking way. We may predict that if the child fails to get models, reinforcers, or the like for adaptive examples of skill $X$, and if he does get many models and reinforcers for maladaptive examples with respect to skill $X$, then his development of skill $X$ will suffer greatly.

These mechanisms are felt to account for a large portion of, but not all of, psychopathology; other contributions are discussed shortly.

### The Matrix as a Structure for Developmental Theories

Anna Freud (1965) has used the concept of "developmental lines"—a number of parameters upon which child development may proceed apace or become retarded. In a sense, each of the competences to be listed in the skills axis can be considered a developmental line: A certain degree of progress in each is to be expected as the child develops, and certain degree of skill in each may be considered approximately average for a given age group. Indeed, some of the competences to be included in the skills axis have been subjected to extensive developmental study. For example, Selman and colleagues (e.g., Selman & Byrne, 1974), following up on the work of Piaget, have studied the progression across age of the ability to see things from the point of view of another person. The methods axis constitutes a set of influences that explain some of the variance in rate of developmental progress: For example, the child who receives much positive modeling of, much practice of, and many reinforcing consequences for the skill of seeing things from another's point of view may be expected to develop more rapidly in this skill.

### The Matrix as a Guide to Preventive Intervention

The most effective clinician will seek not only to deliver favorable influences directly to children, but also to help others deliver such influences. Parent, teachers, babysitters, paraprofessional workers, older peers, and others can learn techniques of promoting psychological skills, as I discuss in Chapter 8. If such influences toward the development of psychological skills can be delivered by many people to many people, we have the wherewithal for primary prevention in mental health. The skills that, when learned in the course of therapy, help reduce psychological symptoms are the same skills that, when promoted in educational or family or other community settings, should prevent the occurrence of those symptoms. The tasks of the preventive mental health specialist are exactly analogous to those of the clinician: first, to determine the skills of highest priority for a given group; second, to determine the best influence methods that promote the development of these skills; and third, to teach these methods to people within the children's natural social units, so that they may multiply the positive effects. Prevention is discussed more thoroughly in Chapter 10.

Thus, with respect to unifying approaches to psychotherapy, explaining and predicting psychopathology, predicting both curative and destructive influences, providing parameters for developmental study, explaining some variation in rate of development, and providing a guide to preventive intervention, our matrix is meant to be a very hard-working one. It is not, however, designed to take the whole world on its shoulders. Let us look briefly at what is outside its scope.

## THE PLACE OF LEARNING-BASED TREATMENT
## IN THE TOTAL ARMAMENTARIUM

The matrix is meant to guide us only with respect to that subset of mental problems that can be called "learning-based." I have elsewhere (Strayhorn, 1982) spoken of three sets of causes and cures of psychological symptoms: biological, situational, and learning-based. Biological influences can result in disturbed behavior, with or without accompanying physical symptoms. Examples include lead toxicity, hyperthyroidism, a brain tumor, or ear infections that disturb hearing. Similarly, biological interventions, such as the treatment of any of these problems, can alleviate behavioral symptoms. Psychotropic medication represents another example in the class of biological interventions. Biological causes and interventions are outside the scope of this book, but should always be kept in mind when choosing treatment strategies.

The second set of influences is situational factors—the aspects of the immediate situations the child has to deal with. If the child is in a classroom in school where the work is over his head; or if the child is in a home where he is being sexually abused; or if the child is in the situation of being shuttled back and forth between two sets of caretakers, each hostile toward the other—then the foremost task of the helping person is to attempt to better the child's life situation. Hospitalization of a child to provide both child and family with respite from a rapidly worsening situation is sometimes beneficial, even when no one learns more adaptive ways of coping with life; hospitalization in such examples constitutes situational treatment. (On the other hand, hospitalization can also constitute a noxious, stressful situation conducive to the increase of symptoms.) This book deals with situational influences only to the extent that a family member's learning of psychological competences constitutes an improved situation for the child. This book does not deal with the extensive issues of residential placment, adoptive placement, custody determination, and other situation revisions.

Learning-based interventions do not include just those based on "learning theory," but any sorts of psychotherapeutic interventions that result in a child's becoming able to handle situations better than before. Helping a child learn not to be so troubled by Oedipal conflicts or oral dependency conflicts, however these are defined, would constitute learning-based treatment. Learning-based interventions comprise not only psychotherapy, but also parent training classes, self-instructional manuals, and any other influences meant to help someone acquire competences such as those to be listed in the skills axis. Learning-based influences, for better or for worse, are delivered by Saturday morning cartoons, the norms of the peer culture, and countless other environmental exposures.

Learning-based treatment in no way excludes biologically based treatment or situationally based treatment. The clinician should apply any of these that are most useful whenever they are useful, according to what the evidence dictates, for any individual child. Biologically based and situationally based treatments are excluded from the present volume for reasons of limited space and time, not ideological opposition.


## ALTERNATIVES TO THE COMPETENCE ORIENTATION

### A Single Task, Aided by the Therapist

In examining the boundaries of the competence-based approach, let us be aware that not everyone sees as the purpose of therapy to become more competent at some psychological skill, or to learn to do anything better.

Sometimes what the person desires from the therapist is not to learn to do something better over and over for the rest of his life, but to get help in handling some one situation better. For example, a divorced parent may want the therapist to help decide whether the other parent should be allowed to see the children, or an adolescent may wish to work on the decision of whether or not to go to college. At other times the one-time occurrence is the handling of a difficult situation, such as a disruption or loss. For example, a child who has been kidnapped and then returned to the parents comes to the therapist; in this case, the chosen goal is not to increase the child's general ability to cope with frightening situations, but to help him cope with this one situation.

Sometimes the single task carried out in such psychotherapy involves making one discovery. For example, a child may be angry at a stepparent ostensibly because of irritating aspects of the stepparent's personality; the child gets insight into the way in which feelings of loyalty to his biological parent have unrealistically required him to be hostile to the stepparent. This one insight may enable the child to cease feeling hostile and solve the presenting problem.

Much more often, however, to continue this last example, the therapy will fall into the rubric of the matrix and will involve the child's learning more general skills, such as accurately perceiving another person's personality, recognizing the origins of one's own feelings, and forgiving oneself and others. In such a therapy the child's ability to deal not only with this situation, but with others like it, should be increased. In my experience, there is certainly a place for the therapist's lending his or her own competence for the successful handling of one given situation. Nevertheless, the major situations that most frequently give people problems are not one-of-a-kind traumas and decisions; rather, the person is overwhelmed by the accrual of the negative effects of situations that repeat themselves over and over. Accordingly, most of the time the therapist shold aim at improving the competence of the person in dealing not only with a particular situation, but with all future recurrences of situations of that sort. A Chinese proverb states, "Give a man a fish and you feed him for a day; teach a man to fish and you feed him for a lifetime." Just as the need for food never disappears, situations requiring the fundamental psychological competences recur continually throughout each lifetime.

Exactly similar considerations apply to the provision of support by the therapist. The presence of an understanding, accepting person, motivated to help, can be a tremendous source of security to the person in trouble and in need. In the short run, provision of this support directly by the therapist is humane and usually necessary if anything is to be accomplished. However, the need for interpersonal support persists over a lifetime, and the therapist usually best serves by promoting the competences necessary to develop a natural support system of friends, coworkers, and family, rather than promoting long-term dependence upon the therapist.

## Catharsis and Displacement

Another alternative to competence acquisition frequently pursued by therapists is catharsis or displacement of painful feelings. This general paradigm has been such a large part of traditional thinking about mental health that it is worth detailed consideration.

In the catharsis/displacement paradigm, the child's symptoms or maladaptive patterns are viewed as caused by negative feelings or urges residing within the child (e.g., anger, depression, grief, fear); the task of therapy is to get these "out," preferably in some way that is not harmful. The assumption is that painful feelings or maladaptive urges cannot simply go away while they are kept in; they must come out if they are to be resolved. According to this theory, when one is angry, it does not do simply to give oneself time to cool off, think rationally, make the best decisions possible, and work toward remediating or learning to tolerate the unwanted situation; something must be done with the anger. To vent one's anger on inanimate objects seems to some to be an immensely wise solution, and punching bags seem to be useful if not essential mental health aids. Another consequence of such a model is an image of what constitutes effective therapy. According to this model, there is little possibility of positive change without a good deal of release of negative feelings. If an individual *has* anger or grief or other painful emotions *inside*, then the logical thing to *do with them* is to export them.

The alternative to this paradigm is that our language about feeling should portray it not as something one *has*, but as something one *does*. By this paradigm, anger-producing thoughts and anger-reducing thoughts can be brought under voluntary control (although the task may not be easy). It is possible, by this model, to quit feeling a certain feeling without having it go anywhere, just as it is possible to quit doing a behavior without having it go anywhere. Novaco (1975) reported a treatment for persons with chronic anger problems that relied upon this paradigm; his subjects were taught to reduce anger by altering their thoughts.

I cannot review here all the evidence on the fascinating and very complex question of when and how expression of painful feelings is useful. However, looking at a few studies may give a sense of the ways in which the issue has been approached empirically. Carol Tavris (1982) and Albert Bandura (1973), among others, have reviewed the specific question of whether expression of anger is conducive to more or less anger and aggression later on. Both of these authors make impressive cases that the catharsis model is contradicted by much empirical evidence. The following studies illustrate.

Feshbach (1956) studied a sample of boys who were not aggressive or destructive. He encouraged them to play with violent toys, kick furniture, or otherwise let out aggression during some free-play hours. According to the catharsis theory, this experience should have made them less aggressive on later observation; in fact, they were much more hostile and destructive on later occasions than they had been previously. Straus (1974) surveyed married couples and found that, on the average, spouses who yelled at each other felt not less angry, but *more* angry thereafter. Verbal aggression and physical aggression were positively correlated with each other; thus the idea that verbal aggression drains off the urge toward physical aggression did not find support. Mallick and McCandless (1966) conducted an experiment in which third-grade children were frustrated by another child. The children were then divided into three groups: Some were permitted to talk with adult experimenters about their anger; some were allowed to play with guns in aggressive play; and others were given a reasonable explanation from the adults for the child's annoying behavior. The children who talked about their anger and those who played with guns were more hostile toward the child and liked her less than those led to understand why the child had behaved as she did.

Ebbesen, Duncan, and Konecni (1975) conducted exit interviews with workers who had been laid off from their jobs. In the exit interviews, the experimenters asked questions that directed hostility in one of three ways: toward the company, toward the supervisors, or toward oneself. Those who in this conversation had been led to "get out their anger" at the company were, according to a later questionnaire, more angry at the company; those who had been led to "get out their anger" at the supervisor were more angry at the supervisor. (Those who had been directed to explore their own failing did not blame themselves more later, perhaps because the layoffs so clearly had nothing to do with the workers' behavior.) Kahn (1966) reported a similar study, in which subjects who had been angered in the experimental situation either voiced their resentment to a sympathetic person or were left to themselves for an equivalent period. Those who expressed their hostility with support and encouragement disliked their annoyer significantly more and were slower to calm down physiologically than the equally angered subjects who were left to themselves. Biaggio (1980) studied the correlation in a sample of college students between quickness or slowness to express anger and other personality traits. She found that the quick expressers of anger were less self-controlled, tolerant, and flexible than students who kept their anger in check; the "repressers" seemed more dependable and socially mature.

The conclusion of all of these studies is the one that Berkowitz (1970) arrived at after reporting a series of experiments on expression of hostility: "Frequently, . . . when we tell someone off, we stimulate ourselves to continued or even stronger aggression" (p. 5). Thus, with respect to the specific question of catharsis of anger, these studies suggest that verbal or symbolic expression of anger is often best viewed as a rehearsal of future hostility, not a purgation of it.

The issue is more complex than this, however. While avoiding simple-minded catharsis notions, we should also avoid the simple-minded notion that "expression of negative feelings is bad." Sometimes expressing painful emotion facilitates the rehearsal of an adaptive skill, and the skills axis can help us understand why. Disclosing one's fears or resentments or feelings of inadequacy to another person can be an example of trusting and depending; this trusting and depending can in turn be a very important skill, allowing the person to receive support from others. Verbalizing one's dissatisfaction with a situation is often the first step in the process of adaptive decision making; disclosing a dissatisfaction to another person is often the first step in skillful conflict resolution. Speaking about a painful mistake or failure one has made may be a crucial step in cultivating the skill of forgiving onself for one's mistakes and failures. In all these examples, focusing on the painful circumstance is not the end in itself; it is the predecessor to practicing an adaptive coping mechanism in response to the situation. It is a step toward competence enhancement.

Thus the skills × methods matrix reappears as a useful construct in making decisions about the usefulness of expression of negative feelings: When such expression is a part of a strategy in which the most useful methods of influence are addressing the highest-priority competences, then such expression is likely to be very useful. As a general rule, however, the most effective method of influence is that which necessitates the least pain. Sometimes it is possible to build up coping skills by practicing with less difficult situations, and thus to avoid altogether the excessive pain of a piece of therapeutic work.

## THE MATRIX AS AN EMERGING FRAMEWORK IN THE FIELD OF MENTAL HEALTH

Although I must take the blame for coining a bit of jargon in speaking of a "skills × methods matrix," I certainly do not claim to be the first to view mental health as a set of skills or to speak of a variety of ways to promote those skills. Rather, I see references to psychological skills and ways of imparting them as having gradually increased over recent decades in all parts of mental health literature. Bower (1966) has conceived of mental health as competence in abilities to work, love, and play, expanding upon Sigmund Freud's famous statement that the mentally healthy person should be able "to love and to work." Bandura's (1973, 1977) social learning theory speaks of skills for interpersonal functioning and sets of ways to teach those skills, with emphasis upon modeling and practice opportunities and feedback. Goldstein (1973, 1981; Goldstein & Pentz, 1984) has been an advocate of the psychological skills training approach to therapy, and has applied this technique assiduously, particularly with aggressive adolescents. Guerney (1977) has argued that psychotherapy is better conceived of as education, that more effective psychotherapy tends to be carried out by more structured education, and that the curriculum of such education consists of certain interpersonal skills.

The literature of social skills training (Bellack & Hersen, 1979; Michelson & Mannarino, 1986) and of cognitive–behavioral therapy (Beck, 1976; Beck, Rush, Shaw, & Emery, 1979; Kendall & Braswell, 1985) shares the orientation I elaborate here; the cognitive therapists have directed our attention to the fact that skillful patterns of functioning include thought patterns as well as patterns of feeling and behavior. White (1975) has applied the concept of psychological skills to infants and toddlers, and has listed specific skills of im-

portance at various developmental stages. The work of Richard Gardner (1971, 1975, 1979, 1983), although originating from a psychoanalytic tradition, is very much oriented toward discovering what
psychological competences a child needs to learn and using a variety
of techniques (most notably fantasy, play, and storytelling methods
closely akin to methods I emphasize in this book) to convey those
psychological skills to the child. Cowen (1984) has emphasized competence-enhancing strategies as central to primary prevention. The
fact that so many theorists have spoken of skills and influences
(although not necessarily in those terms) has impelled me to attempt a
comprehensive and systematic way of sorting through the various
possibilities.

# CHAPTER 2

# *The Skills Axis*

## OVERVIEW

There is no doubt that for various purposes, symptom-cluster-based diagnoses (exemplified by Axes I and II of DSM-III) are quite useful. The present "skills axis," however, which is meant to be a reasonably comprehensive list of psychological skills contributing to mental health, is designed as an important additional axis, especially useful in directing the content of child psychotherapy. If a child's difficulties are caused by deficiency in a certain skill, then he should be taught that skill, even though the symptoms caused by the skill deficiency may be quite diverse.

Skills axis diagnoses are advantageous partly because they are conducive to reasonable and justified movements along the "abstraction ladder." That is, given a set of vignettes describing situations handled poorly by a person, it is reasonable to move up the ladder to the skills axis term abstracting what the specific examples have in common. It is also easy to move down the abstraction ladder, from a skill that is deficient to concrete examples of positive performance in that area. For reasons to be illustrated later, such movement is of great importance.

There are nine groups of skills on the axis: (1) closeness, trusting, relationship building; (2) handling separation and independence; (3) handling joint decisions and interpersonal conflict; (4) dealing with frustration and unfavorable events; (5) celebrating good things, feeling pleasure; (6) working for delayed gratification; (7) relaxing and playing; (8) cognitive processing through words, symbols, and images; and (9) having an adaptive sense of direction and purpose. Clinicians and researchers in many different areas of the mental health literature have written about these skills. If we wish to shorten the skills axis, we may think in terms of the following four skills: (1) being kind; (2) being socially confident; (3) sustaining attention to tasks; and (4) using language with facility. The central vignette of kindness and helpfulness seems related to the development of a surprisingly large number of skills.

---

The *Diagnostic and Statistical Manual of Mental Disorders,* third edition (DSM-III; American Psychiatric Association, 1980), and the revised edition of DSM-III (DSM-III-R; American Psychiatric Association, 1987) are oriented very heavily toward symptom clusters. Symptom-cluster-based diagnosis is carried out by eliciting information on symptoms (e.g., depressed mood, appetite loss, sleep difficulties) and then assigning the diagnostic label that has been defined in terms of a certain number of such symptoms from a list. Various historical factors have been cited to account for the ascendancy of symptom-cluster-based diagnosis at the present (Robins & Helzer, 1986); surely one of them is the extent to which symptom clusters predict response to drug treatments developed in recent decades. The "skills axis" described in this chapter, as well as in one of my earlier articles (Strayhorn, 1983), is meant in no sense as a replacement for symp-tom-cluster-based diagnosis, but rather as another axis that should be added to the diagnostic system. While symptom cluster diagnosis, as in Axis I and II of DSM-III, is very useful in determining the choice of drug therapy, the present skills axis is more useful in determining the content of psychotherapy and other learning-based treatment.

## SYMPTOM CLUSTERS SHOULD NOT DETERMINE DIRECTION OF PSYCHOTHERAPY

It is quite common to encounter patients for whom the DSM-III diagnosis is the same, but who require very different psychotherapeu-tic goals and directions. Conversely, one also frequently encounters patients who have different DSM-III diagnoses, but who require the same general therapeutic goal or direction. As an example of the first situation, consider two children who meet DSM-III-R criteria for Dysthymia. For one child, the chronic unhappiness is inferred (by means discussed in the following chapter) to be a result primarily of the child's inability to socialize comfortably with other children; his lack of skill in social initiations and social conversation leaves him unhappy because of loneliness. For this child, learning how to interact more comfortably and skillfully with peers is the optimum direction for psychotherapy. The other child, with the same symptoms of mood disturbance, can interact with other children and make friends with no difficulty. This child, by contrast, is so perfectionistic that he berates and condemns himself for his slightest academic or athletic mistake. For this child, developing the skill of tolerating his own mistakes and failures is the optimum direction for psychotherapy.

Thus, for these two hypothetical children with the same DSM-III diagnosis, different therapeutic directions are indicated.

Now let's look at an example of the second situation, where the same general therapeutic strategy may be indicated for children with different DSM-III diagnoses. Consider three children, all of whom are greatly deficient in the skill of handling criticism and disapproval. One child reacts by retaliating aggressively, earning a DSM-III label of Conduct Disorder; another reacts by becoming worried and pre-occupied with how he will be evaluated, earning a label of Over-anxious Disorder; and a third, who is diabetic, shows wide variations in glucose metabolism when criticized, earning a label of Psychological Factors Affecting a Physical Condition. Though the symptom clusters are different, the psychotherapeutic direction of helping the children learn to maintain their self-esteem and security in the face of criticism is useful in all three cases. All three can benefit from decid-ing upon adaptive thoughts, feelings, and behaviors with which to handle criticism, and practicing those adaptive response patterns repeatedly.

In these hypothetical examples, and as a rule, the direction of therapy is determined not so much by symptom cluster as by the *psychological skill deficiencies* of highest priority for the person to learn.

## SKILLS CONCEPTS AND THEIR ADVANTAGES

The words "skill" and "competence" are used interchangeably here to refer to patterns of thought, feeling, and/or behavior useful in responding to a certain sort of situation. The skills axis is a com-pendium of such competences, sometimes named by the situation (as in the skill of handling frustration) and sometimes named by the response (as in the skill of relaxation). The skills axis has been com-piled by identifying the competences focused upon in treatment as described in the psychotherapy literature, as well as in my personal experience.

Let us now examine three advantages to the use of the concepts of the skills axis.

### Nonpejorativeness and Usefulness in Mental Rehearsal

First, the skills axis diagnoses are nonpejorative. Most people would feel insulted to be told that they were labeled as having a "personality disorder" or that they were considered "passive–aggressive"; most would probably not feel nearly so attacked if told that some improved skills of negotiation and conflict resolution would be helpful to them. A child who would feel insulted or confused by being told he had an "oppositional disorder" would be more likely to benefit from being told he needed to learn to handle it better when he doesn't get his way.

Second, the "skill" label by its very name may summon to consciousness mental images of the desired pattern that should be rehearsed; thinking in terms of such a label may then constitute a miniature fantasy rehearsal of the desirable pattern. For example, a person who thinks about his need to develop skills in making decisions efficiently and tolerating things that cannot be controlled calls up mental images of the desirable patterns to be rehearsed; if the same person were to think of himself as an "obsessive," a mental rehearsal of the desirable pattern would not be evoked.

## The "Abstraction Ladder"

The third advantage of the skills language has to do with the "abstraction ladder," or the ranking of concepts according to their level of abstraction. This notion was explicated by the semanticist Alfred Korzybski (1933) and lucidly explained by S. I. Hayakawa (1978). I return to it repeatedly throughout this book. The essential meaning of the abstraction ladder has been incorporated into the mental health professions in several forms, one of which is emphasis upon "operational definitions," a term originated by Bridgman (1927); operational definitions are phrased in terms of concepts low on the abstraction ladder.

A concept is at a lower level of abstraction if what it stands for is more directly observable, more directly able to be perceived by the senses; a concept is at a higher level of abstraction if it leaves out more characteristics of one observable thing or event and refers to characteristics held in common by a more disparate population of observable events. Let's look at an example (and thus speak at a lower level of abstraction). To say that Johnny Jones screamed very loudly for 5 minutes in the local supermarket when his mother said "No" to his request of "Buy me some candy," is to speak at a lower level of abstraction than to say that Johnny Jones exhibited low frustration tolerance. To say that Johnny Jones has an oppositional disorder is higher on the abstraction ladder than to speak of low frustration tolerance, and to say that he has a psychological disorder is higher still.

As another example, to say that Mary Smith reported that upon finding that she missed one item on an arithmetic test, she told herself she was a worthless person, felt awful for 3 days, and had fantasies of suicide is lower on the abstraction ladder than to say that Mary Smith had difficulty handling an academic mistake. To say she has a problem handling her own mistakes and failures is at a higher level; to say that she has a harsh and punitive superego is still higher; and to say she has a neurotic disturbance is higher still. Each more abstract concept leaves out some of the characteristics of the specific observed events, so as to encompass a wider range of events.

Hayakawa (1978) makes several useful points about the abstraction ladder. First, if two observers are to agree on the presence or absence of something, that something must be defined in terms of specific observations, low on the abstraction ladder. Second, the meaning of a word is ultimately communicated best (and as some may argue, only) by concepts below it on the abstraction ladder. For example, one grasps the meaning of the color red only by seeing such things as fire trucks, rubies, ripe tomatoes, and so forth, and abstracting the property that those things have in common. If one has never seen a single red thing, it is difficult or impossible to understand the meaning of the word "red." A concept is only as good as its grounding in lower-level concepts; as Hayakawa puts it, "The test of abstractions is not whether they are 'high-level' or 'low-level' abstractions, but whether they are referrable to lower levels" (p. 163).

On the other hand, the process of abstraction is an indispensable convenience, necessary for economy of thought and communication. The process of "leaving characteristics out" is necessary, because our minds cannot hold infinite bits of information and we do not have infinite time to speak. In order to have a science of chemistry, for example, we must be able to think of $H_2O$, leaving out of consideration for the time being the wetness of water, the hardness of ice, the pearliness of dew, and the other observable characteristics of particular examples of $H_2O$. If every time we spoke of something red, we had to say that it had something in common with fire trucks, ripe tomatoes, and robins' breasts without being any of these, our language and thought would be unbearably cumbersome.

The most useful discourse, therefore, is that which can move up and down the abstraction ladder so to provide the mental economy of higher-level concepts while also keeping concepts tied to their moorings of lower-level concepts. In other words, the ladder is only useful if one moves up and down on it, rather than perching permanently at one point.

How is all this relevant to mental health practice? The skills concepts to be presented have the advantage of being at a level of abstraction higher than the molecular behaviors countable by strict behaviorists, and lower than most of the theoretical constructs used by analysts; they are at a midrange. This level is chosen so as to be useful not only to therapists, but to patients, even young children, and to permit ready access to higher or lower levels. Just as the child learns the meaning of red only by seeing red things, the child learns the meaning of frustration tolerance or "putting up with not getting my way" only be seeing concrete examples of this concept. And just as learning the concept of red helps the child to choose a red thing when he or she wants it, learning the concept of frustration tolerance helps a child to tolerate frustration when there is a reason to do so. For the child who primarily needs to learn frustration tolerance, the concept of "adequate ego controls" probably covers too much territory—it is too abstract—as does the concept of "being good." On the other hand, the concept of "talking quietly when your mother doesn't let you have candy" and many other similar examples can most economically be stored in the child's mind when there is some one concept that abstracts what they have in common.

## THE NINE MAJOR GROUPS OF SKILLS

For purposes of mnemonic efficiency, as much as of conceptual clarification, the competences on the skills axis have been divided into nine groups, as follows. Group 1 consists of skills of forming and maintaining social bonds—skills of building relationships, of receiving and giving love. Groups 2 and 3 consist of skills involved in dealing successfully with forces that may weaken or threaten social bonds: separation and interpersonal conflict. Groups 4 and 5 cast the psychologically healthy child as dealing well with frustration, failure, and personal misdeeds on the one hand, and as taking pleasure in success, favorable events, and prosocial deeds on the other. Groups 6 and 7 involve skills of working (delaying gratification) and playing (consuming gratification). Group 8 focuses on the skills of letting thoughts influence action in an organized way. Group 9 focuses on one possible result of such thought—the use of guiding principles and meanings for one's life.

These groups have a rough correlation with certain developmental theories: The infant bonds and learns to trust; the toddler begins to learn to tolerate separation; the preschooler becomes competitive and experiences interpersonal conflict; the preschooler also starts to develop superego (including the capacity for self-praise); the school-age child works and plays; the adolescent develops formal operations; and the young adult generates meaning and direction for life. The concept of stages may be more useful as a mnemonic device than as a guide for action; I believe that all these skills begin to develop by the preschool years.

The complete list of these psychological health skills is presented in Table 2-1. The following sections provide further detail on these skills and link them to some of their roots in the literature on psychotherapy and psychopathology.

## Group 1: Trusting, Closeness, Relationship Building

The first of the nine groups of skills contains some of the crucial ones that allow a relationship with another person to be formed and sustained. The skill of trusting, of accepting help, and of being appropriately dependent is my translation of a variety of primarily psychoanalytic writings, such as those of Erik Erikson (1950) on basic trust versus mistrust, or other psychoanalytically derived writings (e.g., Hine, 1971) on oral dependency conflicts of the sort that make one fear dependency excessively. Many children with conduct problems have never had good practice in depending upon a trustworthy source of nurture; they simply are unskilled at depending, and some are even afraid of it. As a result, to defend against that fear, they have to drive people off—to communicate to people, "Who needs you!" in many different ways. Adults and children who gain the description "borderline" often seem to have deficiencies in the skill of accurately assessing the trustworthiness of another individual along a continuum of possibilities. Their concept of the other tends to be that of "all good, infinitely trustworthy" or "all bad, infinitely deceitful." The skill of making a more realistic appraisal should to some degree protect against such a syndrome.

The skill of sustaining attachment is closely related; Bowlby (1969–1980) has explored that topic extensively. The skill of self-

TABLE 2-1. Psychological health skills axis

*Group 1: Closeness, trusting, relationship building*
1. Accurately assessing the trustworthiness of another person, and trusting when appropriate.
2. Accepting help, being dependent without shame, asking for help appropriately.
3. Tolerating and enjoying sustained closeness, attachment, and commitment ot another.
4. Intimately disclosing and revealing oneself to another in a situation where it is safe.
5. Nurturing someone else: being kind and helpful.
6. Nurturing oneself: delivering assuring or caretaking cognitions to oneself, and feeling comforted by such cognitions.
7. Expressing gratitude, admiration, and other positive feelings toward others.
8. Initiating social contacts appropriately; getting attention from others in appropriate ways.
9. Engaging in social conversation.
10. Listening, empathizing, encouraging another to disclose.

*Group 2: Handling separation and independence*
11. Making decisions independently; carrying out actions independently.
12. Tolerating separation from close others.
13. Handling rejection.
14. Dealing with disapproval, criticism, and lack of respect from others.
15. Having a good time by oneself, tolerating aloneness, tolerating not getting someone's attention.

*Group 3: Handling joint decisions and interpersonal conflict*
16. Dealing with someone's doing or wanting something that conflicts with one's own preferences; deciding how much self-sacrifice, assertion, conciliation, forgiveness, giving behavior, resignation, and/or punishment constitutes the best response.
17. Generating creative options for solutions to interpersonal problems.
18. Recognizing and choosing reasonable solutions to interpersonal problems.
19. Negotiating: talking out conflicts and reaching joint decisions (includes the subskills of being persuasive, using tact, using well-chosen timing, and discerning and explaining the reasons for disagreement).
20. Assertion and dominance skills: sticking up for one's own welfare, taking charge, enjoying winning a competition, exerting one's will over others when appropriate, resisting inappropriate influence.
21. Conciliation and submission skills: giving in, conceding a point, tolerating losing a competition, admitting one was wrong, allowing oneself to be led, allowing another's will to dominate when appropriate.
22. Recognizing and praising the portion of another's behavior that is positive.
23. Tolerating, without needing to control or direct, a wide range of other people's behavior.
24. Forgiving other people, being able to relinquish anger.

*Group 4: Dealing with frustration and unfavorable events*
25. Handling frustration, tolerating adverse circumstances.
26. Handling one's own mistakes and failures.
27. Tolerating a second person's getting something that one wants for oneself; avoiding inappropriately large jealousy.
28. Correctly estimating the danger of situations; being relatively fearless in relatively nondangerous situations.
29. Feeling appropriate fear when danger is present.
30. Feeling appropriate guilt when one has harmed others.
31. Tolerating one's own feelings—including painful feelings—without making mat-

ters worse by fearing them, feeling guilty over them, not permitting oneself any feelings, or otherwise overestimating the danger of the feeling.

32. Tolerating thoughts, impulses, or fantasies that must not be acted on, with confidence that idea and actions are not the same; tolerating less than 100% control of these mental events.

*Group 5: Celebrating good things, feeling pleasure*

33. Enjoying approval, compliments, and other positive attention from others.
34. Celebrating and internally rewarding oneself for one's own accomplishments and successes.
35. Feeling pleasure from doing kind, loving acts for others.
36. Enjoying discovery, taking pleasure from exploration.
37. Feeling gratitude for what others have done.
38. Celebrating and feeling the blessings of luck or fate.
39. Enjoying physical affection without various fears interfering.
40. Having romantic or erotic feelings attached to desirable stimulus situations.

*Group 6: Working for delayed gratification*

41. Denying oneself present gratification for the sake of future gain.
42. Complying, obeying; submitting to reasonable authority.
43. Concentrating on, maintaining attention to, and persisting on tasks.
44. Maintaining healthy habits regarding drinking, smoking, drug use, exercise, and diet.
45. Being honest and dependable when it is difficult to be so.
46. Developing competences that bring approval and acceptance from people: (a) work-related, (b) school-related, (c) recreational.
47. Forgoing consumption in favor of saving; financial delay of gratification.

*Group 7: Relaxing, playing*

48. Relaxing; letting the mind drift and the body be at ease.
49. Playing, becoming childlike, experiencing glee, being spontaneous.
50. Enjoying humor; finding and producing comedy in life.

*Group 8: Cognitive processing through words, symbols, and images*

51. Using words to conceptualize the world: verbal skills.
52. Recognizing and being able to verbalize one's own feelings.
53. Correctly assessing other people's feelings; seeing things from the other's point of view (including the impact of one's behavior on others).
54. Accurately assessing the degree of control one has over specific events.
55. Decision making: defining a problem, gathering information, generating options, predicting and evaluating consequences, making a choice.
56. Thinking before acting; letting thoughts mediate between situation and action.
57. Being organized and planful in the use of time, money, and physical objects: deciding upon priorities, consciously deciding upon and organizing allocations, carrying out those decisions.
58. Accurately assessing one's own skills and abilities in various times, tasks, and circumstances.
59. Accurately assessing the skills and character of others, based upon evidence rather than upon prejudice, overgeneralization, wish-fulfilling fantasies, or other distortions.
60. Being able to use imagination and fantasy as a tool in rehearsing or evaluating a plan, or adjusting to an event or situation.

*Group 9: An adaptive sense of direction and purpose*

61. Aiming toward making circumstances better, in the long run, rather than worse; seeking reward and not punishment.
62. Assigning to activity a "meaning" or "purpose" that allows effort to provide a sense of fulfillment (even in unpleasant circumstances).

disclosure is also closely related to that of appropriately depending, because telling someone about one's thoughts and feelings involves a certain degree of trust and dependency. The skill of asking for help without feeling ashamed of doing so is a subset of the concept of dependency. Most therapists are familiar with children who seem unable to ask for help in direct verbal ways and seem to be asking for help in symptomatic ways, such as by a psychosomatic symptom or by misbehavior.

Self-nurture—the ability to comfort oneself, to console oneself, to praise oneself, to take care of oneself mentally—is a very important skill. It is reasonable to suppose that the ability to generate internal sentences and images that adequately comfort and nurture oneself is fostered by learning both the giving and receiving of nurture in interpersonal relationships. For example, seeing and hearing a nurturing parent should, by modeling, increase the child's skills in being nurturing to others; second, receiving nurture from a parent should provide practice and reinforcement for the child in receiving nurture from someone else. The combination of the skills of nurturing and accepting nurture then enable the child to develop skills of self-nurture.

Initiating social contact is another of these relationship-building skills—one that is often deficient in withdrawn, shy children, or children who are afraid of school. Teaching a child how to make friends is sometimes a very important antidote to school difficulties. Putallaz and Gottman (1983) argue strongly for the strategy of carefully observing what popular and unpopular children do and inferring successful strategies of making friends from these observations, rather than simply deciding from the armchair that certain strategies work better. In this manner these investigators found, among other things, that when initiating social contact with a group of other children, unpopular children tended to disagree, ask informational questions, say something about themselves, and state their feelings and opinions; popular children were more likely to observe for a few minutes to determine the "frame of reference" or focus of attention of the group, and then establish themselves as sharing in this frame of reference.

The skill of empathic listening is one modeled well, although single-mindedly, in the responses of classic Rogerian therapists of former decades (Snyder, 1947). This skill of empathic nondirective listening has been emphasized greatly in parent training techniques such as T. Gordon's (1970) parent effectiveness training or Guerney's

(1980) filial therapy. Proficiency in this skill requires an ability to "take the role of another," which has been widely studied by developmental psychologists and which has been the focus of training programs (Urbain & Kendall, 1980).

### Group 2: Handling Separation and Independence

Psychoanalysts refer to other sorts of oral dependency conflicts, in which the person is afraid not so much of dependence as of independence. The skill of being independent has to do with Erik Erikson's (1950) concepts of autonomy versus shame and doubt and of initiative versus guilt. Can the child make decisions without going to an adult in a clinging manner, and without passively waiting for someone to decide for him? Can the child tolerate separation from attachment figures for reasonable lengths of time? The skill of tolerating rejection is similar: Can the child be autonomous enough to handle the situation when not everybody likes him, when bids for affiliation are spurned? Handling aloneness is a related skill, which involves cultivating enough of an inner life that one is not totally dependent upon other people for good feelings. Mahler, Pine, and Bergman (1975) have provided observations on how the child begins to develop and practice these skills of separation, "individuation," and independence building during early years.

The clinical symptom most closely associated with skill deficiencies in the areas of handling separateness and independence is anxiety. Freud (1905/1953) wrote that "anxiety in children is originally nothing other than an expression of the fact that they are feeling the loss of the person they love" (p. 224). Anxiety may be manifested or defended against in myriad ways; thus a variety of clinical symptoms can arise from this skill deficiency. Inadequate skills in the independence group can also result in an unthinking acceptance of authority or influence, a lack of capacity to take an independent stand.

### Group 3: Handling Joint Decisions and Interpersonal Conflicts

Although the role of "getting anger out" of one's system has been overrated, it is hard to overemphasize the role of anger in the production of clinical symptoms. Clinicians are familiar with such presenting symptoms as suicide attempts that seem to be aimed toward getting revenge on someone; tension headaches that accompany thoughts of how one has been mistreated; and direct shows of hostility and violence.

What skills provide the antidotes for such maladaptive manifestations of anger? One obvious candidate is the group of skills concerned with interpersonal joint decision making and conflict resolution, because, almost by definition, anger is the result of an individual's perceiving himself as not having arrived at a satisfactory conclusion in a conflict of wishes with someone else. Handling joint decisions and interpersonal conflict harmoniously enables people to jointly decide upon ways of handling their wishes *vis-à-vis* other people's wishes without having to resort to great anger or aggression.

Such skillful handling of joint decision and conflict can be broken down into various subskills. The skill of being assertive has received much attention in recent years. As has been pointed out in reviews of this concept (e.g., Linehan & Egan, 1979), the word "assertion" has been used to cover a wide variety of psychological skills, and its use in that broad sense should probably be dropped. The broadening of the concept of assertion illustrates the fact that assertiveness as narrowly defined (e.g., the skill of insisting on one's rights, stating one's wishes forcefully, and driving a hard bargain) is insufficient as an answer to the problem of interpersonal conflict. Other skills have proved to be of great usefulness in this arena as well. Spivack and colleagues (Spivack, Platt, & Shure, 1976; Spivack & Shure, 1974) and other researchers (e.g., Yu, Harris, Solovitz, & Franklin, 1986) have focused with positive results on skills of generating options for the solution of interpersonal problems, predicting accurately the consequences of such options, and choosing wisely among those options. Such problem-solving skills have also been approached by Thomas Gordon (1970) in his parent effectiveness training, under the title of the "no-lose method of problem solving." Such interpersonal problem-solving skills were found to be lower in a sample of depressed children than in their nondepressed peers (Sacco & Graves, 1984). Using positive comments and other means of positive reinforcement with the other person is also a very important skill in the joint decision process, and very often when it is used properly it lets interpersonal influence be carried out without generating an adversarial process at all. Many parents have learned to reduce the conflict with their children by increasing their rate of positive reinforcers for desired behavior (Patterson & Fleischman, 1979; Strain, Steele, Ellis, & Timm, 1982).

Another skill involved in satisfactory handling of conflict is tolerating a wide enough range of other people's behavior. Sometimes clinicians see children who are driven to be constantly controlling of others—children who seem guided by the rule that whatever somebody is doing, it is necessary to get that person to do something else instead. This skill deficiency stimulates many unpleasant conflicts; the antidote for it is the skill of tolerating a wide enough range of other people's behavior. Another skill infrequently mentioned in the mental health literature—but one of paramount importance for mental health, according to my observation—is the ability to forgive people for the harm they inflict. The course of conflict resolution can never work with 100% efficiency, and everyone is wronged by other people sometimes, if not often. Cultivating the skill of forgiving the offender is usually a much more workable and pragmatic solution than trying to purge oneself of the anger via catharsis.

## Group 4: Dealing with Frustration and Unfavorable Events

Sometimes the clinician sees children who condemn and punish themselves excessively when they make a mistake or fail at something; some of these present with symptoms of depression, and some of these are referred to as having overly harsh superegos. Often, clinically, what seems to have happened is that such children seem to have internalized into their imaginary cast of characters one or more harsh, punitive, and excessively critical characters who actually existed or still exist in real life. What these children need is the skill of handling their own mistakes and failures—handling the frustrating events they themselves are responsible for.

Other children have tantrums, become aggressive, or feel inordinately bad when their wishes are not met; they need to strengthen the skill of dealing with frustrating events that arise externally. Cognitive strategies for anger control have brought about reductions in problems with anger through teaching individuals to reduce the sorts of cognitions that blame and condemn others (Hazaleus & Deffenbacher, 1986; Novaco, 1975).

I find it helpful to instruct children (and adults) about strategies of dealing with mistakes, failures, and frustrating events by identifying the following types of responses:

| | |
|---|---|
| • "Awfulizing" | • Not "awfulizing" |
| • Getting down on oneself | • Not getting down on oneself |

| • Blaming someone else | • Not blaming someone else |
|                        | • Listing options and choosing among them |
|                        | • Learning from the experience |

These concepts have been gleaned from the cognitively oriented therapists; the word "awfulizing" is taken from Albert Ellis (1977). The responses in the left column are not always totally inappropriate; very often, however, it is helpful to moderate them greatly in favor of those in the right column.

Inappropriately great jealousy is a fairly frequent complaint about children who come for treatment. Some of these children are referred to by psychoanalysts as having Oedipal conflicts; the child's jealousy is considered analogous to the prototype situation in which the child envies the same-sex parent's receiving attention and love from the opposite-sex parent. This analogy may or may not be useful in specific cases. Sometimes it is sufficient simply to observe that the child needs to improve the skill of tolerating someone else's getting what he wants.

The skill of correctly estimating danger helps a child not to fear excessively situations that are not dangerous; on the other hand, a correct estimation of danger helps the child stay away from situations that are truly dangerous. Beck (1976) has discussed the role of estimates of danger and internal statements about these estimates in determining fear and anxiety. Adjusting the degree of fear attached to certain situations is very frequently adopted as a therapeutic goal; the role of fear in symptom production has been emphasized by Hine (1971).

Feeling guilt when one has hurt someone else is a positive, desirable mental health skill, provided that the guilt is sufficient to deter one from hurtful actions but not so great as to incapacitate oneself. (Thus a little "getting down on oneself" at times is a useful strategy.)

The ability to tolerate one's own bad feelings is a skill whose lack sometimes plunges people into vicious cycles. For example, some people feel afraid, and upon experiencing the fear, think that something terrible is happening to their bodies; they then feel more afraid. Or other people feel sad, and, assuming that it is not normal to feel sad, berate themselves for their weakness; they thus feel worse, and feeling worse makes them feel still worse.

The inability to tolerate less than total control over one's fantasies and thoughts is sometimes prominent in people with obsessive–compulsive problems. The person has an unacceptable fantasy—for example, the image of an aggressive act—and pays so much attention to this fantasy and devotes so much effort to *not* thinking of this specific image that the image begins to intrude all the more. Self-instructions not to have a certain thought are much more difficult to obey than self-instructions to have a certain thought. When the person can tolerate having fantasies of unacceptable actions, in the knowledge that it is still possible to control the behaviors that correspond to them, the fantasies should become less intrusive.

## Group 5: Celebrating Good Things, Feeling Pleasure

The ability to feel pleasure at appropriate times and in connection with certain events is a very important but often underemphasized set of skills. Child therapists have advocated that parents and other adults use praise and compliments to reinforce desirable behavior from a child; however, this strategy presupposes that the child has the ability to feel good about such messages. This ability is not always present. Levin and Simmons (1962; cited in Twardosz & Nordquist, 1983) found that half of a group of emotionally disturbed boys they tested on a marble-drop task stopped responding after praise was made contingent on the response. In a second experiment, there were two groups, and a group that received food only as a reward made many more responses than the group that received food and praise. It would appear that getting praised was downright painful for many of these boys. Deficiency in the skill of enjoying approval is a particularly incapacitating deficiency, because it cuts off a crucial avenue of feedback that regulates behavior.

The skill of response to well-regulated internal approval is a step up on the hierarchy from the skill of responding to external approval. The ability to feel good, even without the benefit of external praise, after doing things good for oneself and others is a tremendous advantage in coping with life. Sometimes this is accomplished by developing an almost unnoticed but powerful internal audience—an imaginary internal cast of characters who can appreciate positive actions. Bandura (1977) discusses under the rubric of social learning theory the notion of self-reinforcement; psychoanalytic writings (e.g., Brenner, 1955) include self-praise as a superego function. A child's feeling good about accomplishments (such as academic successes) helps the child to work toward further accomplishments; conversely, children who are more depressed tend to rate their own accomplishments more negatively (Sacco & Graves, 1984).

Feeling good about doing kind and loving actions for others helps the child to be more loving and prosocial. Garmezy (1984), in reviewing factors that seem to make children resistant to stress, has cited various lines of evidence that helpful, considerate behavior is associated with "ego resiliency," or the capacity to withstand stressful events; the phrase "therapy through helping others" is applicable to such a phenomenon.

Getting pleasure from discovery helps children to be active in the world and to enjoy school; feeling gratitude and pleasure at the helpful acts of others helps them to reinforce other people for doing kind things for them and thus helps sustain the exchange of positive actions that is basic to human happiness. Some depressed children seem to filter out from awareness the appreciation of good things and to focus only on the unfortunate and unpleasant aspects of life. For them, developing the skills of appreciating the blessings of fate, the good things they do, and the good things other people do for them is an important antidote to depression. Beck (1976) uses the "mastery and pleasure list"—a list that the person keeps of times in which he accomplished or enjoyed something—as a treatment method for depression in adults. Learning to say "Hooray" rather than "It isn't good enough" in response to the partially filled cups that life offers has brought increased happiness to many people.

Being able to enjoy physical affection without the interference of negative feelings is a skill important for adult sexuality that probably has its foundation in childhood. Feeling sexual pleasure from appropriate situations (such as loving feelings toward one's mate), as contrasted with the association of sexual pleasure with disadvantageous situations (such as cross-dressing, hostility, or being involved with someone one does not respect), are learned associations that child therapists occasionally deal with. These aspects of sexual association learning more often come to the fore in adolescence.

## Group 6: Working for Delayed Gratification

The skills in Group 6 are closely allied to those of frustration tolerance; they involve voluntarily delivering less pleasurable circumstances to oneself for the present, and tolerating them for the sake of future gain. Delay of gratification was called by Freud (1911/1958) the "reality principle" as opposed to the "pleasure principle." The skills of delaying gratification and sustaining attention to tasks are often deficient in children who get DSM-III labels of Conduct Disorder or Attention Deficit Disorder. At least a portion of the skill of delaying gratification is learned when a child learns to comply with adult requests: These requests often entail following some rule that does not give immediate pleasure other than to get the approval of the adult or to escape the adult's disapproval. Later on, we may hypothesize, the child learns to give himself the approval and disapproval that provides the incentive for delaying gratification appropriately. But a source of external approval and disapproval that is reasonable and potent will be crucial to the development of the internal ability. An adult's approval or disapproval will mean the most when the child has a stable, trusting, and dependent attachment to the adult. By this reasoning, the skill of delaying gratification is linked to the skill of compliance with adult authority, which is in turn linked to the skill of trusting and depending. This theoretical pathway is consistent with the clinical observation that conduct-disordered children often have histories of disrupted attachments.

The skill of sustaining attention to tasks, and the deficiency of that skill that takes the form described in DSM-III as Attention Deficit Disorder with Hyperactivity, seem to have a genetic contribution; however, children with Attention Deficit Disorder seem not to form a genetically homogeneous group (August & Stewart, 1983). Learning-based influences, such as classroom contingency systems, clearly also influence the extent to which children can sustain attention to classwork (Rapport, 1987). Within the experimental literature on selective attention, there is evidence that a person's previous experience with a given set of stimuli and the internal representation that seems to be allocated to them can affect the degree to which they capture and hold attention; such a phenomenon has been called "schematic priming" (Johnston & Dark, 1986). School children's differential histories of experience with words, written materials, sitting at desks, and so forth, must surely influence the degree to which the children can sit and attend to verbal and written information.

The skill of being honest or dependable when it is difficult to be so is another of the delay-of-gratification skills; it certainly does not occupy as prominent a place in the mental health literature as it merits, considering its importance in preventing a multitude of interpersonal and intrapsychic problems. Delinquency is the most obvious of these; there are about five times as many juvenile delinquent arrests for dishonesty (such as stealing) as for aggression (Empey, 1982).

The ability to delay gratification enough to experience some academic success is a very crucial development for a child's mental health. Studies by Rutter and Yule (1977) confirm the relationship between academic success or failure on the one hand and behavioral and emotional adjustment on the other hand.

Delay of gratification with respect to financial matters is seldom written about by mental health professionals, especially those involved with children; this skill is one of greater interest to the preventive mental health professional than to the child clinician. But the anxiety, marital conflict, and stressful situations that proceed from the lack of a saving habit in adults surely contribute to clinical syndromes both in them and in their children. Saving versus spending is perhaps as important a conflict between the "pleasure principle" and the "reality principle" as are more traditionally studied areas, such as sexuality and aggression.

## Group 7: Relaxing and Playing

Despite the importance of the ability to delay gratification and to work, it is also important to be able to consume gratification and to play. Sometimes it is very important to teach some parents that to be silly, to enjoy mirth and hilarity, and to have fun in frivolous ways constitute a positive, desirable skill, not a deficit. The transactional analysts (e.g., Berne, 1961) have spoken of this skill in terms of "natural child ego state." The use of humor is a social skill that is probably greatly underemphasized in facilitating a whole variety of interpersonal transactions, including conflict resolution and the forming of attachments. Mental and physical relaxation is a skill that has been taught to children by researchers hoping to counteract various problems, including a number of psychophysiological disorders, most notably headache (Williamson, McKenzie, Goreczny, & Falstitch, 1987); low academic achievement (Carter & Russell, 1985); anger (Hazaleus & Deffenbacher, 1986); a wide variety of fears (Strauss, 1987); and disruptive classroom behavior (Denkowski & Denkowski, 1984).

## Group 8: Cognitive Processing through Words, Symbols, and Images

Verbal fluency is not traditionally thought of as a psychological health skill. However, the evidence is compelling that helping children to use language more fluently should improve their mental health. There is significant correlation between language problems and behavior problems in children (Behar & Stringfield, 1974; Brown, 1960; Conger & Miller, 1966; Eisenberg, Landowne, Wilmer, & Iamber, 1962; Rutter, 1967; Rutter, Tizard, Yule, Graham, & Whitmore, 1976). Also, there is a strong correlation between language facility and reading ability (Loban, 1963; Norman-Jackson, 1982; Rutter & Yule, 1977), and a similarly strong relation between reading difficulty and conduct problems (Arnold, 1977; Jorm, Share, Matthews, & Maclean, 1986; Rutter & Yule, 1977).

There are several mechanisms by which lack of verbal ability could contribute to conduct problems. First, the repeated experience of frustration, disapproval, and failure at school when the child finds the work too difficult can simply lead the child to get off task more often, or can lead him to get angry and retaliate aggressively. A different mechanism is suggested by Vygotsky's (1962) notion of "verbal autoregulation of behavior," and other more recent theories dealing with verbal mediation between situation and behavior. Camp (1977) found that aggressive boys tended to use more irrelevant or immature speech when participating in tasks requiring self-control, whereas nonaggressive boys tended to use more appropriately self-guiding speech. Presumably, having a certain level of verbal ability is a necessary but not sufficient condition for using internal speech to mediate between situation and response.

Having adequate verbal ability does not insure that the child will be able to go through cognitive steps of decision making. Spivack and colleagues (Spivack et al., 1976; Spivack & Shure, 1974) have with beneficial effects taught children to use systematic steps of verbal mediation in their own decision making. Meichenbaum (1977) has also taught children to interpose some thought between situation and response. Camp and Bash (1981) presented a curiculum to teach self-guiding speech. Therapists who help children to put feelings into words are presumably making such phenomena more accessible to the cognitive reasoning processes of the child; indeed, this mechanism, rather than the "catharsis" mechanism, is one of the major candidates for why "expressing one's feelings" to a therapist often seems to help.

The cognitive component of empathy—the ability to discern how others do feel or would feel in certain situations, particularly in response to one's own actions—is an ability whose stages have been studied by child development researchers such as Selman (Selman, 1980; Selman & Byrne, 1974; Selman, Jaquette, & Lavin, 1977).

Samples of conduct-disordered children have shown, on the average, deficiencies in this skill (Urbain & Kendall, 1980).

The ability to see oneself in control of events, to find ways of mastering one's fate, is important; this has been made clear by studies linking "internal locus of control" to various measures of maturity and adjustment (Lefcourt, 1982; Phares, 1976). However, it is scarcely adaptive to see oneself in control of events that one actually has little power to affect, such as the divorce of parents or the accidental death of someone whom one had wished dead. Thus an important skill is to discriminate which events one can influence and which events must simply be tolerated.

The skill of organizing one's use of time has been written about much more in the business arena than in the mental health arena (Lakein, 1973; Winston, 1978); this skill, however, is working its way into stress management seminars and courses. The anxiety and stressful situations that result from procrastination, failure to plan, taking on too many tasks for the time available, and other time management errors surely can contribute to clinical symptoms. Biglan and Campbell (1981) report that teaching this skill is useful in helping depressed patients initiate activities that are more satisfying and productive. It is interesting that mental health professionals frequently refer, correctly, to certain families as "disorganized"; their use of time, money, and objects approaches chaos most of the time. Yet when such families enter treatment, therapists often focus by reflex upon skills such as expressing feelings. Perhaps it would be much more useful to teach them to make and be guided by organizing systems, schedules, agendas, budgets, and plans. A very few programs have begun to try such a strategy; these are classed as "household organization" training programs and are reviewed by Twardosz and Nordquist (1987).

The ability to accurately assess one's own abilities and skills at any given time is a cognitive skill that, when highly developed, should provide a certain degree of protection from the wide swings from grandiosity to self-hate found in some people called "narcissistic" or "borderline."

The entire set of skills in this group renders the child more able to process the world cognitively, to use thoughts to mediate between situation and response, rather than to be the prisoner of immediate reflex responding. The use of fantasy and imaginative powers is a skill that when highly developed greatly enhances the child's ability to deal with what is not physically present—to render situations and possible courses of actions accessible to mental processes.

## Group 9: An Adaptive Sense of Direction and Purpose

Having a sense of direction, a sense of where one wants to go in life, is useful for children as well as adults. Frankl (1963) has emphasized the search for meaning and direction as a healing force. I have often asked children what they want to do when they get older and who, of all the people they have ever known or heard about, they would want to be like in any way. Often the children who have the biggest problems are those with absolutely no role models or with role models who are antisocial or otherwise undesirable. An appropriate role model can perform the function of making concrete a sense of direction and purpose for a child; the more abstract formulations of life's purpose and direction can come later.

Work with adolescents often presents circumstances in which ill-founded senses of direction and purpose seem to contribute to the symptoms. Could it be that some adolescent girls with eating disorders who are focused almost solely upon the goal and purpose of looking good, of being thin enough, could benefit from refocusing some of their energy upon purposes more worthy of their efforts, such as being of service to others, fulfilling their productive potential, creating joy in interpersonal relationships, or being admired for achievements? Could it be that teenage pregnancy, antisocial behavior, drug abuse, suicidal behavior, and school failure would be greatly reduced if the adolescents in question possessed a stronger sense of purpose—of a desired future they wished to create—with which such behaviors might interfere? Although I am unaware of systematic empirical studies of this question, my experience indicates that an ethically valid "cause" with socially acceptable means of working toward it can be a powerful healing force.

## THE LENGTH OF THE SKILLS AXIS

Even this cursory trip through the skills axis may seem rather tiring; a full exploration of each skill would be much too great a task to undertake at one sitting. Holding the skills axis in memory requires a great deal of study. Is the rather overwhelming number of skills included on the axis a reason to abandon it? On the contrary, I suggest that by accepting the large number of skills necessary for mental health as accurately reflective of the complexity of life, and by comparing that large number to the seven or so bits of new information that can be comfortably held in short-term memory by intelligent people, we can come to some insights about the field of mental health.

There is a story about several blind men who each felt a part of an elephant. Each came away with a totally different impression of the nature of the beast, comparing it to a snake, a tree trunk, a wall, and so forth, depending upon the part that was felt. The central explanation for these differing viewpoints resides in the large ratio of the total body of information to that capable of being apprehended by a given observer. If, in a similar manner, mental health requires a much larger number of competences than are capable of being quickly assimilated in short-term memory, we might expect exactly what we see: differing factions emphasizing differing aspects of mental health competence, each drawing upon a subset of observable data. The complexity and size of the skills axis make it plausible that we might find one group emhasizing the expression of emotion, and another group emphasizing its control; one group aiming by reflex toward the reduction of guilt, and another seeking to foster the development of conscience; one group almost exclusively teaching relaxation, and another teaching the healing power of doing more activities; and, finally, a group avoiding "therapy" altogether and teaching academic and job-related competences. Each group may be right, given the prevailing skill deficiencies of the subpopulation with whom it deals. The problem comes when the subpopulation is not homogeneous, and the therapist must emphasize a totally different skill with one person than with another.

## CONTRACTING THE SKILLS AXIS

Despite the complexity of life and the inevitably large number of skills required to live it well, there is a need at times for a list short enough that people can hold it in memory after hearing it the first time. How may such a contracted skills axis be rationally arrived at?

When researchers have factor-analyzed problem checklists, they have derived broad categories of problems. Four categories frequently appearing are conduct problems, including aggression and other forms of acting out; problems of anxiety, withdrawal, and unhappy mood problems; problems of short attention span; and academic problems (Achenbach & Edelbrock, 1978; Kohn, 1977). If we search for the skills that are the most direct antitheses to these major factors, we arrive at the following: (1) the skill of cooperation and kindness;

(2) the skill of taking pleasure from positive events, including confident social interaction; (3) the skill of sustaining attention to tasks; and (4) the skill of using language with facility. These constitute the short version of the skills axis.

The last skill is perhaps the only one that does not in an obvious way correspond to the problem from which it was derived; however, various studies have demonstrated that facility in the use of language is rather highly correlated with school success (e.g., Loban, 1963; Norman-Jackson, 1982).

The four skills listed in this short form of the axis account for much of the variance in child behavior; they lose a great deal of the richness of the longer list. But for certain purposes—for example, constructing preventive mental health curricula for groups of children, or explaining to parents general goals for raising mentally healthy children—the short list may be quite useful.


## THE CENTRAL VIGNETTE OF HELPING

Finally, before leaving the subject of the skills axis, let us ask whether there is any one experience for children that is of paramount importance for mental health. To some extent, even asking this question is inconsistent with the goals of the skills axis. The axis implies that what children need for mental health is exposure to a wide variety of experiences, wherein they can learn each of the 62 skills on the axis. Nevertheless, if forced to choose one single type of experience, I would include those acts in which the child is a helper, those in which the child is helped, and those in which the child observes kindness between two other people.

I describe the helpfulness vignette in more detail here, to derive from it the reason for its central importance. To begin with, a person has a problem or a need. Another person offers to help the first person, and the first person accepts that help. They devise a way to solve the problem and then implement the plan, facing some unpleasantness if necessary in order to do so. They eventually solve the problem; the helper feels good about having been of use, and the person who has been helped feels grateful about having been assisted. There is an exchange of messages of gratitude and good will between the two.

This vignette is so central partly because so many psychological health skills are modeled in it. The helped person becomes aware of his own feelings, to perceive that a need exists. The helper and the

person helped may practice social conversation skills in their encounter of each other. The helper may practice empathic listening, and the
person helped may practice verbal communication. The person
helped then exhibits appropriate trust and dependency in accepting
the aid of the helper. The support that is illustrated, when internalized, is the antidote to the fear of separateness. The two people
use problem-solving and decision-making skills to determine the solution to the problem. They may delay gratification and work hard to
get the problem solved. Frustration tolerance is often involved when
the solution does not come immediately. Discovering a solution may
entail taking pleasure from exploration and discovery. The helper
feels pleasure from the act of kindness, and the person helped feels
pleasure from the kindness of another; the person helped practices
communicating approval, and the helper practices enjoying another's
approval; both feel pleasure from their accomplishment of the solution to the problem. The expectation that other people will be kind
rather than hostile, which should reasonably be increased by exposure to such experiences, would tend to reduce the fear of social
initiations and to increase the ability to be outgoing and confident in
interaction. The activity of going about helping people forms a decent
answer to the question "What is the purpose of life?" Even the skill of
independence can be fostered, if the person helped internalizes some
of the problem-solving competences modeled by the helper and uses
them to help himself. In other words, much exposure to this basic
"Good Samaritan" vignette, so that it becomes quite prominent in the
child's memory bank, would theoretically tend to increase a wide
variety of psychological health skills. For this reason, I have come to
the conclusion that providing the sort of experiences that strengthen
the child's skills of enjoying the performance of loving acts is almost
always of high priority.

The centrality of the act of helpfulness achieves a validation of
sorts if one considers the world's religions, which have evolved in
order to foster not only social harmony, but also individual mental
health. In each, acts of kindness and helpfulness have received major
emphasis (Smith, 1958).

# CHAPTER 3

# Making Diagnoses
# on the Skills Axis

## OVERVIEW

How does one diagnose degrees of skill deficiency? Various instruments for measuring specific skills are gradually becoming available; obtaining accurate quantification of these concepts is still problematic. However, for clinical purposes, an interview and inference procedure is recommended that relies on the type of thinking often used in single-case experiments. The clinician elicits a number of narratives of specific problematic occasions—situations the person could not handle well. Then these vignettes are examined for the commonalities they contain. The more consistently reports accumulate in which a certain situation was handled in a maladaptive manner, the more certain the clinician can be that the person has a deficiency in handling this type of situation. In going through this process, the clinician is moving from descriptions of events at a low level on the abstraction ladder, and moving to summary statements just one step higher on the abstraction ladder. The sources of information regarding the specific vignettes include the child's own reports of his experiences, parents' reports, teachers' reports, and the clinician's direct observations. Observations or descriptions of responses to role-played or imaginary situations give some additional information, though the clinician should be careful not to generalize too drastically from these. The same processes used to infer skill deficiencies may also be used to infer skill sufficiencies, or strengths.

Carrying out this process of diagnosis on the skills axis requires a decision that some patterns of responses to situations are more adaptive than other patterns. For some of these distinctions, reasonable people may strongly disagree as to which pattern is more adaptive. For most skill areas, more empirical research would be very helpful in shedding light on what patterns do actually work best in what circumstances. However, distinctions can usually be made fairly well between responses at the extremes of the continuum of skill and adaptiveness; in any case, in the absence of someone's deciding that something is better than something else, therapy is impossible.

Determining what skills are most deficient is one decision to which single-case experimental thinking is helpful; determining which skill deficiencies are most causally related to the presenting symptoms is another decision carried out by exactly the same sort of reasoning.

---

Most human beings can benefit from improvement in almost all the skills on the axis. But the therapist faced with people in distress must decide which skills to focus on first so as to remedy the situation most quickly. It is difficult or impossible for a family to work on 62 skills simultaneously; 4 or 5 target skills are a maximum for a family to focus on at a given time. How, then, does the therapist most effectively decide where to focus his or her efforts? This decision entails determining not only which skills are most deficient, but also which skill deficiencies are most related to the symptoms the child has.

## THINKING SCIENTIFICALLY ABOUT SKILLS-ORIENTED DIAGNOSES

Let us consider how conclusions about skills-oriented diagnoses can be made in a *scientific* manner. The word "scientific" refers to methods wherein hypotheses may be subjected to the test of repeated observation, and wherein conclusions are believed with a degree of certainty proportional to the amount of observed data supporting them.

One way of repeating observations is by making them across many individuals—for example, through experimental designs involving group comparisons. Just as legitimate, however, and more relevant to the clinician in his or her work with one family, is the process of repeating observations over time with one individual. The latter process is the central strategy of "single-case studies" or "intrasubject replication designs" or "one-subject designs" (Hersen & Barlow, 1976; Kazdin, 1980; Strayhorn, 1982). In this strategy, there are repeated measurements of a dependent variable over time, while the independent variable is allowed to vary or is actually manipulated. A typical example is the design in which treatment is given and withdrawn over time, and the level of the symptom is measured.

This sort of thinking is central to diagnosis of skill deficiencies or sufficiencies: The sort of situation requiring a skillful response is the independent variable, and the skillfulness of the person's response is the dependent variable. For example, if we hear about or observe an incident in which a child, after encountering some minor criticism, became so upset that he was unable to function for several hours, we have one observation suggesting that the child's skill in handling criticism is low. If further observations produce more and more similar pieces of data, our hypothesis is strengthened. Our $p$ value, to use statistical language, gradually becomes smaller and smaller; in other words, it becomes less and less likely that all these examples of maladaptive responses to criticism could be simply random aberrations. If, on the other hand, we accumulate examples in which the child does a skillful job of handling criticism, our hypothesis must be rejected or modified. Over time, we can accumulate quite a large set of observations about how the child characteristically responds to criticism. Even though the $n$ of subjects remains 1, the $n$ of observations can grow quite large over time. Psychotherapists can, in the course of treatment, arrive at thoroughly grounded conclusions about someone's psychological health skills.

Theoreticians who deal with diagnosis have debated the merits of "categorical" versus "dimensional" diagnoses: That is, should our diagnoses be all-or-none decisions, as the categories of the DSM-III require, or should they be perceived as varying along a continuum, as the results of a rating scale do (so that one is not only depressed or not depressed, but may be mildly depressed, moderately depressed, etc.)? Keeping in mind the fact that the skills axis is designed for use in psychotherapy, I believe that it is very important that the skills be conceived of as dimensions rather than categories. In this way, the patient and therapist can recognize and celebrate the fact that the patient has gained a little more skill and has moved along the continuum in a positive direction, even though he may not have arrived at the goal level yet. Much more is said about the process of celebrating small positive steps in later chapters.

## GATHERING INFORMATION FOR
## SKILLS-ORIENTED DIAGNOSES

What are the sources of data for skills-oriented diagnoses? There are four major ones: the reports of parents, the reports of the child's teachers, the reports of the child, and the therapist's firsthand observations of the child and the family.

The process of information gathering oriented toward skills-oriented diagnoses recalls the notion of the abstraction ladder mentioned in Chapter 2. It is usually necessary for the therapist to start with a parent's or a teacher's abstraction about a child, to move down the abstraction ladder to concrete examples, and then to move back up the ladder to a new abstraction in skills language.

For example, parents sometimes describe their children as "bad" or even "evil." A desirable reflex response for the interviewer is to call for a move down the abstraction ladder: "Can you give me an example?" or "See if you can remember a specific time when he acted that way, and tell me about it."

The therapist should move down the abstraction ladder until the descriptions evoke specific visual and auditory images of the child's response to a specific situation. If the response of the child is a thought or a feeling, then concreteness should still be pursued, until the thought is put in terms of what the child said to himself or what visual image the child presented to himself.

When one example has been obtained in fullness, the therapist should not stop at that point, but should obtain more examples of the problematic concerns. In each of these examples of situations and responses, the therapist should ask himself or herself what skills could have been usefully employed that were not employed. The skills that crop up over and over as the answer to this question are the ones whose deficiencies are most obvious. It is only when several examples have been obtained that the therapist can then look for commonalities among all the examples, and form his or her own abstraction.

When the therapist moves back up the abstraction ladder, if the information-gathering work has been done well, the abstraction arrived at may be considerably more useful than the one the child or parent started out with. The child who at the beginning was labeled "evil" by the parent may, after the trip down the abstraction ladder and back up again, be considered unskilled in knowing when to comply with adult authority, or incompetent at feeling appropriate guilt. On the other hand, the examples given may be those of normal temporary grumpiness, of appropriate self-assertion, or of appropriate independent decision making.

The interview, as described so far, may to an outside observer very much resemble the "unstructured" sessions that often constitute the first interviews by therapists. It is quite appropriate that this should be so, since concepts very similar to those on the skills axis are used by most therapists; the skills axis and the skill-oriented interview are conceptualizations of what most good therapists do to some extent already. Children or parents who are being interviewed in this way should have the feeling that they are free simply to talk about their lives and their problems, and the situations they handle poorly and the situations they handle well, without having the feeling that they are waiting for the therapist to introduce the next question.

Asking for specific examples of problematic incidents is only one of the interviewing techniques that should be applied in making skills axis diagnoses. It creates hypotheses in the mind of the interviewer, which then can be confirmed and denied by further information. When the interviewer hypothesizes that a skill deficiency is present in the child, he or she should ask of the parents, the child, and the teachers, as well as of the accumulated memory of his or her own observations, "Have you ever seen the child handle this sort of situation very well?" Now the therapist is asking for evidence of the skill, instead of evidence of the skill deficiency. Sometimes this line of questioning will uncover evidence for the skill; when it fails to do so, the hypothesis of the skill deficiency is strengthened.

## ABILITY VERSUS MOTIVATION, AND SELF-MOTIVATION AS A SKILL

In conversations about children's behavior and skills, this notion is often advanced: "The child does not lack the skills necessary to do $X$ [get along, stay out of trouble, make friends, stay by himself at night, etc.]—he just doesn't *want* to do it. His problem is motivation, not ability." For example, a child may possess the skill of doing helpful deeds when immediate reinforcement is present, but may not invoke this skill when immediate reinforcement is not present. One could say that there is no skill deficiency, only a deficiency of motivation. It certainly is important to recognize this type of distinction, because the therapeutic approach to the two situations should be different. However, I believe that both situations can, under our broadened definition of the word "skill," be referred to as a skill deficiency. We may refer to two separate skills, one being the skill of performance, and the other being the skill of internally motivating oneself for the performance. For example, the skill of *performing* kind acts may be in the repertoire, but the skill of *feeling good* about one's acts of kindness—that is, of generating internal reinforcement for such acts independently of external events—is a skill that is actually deficient.

What is the usefulness of such hair-splitting? One benefit is that it discourages us from reaching premature closure on certain questions of treatment. Some clinicians are in the habit of thinking, for example, that modeling is useful for getting a pattern into someone's repertoire, but that only a manipulation of consequences is capable of motivating someone to use a pattern already in his repertoire. But if the unmotivated person is conceived of as lacking the skill of internal motivation, and can be shown how to feel good about a performance and celebrate it, such modeling may be just what is needed. To be specific, a child might benefit from being shown examples (in a way to be discussed in later chapters) of someone's doing a kind act and delivering himself internal reinforcement for the act.

## INFERENCES CONCERNING THE "FANTASY REPERTOIRE"

Within the interview situation, there is another interesting way of seeking to confirm or disconfirm a hypothesis about a child's skill deficiencies, involving the examination of the child's fantasies. This topic is one that could demand much attention. Projective tests have absorbed much energy by clinicians and researchers, but have mainly produced unreliable results. Most psychometric researchers (e.g., Anastasi, 1976) are not great enthusiasts for these sorts of measures. The problem, as I see it, is not that fantasy does not have "meaning" concerning the person's life experience. Rather, so many different factors can influence fantasy that there is a huge amount of variance in the types of fantasies that may be elicited across different times and circumstances. Because fantasy productions are so multidetermined, it is dangerous to reason backward from fantasy to cause, to infer that a given fantasy character stands for a given real-life character, and so forth.

Rather than using fantasies to make sweeping inferences about the child's psychological makeup, it is epistemologically more justifiable to use the child's fantasies to make inferences about the child's fantasy repertoire, if "fantasy repertoire" is defined as the set of interactions and of thoughts, feelings, and behavior patterns that the child is capable of conjuring up in his imagination. If we ask the child to make up a story or watch the child construct plots with toy people, we are justified in inferring that the pattern the child enacts is in the fantasy repertoire. If it is a useful pattern, then its presence in the fantasy repertoire at least suggests that it is relatively more available for translation into behavior than if it were not present in the fantasy repertoire. The literature on "rehearsal in fantasy" leads us to feel fairly comfortable in assuming that repeated fantasy rehearsals of a pattern should make the pattern easier to carry out in real life, should the motivation ever arise (Cautela, Flannery, & Hanley, 1974; McFall & Twentyman, 1973; Suinn, 1972).

The inference that a certain pattern is *not* in a child's fantasy repertoire is difficult or impossible to make with certainty. However, when the therapist has heard a great many of the child's fantasies, and the child seems very comfortable revealing them; and when the therapist can successfully direct the child to enact certain types of fantasies, but certain types seem to draw a blank with the child—in such cases, the therapist may reasonably estimate that the salience of that pattern in the child's fantasy repertoire is low. At least, this inference may be made with enough confidence to act upon it with more chance of helping than of harming, especially if the response is the rather low-risk one of providing models designed to introduce the adaptive patterns into the child's fantasy repertoire.

## QUESTIONNAIRE INFORMATION REGARDING PSYCHOLOGICAL SKILLS

Now let us return to the main subject at hand—that of making inferences about the child's skills on various dimensions of the skills axis. The interview methods described earlier have the advantage of getting to very concrete images and leaving it up to the therapist to make the more abstract inferences about psychological skills. But there is something to be said for the straightforward question, "How skilled is the child at this?", using the midlevel abstractions of the skills axis. The Psychological Skills Inventory, presented in Table 3-1, simply asks a parent, teacher, or the child himself to rate the child's level of proficiency in the various skills. There are versions for parents and teachers, and versions slightly reworded so as to appropriate for self-report. Table 3-1 presents one version of the parent–teacher questionnaire. In the interest of brevity, this questionnaire does not attempt to assess all 62 skills on the axis, but looks at 22 skills most commonly at issue with children. There are three items for each of these 22 skills. Psychometric data on this measure are available from me.

In addition to this 66-item questionnaire, I have used with older children a simple list of the 22 skills as an aid to the interview. These

TABLE 3-1. Psychological skills inventory, Form A

---

Each of the following items will ask you to rate this child's skill in a certain area. Please rate each item according to the following scale:

$$5 = \text{Exceptional skill at this}$$
$$4 = \text{Very much skill at this}$$
$$3 = \text{Moderate skill at this}$$
$$2 = \text{Not much skill at this}$$
$$1 = \text{Almost no skill at this}$$

Please blacken a number from 1 to 5 for each item, using the answer sheet provided. Please rate all items.

Rate the child's skill at:

1. Getting to know other people his own age.
2. Making well-thought-out decisions.
3. Communicating appreciation to others.
4. Learning from and making the most of his own mistakes or failures.
5. Talking about feelings.
6. Getting satisfaction out of accomplishments.
7. Making the most of it when things don't go his way.
8. Being understanding and concerned about the feelings of other people.
9. Tolerating or enjoying making a sacrifice for others.
10. Talking out conflicts with other people his age in a rational way.
11. Sticking up for his own way.
12. Enjoying doing something nice for someone else.
13. Being, at times, calm and settled.
14. Tolerating criticism.
15. Enjoying being alone.
16. Obeying reasonable authority people.
17. Being able to trust and depend on someone.
18. Experiencing glee.
19. Holding himself back from getting or doing something fun now, to get a greater reward in the future.
20. Being honest when it is difficult to be honest.
21. Paying attention to a task for a reasonable length of time.
22. Handling situations without letting fear get in the way.
23. Meeting strangers.
24. Generating good ideas for solutions to problems he comes up against.
25. Expressing gratitude to others.
26. Experiencing his failures or mistakes without getting too down on himself.
27. Putting his own feelings into words.
28. Feeling pleasure when he has a success.
29. Experiencing unwanted events without getting overly disturbed.
30. Recognizing how others are feeling.
31. Giving in and compromising.
32. Negotiating with other people for solutions of disagreements.
33. Being firm; holding his ground.
34. Taking pleasure in doing acts of kindness to others.
35. Getting free of tension and nervousness.
36. Handling it when someone disapproves of something he had done.
37. Having fun in solitary play or work.
38. Doing what a reasonable leader says to do.
39. Getting support or aid from other people without being embarrassed.

40. Enjoying being silly.
41. Working hard now for benefits that come only later.
42. Telling the truth even when lying would pay off in the short run.
43. Keeping his concentration focused on a job.
44. Remaining unafraid at times when it is good not to be afraid.
45. Making social conversation.
46. Making thoughtful choices on problems of living.
47. Giving compliments to other people.
48. Not being too hard on himself when he makes a mistake or fails at something.
49. Expressing feelings verbally.
50. Feeling good about praise or compliments.
51. Tolerating not getting what he wants, without getting unduly upset.
52. Acting as a listener for someone else.
53. Letting other people have their way, when appropriate.
54. Using reasoning, expressed verbally, as a way of dealing with interpersonal problems that come up.
55. Avoiding being taken advantage of.
56. Getting pleasure out of helping other people.
57. Getting himself relaxed and calm.
58. Dealing with it when someone asks him to change something he is doing.
59. Enjoying doing things by himself.
60. Complying when a reasonable authority person sets a rule.
61. Asking for help when appropriate.
62. Enjoying childlike play.
63. Using self-discipline.
64. Being truthful, even when he knows that telling the truth will bring disapproval from someone else.
65. Focusing on something without getting distracted.
66. Keeping himself from getting scared unnecessarily.

*Key:* Getting to know other people, 1, 23, 45. Problem solving and decision making, 2, 24, 46. Expressing positive feelings to others, 3, 25, 47. Handling mistakes and failures, 4, 26, 48. Talking about one's feelings, 5, 27, 49. Celebrating one's successes, 6, 28, 50. Tolerating frustration, 7, 29, 51. Being empathic, 8, 30, 52. Letting the other do what he wants, giving in, 9, 31, 53. Talking out conflicts, 10, 32, 54. Being assertive, 11, 33, 55. Enjoying acts of kindness to others, 12, 34, 56. Relaxing, 13, 35, 57. Tolerating criticism, 14, 36, 58. Having a good time by oneself, 15, 37, 59. Complying with reasonable authority, 16, 38, 60. Depending, getting help when appropriate, 17, 39, 61. Experiencing glee, 18, 40, 62. Using self-discipline, 19, 41, 63. Being honest, 20, 42, 64. Sustaining attention to tasks, 21, 43, 65. Not letting fear get in the way, 22, 44, 66.

are the summary terms used in the key (see footnote to Table 3-1). I hand the child the list and ask how good he or she is at each of the skills. If the child claims to be very good at a certain skill, I ask for examples. If the child claims not to be good, I will ask for examples of times when the deficiency in that skill has caused a problem.

Other standardized instruments certainly provide information on a variety of the skills. Perhaps the easiest skill to measure with standard instruments is general verbal ability. In the interpersonal arena, things are much more complex. Factor analysis of several inventories meant to assess "assertiveness" in adults taps into several different areas of the skills axis besides the restricted meaning of "assertiveness" given there: Skills of expression of feelings, social initiations, giving praise and compliments, and others have been split off from inventories meant to measure the broad concept of assertion (Henderson & Furnham, 1983). Assertiveness scales for children (Deluty, 1979) and for adolescents (Lee, Hallberg, Slemon, & Haase, 1985) have been constructed that ask the subject to choose responses to hypothetical situations. Other measures (reviewed by Kendall, 1985) have been constructed to assess social competences by giving the subject situations and asking him to role-play a response. Unfortunately, the results of such tests seem to have a low-magnitude relationship to criterion behaviors also thought indicative of the competence in question. A number of other measuring procedures also reviewed by Kendall (1985) attempt to measure the content of subjects' cognitions; several of these take the form of a list of self-statements, with instructions for subjects to endorse how often they think these thoughts or how much they agree with them. The task of arriving at reliable and valid measures of each of the skills on the axis is complex and difficult and has by no means been accomplished, but progress in that direction does seem to be occurring.

## DIAGNOSIS OF SKILLS SUFFICIENCIES

Finding out children's "skill sufficiencies" is often a useful maneuver. If children can be led to appreciate and feel good about the skills they have already developed, they are in a much better position to motivate themselves to develop the remaining skills. Skill sufficiencies are inferred by interview and by questionnaire in just the same ways as skill deficiencies are inferred. The major way, of course, is to hear of specific situations that a child has handled well; when a certain number of these examples have accumulated, the therapist can infer that a certain skill is well developed in the child.

## SKILLS-ORIENTED DIAGNOSIS WITH FAMILIES

Family theapists rightly counsel that we should not devote sole attention to diagnosis of the child's skill levels, to the exclusion of assessing the skills of the family members and of the family as a system. Such factors have great bearing upon the skills the child develops, and it is important to notice these. Thus, while the therapist is interviewing the parents, the therapist also hears about situations that came up for each of the parents and for the couple or the family as a unit, and notes the responses made to those situations. From these concrete observations, abstractions can be made about the skills of family members and of the family unit with respect to each of the items on the skills axis. However, it is then useful to conceptualize these skill levels as contributing to an ongoing "intervention" in the life of the identified patient. That is, even before treatment begins, the parents are using reinforcement patterns, modeling, practice opportunities, and the other of the nine influence mechanisms I describe later. These influences may already be either favorable or unfavorable, and the greater the psychological skills of the people in the child's environment, the greater the chance of favorable influence. The system of influence on the child does not simply include the parents, but also includes peers, other relatives, the peer culture, teachers, other friends, and so forth. As I also describe later, one of the therapist's major goals is to teach *someone* in the child's influence system to intervene in a favorable manner with the child. It is useful (though not always essential) to understand the current intervention before trying to improve it.

One corollary of the preceding paragraph is that the therapy will sometimes primarily focus on improving the psychological health skills of someone other than the child. If, for example, a parent constantly models low skills of conflict resolution, it may be more important to teach the parent conflict resolution skills than to work directly with the child. If the parent is so low in the skill of tolerating a wide range of behavior from others that the parent is constantly feeling bad about the child's normal immaturity, work with the parent on this skill may be what helps the child the most.

I have referred above to the inference of skill deficiencies or sufficiencies in the family as a unit, as well as in the individuals it comprises. The therapist may look at the family's response to situations, and collect examples of how the family does or does not handle failure, celebrate success, delay gratification, get help, and so forth. In certain families described by Minuchin (1974) as "enmeshed," a characteristic pattern is that when one person in the family is distressed by something, the other members take on that distress and even amplify it; the family's boundaries are insufficient to enable the problem of one member to remain that person's primary problem.

Within the conceptual system described here, we might say that the family as a unit has low skills in dealing with frustrating events (i.e., the ones that cause the original distress) and particularly low skills in tolerating bad feelings (of other family members, in this case, rather than in oneself) without feeling bad about them and getting a vicious cycle started. Here the vicious cycle is perpetuated among different family members rather than within one individual.

As this example illustrates, there is nothing about the skills axis that requires that it be applied only to individuals. One can look at the functioning of any system, whether it be an individual, a family, or an organization, and ask how the basic tasks get carried out either successfully or unsuccessfully. One can ask about a school, a corporation, a legislature of a country, or a world court the same basic skills questions one asks about an individual: How well does it do at forming relationships and affiliations? How well does it tolerate rifts and losses of important affiliations? How well does it resolve conflict? How well does it tolerate adverse times, and how well does it generate positive affect from its successes? Is it able to get its work done, and is it able to foster relaxation and play? How organized is its planning and decision making, and does it have a set of superordinate goals that give meaning and purpose to its activities?

## DEFINING A SKILLFUL RESPONSE

One large challenge to the success of the skills axis notion is that it requires someone—the clinician, or whoever is filling out the questionnaire—to have a correct notion of what constitutes an appropriate and skillful response to a variety of given situations. If an adequately nourished child were to scream at the top of his lungs for 10 minutes after being told that he could not have a candy bar, I would regard that as an example of an inappropriate response, one exemplifying low skill in frustration tolerance. If someone else, however, were to argue that this response was an appropriate response, and an example of high skill in expressing feelings and in conflict resolution, it would be difficult for me to cite concrete data to show that I was correct with respect to this particular situation and this particular response. I would need to fall back upon "clinical judgment," or even the judgment resulting from nonclinical experience in human relations. How, one might ask, can diagnosis or treatment be based on something so subjective?

One answer to this question, which has been argued forcefully by Putallaz and Gottman (1983) among others, is that our field has been quite remiss in focusing so exclusively upon research in how to promote change, rather than more thoroughly researching first what sorts of changes we ought to promote. These investigators give an example in their own work of the second sort of research: They carefully observed how popular and unpopular children gain entry into social groups. Such observations are thought to provide a more informed basic for intervention with unpopular children than armchair decisions about what should or should not improve popularity.

I very much agree with the need for more research on what patterns of thought, feeling, and behavior actually work the best in life's situations, and in a later chapter I propose a method by which this question may more efficiently be studied. However, until many more rich empirical data accumulate, what should be done? Must therapists take a "know-nothing" approach to the question of what is skillful and what is not?

Clearly, it is easier to make distinctions among patterns at the extreme ends of the spectrum of adaptiveness or maladaptiveness than to make subtle distinctions among those in the middle. To give some very concrete examples, a child's fear of picking up an ordinary teddy bear is (barring unusual circumstances) clearly maladaptive; a child's fear of touching a rattlesnake is clearly adaptive; and a child's fear of approaching an unfamiliar German shepherd dog is one that is more debatable. To give another, slightly less concrete example, let us suppose that a child is playing with a toy that another child is also interested in. If the first child talks with the other child and arranges a way in which they can both play with the toy more enjoyably than either could use it alone, that is clearly good conflict resolution; if the first child, in anticipation of the other child's wanting the toy, bloodies the other child's nose, that is clearly overly aggressive conflict resolution; if the first child, realizing that the other child is not very responsive to cooperative negotiations, clutches the toy and shoves the other child away, that is more debatable.

There are definite problems with the empirical approach to discovering, in the subtle middle range, what types of responses work best. One of the main problems is the sheer enormity of the task, given the huge range of situations one can encounter in life and the fact that what is appropriate with one type of person or one group may be totally inappropriate with another person or another group.

In addition, a huge range of responses to a given situation may be workable and adaptive, given proper follow-up in subsequent responses.

Accordingly, a different approach is to focus on the higher-order skills of information gathering, generation of options, prediction of consequences, and learning from experiences, so as to teach "how to think" rather than "what to do." Among those who have tried this approach have been Weissberg *et al.* (1981); their careful observations pointed to the conclusion that content-free instruction does not inevitably lead to adaptive solutions. Teaching suburban children to brainstorm about possible solutions to interpersonal problems tended, in the eyes of the teachers, to produce more creative solutions; however, a group of lower-class inner-city children, when brainstorming, seemed to generate so many aggressive solutions that, in the eyes of the teachers, class discipline was negatively affected. Experimental children declined significantly on five out of nine rating dimensions. Perhaps if the instruction had assigned greater value, greater adaptiveness, to certain alternatives than to others, the program would have been more helpful. In my own less clearly documented forays into teaching of problem-solving skills, the same conclusion has emerged.

Regardless of the problems in doing so, the need to decide that some responses are better than others in specified circumstances is inescapable in the enterprise of psychotherapy and preventive mental health. The more information we have to help us, the better, but we will never have enough information to make foolproof decisions. I believe that in the meantime we can make fairly reliable decisions on skills axis diagnoses simply by taking advantage of fairly widespread agreement upon responses at either end of the adaptiveness spectrum. The more the therapist, as a result of life experience and exposure to wisdom of all sorts, is able to decide very accurately what is adaptive and what is not, the better the patients will be served.

## INFERRING CAUSAL RELATIONS BETWEEN
## SKILL DEFICIENCIES AND SYMPTOMS

The simple inference of a skill deficiency does not necessarily prove a causal relationship between that deficiency and the symptoms with which the child presents for treatment. For example, the child may be poor at handling criticism, but the presenting symptoms may be determined by his inability to sustain attention. Thus with respect to a symptom, a skill deficiency can be causal, or it may be an epiphenomenon. In order to infer causal relationships between skill deficiencies and symptoms, we must return to the model of one-subject experimental thinking mentioned earlier. Now we let the symptom be the dependent variable, and the occurrence of unskillful coping be the independent variable, and we search for repeated associations between the two.

Sometimes our inferences are easy to make. For example, if the parents' main complaint is that the child has tantrums, and the tantrums reliably occur in situations when the child's wishes are frustrated, it is easy to infer that reduced skills of frustration tolerance are causally related to the presenting symptoms. Here the symptom and the unskillful coping are identical. This is not always the case, however. With more distal effects such as physical symptoms, the causal inference can be more difficult. Nevertheless, with transient physical symptoms, the inference can sometimes be made with validity. If, for example, a diabetic patient has major problems in the skill of conflict resolution, and episodes of unskillful coping with conflict are regularly connected with episodes of diabetic ketoacidosis, the recurring temporal pattern enables the hypotheses of association to be verified over time. For certain other hypothesized relationships, such as with physical symptoms of long duration, causal relationships may remain hypothetical. For example, a child who is chronically afraid of separation, criticism, and rejection develops an ulcer. Whether there is a causal relationship between the psychological skill deficiencies and this physical illness may be impossible to decide for certain. In such cases, the logical strategy for the therapist is to attempt to improve the psychological skills, in the reasoning that if there is a causal relationship the illness may be helped as well, and if there is not a causal relationship, then at least relief of psychological distress has been achieved. In such cases, even if the patient's ulcer gets better as his psychological skills increase, the causal relationship has still not been demonstrated to the criterion of replicability. It is very important for the field that we not make inferences when the information on which to base them is not sufficient. However, it is quite rational to act on hypotheses when there is much to gain if the hypothesis is correct and little to lose if it is incorrect.

# CHAPTER 4

# Skills-Oriented Contingency Programs

## OVERVIEW

The therapist and the parents and child choose four or five high-priority target skills to promote, basing their decision upon which skills are most deficient, which seem most causally related to symptoms, which the family seems most immediately motivated to work on, and which are likely to give some signs of rapid improvement. It is usually best to give the parents a rating scale listing the four or five target skills, and another piece of paper with very concrete examples of each target skill. The parents are further prepared by practicing (if necessary) regulating tones of approval versus disapproval, and rehearsing in fantasy positive responses when the child does well in a "trigger situation" that has habitually touched off a maladaptive response. Then at home, whenever they see the child perform a positive example of a skill, they give immediate attention and approval, and note the example either mentally or on paper. The parents then tell each other, in the child's hearing, about the positive examples they saw. Each night parents review the positive examples with the child, to provide further rehearsal and reinforcement of the adaptive pattern. They bring their records in to the therapist, where the positive examples are remarked upon further in the child's presence.

This procedure is modified according to how much effect the parents are capable of expending; the burden is lightened to the point where the parents cease to feel a persistent sense of failure. Usually it is a good idea to avoid tangible rewards for the child's positive behavior. If social attention and approval are not reinforcing for the child, often the best strategy relies upon improving the child's relationship with the adult through fostering mutually gratifying activities. Another very important strategy is to reduce to a minimum the number of commands and requests the child is given; exercises in practicing with hypothetical situations may help parents discriminate necessary from unnecessary commands. In dealing with the child's undesirable behaviors, it is useful for therapist and parent to decide ahead of time upon consequences for specific behaviors: ignoring, time out, a reprimand, physically moving the child's body, or other consequences. Delivery of such consequences with low emotional arousal is quite useful. The delivery of consequences may be rehearsed in fantasy and role-playing exercises. The therapist should try to make sure the parent or parents get adequate reinforcement for their efforts, either directly from the therapist, or (preferably) from each other and from their own social network. If the program has been constructed efficiently, it may not have to be faded, but may continue as a permanent change in parent–child interaction patterns.

---

Having discussed the assessment process, which is aimed at deciding upon four or five skills that are of highest priority to promote, let us now move to one strategy exemplifying the treatment relevance of this diagnostic decision. A brief summary of the overall strategy described earlier may be in order: After deciding that learning-based treatment is indicated, the clinician (in conjunction with the parents and child) decides what skills are of highest priority to promote; then he or she selects among nine sets of ways of promoting these skills; then the clinician teaches those methods to parents or other available lay people who can work with the child.

In the following chapter, we finish defining the skills × methods matrix by looking at each of the nine influence methods. But before making that next foray into theory, let us survey one highly useful clinical strategy: teaching parents to use reinforcing consequences for examples of skills.

## CHOOSING TARGET SKILLS FOR TREATMENT

Deciding upon target skills involves more than diagnosis of skill deficiencies and determination of which skill deficiencies seem most causally related to symptoms. The clinician must also take into account what skills the family members are most motivated to work on. In addition, the clinician should give some weight to the question of what skills may be improved most rapidly. To see some rapid improvement at the beginning or treatment, especially improvement that reduces symptoms, is often a boost to parents' morale, and provides them with the energy to take on the more recalcitrant skill deficiencies.

Sometimes the direction in which parents would like to move with their child is diametrically opposed to the one the therapist determines to be most useful. If a therapist feels that the symptoms of a 4-year-old child are most related to skill deficiencies in trusting, depending, and accepting help, whereas the parents would like to foster independence by rather harshly insisting that the child do things for himself (e.g., prepare his own meals, awaken in time to get to preschool, and dress without assistance), then some of what I later call "goal setting" with the parents is a necessary preliminary to agreeing upon target skills. Sometimes the clinician needs to spend quite a bit of time summarizing evidence for the parents; persuading them that certain skills are worth working on; and leading them through the same evidence, the same observations, the same reasoning process that have enabled the therapist to adopt certain target skills.

## KEEPING RECORDS

When the therapist and the parents agree upon a set of four or five skills that are worthy of concentrated focus, it is then useful to construct a form that asks for positive examples of the child's target skills, of the type illustrated in Table 4-1. In addition, the form may ask for a daily rating of the skills, so as to quantify how well the child is doing.

The clinician includes on a form such as this whichever of the 62 skills on the axis have been assigned highest priority.

## MOVING DOWN THE ABSTRACTION LADDER
## TO POSITIVE EXAMPLES

Let us review the movements along the abstraction ladder that the therapist has made so far. If the parents have entered treatment with a negative generalization about the child, the therapist promotes a move down the ladder to lower levels of abstraction by asking for specific examples. Then the therapist moves back to a higher level of abstraction in making a skills axis diagnosis and choosing target skills; we may hope that this abstraction is more useful than the original negative abstraction about the child. The therapist then constructs the form illustrated above.

At this point, it is usually very important for the therapist and parents to move back down the abstraction ladder to concrete positive examples of the targeted skills. For each skill that is targeted, the

TABLE 4-1. Example of a positive behavior scale

Name: _____

Date: _____

Please rate each of the items below, using the scale that is given. Then please try to write in the "examples" space one or more incidents illustrating *positive* behavior in the area in question.

> 0 = None
> 1 = Only a little
> 2 = Some
> 3 = Pretty much
> 4 = A lot
> n.a. = Not applicable

1. How much did he seem to enjoy doing or saying some nice, helpful, friendly, or kind things? ____
   Examples: _____

2. How much did he comply with the requests given by adults? ____
   Examples: _____

3. How much did he put up with not getting what he wanted, without getting too upset? ____
   Examples: _____

4. How much did he do something brave? ____
   Examples: _____

5. How much did he keep at something long enough to see some results? ____
   Examples: _____

Total points from these items: ____

therapist and parents should write a list of such examples. In my experience this list is best constructed in the therapist's office, and not assigned as "homework." That is, the parents go home from the therapist's office with two different documents: one listing the target skills and leaving space for the positive examples they see, and the other listing the sorts of positive examples that should be looked for.

Examples should be chosen so as to include not only large and moderate improvements from the child's current level, but also small improvements and positive examples the child now already carries out. In this way the child can move along a hierarchy, rather than having to take a great leap into more adaptive behavior.

Why are these movements along the abstraction ladder necessary? What happens if they are skipped? Suppose, in initiating a positive reinforcement program, that the clinician simply asks the parents to generate a list of positive behaviors that they would like to see their child doing more often. Often, in my experience, the behaviors listed as desirable have little to do with the reason the child has come to treatment. For example, the child comes in because he cannot tolerate criticism and becomes aggressive when criticized, and the desirable behaviors the parents pick have to do with household chores such as emptying the garbage and making his bed. The child's failure to do household chores is the least of anyone's worries, yet the parents have selected these behaviors. Why? Often, I believe, it is because the therapist has not helped them to make a cognitive bridge between their complaints about the child and the positive behaviors they choose. The bridge I refer to, of course, is the abstraction, the skills axis diagnosis.

Suppose that the therapist comes to a skills axis diagnosis, but omits moving down the ladder to the specific examples. In other words, suppose the therapist simply tells the parents to watch for examples of frustration tolerance or compliance and to reinforce them upon seeing them. In this case, parents often simply fail to recognize many positive examples. In looking for examples of frustration tolerance, they may have a mental image of the child's reacting calmly when a request is refused, but may overlook the times when the child is expecting something in the mail and it doesn't come, or when a sibling has misplaced one of the child's possessions and the child cannot find it immediately, or when the child has to interrupt a favorite activity to come to supper.

The list in Table 4-2 is a sample of the concrete examples the therapist and the parents might generate, to illustrate for a given child each of the five skills on the positive behavior scale given above.

## BASELINE OBSERVATIONS

It is sometimes helpful for the parents to start keeping the records each day *before* starting to do anything differently. If both parents are interested and energetic, I encourage them to follow a procedure for 3 or 4 days in which they test their "interrater reliability." That is, each evening they do the ratings independently of each other, and then compare their results. For the first 3 or 4 days to a week, they simply fill out the form in the evening, and do nothing else any differently than they did before. This way they get some baseline data on how things are going before intervention is more formally begun.

TABLE 4-2. Specific examples of skills

*Doing kind things*
Seeming to enjoy reading his brother a story; saying "Thanks for the supper" to his mother; picking up something his mother drops and giving it to her; saying "Good morning" in a cheerful tone to his father; speaking gently to the dog and petting it nicely; saying "That's OK" in a gentle manner when a parent forgets to do something he wanted him or her to do; saying "That's interesting" when his sister mentions some of her thoughts; saying "Don't worry about it, you'll get it sooner or later" in a gentle way when his brother seems to feel bad about a mistake he made in a game; giving his brother a piece of his dessert when his brother wants some more; saying "What have you been up to?" and listening nicely to his sister when she tells him about her day; offering to help his mother carry in groceries; saying "You're welcome" in a gentle way when she thanks him for helping her.

*Obeying*
Saying "OK" without arguing when his father tells him it is time for bed; getting ready for bed after being asked to, without having to be reminded again; remembering to keep his voice low when his mother is trying to work, as she has asked him to; playing inside on a rainy day for an hour and following the "no throwing the football inside" rule; starting to work on his homework when his father suggests he should; playing gently with his friend after his mother tells them to stop wrestling.

*Putting up with not getting his way*
Saying "OK" in a nice way when he asks for some candy and is told he can't have any; keeping cheerful when the rain spoils his plans to play outside with his friend; handling it without yelling when his brother breaks one of the things he owns; looking for something he has lost in a calm way, without losing his temper; not yelling when he has to stop watching a television show to come to supper or to go out somewhere with a parent; remaining calm when his little brother grabs something out of his hand (getting it back, if he wants, but not yelling or hitting); being cheerful when he doesn't get a present that he has asked for; being cheerful when he has to come in from playing outside at night.

*Doing something brave*
Going up to a boy he does not know at the swimming pool and striking up a conversation with him; sticking up for one of his friends by saying "He's my friend" when someone at school is teasing the friend; disagreeing with what another boy with very strong opinions thinks about a movie; sticking up for his religion when some boys in his neighborhood are putting it down; feeling safe by himself in his room at night; hearing a screech owl out the window at night and not being scared of it; seeing lightning without being upset; calling up some friends to ask them to his birthday party.

*Keeping at something long enough to see results*
Finishing reading to himself one of his *Famous Myths and Legends* stories; finishing a homework assignment; having a long chat with one of his parents without having to run off to get into something else; working on his model of the human body for half an hour without getting distracted by something his brother is doing; listening to his mother read a chapter of *Mrs. Frisby and the Rats of NIMH* to him, and paying attention the whole time; finishing a game of chess he plays; practicing playing his guitar for half an hour.

The advantage of baseline observations is that they provide a standard of comparison for future reference; the disadvantage is that valuable time is wasted. Often the very beginning of the intervention is the time of highest motivation for the parents, and it is sometimes useful to seize the opportunity while it presents itself, giving only those directives that will make things better. If the therapist takes a detailed history in the assessment interview, this may sometimes provide enough baseline information to detect the major positive change that is sought.

## PREPARING TO REINFORCE POSITIVE EXAMPLES

The next step for the clinician is to make sure that the parents are both willing and able to deliver attention and approval immediately upon seeing a positive example of a target skill. In my experience, the ability to use positive reinforcement with children varies tremendously among individuals. The clinician observes and asks about the frequency with which the family already gives positive reinforcement. Then, if necessary, the clinician educates the family as to the value and importance of positive reinforcement, as well as necessity of its following fairly closely in time the behavior that it is meant to reinforce. The "tones of approval" exercise and the "shaping" game, which I describe in a later chapter, may be used at this point to give concrete practice in the use of positive reinforcement. The therapist assigns the parents the following task: They are to compliment, recognize, or otherwise positively reinforce the child *immediately* after they see any positive examples of the skills on the list that they have constructed. The therapist may need to rehearse or model with the parents the types of reinforcing responses that are likely to make the child feel good.

The therapist can ask the parents to say exactly what they would do or say if the child were to perform a certain positive example. For example, the therapist might say, "Let's suppose you asked the child to put up his coat and he did so. What sort of positive response do you think would feel natural to you?" Or: "Let's suppose the child asks for you to buy him some candy in the grocery store and you said no, and he didn't whine or fuss. What sort of response would feel natural to you?"

If the parent can think of nice things to say to the child fairly easily, then little additional time needs to be spent on this. If the parent cannot do so, then the therapist should model such responses for the parent.

In addition to such one-on-one instruction, it is useful to let parents listen to an audiotape on positive reinforcement produced by Patterson and Forgatch (1975), or a videotape produced by Webster-Stratton (1984). These materials provide many examples of positive reinforcement. Hearing or watching them is an excellent way for a parent to use time while the therapist is in an individual session with the child.

A potent means of reinforcement for parents to use is to give the child positive messages via a third party. It is very pleasing to the child if one parent (the one who saw a positive example) will talk to someone else, in the child's hearing, about the child's positive behaviors. For example, upon the arrival home of the father, the mother calls out, "Guess what Johnny did today! He kept working at his homework for an hour without stopping, and he did a good job on his math problems and his English exercises!" In this way, parents can use delayed reinforcement as well as the immediate type. There have been times when I have gotten parents to call my office on the telephone and leave a message for me when the child has done something particularly worthy of reinforcement. The one situation in which reinforcement by positive messages via a third party may backfire is in the case where jealousy is an issue—for example, with siblings close in age to the child being reinforced. If the parent exultantly compliments a child before a jealous sibling, the repercussions of the jealousy may greatly dilute the positive effect of this comment. If the family unit is quite skilled at celebrating positive events, the sibling will be able to celebrate the other sibling's success in the knowledge that this does not diminish his own worth and is not meant as a message of "Why can't you be like this?" But many family units have not developed this skill to this point. Thus, the use of this type of reinforcement with siblings will have to depend on an individual prediction of what effect it will have.

## HELPING PARENTS TO RECOGNIZE "TRIGGER SITUATIONS"

It is not easy for parents to remember to give approval when they see positive examples—particularly the examples in which being more skillful makes less noise. Some skills are obvious and attract attention (e.g., overt acts of kindness or helpfulness, delay of gratification through much hard work, or appropriate social conversation with a peer). However, other skills tend to attract attention only when they are *not* carried out. Frustration tolerance is a prime example of one of these. Suppose the child asks for a candy bar and the parent says, "No, you'll have to wait until you get home to get anything to eat." Suppose the child does not say anything at all, but continues to walk along with the parent. If in the past, the child has been in the habit of having a tantrum in such a situation, the parent is definitely seeing relatively skillful frustration tolerance that should be reinforced. But since the child does not announce to the parent, "OK, I will tolerate frustration better than before and not have a tantrum," there is no overt behavior to signal the parent. The parent tends, therefore, not to comment upon or give attention to such examples. The parent needs to mentally rehearse with the therapist the process of recognizing the "trigger situation" of denying a request, and being ready in such situations to notice quiet but desirable responses. The therapist and the parent generate images of a concrete set of trigger situations, and mentally rehearse reinforcing the child for a desirable response. Thus there is a "slot" or a "file" being created in the parent's consciousness for such situations—an allocation in the parent's memory bank—so that silent examples of skills will not be passed over in silence.

Other skills are also often manifested in ways that tend not to attract attention. Harmonious conflict resolution is often quiet and routine. The parent who is reading a magazine will hardly notice siblings resolving differences harmoniously, but will have his or her attention attracted to the loud failures of harmonious resolution. Again, the parent needs to mentally practice listening for situations where children's wishes conflict, so that harmonious solutions can be noticed with approval.

The process of creating suspense about the response to trigger situations can be transmitted not only from the therapist to the parent, but also from the parent to the child. When the child who is low in frustration tolerance demands, "I want a candy bar!," the parent can say, "Here's a chance to see how well you can put up with not getting your own way. You'll have to wait until we get home to have something to eat. Let's see whether you do another good example for us to go over tonight, or not." Now the child knows that more is at stake than the candy bar: He has been reminded of a chance to practice a skill whose successful performance gets lots of positive notice.

## ESTABLISHING ROUTINE NIGHTLY FEEDBACK AND REVIEW

It is useful if the information stored on the rating form can be used each day for delayed as well as immediate reinforcement. The parents sit down with the child for 5 or 10 minutes each evening, and review with the child how the day has gone. They ask the child to recall any deeds or actions that he is proud of. The parents list the examples of positive behaviors that they are proud of, using the rating form to jog their memories. They can give a total rating to the day by adding up the scores for each of the items on the scale. Thus the child is being reinforced for the positive examples again, and the child is also rehearsing in his memory the image of those positive examples. Furthermore, the child is calling upon his own stored memories to retrieve positive examples that the parents may not have seen. This technique harnesses the power not only of positive reinforcement, but also of mental rehearsal: Going over the positive examples in one's mind is a rehearsal for future performances of these or of similar examples. In addition, the procedure gives practice in reflecting on the day's accomplishments and celebrating them—a very adaptive habit that the child can use throughout his life.

A variation on this procedure is for the parents to pick some skills that they would like to improve in themselves, and to use the evening celebration procedure with their own examples as well as the child's. In this way, the parents are able to provide models for the child, as well as reinforcement and practice. When the parents get in on the act, the procedure becomes more of a family growth activity and less of a clinical procedure focusing upon the identified patient. The process of operationally defining one's goals for self-improvement, monitoring and reflecting upon one's performance daily, and celebrating improvement is exceedingly useful as a routine procedure for people of all ages.

This process was described in a charming manner by Benjamin Franklin in his *Autobiography*. Franklin monitored himself in 13 skills; he referred to these as "virtures" rather than "skills," but the concept is very similar. His virtue of "tranquility" for example, corresponds roughly to the skills axis concept of frustration tolerance: Franklin's definition was "be not disturbed at trifles, or at accidents common or unavoidable." He kept daily records of his performance over a long period of time. He heartily recommended the procedure, stating, "It may be well my posterity should be informed that to this little artifice, with the blessing of God, their ancestor ow'd the constant felicity of his life, down to his 79th year, in which this is written" (Franklin, 1784/1950, p. 101).

## RAPID IMPLEMENTATION OF THE MONITORING AND REWARDING PROCEDURE

Sometimes, when a child's parents are very cooperative and the telephone intake conversation and first office visit have been fairly long, I have sent the parents out of the office after the first session with a week's supply of forms and a fairly good plan for what the reinforcement program will ultimately be. This general strategy is a way to get moving very quickly, and a way that can help the child a tremendous amount. The strategy puts into effect, via one simple set of maneuvers, a strong influence on the parent to start looking for the positive behaviors of the child and to start calling attention to these behaviors. In addition, if the therapist has done his or her diagnostic job right, the parents are working on just the skills that the child needs the most to work on. Furthermore, the records will provide a quantitative measure of the target parameters of the treatment, which the therapist can then use to keep track of the child's future improvement. Several important treatment principles have been accomplished efficiently.

## DECIDING HOW MANY DEMANDS TO MAKE UPON PARENTS

The procedure that I have just advocated is not overly difficult for a well-organized parent who has the motivation and energy to devote a few extra minutes a day to the procedure. However, it is very common in clinical practice that parents are functioning in a state of chronic disorganization of time and tasks, and/or a state of chronic exhaustion because of an overwhelming amount to do with too little help. When such is the case, the clinician should tailor the procedure so that the parent does not feel as though it simply constitutes one more time demand that he or she will probably fail to meet.

Accordingly, the clinician should find out, before assigning more tasks, how overwhelmed the parent is to begin with. The clinician might ask the parent to describe a typical day in his or her life; might ask how many unfinished tasks are presently looming over the parent; might inquire how comfortable versus overwhelmed the parent feels with the number of tasks to do and the amount of time in which to do them; and might inquire directly what the parent's reaction would be to a request to keep certain records each day.

After this conversation, the clinician may assign tasks to the parent that are more nearly proportional to the time and energy the parent has available. For the most overwhelmed parents, it may be desirable to require no record keeping at all. The therapist may simply send the parent home with a piece of paper with the names of one or two target skills on it, and a list of concrete examples of each of those skills; the parent's job is simply to post that list and read it occasionally, watch for the positive examples, and approve of them when they occur. At the time of the next visit the parent is asked to remember one or two of the positive examples if possible, and to tell them to the therapist in the presence of the child. The therapist relies upon work done in sessions with the parent to increase the parent's reflex tendency to notice those positive examples and reinforce them. If the therapist desires to use the positive behavior scale (see Table 4-1), he or she may ask the parent to recall examples and give a rating for the child's performance during the preceding week, rather than asking for daily feedback. I believe something is lost by reducing the demands on parents, but more may be gained if doing so keeps the overburdened parent from feeling that yet another failure is in the making.

Another approach to the overburdened parent is to focus less attention upon the child, but to devote some energy to time and task management skills with the parent. I present techniques for doing this in a subsequent chapter.

## NONTRADITIONAL ASPECTS OF THE PROCEDURE

### Specificity of Reinforcement to Highest-Priority Skills

The procedure just described represents variations upon behavioral programs widely used with oppositional children (reviewed by Gard & Berry, 1986). But some of the differences between what is described and what is often carried out in behavioral programs are worthy of comment. In my observation, the attempt to find positive behaviors to reinforce in a child with many undesirable behaviors often leads the therapist and parent to focus on behaviors such as making the bed, taking out the trash, and so forth, when the child's nonperformance of these tasks is the least of anyone's concerns and they are low-priority, "icing-on-the-cake" goals. Skills-oriented diagnosis and generation of positive examples of high-priority skills, with the moves up and down the abstraction ladder that these processes require, are meant to get parents reinforcing children for just the behaviors that most need to be reinforced. This practice enables the method to be generalized to any skill on the axis, and not to be used just for cooperation and compliance.

## Global Ratings

A second departure from procedure sometimes recommended has to do with using global ratings versus frequency counts of behavior. Therapists sometimes insist that parents count each compliance and noncompliance, each instance of prosocial behavior, each instance of aggression, and so forth. Anyone with actual experience in counting behaviors realizes that the task is not only a full-time job, but also very draining; it is just the sort of task that most stressed parents cannot take on. Even giving global ratings each day is often too laborious a task for some parents.

## The Issue of Tangible Reinforcers versus Social Reinforcement

A third difference between what I am suggesting and what is done in many traditional behavior modification programs is the reliance on social reinforcement (i.e., verbal recognition, approval, attention) rather than toys, food, or tangible reinforcers. This is an issue of some complexity; let us examine it more thoroughly.

Parents often object to the use of tangible prizes as reinforcers. My clinical experience has taught me that there is much merit in these objections, and that the reluctance of a parent to use "bribery" is not simply something to be educated away by the therapist. If quick results are the criterion, reinforcement with toys and other material prizes is often quite successful; yet I advise the use of tangible rewards only as a last resort. Why?

### DISADVANTAGES OF TANGIBLE REWARDS
Several untoward side effects have been known to occur with tangible rewards. First, parents often find it quite aversive that their child

seems to become interested in being good only for what it gets him. The child sometimes very reasonably expects that some rewards will come for positive behaviors not included in the program, and when asked to do something will respond by inquiring, "What do I get for it?" If he is getting paid for performing behaviors previously expected for free, it is reasonable from his point of view to expect payment for other desirable behaviors as well, and it is only good business practice to withhold those behaviors until payment is promised.

Second, it is entirely within the realm of possibility that some children will figure out the advantages of behaving badly: They enjoy being on a reinforcement program, and they know that the program is in place because they are behaving badly and presumably will be faded if their behavior improves for long enough. Baruch (cited in Ginott, 1965) quotes a boy who did just that: "I get what I want by keeping mother thinking I'll be bad. Of course, I have to be bad often enough to convince her she is not paying me for nothing" (p. 55). This possibility is also intensified when a tangible reinforcement program is used for only one child in a group of children—for example, the sibling who is behaving the worst. The other children also can figure out that the child has begun getting rewards for good behavior because the initial behavior was bad, and it seems to them only reasonable business practice for them to act out to get the same set-up.

A third disadvantage of tangible rewards is that the process of keeping track of points, finding rewards that are truly reinforcing, deciding how many points are needed for the next reward, delivering the reward on time, keeping the reward from being delivered before the requisite number of points have been made, and so forth is a lot of work. The fact that it is a lot of work implies that very few parents will be able to continue it for as long as a few months. And there are several problems associated with a temporary program. One is that when it is discontinued, the child sometimes feels deprived of what must have been his rightful due; otherwise, why would it have been offered? The child may feel somewhat like the paid employee who is told he is being made a volunteer—a quite different feeling from that of the worker who has been a volunteer from the beginning. Another disadvantage of the temporary nature of the set-up is that if the program is discontinued because it is too much work and not because the child's improved behaviors have become independent of the tangible rewards, one should expect to see exactly what occurs with the typical ABAB design: When the rewards are withdrawn, the maladaptive behavior returns to baseline levels. O'Leary, Poulos, and Devine (1972), in a review, cite five studies of token economies in which the tokens were the major reinforcers for positive behavior, and in which the withdrawal of the token contingency resulted in a decline in appropriate behavior. A final negative consequence of the work involved in tangible reward programs is that the time and effort spent in that way compete by necessity with time that the parent could spend in other pursuits, such as reviewing positive accomplishments, presenting positive models, and doing enjoyable activities with the child.

Accordingly, I believe that it is rarely the best strategy *in the long run,* although very pleasing in the short run, to use toys and other presents as reinforcers.

I would exclude from the category of tangible reinforcers the colored stars that can be stuck onto a chart for preschoolers and young grade-school children. These I regard as a record-keeping method and method of graphic display that can be used with little effort and that results in few or none of the harmful effects listed above, especially if it is used with all children in the family. Special trips to the park or to a restaurant, in which the real reinforcer is more time with the parent, have a few of the disadvantages of tangible reinforcers; the advantages of such a plan sometimes outweigh the disadvantages, however.

WHEN APPROVAL AND ATTENTION ARE NOT REINFORCING

When the approval and attention the child is given for positive examples of high-priority skills do not seem to be rewarding for the child, should the therapist then go to a tangible reinforcement program? In my experience, it is usually better to examine ways of improving the relationship between the adult and the child.

First, the child may enjoy attention or approval, but just not the particular brand that is being dispensed. Quiet interest and observation may, for example, be much more rewarding at times than gushy praise. An interested tone of voice may be much more rewarding at times than a "You did well" statement. A simple comment on what someone did may be more reinforcing than a hug or applause. The adult must be able to accommodate himself or herself, in the short run at least, to the child's preference for certain types of attention or approval, while in the long run hoping to broaden the child's range of receptivity.

Second, some children who do not seem at all influenced by adult attention or approval seem never to have had a very good relationship with an adult, or with the particular adult who is to provide the social reinforcement. When the adult meets some of the child's needs, gratifies some of the child's wishes, gives the child pleasure, lets the child have fun with him or her, enjoys being with the child, and is reliable and dependable, the conditions are then ripe for the child to come to rely on the adult in such a way that the adult's approval or disapproval, and attention or inattention, will really make a difference to the child. A corollary of this principle is that if the therapist discerns that the parent and child almost never engage in mutually gratifying activities, and if the therapist can successfully promote such activities, the social reinforcement the parent gives should become much more potent. The story reading and dramatic play activities to be discussed in future chapters can sometimes be just such activities.

An interesting allusion to the necessity for first establishing a positive relationship with the child was made by Harris, Wolf, and Baer (1967) in a set of case reports on the use of preschool teacher attention to modify behavior. The authors stated,

> Actually, for a few children observed at the preschool, it has been thought that adult attention was a negative reinforcer. This seemed to be true, for instance, in the case of [a child whose lack of vigorous play was a problem]. Before the study was initiated, the teachers spent several weeks attempting to make themselves positively reinforcing to the child. This they did by staying at a little distance from him and avoiding attending directly to him until he came to them for something. At first, his approaches were only for routine help, such as buttoning his coat. On each of these occasions they took care to be smilingly friendly and helpful. In time, he began making approaches of other kinds; for instance, to show a toy. Finally, when a teacher approached him and commented with interest on what he was doing, he continued his play instead of stopping, hitting out, or running off. However, since his play remained lethargic and sedentary, it was decided that special measures were necessary to help him progress more rapidly. It was the use and effects of these special measures that constituted the study. Clearly, however, adult attention must be or become positively reinforcing to a child before it can be successfully used to help him achieve more desirably effective behaviors. (Harris *et al.*, 1967, p. 155)

This is a nice description of a therapeutic task carried out prior to the research study that sounds even more important than the study itself. The child was informally taught skills of appropriately depending and of enjoying the approval and attention of adults; once he gained these skills, the adults could help him learn improved play behaviors. The moral to this story—that the adult needs to first establish a kind, dependency-gratifying relationship with the child before the contingent use of approval can be very potent—is often overlooked by those who set up behavioral programs.

## DEALING WITH UNDESIRABLE BEHAVIORS

Despite the great emphasis this book places upon the positive, it is almost always necessary for the therapist and the parents to make conscious decisions about how to deal with the child's harmful or undesirable behaviors.

In keeping with the emphasis on the positive, many if not most of children's undesirable behaviors can best be dealt with by ignoring them; they will wither away from inattention rather than being crushed by punishment. Ignoring the child's undesirable behavior is very useful, but more difficult to carry out than one might think. Many parents have to be taught how to ignore: Ignoring does not mean glaring silently at the child, and it does not mean saying something like "I'm not going to do it for you until you can ask nicely." It does mean turning one's attention to something else without giving the child eye contact or a verbal response.

Another nonpunitive means of reducing defiant behavior is to eliminate all unnecessary requests or commands. I have found it a useful teaching tool to tell parents about a couple of studies suggesting that the more commands one gives children, over a certain threshold, the worse they behave. G. K. Lobitz and Johnson (1975) found that in a sample of children and parents, the children who behaved worse were given more commands by the parents. This finding, of course, does not tell us whether the children behaved worse because they got more commands, or whether they got more commands because they behaved worse. In a second study, W. C. Lobitz and Johnson (1975) found that the parents of nonproblem children were able to make their children behave worse by issuing more commands to them. (The Spearman rank-order correlation between changes from normal to worse behavior and increases in the number of commands was .62—a rather substantial correlation.) I have also found it useful to go over a set of commands or requests and let parents practice discriminating the necessary ones from the unnecessary ones. Chapter 8 contains some exercises of this sort, plus some exercises in chatting with the child and regulating the tones of approval and disapproval that are sent to the child.

When ignoring is not sufficient, sometimes it needs to be supplemented by gently physically moving the child's body to enforce a command. For example, the parent says, "Please put the book down and come with me." When the child does not comply, the parent gently takes the book out of the child's hand, takes the child by the hand, and leads the child along. This method, which is of course more applicable to young children, relies on the fact that most children do not like to be physically made to do something, and will comply if they know that the alternative to compliance is to be physically made to comply.

When ignoring and physically moving the child's body are not sufficient to stop the child from doing harmful things, the parent must often resort to punishment. If the parent is punishing severely enough and frequently enough, the child tends to rebel, perhaps as a manifestation of the universal human tendency to reciprocate; in this case, punitiveness is being reciprocated. The ideal form of punishment is one that is mild enough that the parent can apply it without feeling guilty, and the child can accept it without feeling excessively frightened or angry. Furthermore, it is necessary that the punishment not constitute a model for very undesirable behavior, as does physically hitting someone in anger. A form of punishment that meets these criteria fairly well is "time out": The child is made to stay in an uninteresting place, preferably in a room by himself, for 2–5 minutes, without receiving any attention or reinforcement during that time. The time-out program is initiated by a conversation in which the child is told, "Each time you do X, you will have to take time out." The concrete details of time out are reviewed and rehearsed with the parents, who in turn review and rehearse it with the child before the first time out is given. It is particularly important to communicate that time out need not last a long time; research has demonstrated that time-out periods longer than 15 minutes are no more effective than the shorter periods and may even add to the disruptive behavior (Benjamin, Mazzarius, & Kupfersmid, 1983). A videotape by Patterson (1982) on time out is particularly useful in teaching parents this technique.

Time out is certainly not the only form of punishment that is useful. A reprimand is probably even more effective with children who have not been habituated to disapproval. Reprimands are best delivered when the child is removed from a group, and when the adult states very clearly what the undesirable behavior was, why it was undesirable, and what the desirable behavior would have been. I have found it quite important that reprimands, as well as other forms of punishment, be delivered with low emotional arousal. Excitement and high-pitched, high-volume vocal tones often escalate or reinforce misbehavior. Ideally, the nonverbally communicated disapproval of the parent is very skillfully regulated in response to the contrition that the child feels. But many children who present clinically have been desensitized to disapproval by having heard too much of it, applied too indiscriminately. Withdrawal of privileges (e.g., television, bicycle) is another form of punishment that often proves effective, especially as a "backup" if the child refuses to go to time out. It should be emphasized to parents, however, that with much positive modeling, much positive reinforcement for positive skills, keeping requests and commands to a minumum, and ignoring or physically moving the child in response to undesirable behavior, punishment of any sort should eventually become only rarely necessary.

## A CHECKLIST FOR CONTINGENCY PROGRAMS

The checklist in Table 4-3 has been put together by analyzing a number of contingency programs that did *not* work, and searching for the crucial element that might have turned failure to success. If the parent reviews the checklist each week, and can answer "Yes" to all the questions in this list, it is likely that the contingency program being examined will help.

## WHO REINFORCES PARENTS?

All the things described in this chapter are work for the parents. The total time spent in keeping records is rather small, but the energy spent in revising one's personal habits may be fairly substantial. Therefore the parents need to be reinforced for the labor that they put into this task. Who is to reinforce the parents? Our society provides a rather scant degree of approval, not to mention applause, for conscientious parents. It would be ideal if natural support systems could reward the parents' work; however, pragmatically, for families in therapy, the deliverer of reinforcement for the job of parenting most often turns out to be the therapist.

TABLE 4-3. A checklist for contingency programs

1. Did you have in your mind (or, better still, written out) a list of concrete, specific examples of the sorts of behaviors you wanted to see your child do *more* often?
2. If there were some things you wanted to see the child do less often, did you decide what the "trigger situations" are that usually bring out the undesirable behavior? Did you rehearse in your mind recognizing it when the child does anything acceptable in response to those trigger situations?
3. Did you break the big goals down into very small steps, so that you were set to reward examples that the child was already able to do?
4. Was the child aware of the examples? Could the child name some examples?
5. Did you watch carefully for these positive examples, and give the child some attention and approval (smile, pat on the back, praise, attention, interest) whenever you saw an example?
6. Except when it would embarrass the child in front of peers, did you give the child approval for the positive example *immediately* after you saw it?
7. Were you able to regulate the tone of your voice well enough to give the inflections of approval as well as the words?
8. Did you sometimes tell someone else about the positive examples you saw, in the child's hearing?
9. Did you go over with the child at the end of the day the positive examples that you could both remember?
10. Have you been dependable enough in meeting your child's needs and sustaining a consistent attachment that your child cares about whether you approve or disapprove?
11. For undesirable behaviors, did you decide ahead of time what you want to ignore, what you want to reprimand, what you want to give time out for, and what you want to use other consequences for?
12. When one of the undesirable behaviors happened that you wanted to ignore, were you able to pay no attention to it at all?
13. Had you told the child ahead of time what behaviors would result in time out? Had you rehearsed the time-out procedure in moments of calm?
14. When you used time out, did you use a place that has no interesting things in it?
15. Did you use time out every time you saw the undesirable behavior?
16. Did you use a short length of time for time out (e.g., 2–5 minutes)? If you used some other punishment, did you make it last as short a time as possible?
17. Did you use a kitchen timer to signal the end of time out, so that there was no conversation with the child about when time out was to end, or about anything else, during the time out?
18. Did you respond to your child's negative behaviors with low emotional arousal, communicating low-excitement emotions (such as disappointment) rather than high-excitement emotions (such as loud frustration and anger)?
19. Did you do something fun with your child?
20. Did you model, in real life, the skills you most strongly want your child to improve in?
21. Did you give as few commands as possible, only when necessary?
22. Did you enforce every command you made?
23. Are you in control of your own stresses enough that you have the energy to pay attention to these things?

How does the therapist reinforce the parents? The parents' homework assignments, such as filling out the forms and going over them with the child and so forth, are a very important part of the therapy. Whenever homework is assigned, the therapist is obligated to collect and check it. Therefore, as long as records are being requested, the therapist should without fail ask to see them. Putting the numerical results into a graph will further strengthen the idea that these are to be done every time without fail. I like to look at the parents' records at the beginning of the session, with the child present, and read to the child some of the positive examples of his behavior that the parents have recorded. Doing this has two favorable effects: It reinforces the child for whatever the behaviors are, and it reinforces the parents for recording the positive examples. Asking about the celebration that the parent has had with the child for positive behaviors helps to insure that such recognition continues to take place. The therapist should feel no hesitation about congratulating the parents for the work that they have put into the program; applause and cheers are very much in order. Brief telephone conversations may be very useful in sustaining motivation and in troubleshooting at the beginning of the program.

Even more important than the therapist's appreciation for the parents' effort is that which they give each other. If one parent is unable to participate as fully as the other, the therapist may at least exhort the less active parent (by a telephone conversation if that is all that is possible) to show appreciation to the other parent for his or her efforts.

The overstressed parent can often use help in a variety of psychological skills. On many occasions much time is saved by the therapist's simply teaching these to parents, without insisting that the parents see a separate therapist for "their own issues." Often some attention to such nonthreatening areas as time management skills and relaxation skills can help parents avoid the chronic "I'm at the end of my rope" syndrome. A later chapter goes into greater detail on skill training for parents.

## FADING VERSUS CONTINUING CONTINGENCY PROGRAMS

One often sees advice that a contingency program be gradually faded—in other words, that the rewards come gradually less and less frequently. An alternative is to try to structure the program from the beginning so that it can be continued indefinitely. With the use of social approval and no tangible rewards, and the emphasis on recalling and celebrating specific positive examples rather than giving points, the program may be seen as not something to be done for a time and faded, but as a permanent change in the family interaction patterns.

## WHEN THE PROBLEMS EXIST AT SCHOOL AND NOT AT HOME

I have written this chapter with the assumption that the child's skill deficiencies manifest themselves at home, in the presence of parents. Sometimes, however, some other setting—most often the school—is the site where the problem shows itself.

In such circumstances, it is prudent not to expect that rearranging consequences in one setting will produce changes that automatically generalize to the next setting. If a teacher is reinforcing or provoking maladaptive patterns, sometimes nothing parents can do will override the negative effect. Sometimes the therapist can best serve by consulting with a teacher and advocating contingency programs similar to those advocated to parents.

# CHAPTER 5

# The Methods Axis

OVERVIEW

Arranging consequences, as discussed in Chapter 4, is only one of nine methods of influence that constitute the "methods axis." The most complex of these methods is promoting goal setting. Much of insight-oriented therapy, when examined closely, is directed toward understanding how symptoms may be linked to specific skill deficiencies; this understanding serves to link the motive of reducing the symptom to the motive of increasing the skill. At other times, goal setting involves a person's becoming aware of what he is presently in the habit of doing, thinking, or feeling; at other times the person best forms goals by learning concepts that are cognitive handles for the various choices open to him. At still other times the person becomes persuaded that a certain goal is worth achieving.

The other processes on the methods axis include the following: forming a hierarchy, or devising a series of small steps toward the goal; modeling, or giving examples of how to move toward and accomplish the desirable pattern; providing instruction, or explaining how to carry out the desirable pattern; providing practice opportunities; controlling stimulus situations; monitoring and providing feedback on progress toward the goal; controlling or communicating reinforcement contingencies; and attributing to the person the traits that are consistent with the desired thought, feeling, or behavior patterns. In examining these various processes, certain interesting facets become evident, as follows. Modeling, practice, and communication of consequences may be carried out in fantasy and role playing as well as in real life. The process of monitoring progress and giving feedback is sometimes effective even without additional reinforcement. Attention from an adult is often a reinforcing consequence for a child, even when it is not intended to be. Communication of consequences can influence behavior, even though the particular reinforcement or punishment may never once have been delivered.

When the methods axis is combined with the skills axis to form the skills × methods matrix, I believe it is possible to place nearly all that is useful in all schools of psychotherapy in the cells of the matrix. Since nearly all psychotherapeutic orientations provide the opportunity for a flexible therapist to use the nine methods of influence with any of the skills, we would expect to find exactly what has been found—namely, that comparative studies of different types of psychotherapies tend not to yield significant differences.

It is my contention that the skills axis is a guide to differential action, and that the methods axis designates possibilities for what those actions should be. That is, when high-priority skills are chosen, those skills become the content for goal setting, hierarchy formation, modeling, and the other methods of influence.

---

Chapter 4 has focused primarily upon one method of promoting change—namely, the use of consequences, of reinforcement contingencies. Invoking the principle of reinforcement by itself often brings about major positive changes. But to assemble the full range of ways of promoting skills, we must look at a broader range of methods. This chapter examines nine sets of influence methods that constitute the "methods axis."

## GOAL SETTING

The first method of influence or way of promoting skill development is one of the most complex: It is helping a person to consciously adopt the development of a certain psychological skill as a goal for himself.

Sometimes this process involves promoting *insight* into the causal relationship between a competence and a symptom. The parents who come to understand that a child misbehaves as a way of asking for attention and social contact, and that such a request is in turn motivated by a fear of being alone, are much more likely to set as goals for their child the development of appropriate ways of initiating social contact and more competent ways of enjoying solitude.

The process of "insight-oriented" therapy is primarily aimed at proper goal setting, though these two phrases have not been linked in any literature of which I am aware. But the desired end of an insight-oriented exploration is almost always the setting of a psychological growth goal that will be most "on target" in reducing distress and promoting growth. For example, suppose an adolescent comes to treatment complaining of unhappiness and suicidal ideation. None of the skills on the axis is on his priority list; he simply wants not to be so miserable. In a series of insight-oriented conversations, the adolescent realizes that he has marked difficulty in forming close and trusting relationships, and tends to break off such relationships as soon as they begin to blossom; the main reason he is so miserable is that he lacks close friends. Furthermore, he realizes that some very important caretaking figures in his life have been very untrustworthy, and that putting trust in these people in the past repeatedly led to disappointment; the transference of the fear of trusting gained from these experiences into present-day relationships causes the current fear of trusting, even when it is not justified by the circumstances. The implicit goal set by these insights is to discriminate among current relationships so as to decide how much trust is justified, and to trust those present people who are trustworthy, without transferring to them the feelings meant for people in the past. Does this insight instantly accomplish the task of gaining this competence? No—but now the adolescent has the goal in mind, and is therefore much better equipped to attain it than he was before.

Another means by which goal setting may be facilitated is by helping the person observe what thought, feeling, and behavior patterns he is presently enacting. For example, a depressed youth may enter treatment with the simple goal of getting less depressed, but without any goal of thinking fewer self-deprecating thoughts. When, however, the youth is asked by the cognitive therapist (e.g., Beck, 1976) to keep a record of the automatic thoughts that occur in certain circumstances, it becomes clear what the present pattern of thoughts is, and from there it is a small step to the goal of changing those thought patterns.

At other times, the goal-setting procedure primarily involves what I have come to call "conceptual sharpening." That is, the therapist helps the person incorporate into his vocabulary and cognitive repertoire the concepts necessary to distinguish between the competent pattern and the less competent pattern. For example, with a child who has great difficulty in the skill of tolerating frustrating events, the therapist defines some ways in which people talk to themselves in the face of frustration, and names them "awfulizing," "not awfulizing," "getting down on oneself," "not getting down on oneself," "blaming someone else," "listing options and choosing among them," and "learning from the experience." When the child has these concepts available, he is much better equipped to aim toward doing more of some and less of others.

Sometimes the word "persuasion" better describes the movement toward goal setting. Suppose a therapist is working with a child whose defiance gets him into much trouble at school. When a teacher asks the child to hand out some papers, his typical response is "I'm not your slave. You hand them out." Suppose the therapist hears the parent state in several different ways that children are equal human beings and should never be ordered around by adults. Suppose the therapist decides that the child would really be a lot happier in the world if he were to develop further the skill of submitting to authority at appropriate times. The therapist cannot simply put the skill of compliance with authority on the target skills list and expect the parents or the child to join in wholeheartedly. The therapist first must present the evidence in some manner or another to the parent and to the child, particularly the parent, and very tactfully bring them to the conclusion that it would be useful if this child did not have to take on his own shoulders the job of righting all the power imbalances in the world. Not until the parents are convinced that submitting to authority is sometimes a useful skill will they become allies in the treatment program. Thus goal-setting conversations, at least with the parents and possibly also with the child, should precede the use of modeling, reinforcement, and the other techniques to be enumerated later.

Here is another example. Suppose that through astute observations, the therapist determines that a certain child's opposition and defiance have to do with his fear of appropriate dependence. The therapist decides that if the child were much more able to depend, to get help, to disclose his weaknesses, then he wouldn't have to drive people away so much. For the parent and the child, however, appropriate dependency may not appear on the priority list at all. So the therapist's first task is to start persuading the parent that appropriate dependency is a useful skill for this child. One approach to this task is to share with the parent the same sort of evidence that has led the therapist to that conclusion.

I place goal setting first on the list of influence methods for good reason. If, for example, an overly aggressive child is asked to practice responses to conflict situations without having first persuaded himself that less aggressive responses are desirable, the child may use the practice opportunities to come up with more aggressive and harmful responses, thus further ingraining the habit of aggression, rather than practicing an improved style of conflict resolution. If the child is exposed to many fictional examples of kind and cooperative behavior, before deciding upon such behavior as a goal, he may simply deride the fictional characters as sissies, thus practicing rejecting the cooperative behavior rather than being influenced toward it.

This is not to say that the child must always have consciously decided to adopt skill development in a certain area as a goal before anything else is done. For example, the therapist who works with preschool children may confidently begin presenting models of desirable patterns without trying to get the children to agree to a certain goal that may be too abstract for them to verbalize. But as children get older and their powers of resistance become more developed, goal setting becomes more and more important.

## FORMING A HIERARCHY

The second ingredient of effective change is forming a hierarchy with respect to the skill in question, recognizing where the child is now on that hierarchy, and arranging to move up the hierarchy in steps that are small enough. The hierarchy for a psychological health skill is the same sort of hierarchy that teachers form when they are teaching mathematics: The child must first master multiplying integers before starting to multiply fractions. Making available a set of steps that enables someone to reach a goal in small jumps rather than by a great leap is sometimes the only missing element for achieving competence.

The concept of hierarchy is quite relevant to therapeutic decisions. Suppose a therapist is working with a child on frustration tolerance. In the therapist's office the child asks to take a certain toy home with him, and the therapist responds, "You can play with it here, but you'll have to leave it here between sessions." Suppose the child stamps his feet, folds his arms, sticks his lower lip out, and says, "That's no fair," then gradually focuses his attention on something else. Should the therapist reward this response by congratulating him or by patting him on the back, or should the therapist ignore this response? The answer depends on whether this response is a step up or a step down from, or at the same level as, the child's previous habitual level of skills. If the child in similar situations before has cried, said "I'll never be your friend any more," and tried to slap and kick the therapist several times, then a short pout would represent cause for celebration; congratulations would be in order. On the other hand, if the child has progressed to a point where he habitually accepts frustration in much better ways, the therapist would probably ignore the brief pout. Part of the art of therapy—a part that many therapists perform intuitively—is to constantly keep track of how far several of the child's skills have progressed along their respective hierarchies, so that the therapist can know when to celebrate and when to ignore. By making these formulations explicitly in their minds, therapists can increase their therapeutic potency quite substantially.

The concept of hierarchy often dictates that adults should settle for whatever allows a child to get success experiences at or slightly above his current level on the hierarchy, rather than failure experiences at the level at which the child "should" be functioning. For example, the shy and socially awkward child might benefit greatly from playing with younger children, where less skill is demanded. It would be a shame to insist that such a child play with older children on the grounds that he "should" practice interacting well with them, while in reality forcing him to practice being ostracized, feeling humiliated, and increasingly fearing social interaction.

## MODELING

The third change mechanism on our list is modeling. A great deal of research on modeling has been done in recent years. Human beings of all ages—as well as a variety of animals, including rhesus monkeys (Mineka & Cook, 1986) and laboratory rats (Galef, Kennett, & Wigmore, 1984)—do tend to imitate behavior patterns that they see.

With children, not only parents' examples, but also those set by peers and by fictional characters, have proved important. In teaching skills, it is therefore highly useful to expose the child to images of skillful examples of the competence in question.

### Empirical Literature on Modeling

Since the use of modeling is very heavily emphasized in the rest of this book, much more than in most other treatises on psychotherapy, let us look at some of the empirical literature on modeling. Modeling has been used successfully both with problems of anxiety and withdrawal and with problems of aggression and defiance. I discuss each in turn.

Modeling has been used to reduce children's fears. The strategy is simply to show a child models who fearlessly deal with the stimulus, or who start out fearful and gradually get over their fears. Such procedures have proved useful with children fearful of dogs (Bandura & Menlove, 1968), of swimming (Lewis, 1974), and of dental procedures (six studies cited by Kirkland & Thelen, 1977).

Modeling films have also been used with preschool children in the teaching of social skills. O'Connor (1969) selected a group of preschool children with long-standing problems of social withdrawal. Half of these children were shown a 23-minute film in which an initially withdrawn child engaged in increasingly complex social interaction in a preschool setting. The model child in the film gradually began to play with peers, and to enjoy the pleasant consequences of increasing social confidence. The other children in this group were shown a film unrelated to peer interaction. Classroom observers found that immediately after the films, those children who had viewed the experimental modeling film showed a dramatic increase in the frequency and quality of their social interactions. Only one of the six children in this group continued to be rated as socially withdrawn by the teachers. The children who had viewed the control film continued to be withdrawn. Two later studies using the same film (Evers & Schwarz, 1973; O'Connor, 1972) replicated the favorable effect.

In discussing his results, O'Connor (1972) surmises that modeling may be particularly useful in introducing new patterns into a child's repertoire, whereas reinforcement contingencies may have their greatest effect on behaviors already within the repertoire of the individual. Thus, the distinction is drawn between learning and performance (in the words of Bandura), or, in other words, between knowing how to do something and being motivated to do it.

Keller and Carlson (1974), however, found that when they used modeling films to teach a number of social behaviors (e.g., smiling, sharing) to socially isolated children, only those specific behaviors that had been highest in the children's pretreatment hierarchy of social skills increased in frequency after the modeling. In this study, at least, modeling seemed more effective at bringing out responses already in the children's repertoires than in getting new responses into their repertoires. In other words, modeling may be just what children need to elicit behaviors they are already capable of.

What is the evidence that modeling reduces problems with aggression and acting out, or that it increases cooperation and kindness? Staub (1978, 1979) has extensively reviewed research on the influence of modeling on positive behaviors, such as sharing, giving, complimenting, and helping. Exposing children to the behavioral example of other people does affect positive behavior immediately following the children's exposure; this finding has been repeated many times. Fewer experiments have demonstrated the long-term or generalized effects of modeling procedures on prosocial behavior; however, those that have looked for such effects have usually found some. Rushton (1975) found that children who had been exposed to generous models were more willing to donate to needy people when tested 2 months after the modeling exposure. Midlarsky and Bryan (1972) found similar results.

Chittenden (1942) conducted a study designed to teach children nonaggressive reactions to frustration. She exposed children to a series of plays depicting first aggressive and then cooperative solutions to interpersonal problem situations; the experimenter facilitated discussion of the advantages of cooperation. The children who observed the modeling plays showed a decrease in domination and aggression in response to frustration at nursery school. G. M. Thomas (1974) used modeling via videotapes to improve the attending behavior of highly distractible first-graders. Meichenbaum and Goodman (1969, 1971) trained impulsive children to make slower, more reflective responses on cognitive tasks by training the children to talk to themselves and guide themselves verbally through the tasks; this training involved exposure to models. Coates, Pusser, and Goodman (1976) found that exposing preschool children to segments of the television show *Mister Rogers' Neighborhood* that contained many models of giving positive reinforcement significantly increased the children's giving of positive reinforcement to other children and adults in the preschool. Alvord and O'Leary (1985) found that the sharing behavior of preschool children could be increased by exposing children to models of sharing through stories and slide–tape shows of modeled sharing. Thus modeling has had success in helping children to increase cooperation and compliance, as well as to reduce anxiety and withdrawal.

In a discussion of the power of modeling effects, we must mention the still-controversial but voluminous evidence on the relation between television violence and aggression in real life. There is no doubt that a correlation exists between real-life aggressive behavior and a preference for violent television; most researchers seem to conclude that the weight of the evidence favors bidirectional causality, in which viewing influences aggressive behavior, and aggressive personality traits lead to a preference for violent entertainment. (For the "pro" and "con," respectively, of the notion that viewing causes aggression, see Freidrich-Cofer & Huston, 1986, and Freedman, 1984, 1986. For other reviews of this subject, see Eron, 1980; Liebert, Sprafkin, & Davidson, 1982; Pearl, Bouthilety, & Lazar, 1982; Singer & Singer, 1983, 1985.) My own reading and experience leads me routinely to advise parents of young children to try to influence children's diets of television and other symbolic presentations so as to include the highest possible ratio of prosocial to antisocial models.


## Factors Contributing to the Effectiveness of Modeling

Assuming that one wishes to use modeling to help children learn psychological skills, what particular factors seem to contribute most to the effectiveness of the procedure? Kirkland and Thelen (1977) have reviewed several such factors; I summarize the findings here.

With respect to subject or client characteristics, modeling works best with younger children, with more dependent children, and with less resistant children. Two studies (Gelfand, 1962; Kanareff & Lanzetta, 1960) suggest that children who have experienced failure in the activity relevant to the modeling imitate models more than do children who have experienced success in the activity.

With respect to model characteristics, those models who seem nurturing, who express positive emotion, and who powerfully control resources of value to the child seem to elicit a high rate of imitation. Both adult and same-age models have successfully elicited imitation; Kirkland and Thelen (1977) found that with young children, the data do not permit a definitive statement as to whether adult or child models are most potent, nor as to whether same- or opposite-sex models are superior. Multiple models seem more potent than a single model (Bandura & Menlove, 1968; Marburg, Houston, & Holmes, 1976). Meichenbaum (1971) found that models who initially showed some difficulty with the task and then gradually mastered it were more effective than models who demonstrated immediate mastery. Models who talked to themselves about their coping responses (i.e., who used "self-verbalization") were also more effective. Yarrow and Scott (1972) found an interaction between the nurturant or non-nurturant style of an experimenter and the content of the modeled behavior that children chose to imitate. Adults were trained to supervise groups of children in either nurturant or non-nurturant ways. All of these adults modeled both nurturant and non-nurturant behaviors toward toy animals. The children who were supervised in a nurturant way imitated more of the nurturant activities toward the toys, and those supervised in a non-nurturant way imitated more of the non-nurturant activities toward the toys, despite the fact that both groups of children were exposed to the same models of behavior toward the toys. The conclusion is that children may selectively imitate the symbolic models of adults that are most consonant with the adults' real-life behavior. If we may extrapolate these findings, children should more frequently imitate prosocial stories parents read to them if the parents also carry out prosocial actions in real life.

With respect to consequences that ensue for the models, models who are rewarded for their behavior elicit more imitation. Selective reward and punishment of models has been used to help the child discriminate which behaviors to imitate and which to avoid. The importance of consequences to the model implies a corollary: Modeling is more potent when children perceive that their peer group or some other valued group admires the model. In other words, if the model gets the admiration of a real audience or the child's "imaginary audience," the model is more likely to be imitated. By contrast, if many positive models are shown to a child who is in a group of peers, and the peers deride the models and think of them as sissies and wimps, the net effect may be negative. (One could examine this hypothesis by enlisting children as confederates of the experimenter so as to make positive or negative comments on the model during the viewing of the modeling stories, and then testing the behavior or attitudes of the real subjects after such experiences.)

With respect to adjunctive instructions, asking the subject to describe the actions of the model seems to elicit greater imitation (Bandura, Grusec, & Menlove, 1966). In one study, giving subjects direct instructions to imitate the model also tended to increase imitation (Rennie & Thelen, 1976). Sometimes the person providing the influence does not actually need to present the model, but can instruct the child to recall the image of a model from his or her own memory bank, and use that model for imitation. This strategy was studied by Hartley (1986), who asked school children to choose someone they thought was very clever, and to imitate that person while performing cognitive tasks; this procedure improved children's performance.

The implications of the principle of modeling are quite far-reaching. One implication with respect to parent training is that when the parents and the therapist arrive at a list of target skills that the parents are to reinforce with their child, they should also be encouraged to model these skills in real life in any way that they can. I speak of this more in a subsequent chapter.

Another implication of the principle of modeling is that the world's collection of fictional and biographical narratives, songs, and poetry—an enormous set comprising written, filmed, taped, or otherwise recorded thoughts, feelings, and behaviors—are in a sense a huge data base, a massive repertoire capable of being transferred from their stored media to the actual enactments of people. How best to organize and retrieve desirable patterns from this huge data bank, and how to add to it systematically the patterns that people need the most, constitute a challenge for coming generations.

## PROVIDING INSTRUCTION

The fourth change mechanism on our list is instruction—unabashedly teaching someone how to do something. I think that among nondirective therapists there has been far too much of a taboo on directly telling someone how to do something better. In my experience, when families come for help they expect and want to be given some advice and instructions, and most of the time they do their best to try what they are given. I have heard therapists justify the withholding of instructions on the grounds that if instructions were helpful, the patients would have solved their problem before coming to the therapists' offices. One has only to ask patients what sort of advice they have received to realize the falsehood of this reasoning; very seldom, in my experience, have clients received the sort of advice that is optimally useful.

I find that written, audiotaped, and videotaped instruction materials for parents are very helpful. I regard it a great waste of time for a parent to be asked to sit in a waiting room while the therapist is with the child; if the parent is not watching the interaction and learning from it, then I routinely ask the parent to take in training materials most relevant to the child's problems. Appendix 1 of this book contains suggestions for parents that have proved quite useful. Chapter 8 contains some instructions and practice exercises on commands, chatting with the child, and regulating tones of approval and disapproval. A set of audiotapes, the *Family Living Series* (Patterson & Forgatch, 1975), and some videotapes (Patterson, 1982; Research Press, 1983; Strayhorn, 1984; Webster-Stratton, 1984), have been quite useful as instructional tools.

Instructions delivered directly to children have in some studies proved effective in increasing social interaction skills, especially when the instructions have been combined with modeling, practice, and reinforcement. Zahavi (1973, cited in Hartup, 1979) found that having a 15-minute individual session with nursery school children in which instructions were given about aggression tended to reduce the aggressiveness of the children as compared to that of a control group. The instructions were to the effect that (1) hitting others causes hurt; (2) other children do not like children who hit; and (3) it is wise to think of alternatives to hitting. Oden and Asher (1977) provided instruction to children with few friends on how to play well with peers. The instructions centered on (1) participating fully in the play; (2) showing interest in the other person; (3) cooperating; and (4) maintaining communication. The children receiving the instructions increased significantly in attractiveness as playmates, as contrasted with a control group.

Instruction, exhortation, and explanation are difficult to use well with children, partly because it is sometimes difficult for the adult to separate these from punishment and disapproval. Suppose Johnny grabs a toy truck away from Nancy, and the adult says, "Johnny! Give that truck back to Nancy! What did I tell you about grabbing things like that? She had it first!" These instructions are embedded in a context of verbal disapproval, together with attention to the child contingent upon an undesirable action. By contrast, suppose that Johnny comes to the adult wanting some attention, an hour or more after his episode of grabbing, and the adult says, "Johnny, do you know something? Here's one way I like to see boys and girls play with each other. I like it when a boy goes up to a girl playing with a toy truck and just watches for a while, and then says, 'Why don't you roll it to me, and I'll roll it back?' I like it when the boy doesn't grab the truck away from her." These provide a more "pure culture" of instruction, without also modeling punitive tones and rewarding undesirable behavior with attention.

## PROVIDING PRACTICE OPPORTUNITIES

Fifth on the list of change mechanisms is the provision of opportunities for practicing the skillful patterns. A child who needs to learn to have better social interaction skills might practice the skills with the therapist during the session. Once the child reaches a level on the hierarchy at which he is capable of some success experiences with other children, exposure to whatever groups he can be successful with will be very helpful.

One of the major premises of the methods espoused in this book is that practice can usefully be carried out in fantasy and role playing as well as in real life. This principle is an extremely important one, since it implies that a therapist can systematically import practice opportunities into any session, without having to wait for them to occur in real life. Because this principle is so important, let us examine briefly some studies connected with it.

The technique of carrying out desirable patterns of thought, feeling, or behavior in the imagination, in order to facilitate their performance in real life, has been given several labels. Among these are "goal rehearsal" (Lazarus, 1977), "covert rehearsal" (McFall & Twentyman, 1973), "behavior rehearsal" (Suinn, 1972), and "covert modeling" (Cautela et al., 1974). Most of the studies of this technique have been with adults. Suinn (1972) found that with competitive skiers, the technique of skiing a course in the imagination was helpful in improving performance. Cautela et al. (1974) found that fantasy practice was just as effective as live modeling in reducing avoidance behavior in college students. McFall and Twentyman (1973) found covert rehearsal no different from overt rehearsal in promoting the ability to refuse unreasonable requests; both methods of practice improved the subjects' abilities in the target behavior. Kazdin (1974a, 1974b, 1974c, 1974d, 1976) found covert modeling superior to no treatment in reducing avoidance of harmless snakes and in promoting assertive behavior.

Studies have also examined some of the parameters of fantasy rehearsal that seem to make it more effective. If subjects' fantasy sequences had the protagonists rewarded for performing the desired behavior patterns, the fantasy rehearsal seemed more effective (Kazdin, 1974a, 1974b). Subjects' imagining themselves performing the activity and imagining someone else doing so both produced improvement (Kazdin, 1974c). Imagining someone of the same sex and similar age performing the desirable pattern improved the effectiveness of the procedure, as opposed to imagining someone much older and of the opposite sex (Kazdin, 1974d). Imagining someone initially carrying out the desired pattern with some hesitation or difficulty (as the subjects might do themselves in initial trials) seemed to enhance the effectiveness of the procedure (Kazdin, 1974c).

The studies described above were done with adults. Meichenbaum (1972, cited in Singer, 1974) reported that imagery methods were helpful in teaching impulsive children to do more thinking before acting. The children, for example, were taught to remind themselves, "I will not go faster than a slow turtle, slow turtle." Imagining the turtle constituted a form of fantasy practice.

Role playing, which adds a motor component to the imaginary practice, has been used many times with children and adults. Staub (1971) led kindergarten children to enact situations in which one child needed help and another provided help; this intervention increased children's tendency to offer help 1 week after the intervention. Barton (1981) found that detailed instructions and peer modeling of sharing, with praise to the model, were not potent enough to facilitate preschoolers' sharing. When behavior rehearsal through role playing was added, there were dramatic and immediate increases in sharing. Rehearsal through role playing is a basic ingredient of social skills training programs (e.g., Goldstein, 1973, 1981; Goldstein & Pentz, 1984).

## CONTROLLING STIMULUS SITUATIONS

The notion that the habit strength of skillful patterns increases with the number of rehearsals the person carries out implies that eliciting those skillful patterns by any means tends to strengthen the skill. Some situations, because of either biological programming or the programming of prior learning, predictably elicit certain types of responses in a given child. Manipulating these stimuli so as to maximize positive rehearsals is another major means of influence, which I call "controlling stimulus situations." If a child is trying to learn a specific sort of delay of gratification, such as avoiding junk food between meals, removing junk food from the house provides a situation conducive to the exercise of the skill. The child gets to practice the skillful behavior and build up habit strength, before eventually moving up the hierarchy so as to be able to avoid such food even when it is present.

Another prime example of stimulus situation control with young children (e.g., preschoolers) has to do with arrangement of the child's environment, such that it is not necessary to say "no" so frequently to the child. I have seen troublesome children transformed to cooperative ones as if by magic, when placed with a skilled adult in a situation with the following characteristics: (1) The room is empty, except for materials that are desirable for the child to explore and play with; (2) one adult and one child inhabit the room; and (3) there is a shelf or a box whereby the adult can get out of immediate reach those materials that are not the current focus of attention. In such conditions, the adult usually has only to wait for a few seconds before the child requests to see some of the objects (e.g., toy people, storybooks). The adult can reinforce the child's interest in these materials, and does not need to punish or discourage the child's interest in anything. The adult can regulate the materials on and off the shelf so that the child is not distracted from one set of materials by the presence of the others.

For young children, toys are important stimuli influencing the content not only of imaginative play, but also of real-life activities accompanying the play. Turner and Goldsmith (1976) found that preschool children exhibited a higher rate of antisocial behavior (e.g., hitting, kicking, pushing, threatening, cursing) when they were given toy guns to play with than when they were given toy airplanes. Feshbach (1956) found similar results.

Another important stimulus situation, especially for the young child, is the degree to which the home has been "child-proofed." When poisons, firearms, knives, medicines, matches and lighters, and other harmful things have been locked up; when valuable breakables have been put out of reach; when the temperature of the hot water has been set at a nonscalding level; when electrical outlets have been covered; when mechanical devices keep cabinets and drawers unavailable to the exploring youngster—then the parent is greatly freed to enjoy the child more and to spend less energy commanding the child to stay away from something. Such changes can make an enormous difference in the emotional environment, not to mention the safety of the child.

R.V.G. Clarke (1985) has argued that, according to empirical evidence, stimulus situation control is more effective in preventing delinquency than are individually delivered interventions. Specific environmental manipulations that reduce the opportunity for crime include vandal-resistant materials and design, defensible-space architecture, "no-change" systems on public transport, closed-circuit television surveillance, and the employment of security guards. While most of us would be idealistic enough to hope that some day internal controls in individuals will be prevalent enough to make these environmental manipulations unnecessary, the power of environmental stimuli must be acknowledged.

The most complex sort of "stimulus situation" is that set of conditions conducive to the child's developing skills of appropriate dependency, attachment, and trust: a caretaker who gratifies a reasonable portion of the child's needs; who is not cruel to the child; who has reasonable, age-appropriate expectations of the child; who communicates affection for the child; and whose continuing presence for the child is assured. This complex set of stimuli also tends to reward the child for trusting and developing a "secure attachment"; however, one can make a case that reinforcement alone is not sufficient to explain the phenomenon of attachment. The above-named conditions perhaps elicit trusting attachment not through a process of trial and error, but through programming of the brain that has occurred throughout centuries of evolution.

The stimuli that elicit these difficult-to-measure but probably crucial skills of trusting and depending deserve much study. Another hypothesis raised by my observation of children is that the appearance of an adult in the child's life with temporal regularity, such that the child can develop expectations of the person's arrival and have those expectations regularly met, is a "stimulus situation" tending to elicit positive examples of trusting and depending.

Another well-known connection between eliciting stimuli and response is that between overwhelming threat as a stimulus and flight or fight as a response. The child who is regularly threatened with danger, such as abandonment or physical violence, has evoked in him or her the responses of fear, age, or both that are not just rewarded by such threat situations, but elicited by them.


MONITORING PROGRESS

Seventh on our list is making sure that the child who is practicing a skill gets enough informational feedback on his performance to be able to learn the maneuvers that produce the desired outcomes. A youngster practicing basketball foul shots can hardly be expected to improve if he or she is blindfolded and thus unable to see whether a shot goes into the basket. Conversely, a child learning to be less critical of people may benefit from getting feedback on how critical he was during the most recent time interval; a child learning to negotiate conflict situations may benefit from having the role-played negotiations rated according to a standard scoring system; a depressed adolescent attempting to have more mastery and pleasure experiences may benefit from keeping a list of such experiences; and so forth.

Monitoring progress is intimately connected with providing consequences, because it is impossible to provide consequences in a rational manner without monitoring progress. On the other hand, monitoring progress without supplying any external rewards is sometimes potent in the process of behavior change (Christie, Hiss, & Lozanoff, 1984; Dolliver, Lewis, & McLaughlin, 1985; Reiter, Mabee, & McLaughlin, 1985).

## CONTROLLING OR COMMUNICATING CONSEQUENCES

Eighth on the list is controlling or communicating the consequences of behavior, or reinforcement contingencies. Let us include in this category contingencies of reward, punishment, and nonreward. Regardless of whether the therapist is a behaviorist, a Sullivanian, a Rogerian, or a Reikian, whenever the therapist acts in therapeutic sessions there is an outpouring of either reinforcement, nonreinforcement, or punishment: The therapist makes responses that the child either likes, does not care about, or dislikes. The therapist who can either intuitively or consciously regulate attention and approval so as to reinforce the adaptive patterns is greatly improving his or her therapeutic potency. But the expanse of circumstances in which consequences are operative is much broader than that of therapy. Whenever people interact, they are constantly responding to another in ways that produce pleasure, displeasure, or the absence of pleasure. Movements of the eyebrows, the mouth, and the head provide messages that constantly say either "Yes, do more of that," "No, do less of that," or "That doesn't interest me." The influences of this type that a person encounters in a typical day are probably numbered in the thousands. The accumulation of rewards, punishments, and nonrewards occurring over a course of years may have a tremendous influence on the developing personality.

### The Reinforcing Power of Attention

As I have discussed in Chapter 4, workable approaches to children's problems can center on teaching parents to give approval and attention to the positive, to ignore much of the negative, and to punish that portion of the negative that must be punished, so that consequences work in favor of the child's psychological growth.

In teaching parents (and therapists) about the use of reinforcement, the least obvious point is that attention to a child is often reinforcing even when it is meant to be just the opposite. "Stop doing that!" often has the effect of leading the child to "do that" more often, even when in the short run the child does obey the command. I find it very useful to summarize a couple of studies (Madsen, Becker, Thomas, Koser, & Plager, 1968; D. R. Thomas, Becker, & Armstrong, 1968) that demonstrate this point. In the first study, Madsen et al. (1968) studied out-of-seat behavior in classrooms as a function of teachers' requests to sit down; the researchers counted the number of children out of their seat each minute. First, there was a baseline observation. Then the teachers were instructed to respond immediately, each time a child got out of his or her seat, by saying "Sit down." After that, the teachers were requested to go back to their original pattern, and more counts were taken. Then the teachers were instructed to go back to immediately issuing a "Sit down" command to out-of-seat children. Finally, the teachers were instructed to *ignore* all out-of-seat behavior, and to pay attention to those children who were doing their work in their seats. What results were obtained? The condition of immediate "Sit down" instructions produced a *rise* in out-of-seat behavior each time it was applied. When the teachers ignored the out-of-seat behavior and paid attention to the children in their seats, the out-of-seat behavior fell to its lowest levels. In the second study (D. R. Thomas et al., 1968), the behavior under study was "off-task behavior"; the results were the same.

Both these studies illustrate the point that is seen clinically over and over: Adult attention often has the long-run effect of reinforcing the behavior it follows, even when the adult attention is critical or negative in quality, and when it consists of instructions to stop the behavior. These studies also illustrate a second point: When an adult asked a child to sit down, the child in almost all cases actually did sit down. Such immediate compliance tends to reinforce the adult repeatedly for giving the command, despite the fact that the command is counterproductive in the long run. Thus the situation has a built-in contingency, teaching the adult to do the wrong thing! The parent who understands this complex trap can get out of it more readily. These points are discussed very clearly in a widely used parent training text by Becker (1971).

Nonreward (or inattention, ignoring, a bland response, or extinction) is often greatly underused by both therapists and parents. A vast number of children's misbehaviors can be dealt with if therapists or parents can insure that the misdeeds are not followed by anything particularly interesting or rewarding to the children. However, parents should be prepared for the well-known *increase* in frequency of unrewarded behavior that heralds the first leg of an extinction curve.

In other words, they should be warned that when ignoring begins, things may get worse before they get better. (One very interesting question is whether it is possible to avoid this upward "blip" of the extinction curve by using fictional models to communicate the altered contingencies to a child; I speak more about this later in Chapter 6.)

## Factors Contributing to the Effectiveness of Reinforcement Contingencies

The literature provides various guidelines on how reinforcement contingencies may be most powerfully used. Reinforcement seems more potent if it occurs as soon as possible after the behavior in question (a phenomenon referred to as the "time gradient" of reinforcement) (Bijou & Baer, 1961). Continuous reinforcement, or reinforcement for every response of a certain sort, builds up a habit most quickly, and intermittent reinforcement produces the most resistance to extinction (Bijou & Baer, 1961). Thus the therapist or parent should in the first stages of teaching a psychological competence use immediate and continuous reinforcement, and then gradually make the reinforcement less predictable as the child's competence increases.

Determining just what is a pleasant and rewarding consequence for a given child requires some sensitivity. The mother of the 11-year-old who hugs and kisses her son while he is playing baseball with his comrades might conclude from his response that adult attention is not reinforcing after all; there is a subtle code that governs what is appropriate in what circumstance with respect to adult attention, and this code becomes more complex as children grow older. Similarly, the adult who mouths phrases of approval insincerely, too often, or when the child is aware that praise is not warranted may only tend to diminish the value of praise for the child. The question of whether praise becomes less valuable to a child as the supply of it becomes greater is an important one, one subject to empirical investigation, and one that (to the best of my knowledge) is uninvestigated.

Praise can also backfire when it has the effect of turning into a performance situation behavior that has been simply exploratory and curiosity-motivated. Conceivably, for example, a child who has drawn pictures simply as a playful activity could experience displeasure upon getting lots of praise for a picture, in that the praise communicates that a similar level of performance is expected for future drawings, and that other drawings may fail to meet the standard set by the one that elicited the praise. Anecdotes have also been relayed concerning situations in which the child believes that he is not worthy of praise, and, upon getting some praise, actually acts worse in order to prove this (Ginott, 1965). Some (e.g., T. Gordon, 1970) have for such reasons actually advised adults to *avoid* praising children, except in carefully worded statements. This prescription seems to me to be based on the exceptions rather than the rules, and the vast majority of empirical literature suggests that praise is very useful and should be given freely. Those children who are globally unable to feel good about praise, who have fear of failure evoked by it, or who seek to prove themselves bad people are children with skill deficiencies that in my observation are fairly rare. Adults should not overgeneralize to all children from this fairly small subset.

The reinforcement delivered by adult attention and approval is one of the least subtle and most manipulable forms. But other ingenious ways of making various skills reinforcing are also quite potent. One example is the setting up of "rules of the game" in such a way that cooperation is reinforced by the successful completion of a task by a group. For example, a "jigsaw technique" has been used in schools, such that each member of a group is responsible for the gathering of a certain set of information and teaching it to the other group members. Only when all the group members have made their contribution can the group's task be completed. Or, to give a different example, the deliberate setting up of competitive games with ambiguous situations (e.g., poorly demarcated boundaries or nondiscrete criteria for points) requires for the continuation of the game a successful series of negotiations and compromises throughout the whole activity. Successful compromise is reinforced by the continuation of the game; unsuccessful negotiation is punished by the frustration of the game's delay or interruption.

The presence of group approval contingent upon a certain pattern of thought, feeling, or behavior is a very potent influence. Various ways of eliciting group approval for adaptive patterns have been described. One such method is rewarding all the members of a peer subgroup for the improvements made by individual members; thus peers come to socially reinforce each other for the improvements they make. The approval of a social group of which one is a member is exceedingly potent, for better or for worse; I believe that the mental health professions have only just begun to tap the power of this method of influence. In a classic experiment, Asch (1955) assembled a group of confederates to give wrong answers on a task of comparing lengths of lines. He found that 37% of the selections of experimental subjects were erroneous, so as to concur with the answers of group members; by contrast, in the absence of group influence, nearly 100% of the selections were correct. If groups, with their implicit approval and disapproval, acceptance and rejection, are so potent, how can this force be ethically and economically harnessed to the service of enhancing competence? This is a question in which there is room for much exploration.

When therapists or members of the hospital staff are warm, empathic, and genuine, their very contact with their patients may be very reinforcing. Accordingly, one of the major challenges in the mental health system is mitigating the negative effects of a contingency in which a patient is actually reinforced for getting worse, by renewed or more intense contact with helping professionals.

Another important concept with respect to reinforcement contingencies is what Baer and Wolf (1970) have called the child's "natural community" of reinforcement—the rewards and punishments that those in the child's environment, including the peer group, hold out. Sometimes training by a parent or therapist in social skills, for example, enables a child to receive further "training" from peers, whereas the child previously may not have been skilled enough to receive much except punishment from them. The therapy thus has the task of getting the child up to a threshold where everyday life can then take over. Natural communities of reinforcement can be negative as well as positive influences; for example, children who are placed with aggressive peers tend to become more aggressive (Patterson, Littman, & Bricker, 1967). The parent and therapist should take the child's natural communities of reinforcement into account. The parents can to some degree select these communities, especially when the child is young, so as to provide the most favorable reinforcement contingencies.

Communicating Contingencies of Reinforcement:
The Importance of Information Transfer

When a man pointing a gun says "Give me your money or I'll shoot," a powerful method of influence toward obedience has occurred, despite the fact that the gunman may have never delivered one punishment for disobedience. The information transfer regarding future contingencies is the crucial element of the influence. In nonhuman animals, to whom language is not available as a means of information transfer, the repetitive history of situation followed by consequence is the means by which such information transfer may be carried out; in humans, however, the availability of language adds a new dimension to the communication of contingencies, and permits contingencies to be communicated without an individual's ever having experienced the association between behavior and reinforcement.

The emphasis on information transfer permits us to understand how people often act as if they have been repetitively reinforced or punished for an experience, when such direct experience is totally lacking. We may understand how a child may become phobic of strangers without ever having been harmed by a stranger, if the adults around that child repetitively communicate that strangers are dangerous and to be feared, and if adults demonstrate highly fearful responses when the child tells of a harmless encounter with a stranger. Or the child may act as if reinforced for violence after repetitively hearing the admiration in others' voices for fictional and real-life violent heroes. Or in ordinary conversation, when the child hears teenagers speaking with great positive excitement about a teenage friend who will have a baby, or, alternatively, about a teenager who has made high academic achievements, information transfer is occurring, even though the child is not being directly reinforced for anything.

## ATTRIBUTION

The ninth and final method of influence on our list is what I call "attribution." By this I refer to the way in which telling people what sort of people they are often tends to make them become more that sort of people. For example, the parent who tells a child, "You are no good; you will never amount to anything," is probably helping the child attain just that outcome. The therapist who says, "I don't think you like yourself very much," is probably (all other things being equal) influencing the child not to like himself. The therapist who says to the child, "You have the power to be braver than you ever thought you could be," or "I think that down deep inside, you have the power to really like people, and to really get a kick out of making them happy," or other such positive attributions, is probably encouraging those attributions to come true.

A parent I know skillfully used attribution to avoid power struggles over eating and to help his son like various different sorts of foods. He occasionally remarked to other adults in his son's presence, "That son of mine is a big boy. He likes all sorts of vegetables, and all kinds of foods that big people eat." After hearing such a positive trait attributed to him in such glowing terms, the son made sure to live up to it.

It should be mentioned that a dishonest positive attribution is worse than none at all. Children who hear positive traits attributed to them, knowing that they possess not the slightest traces of those skills, will realize that adults making such attributions are trying to trick them and will accordingly trust the adults less. Positive attributions are useful and ethical when children have demonstrated some evidence of capacity for the skills in question.

The use of the word "attribution" to refer to this influence mechanism is a special case of what is spoken of under the rubric of "attribution theory." Attribution theory (reviewed by Harvey & Weary, 1984) provides explanations of the ways in which people attribute causes to the events they observe. One important class of attributions is that of explaining the behavior of an individual by reference to a fixed trait. Ross (1977, p. 184) has argued that the intuitive psychologist's "tendency to overestimate the importance of personal or dispositional factors relative to environmental influences" in controlling behavior is the fundamental attributional error. The notion that the expectancies set up by such attributions may influence behavior so as to become self-fulfilling prophecies has been reviewed by Miller and Turnbull (1986). The "Pygmalion effect," wherein manipulation of adults' (most often classroom teachers') expectancies of children actually influences the outcomes for those children, has been expounded by Rosenthal and Jacobson (1968); although still controversial, the effect has found some validation in studies attempting to replicate it (Rosenthal & Rubin, 1978).

## THE SKILLS × METHODS MATRIX AS A GENERAL FRAMEWORK FOR MENTAL HEALTH PROMOTION

The nine methods of influence discussed in this chapter are as follows:

1. Promoting goal setting
2. Forming a hierarchy
3. Modeling

4. Providing instruction
5. Providing practice opportunities
6. Controlling stimulus situations
7. Monitoring progress
8. Controlling or communicating consequences
9. Using attribution

When this methods axis is combined with the skills axis discussed earlier to form the skills × methods matrix, a wide variety of psychotherapeutic techniques can be subsumed under this theoretical umbrella—in fact, I would argue, almost everything that is useful in psychotherapy of any orientation. The client-centered therapist (e.g., Axline, 1947) provides a constant stream of models for the skills of empathic listening, use of words to conceptualize the world, and toleration of a wide range of the other's behavior, as well as a set of stimuli that tends to elicit cooperative and nonfearful behavior from the child. The Jungian analyst who focuses upon a character in a dream, and designates that character as representing a positive trait that is present in the patient but not currently expressed, is in effect using attribution to bring out expression of the desirable skill. The transactional analyst who teaches an adolescent about the parent, adult, and child ego states may be providing some conceptual tools for the patient's goal setting, some instructions as to how to shift from one mode of acting to a more preferable one, and some implied contingencies for gaining the therapist's approval. The behavior therapist who uses desensitization to help a child get over a fear is providing a series of hierarchical steps, as well as opportunities for the child to practice handling the situation fearlessly.

How the Theory Explains the Nonpredictiveness
of Therapeutic "Orientation"

Reviews of therapy literature have for years raised the hope that the relevant question is not "Does therapy work?" but "What sort of therapy is most useful for what sort of problem?" There have been hopes that outcome research would show that psychoanalytic therapy is most useful for a certain type of problem, Gestalt therapy for another type of problem, behavior therapy for another, Rogerian therapy for another, and so forth. Instead, when the empirical results have come in, the most general conclusion has been that the orientation of the therapist is not a factor that predicts outcome. "All have won and all must have prizes," as one review article concluded (Luborsky, Singer, & Luborsky, 1975, p. 995), gives us no help in deciding what to do in what circumstances.

The competence-based theory provides a mechanism to explain this state of affairs. It is true that the various orientations perhaps bias therapists toward certain skills and certain methods of influence (e.g., the psychodynamic therapist tends to emphasize goal setting through insight more than the behavior therapist does; the behavior therapist tends to emphasize manipulation of consequences more than the psychodynamic therapist does). Despite these predispositions, a wise therapist of any orientation can choose the correct skills to work on, and can choose any of the nine methods of influence to promote them; the correct choice of skills and methods can cut across a wide variety of therapeutic orientations. Some methods, such as goal setting, defining a hierarchy, monitoring progress, and giving consequences of subtle approval for positive movements, can conceivably be used intuitively by the therapist without any conscious decision to do so, while conscious attention is focused more on the distinguishing characteristics of the particular orientation.

### The Skills Axis as a Guide for Differential Action

According to Achenbach (1982), "No taxonomy for children's behavior disorders has yet proved itself a valid guide for differential action" (p. 32). This is indeed a rather severe indictment of our classification systems: After all, if we are not prepared to do something differently as a result of our classification, why go through the exercise of classifying in the first place?

The skills axis seems to be a likely candidate for a guide to differential action in learning-based interventions (it should be reiterated that biological and situation-based interventions are outside the scope of this book). Something akin to it—some informal and probably less detailed mental representation of it—probably already forms the guide to differential action that is used by many if not most child psychotherapists. When the child is most deficient in skill $A$ and has symptoms that seem to be caused by the deficiency in skill $A$, and the opposite is true for skill $B$, then it makes eminent sense to make skill $A$ and not skill $B$ the skill for which the therapist uses his or her models, consequences, instruction, and so forth.

# CHAPTER 6

# Techniques for Sessions with Young Children

## OVERVIEW

Some or all of the techniques of influence discussed in this chapter may be used by the parents of young children, depending upon the parents' skills and motivation. Accordingly, the therapist's sessions not only may provide direct benefit, but also may lay the groundwork for sessions carried out by the parent. The approach recommended is diametrically opposite to those warning against "contamination" of the child's fantasies; rather, the child's fantasies are seen as a vehicle by which such methods of influence as modeling, practice, and communication of contingencies may be carried out in a developmentally appropriate manner.

A very basic technique is that of chatting with the child. Therapists for young children are encouraged to tell about their own experience as a way of showing children how to talk about their experience; when a child does so, paraphrases and follow-up questions tend to keep the child's conversation going. Using tones of approval is important in maintaining the child's conversation flow. In addition, the reticent child may often be brought out by the technique of delivering a prompt, waiting an adequate length of time for the child to respond, and replying quickly and enthusiastically when the child does respond; I refer to this sequence as "prompt, wait, and hurry."

The therapist may retrieve from a master file illustrated stories that provide symbolic models (very low on the abstraction ladder) of skillful performance in the child's high-priority target areas. These modeling stories, as well as modeling plays (to be performed by the adult with toy people for the child), place the desirable patterns in the child's memory bank. Modeling plays of desirable behaviors that the child has carried out and the parents have recorded (as described in Chapter 4) may also be constructed and performed for the child.

The technique of "tracking and describing" consists of watching and verbalizing what the child is doing. This totally nondirective commentary tends to reinforce the child's spontaneous play, particularly fantasy play. When tones of greater interest and approval are applied to the more desirable patterns, tracking and describing may exert, through the medium of differential attention, another positive influence on the patterns the child enacts.

The therapist may promote fantasy rehearsal of adaptive patterns by eliciting original stories from the child. In addition, the therapist may construct new modeling stories tailored to the particular child's needs.

Spontaneous joint dramatic play with a child is indeed a fine art. The artful therapist constantly keeps in mind the high-priority skills of the child, and makes choices about the direction of the play's plot so as to model or provide practice in these high-priority skills. Artistry in this activity also requires an optimum balance between use of influence and allowing the child to follow his own lead. An equally subtle activity is that of embedding models, practice, communication of reinforcement contingencies, and other methods of influence smoothly and naturally into free-flowing conversation.

The empirical literature gives quite positive indications of the benefits that young children can derive through the media of fantasy and dramatic play.

————————

This is the first chapter that explicitly discusses activities the therapist engages in directly with the child. The skills × methods matrix dictates scores of possible strategies; this chapter examines some promising ones. First, I present some ways of looking at the purposes of such activity; second, discuss specific therapeutic techniques, in the order of simplest to most complex.

The strategies in this chapter are appropriate for young children. By "young children" I mean those who do not feel that they are too grown up to engage in make-believe play with toy people or puppets, or to have stories read to them. Obviously, it is not possible to state an upper age limit for these activities; their suitability varies from child to child. Children in third grade and under usually feel at home with such techniques, and many older children may as well.

## MOVING DOWN THE ABSTRACTION LADDER USING FANTASY

The sessions to be described here are aimed not at getting diagnostic information from the child, but at promoting the development of the high-priority skills as quickly as possible. Accordingly, the therapist uses any of the nine methods of influence that are available, and applies them to this child's target skills.

As I have mentioned in previous chapters, the target skills are abstractions that benefit from concrete illustration for anyone who uses them. This is particularly true of young children; in fact, most of the time, skills axis abstractions have meaning to young children only to the extent that very concrete examples are provided. Such concrete examples can come from direct observation of here-and-now real-life circumstances, or they can come from fantasied, hypothetical, or remembered circumstances. Human beings are distinguished by their power to use symbols in order to deal with situations not actually present. The symbolizing capacity of the child vastly increases the power of the therapist to provide models, furnish practice, and find positive patterns to reinforce. Rather than having to wait for certain sorts of situations to come up in real life, the therapist and child can, with the use of imagination, bring literally any conceivable circumstances and characters into the office.

The symbolizing capacity of adults or older children can often be harnessed simply by talking about situations; with young children, visual aids are often needed to supplement their budding language skills. Many of the techniques described in this chapter are ways to make it easier for the young child to get models, practice, and reinforcement of skills through symbolic media.

## THE THERAPIST'S SESSIONS AS LAYING GROUNDWORK FOR PARENTS' SESSIONS

The sessions that the therapist has with the child are meant to serve two goals other than the obvious one, (i.e., the direct influence of the child). In addition, the therapist uses the sessions to find the particular combination of symbolic modeling, fantasy practice, and other techniques that is most useful for the particular child. The therapist can try several variations on the themes that I mention in this chapter, and can discard some and adopt others. Then once this is accomplished, the therapist can use the sessions for a second goal: to model for the parents or for some other lay person how to work best with the child. If a particular way of working with the child seems to be very helpful, it is often very useful to videotape the sessions and to show them to parents or other lay people so that they can imitate the useful techniques that the therapist has refined.

## "CONTAMINATING" THE CHILD'S FANTASIES: PROBLEM OR TOOL?

The techniques to be described make great use of fantasies and imagery; they share this aspect with the psychoanalytic methods. However, the attitude toward the fantasies is quite different from that of many traditional psychoanalysts. Traditional psychodynamic teaching in some quarters is that the therapist should try to avoid "contaminating" the child's fantasies with his or her own influence. From the child's fantasies, the therapist infers the psychodynamic conflicts that influence the child's behavior and interprets them to the child, who gets insights into the pattern and changes them because he now understands them. My experience leads me to the following conclusions. First, even in the face of a therapist's determined efforts to influence the child's fantasies, a large fraction of what the child produces bears the child's own distinctive stamp and is just as available for obtaining insight as those fantasies that have been less influenced by the therapist. Second, according to my observations most interpretative comments delivered during fantasy play to young children (especially preschoolers) seem to go over the children's heads and produce no visible impact either at the time or later. Third, by contrast, the patterns the therapist presents to the child in fantasy play are very frequently imitated in the child's subsequent fantasy play, and often in real-life behavior. The more frequently and joyously the child carries out these patterns in fantasy, the more likely it seems that the child will carry them out in real life. Thus, to sacrifice the chance to influence the child's fantasies upon the altar of accurate interpretations seems to be far too large a price to pay.

The permissibility, desirability, and centrality of influencing the child's fantasies in this therapeutic model does not mean that the therapist is to get so enthusiastic about presenting models that the child is overwhelmed and does not have time to practice creating his own fantasies. Above all, it does not mean that the therapist nags the child to enact vignettes of desirable patterns and criticizes the child if he enacts undesirable patterns.

## THE CONCEPT OF A "VERSATILE VEHICLE"

There are 62 skills listed on the skills axis; does this mean that there needs to be an equal number of independently conceived training programs for skill development? That is, do we need entirely separate means of promoting problem solving, promoting frustration tolerance, and promoting enjoying being alone? Or are there general templates onto which we can superimpose training in whatever skills are desired? The techniques to be discussed are meant to illustrate the second alternative. They are meant to be "versatile vehicles" that can carry quite disparate loads of skill information. Such versatile vehicles greatly reduce the burden of cumbersomeness imposed by the lengthy skills axis.


## THE TECHNIQUES

In the remainder of this chapter, I describe the following techniques for creating imaginary arenas for skill promotion; I have arranged them roughly in the order of simplest to most complex. The simplest ones are especially useful, in that they may be taught more quickly to a larger fraction of parents. The hierarchy of difficulty is different for each adult, however, depending upon the feelings and images associated with each activity. The hierarchy may be individually determined for any given adult.

0. Chatting with the child in a positive way.
1. Reading "modeling stories" corresponding to target skills.
   1.1. Promoting the child's retelling the modeling stories.
2. Performing prewritten "modeling plays" corresponding to target skills.
3. Creating "modeling plays" from reports of the child's own actions.
4. Encouraging the child's spontaneous play: "tracking and describing."
5. Combining tracking and describing with differential reinforcement.
6. Eliciting stories from the child.
7. Constructing stories and plays tailored to the particular child's needs.
8. Participating in jointly created dramatic play.
9. Using fantasy models, imaginal rehearsal, and reinforcement in spontaneous conversation with the child.

Chatting with the Child in a Positive Way

I list the first activity as number "0" above because it need not involve the use of fantasy for modeling or practice. Rather, chatting with the child in a positive way is a very basic activity that is interlaced among all the others.

TELLING, PARAPHRASING, AND FOLLOWING UP

When teaching the art of this activity, three types of utterances by the adult are emphasized: (1) telling about one's own experience, (2) paraphrasing the child, and (3) asking "follow-up" questions of the child. Perhaps the largest departure from traditional psychotherapeutic technique is telling about one's own experience. But it has been my repeated clinical observation that an adult's disclosures about events he or she has recently experienced are the fastest way to help a young child begin to tell about his own experience. Children begin to talk about their experiences much more readily when shown how to do so by modeling rather than when asked "new-topic" questions. The disclosures of the adult need not be intimate ones; simple, everyday events will show the child how to do it. For example, the adult may say, "Guess what I saw this morning—I saw a big dog. He was in a pen by someone's house. I wondered if the dog would bark at me, but he just looked sleepy." The child may or may not know how to respond to such conversation at the beginning, but after repeated modeling—without performance pressure for the child to respond, and with frequent several-second periods of silence in which the child can respond—the child will begin to tell about his own experience, perhaps by saying, "My next-door neighbor has a dog." At this point, the adult can nondirectively encourage the child to continue by using a paraphrase: for example, "Oh, right next door to you, someone has a dog, huh?" Alternatively, the adult might use a "follow-up" question (one that, in contrast to a new-topic question, pursues a topic that the child has already expressed an interest in speaking about). For example, the adult might say, "How big a dog is it?"

These three types of utterances—telling about one's own experience, paraphrasing, and asking follow-up questions—often provide the child with an interaction experience that is quite new. Many parents, and even many mental health professionals, issue to children a conversational diet consisting predominantly of commands and requests and/or new-topic questions.

In addition to choosing types of utterances that tend to bring out the child's conversation, a second crucial contributor to a productive chat with the child is using a vocal tone consisting primarily of approval and enthusiasm. The "tones of approval" exercise (see Chapter 8) is useful for adults who need to practice this.

The adult should be ready to interrupt any of the subsequently described activities in order to chat with the child. Children's learning to talk about their experiences is a great facilitator of their learning to think about their own experience; this, in turn, is crucial to many of the psychological skills on the axis (e.g., thinking before acting, decision making, accurately assessing the skills of oneself and of others). In addition, chatting provides the opportunity for direct practice in the skills of social conversation, empathic listening, seeing things from another's point of view, taking pleasure from exploring, using positive reinforcement, and a variety of other skills.

THE "PROMPT, WAIT, AND HURRY" APPROACH
TO PROMOTING RECIPROCAL INTERACTION

One of the distinguishing features of an interaction gratifying to the child, whether it be chatting, dramatic play, or any other activity, is a reciprocal or "ping-pong" quality: Child and adult take turns responding to each other. If the only way this sort of interaction can take place is by an argument, even then it often seems to both parent and child to be preferable to no reciprocal interaction at all.

Reciprocal interactions with young children are sometimes difficult for adults to promote. Shy and withdrawn children sometimes have not yet learned the skills of alternating responses. The "prompt, wait, and hurry" approach is the name I have given to a fairly complex set of adult behaviors that seems most effective in facilitating reciprocal interaction with a shy child.

By the "prompt," I mean any behavior of the adult that tempts the child to respond to it. In conversation, the adult's telling about his or her own experience can be a prompt, as can asking the child a question or making a request of the child. In a dramatic play, the adult may put a little ball behind something in the child's plain sight, and then have a character say, "Now let's see, where did I put that ball? I can't find it anywhere," while the character looks for it. In story reading, the adult may spread out several books on the floor where the child is sitting and say, "We can look at any of these. If you pick one, I'll read it to you."

The "wait" is a crucial part of the sequence that is frequently eliminated. After actively and enthusiastically giving a prompt, the adult sits serenely for some 10 seconds and waits for the child to respond. Sometimes the child needs this long to understand that it is permissible to respond, or to figure out how he wants to respond, or to summon the courage to respond. If the adult does not tolerate silence, but barges ahead with nonstop prompts, the child never gets a chance to respond.

The "hurry" comes if the child does respond to the prompt: The adult hurries to respond positively and enthusiastically to the child's response (and, by so doing, usually delivers another prompt). For example, when the first prompt has been the adult's telling about an experience, and the child has responded by saying something about his own experience, the adult may hurry with an enthusiastic para- phrase. Or in the dramatic play example given above, if the child's character finds the lost ball and gives it to the adult's character, the adult may hurry to say, "Oh, thank you! You found it for me! Do you want to kick it back and forth with me?"

What if, after the wait, the child does not respond? Then the adult can deliver another prompt or can wait longer, using his or her judgment as to what will work better.

In my experience, this approach is usually very quickly effective in helping the withdrawn and scared child to blossom into enjoying reciprocal interaction, especially if the activities available for the child are pleasant and developmentally appropriate. The skill of "prompt, wait, and hurry" is a fairly complex one, but can be learned readily with modeling, instruction, and practice.

## Reading "Modeling Stories" Corresponding to Target Skills

Young children tend to like stories, especially illustrated ones. Ac- cordingly, it makes sense to take advantage of this developmental fact and to use stories to show the children how to enact the skills that are of highest priority for them. Stories provide a very convenient way for concrete positive patterns to be imported into the child's memory bank.

Let us imagine, as part of the ideal therapeutic armamentarium, a "master file" of stories for children, arranged according to skill. Let us assume that in this file there are some 10–20 stories modeling each of the skills on the skills axis. When the child's four highest-priority target skills have been determined, the therapist can take from the master file the 40–80 stories that illustrate these skills. The therapist can begin reading these stories to the child. With each repetition, the child experiences one more imaginary visualization of the desirable pattern in question.

I have been gradually accumulating such a master file of stories I have composed specifically to model the skills on the axis. Some sample stories (the nonillustrated versions) are presented in Appendix 2 of this book. The illustrated versions are much more effective with preschool children.

Stories are capable of modeling cognitive patterns and feelings for the child whose vocabulary may not even include the words for those patterns. For example, illustrated stories can portray a character as considering several options for the solution to a problem, and the child can understand the stories, before the child even has the words "options," "problem," and "solution" in his vocabulary. When characters model decision-making skills, they may have "thought bubbles" over their heads with pictures of the various options they are considering. Feelings may be represented by facial expressions for children too young to have much of a vocabulary of "feeling words." For the child with more highly developed verbal abilities, characters can model through soliloquies adaptive patterns of self-talk that produce desirable emotional responses.

Comments that characters make in modeling stories can represent movements back up the abstraction ladder, from the concrete event being modeled to the skill concept it is illustrating. For example, after a character exhibits frustration tolerance, another character might remark, "You're really good at putting up with not getting your way." Or after a character has enjoyed a kind act for another person, the character may say to himself, "It really feels good to have been able to help that person out." Although it is difficult to muster empirical proof at this time, it seems reasonable to suppose that such abstractions will make the effect on the child more general, so that perhaps the story will make more likely not only the specific act of frustration tolerance or enjoying kindness that has been modeled, but other acts of frustration tolerance or enjoying kindness.

The construction of modeling stories should take into account principles found empirically to foster the effectiveness of modeling, as discussed in Chapter 5. Multiple characters can be used, to harness the possible increased power of multiple models; the model can experience reinforcing consequences; the model can be presented as an admirable character within the context of the child's cultural group; the model can experience some of the same difficulties the

child is likely to have in enacting the skillful pattern for the first time,
and model how to overcome them; and the model can give himself or
herself self-instructions while coping with the situation.

TECHNIQUES FOR USING THE STORIES

The tremendous advantage of having a master file of stories is that
stories may be given to the parents and read to the child at home.
Frequently children have asked to be read some story many times
over, as many as 40 or 50 times. Thus the number of mental rehearsals may be vastly multiplied by teaching the parents to use the stories
with the children.

What is meant by "teaching" parents or other adults to use the
stories with their children? Upon first glance, it would seem that if the
stories are of a length and complexity appropriate for the child's
attention span and verbal ability, and if they are well written and
enjoyable, it should present no difficulty for anyone to read them to a
child in a mutually enjoyable way. Having watched many adults and
children reading stories together, however, I can testify that even this
seemingly simple activity can be spoiled in many ways, and that some
degree of training is often in order. This statement applies even to
therapists and therapists-in-training.

The following suggestions regarding skill-oriented story reading
have been found most helpful.

1. The adult should avoid urging the child to listen to the stories,
   especially if the child is not interested at the time. Control of
   the stimulus situation can be used to tempt the child to become interested in the stories. It is important that the child not
   come to regard the stories as something "good for me" that
   are foisted upon him, like foul-tasting medicine. The reader
   should arrange the situation such that the child asks to be read
   to, and is not requested to listen to the story. This can usually
   be accomplished in the therapist's office by removing from the
   environment other, more tempting objects; by placing the
   stories within easy reach; by making sure that the stories have
   interesting pictures on their front covers; and by simply waiting for the child to become interested in them.

2. The adult should use a very enthusiastic and expressive tone
   of voice while reading. Such positive emotion will reinforce
   the child's attending to the story.

3. The adult should give the child occasional eye contact while

reading; this way the child will feel that the adult is paying attention to the child and not just the book.

4. If the child's attention wanders, the adult should not nag or command, but should wait for the return of the child's attention. Reading can be resumed if the child's attention returns to the story. Thus the process of "differential attention," or giving more attention to the desired behavior than to the undesired behavior, tends to influence the child to pay attention to the story. Even more important, the adult should avoid a punitive or commanding response of "Come back here and listen to this story," which would serve to punish the child for agreeing to listen to the stories in the first place.

5. At the end of the story, the adult should use an approving tone of voice that tends to reinforce the child's paying attention to the story to the end. The adult's utterance does not have to praise the child for paying attention to the story, but can contain approval only in the nonverbal content. For example, if the adult looks at the child, smiles, and says in an approving tone, "And that's the end of the story," the child is certainly adequately reinforced.

6. In general, the adult should stop reading before the child is bored rather than after. The adult is to aim at gradually increasing the child's appetite for books, not at reducing the child's appetite by going beyond the point of satiety.

7. If the reader is the child's parent, it is helpful to let the child sit in the lap or otherwise be physically affectionate while reading. This provides yet another incentive to the child to listen to the stories.

8. If the reader is the child's parent, it is helpful to read to the child at bedtime; this practice harnesses the very frequently seen motive of the child to postpone bedtime separation by hearing another story.

Given this combination of factors and some concise, fast-moving, well-illustrated, and dramatic stories, very few children will resist getting "hooked" on them.

If the child rather unambivalently likes the therapist, it is helpful for the therapist to make some comments about the character in the story or the act modeled, in order to give vicarious reinforcement for the act carried out: "Boy, I sure would feel proud of myself if I had done something like that," or "I really like people who do things like he did." By thus commenting, the therapist also models the behavior of commenting on the story, so that the child may feel freer to engage in conversations about the stories. On the other hand, if the child transfers to the therapist feelings derived from overly pushy or preachy parents or teachers, it may be the best part of wisdom simply to read the stories and let the approval of the protagonist's act come only in the vocal inflection.

PROMOTING THE CHILD'S RETELLING THE MODELING STORIES
Many young children at some point spontaneously decide that it is time for them to read a story to the therapist. This occurs frequently with preschoolers, who pretend to read by looking at the pictures and narrating the plot from memory and the picture cues. This activity should meet with great celebration, since it allows the child to re-hearse the positive pattern by expressing the story rather than simply hearing it. If the child listens to stories for several weeks without retelling spontaneously, the therapist can very mildly prompt the child by saying, "Can you remember what happened in the story? Maybe some day you will be able to tell me the story." Or the therapist may turn to the beginning of a very familiar story and say, "Let's see, how does it start out?" If the child does not start to retell the story, the therapist can retell it and ask the child to fill in only the easiest details. When the child does contribute to the telling of the story, the therap-ist celebrates this greatly, with tones of approval and interest. After a few experiences of thus being gently shaped, the child will usually initiate the activity of retelling. After the child has come to enjoy this activity, he may do it as often as is desired, but the retelling should of course not crowd out the reading of stories by the adult.

Performing "Modeling Plays" Corresponding to Target Skills

The second way for the therapist to provide concrete models of the high-priority skills, with visual supplementation of the verbal com-munication, is through plays performed with toy people. In my work with preschool children I have found very useful the toys that supply, in addition to characters, a setting for the fantasy activity (e.g., a house, a farm, an airport, a boat). It is a great advantage to have toy people who can "stand" wherever they are placed, and who can simply be picked up and moved to indicate that they are speaking. Such props permit a fluidity of the drama that is not possible with puppets: The actor can change from one character to another in an instant, without having to take one puppet off the hand and put another puppet on.

A master file of very short modeling plays, with the same characteristics as the master file of modeling stories, is a very useful therapeutic tool; some of the plays I am accumulating are included in Appendix 3 of this book. As with the stories, the ideal method is to choose the plays illustrating the high-priority skills for the child. The adult does not read the exact lines to the child, but rather gets the plot of the play in mind and acts it out using his or her own words.

Seeing a modeling play can be a treat for a child just as hearing a modeling story can be. Children will develop preferences for certain plays and ask to have them performed repeatedly, just as they ask for certain books to be read to them over and over.

When introducing this activity to the child, the therapist need only say something like "I'm going to put on a play," or "Now it's time for me to put on a show for you." It is useful to have very clear discriminative stimuli that communicate to the child whether he is to be a spectator or a participant in the dramatic play. When the child is to be a spectator, it is useful to ask him to sit in a certain chair, out of reach of the characters, and watch the play. The adult then puts on the play, acting out all the parts. Speaking in slightly different voices for different characters, as well as moving the character who is supposed to be speaking, will help the child follow who is speaking to whom. It is important to move the action along very briskly, especially if the child has a short attention span. The therapist keeps in mind where the child is on the hierarchy of sustaining attention to such plays, and chooses the length and pace of the plays accordingly.

Other recommendations that lead a child to enjoy the plays are similar to those regarding the stories:

1. The adult should make the plays seem to be a treat, rather than something that is work for the child to watch.
2. The adult should use expressive tones of voice.
3. The adult should give the child eye contact.
4. The adult should use differential attention if the child's interest wanders.

5. The adult should announce the end of the play with tones of approval.
6. In stopping the activity, the adult should err on the side of finishing too soon rather than too late.
7. The adult should be prepared not to require validation or applause for his or her acting talents. The adult should supply such reinforcement from within, and not depend upon the child for it.

The end of the planned modeling play is often the logical time for the child and the adult to engage in jointly created dramatic play, which I discuss later. It is beneficial for the adult to give a very clear signal that permits the child to play with the toys; for example, the adult sits on the floor with the toys and invites the child to sit on the floor too.

Many children, after seeing a modeling play, will spontaneously imitate it when they start to play with the toys. I have been amazed to observe that children sometimes spontaneously imitate plays for weeks after the original showing of them, sometimes after long periods without any rehearsal.

## Creating "Modeling Plays" from Reports of the Child's Own Actions

A variant of the planned "modeling play" technique is to use the child's own positive examples as models, with the child portrayed by a toy character. For example, the parents bring in to the therapist's office their records of the child's positive behaviors in the target skills, as described in Chapter 4. The therapist hears an account rendered in the presence of the child, and then, after getting the details straight, acts out the positive event with the toy people. If the child wants to show the therapist what happened more accurately, and to demonstrate with the toy people exactly what was done, then the child gets another practice, another visualization, of the desirable pattern.

Another variant of this technique is that when a parent notices a positive example that the other parent did not see, the parent who saw the example can act it out with toy people to show the other parent, in the presence of the child. Finally, the parents can routinely act out one of the child's positive actions each evening, at the time for review of the day.

## Encouraging the Child's Spontaneous Play: "Tracking and Describing"

When the child has witnessed the adult's demonstration of models through plays with toy people, the child will in most cases wish to play with the people and act out his own vignettes. When this occurs, the adult may nondirectively encourage the child's use of imagination by what I call "tracking and describing." "Tracking and describing" means that the therapist watches what the child does in his dramatic play (i.e., "tracks" the activity) and then verbally describes what is going on. For example, the child puts first one person, then a second person, in a toy car, and rolls the car a short way. Then he takes a pipecleaner and sticks it in the hole in the car and makes a noise like gas going in. Meanwhile, the adult is saying things like "Hmm, I wonder where you're going in your car. Oh, he's going to get in and go with you. . . . Off you go! . . . Hmm, you need some gas, don't you? . . . There goes the gas, right into the tank!" The advantage of tracking and describing is that the child is not being asked to pay attention to something other than what he wants to pay attention to at the moment. Therefore, the child gets to have fun acting out his own fantasy. The adult's attention tends to keep the story going for much longer than the child would continue it if ignored. For the child who has not yet learned to have a verbal commentary going on while he physically manipulates the toys, the therapist models this verbal commentary. By this activity, the child learns to have words go through his mind that encode the physical actions being carried out.

Notice that in the example above, the therapist is tracking and describing in the persona of a toy character speaking to the other characters, not in his or her own persona speaking to the child. This custom is of great aid when jointly created dramatic play is to be carried out, as I describe later.

Tracking and describing can be used with any sort of exploratory behavior the child does, not just dramatic play. For example, suppose the child is examining the therapist's briefcase in which books and toys are kept. As the therapist watches the child, the therapist may keep up a commentary such as this: "We can open it if you want. It's a tricky thing to get open. Maybe you can figure it out. Pushing that button seems to do something. You got it open! Now you've found a lot of things inside."

Tracking and describing should be alternated with some periods of silence, so that the child can reply to the therapist's tracking and describing comments and can begin to start tracking and describing for himself as well as speaking for the characters.

## Combining Tracking and Describing with Differential Reinforcement

Regulating the time and manner of tracking and describing can selectively reinforce certain sorts of activities that the child acts out with the toy people. The therapist can describe the enactments of positive skill patterns with great enthusiasm and approval; the less desirable patterns can be described in a more bland and neutral way or can be ignored altogether. The results of violent activity, for example, may be described in tones of grief. By these means the adult can influence the direction that the child's fantasies take, without making heavy-handed prohibitions on the content of fantasy play.

Even though important influence may be embedded in tracking and describing, its expert use looks very similar to the "nondirective play therapy" of Axline (1947) and Moustakas (1959). Studying transcripts of these nondirective therapists is beneficial for learning to let the child "take the lead" so as to find the activities of the sessions more enjoyable.

## Eliciting Stories from the Child

There is another way to elicit practice of desirable patterns by promoting fantasies that are influenced by previously viewed models. This is to elicit stories from the child after the child has heard a number of positive modeling stories at some point in the past, and a couple of modeling stories immediately before being called upon to construct his story. In other words, after simply reading stories for some time, the therapist might say, "This time let's read a couple of stories, and then you can make up one for me."

If the child is reluctant to make up a story, a technique described by Richard Gardner (1971) is very useful in helping the child get started. The therapist uses a real or simulated microphone and says, "OK, let's make up a story together. I'll start it out, and when I point the microphone to you, you tell part of it. Ready?" Then the therapist mainly supplies connectives, letting the child supply the substantive elements of the plot. For example, the therapist might say, "Once upon a time there was a \_\_\_\_\_," and point the microphone to the child. When the child fills in the blank, the therapist continues, "And then, one day, this \_\_\_\_\_ had something happen, which was that _____." After a few such exchanges, the child is usually off and running on telling the story.

With a child who is a good storyteller, the therapist might explicitly ask for stories that illustrate one or more of the child's target skills. For example, the therapist says, "If you can think up any story, we'll celebrate that, but if you can make up a story about someone putting up with not getting his way, we'll *really* celebrate." The task of making up stories that illustrate a particular psychological skill is one that will challenge the brightest child; after appropriate models, however, it can be accomplished by a wide range of children, especially those of grade-school age.

If the child makes up a story that aptly illustrates a target skill, it is helpful for the therapist to type it out and give a copy to the child to take home. If the child is proud of the story and gets his parents to read it, and if it is prominently displayed, the child gets multiple exposures to the positive skill in question.

## Constructing Stories and Plays Tailored to the Particular Child's Needs

The master file of stories and plays, arranged by skills, allows the therapist to tailor the stories and plays to the particular needs of a child simply by choosing the sets that correspond to the child's target skills. Sometimes an even closer fit is desired, and the therapist can compose stories and plays that form more exact metaphors for the child's situation.

Such stories and plays are often useful with children who have experienced a traumatic event. At times, I have attempted in such cases to construct stories that correspond in enough facets to the child's situation to strike a chord of recognition, but that do not duplicate the child's circumstances so obviously as to provoke a defensive reaction. The stories and plays are also meant to demonstrate at least one possible method of coping with the difficult circumstances. I have found that if these stories and plays are constructed well, the child often seems to become fascinated with them and wants repeated exposure to them, as though mastery may be achieved through the repetitions. This is indeed the desired result of this technique.

On a more mundane level, particular stories and plays can present models for a child that do not require large generalizations from one situation to another. For example, if the child is working on acts of kindness and cooperation, and the parents have generated a list of cooperative behaviors they would especially like to see with this child, those very behaviors can be modeled through stories and plays.

### Participating in Jointly Created Dramatic Play

Engaging in jointly created dramatic play with children is a fine art. The artistry of the adult can make the difference between an interaction that is exciting, pleasant, and filled with models and reinforced practice of just the skills the child most needs to learn, and an interaction that is dull, unpleasant, and filled with negative models and practice.

The skills required for a decent interaction between adult and child—an interaction that will promote positive movement—are sufficiently elementary that most motivated adults can learn them fairly quickly; I speak about these skills in Chapter 8, when discussing the teaching of parents and other adults. However, the skills for really making maximum use of the dramatic play, like any other art, require a great deal of work to refine and probably some pre-existing talent.

SUGGESTIONS FOR INVOLVING CHILDREN IN DRAMATIC PLAY
First of all, it is necessary that the child get deeply involved in the dramatic play. There is an easy-to-recognize electricity in the air when a child and adult are fully using the medium of dramatic play—when the medium has really tapped into the resources of both minds. Four suggestions will greatly improve the chances of the child's becoming deeply involved in the dramas.

1. *The adult should pick up the toy people and speak in their roles to other toy people, rather than speaking in his or her own persona to the child.* For example, the therapist's utterances should not be of the form "Where are they going in their truck, Johnny?" but of the form "Hey, Mr. Farmer! Where are you going in your truck?"

2. This piece of advice is crucial in preventing the play from falling flat if the child is shy at the beginning, or unfamiliar with the medium. *If the child does not have characters respond to the utterances of the therapist's characters, the therapist blithely picks up another character and has that character continue the conversation.* The therapist, therefore, is not

depending upon the child to get the dramatic play rolling. The therapist models for the child how to get very involved in the conversations between imaginary characters, and models a convention in which the players can shift from one character to another in a very fluid manner.

3. Another piece of advice tempers the preceding one. This is important to remember if the child is slow to get into the dramatic play, and the therapist is modeling by having the characters talk to one another. *If the child is reticent, the therapist should frequently be silent for 10 seconds or so, to give the child a chance to make a move into the play.*

4. The final piece of advice has to do with consequences. *When the child begins to have the characters speak to one another, the therapist has a character respond quickly and enthusiastically, often by repeating or paraphrasing what the child's character said.* For example, the child's character says, "Let's put this up." The therapist's character responds, "You want to put the fence up? OK! I'll be glad to help you put it up." Most of the therapist's utterances should have an enthusiastic tone, if the reluctant child is to become "hooked" on dramatic play.

The combination of the last two suggestions is what has been spoken of earlier as the "prompt, wait, and hurry" approach. The adult models a segment of dramatic play that tempts the child to get involved; this is the "prompt." Then the adult provides 10 seconds or so for the child to respond; this is the "wait." If the child does respond, the adult very quickly responds in a positive manner to the child's utterance or movement; this is the "hurry." If, on the other hand, the 10 seconds go by without the child's responding, the adult returns to another prompt-and-wait cycle. Using this approach can usually involve even the shyest child in dramatic play fairly quickly.

An additional suggestion is that the therapist must develop a flair for developing interesting plots, not the same plots over and over. This, of course, is sometimes more easily said than done. The adult's creativity may be greatly enhanced if he or she becomes familiar with the plots of prewritten modeling plays (such as those in Appendix 3); "priming the pump" with these ideas provides many themes upon which variations can be constructed. But when the therapist and child are jointly and spontaneously creating plots, the therapist must be flexible enough to change directions quickly, following the lead of the child. In other words, the adult may have a direction for the plot in mind, but if the child turns it in a different direction, the adult follows. The child who sees the adult doing this should in time learn to do this himself, so that the plots become mutual creations.

If these suggestions are followed skillfully, almost all children can be drawn into the medium of dramatic play. Carrying out these suggestions, however, involves a series of judgment calls. The therapist must be able to find an optimum midpoint, for any given child, between being too active and not being active enough; between exerting too much control over the child and not exerting any influence; between talking too much and talking too little; and between showing no approval of the child and approving so indiscriminately that the child comes to discount the approval.

RESPONDING TO VIOLENCE OR OTHER UNDESIRABLE
BEHAVIORS IN DRAMATIC PLAY

How should the therapist respond to violent content in the child's dramatic play? As noted in the discussion of the catharsis theory in Chapter 1, I do not delight in having a child "get out aggression" in fantasy play; I am concerned that the child may be rehearsing aggression more than getting it out. On the other hand, I usually consider it a long-term goal, and not a matter of urgency, that the violent fantasies decrease. If the child has characters doing violent or sadistic things to each other, I usually fail to reinforce this type of action by failing to comment on the vignette for a few seconds. After those few seconds of nonreward, I try to find a way to model or elicit the child's high-priority skills. For example, if being kind and helpful is high on the priority list, it is useful to have one of the characters give nurturing attention to the person who was hurt in the violent episode (e.g., taking the person to the doctor, having the doctor be kind and helpful to him). If the high-priority skill is expressing feelings, I may have a relative of the hurt person come and express feelings about the whole incident. If the high-priority skill is generating options for solution of a problem, I may have a character think out loud about various ways of helping the hurt person. Often the child will join in and assist in these constructive attempts, even when it was the child's character that did the original damage; such is the beauty of a dramatic convention in which the players can switch characters in a fluid manner. The nurturing side of the child can be brought out within seconds after a demonstration of his hostile and aggressive side.

The notion of dramatic play as a way of rehearsing responses to situations causes the therapist to walk a very interesting tightrope, and to exercise intuitive judgment in an artistic manner. On the one hand, the notion of dramatic play as the practice of responses dictates that the therapist should not be comfortable if all, or almost all, of the child's interpersonal behaviors in the dramatic play are hostile, bossy, threatening, or otherwise unpleasant. On the other hand, it is impossible to practice a response to a situation unless that situation is portrayed. So the child who needs to learn to respond to bossy or threatening people must practice dealing with bossy or threatening characters, and if the adult does not create them, often the child himself creates them. I then like to view the unpleasant interpersonal behaviors of the child not by thinking, "Here are some undesirable behaviors to be discouraged," but "Here are some undesirable behaviors the child will do well to know how to handle." I then attempt to model for the child as adaptive a response as possible to the unpleasant behaviors the child has served to me.

With such an attitude, the therapist may respond to maladaptive behaviors of the child's characters in dramatic play, in a way that avoids overly encouraging those behaviors (and thus encouraging transfer to real life) or being overly punitive toward them (and thus weakening the power of the medium of dramatic play).

THE BALANCE BETWEEN FUN AND PRODUCTIVITY

The therapist should keep in mind another balance between two goals: that of keeping the child thoroughly "hooked" on dramatic play, and that of eliciting and modeling the high-priority skills. The attempts to influence the content of the child's fantasies to some degree should not interfere with the child's ability to experience true gleefulness and silliness in the course of this fantasy play. (After all, being gleeful and silly is one of the skills on the axis.) The therapist should not be so impatient to get positive vignettes of one specified type into the fantasy play that the experience becomes boring for the child. This warning notwithstanding, if the therapist looks carefully for chances to do some sort of positive model in an unobtrusive way, literally scores of opportunities may come in a couple of hours of dramatic play.

One way of the therapist to balance the goals of fun and productivity is by relying upon the notion of hierarchy. When the child is only beginning to get involved in dramatic play, the therapist's foremost goal should be that the child be delighted with using the medium of dramatic play. Once the child has progressed so as to greatly enjoy using this medium, the therapist can start to focus more directly on the hierarchies of the target skills.

MAKING SKILLS-ORIENTED CHOICES REGARDING THE PLOT
OF A DRAMATIC PLAY

A given choice point in spontaneous dramatic play presents the therapist with an infinite number of options. How does the therapist choose what to have the characters do in the drama?

The most general answer to this is that the therapist constantly refers to the skills axis diagnosis—the list of high-priority skills that the child needs to learn. The therapist asks himself which of the characters at any given choice point in the play can best model these skills. The therapist also looks for characters' actions that will stimulate the child's characters to practice these skills. (Here ever more artistry is needed, because the therapist's intuitive prediction of how the child will react to a given stimulus interaction determines whether it should be tried. If it is likely to induce a skillful, adaptive response from this particular child, it is indicated; if it is likely to induce a maladaptive response from the child, it is usually not indicated.) And if the child carries out an example of the skill, the therapist looks for ways in which the characters in the drama (not the therapist himself or herself) can reinforce the positive act.

I have given one example of this way of thinking when speaking earlier about the therapist's response to the child's violent fantasies. Let's look at another example, a microevent in the course of dramatic play. Suppose a therapist is involved in a play with farm characters (e.g., using the Fisher–Price toy farm) with a preschool child. Suppose the child, who is playing the part of the sheep, gleefully runs away from the rest of the characters; the farmer, played by the therapist, calls, "Mr. Sheep! Mr. Sheep!" but the sheep replies, "I'm running away!"

Suppose that for the sake of simplicity, we overlook any other evidence that would give clues into the meaning of the sheep's running away. Suppose that the therapist is choosing a response to this point in the drama.

At this point, the therapist recalls the high-priority skills list for this given child. Suppose, for example, that the child's highest-priority skill is that of being able to ask for help, to trust and depend appropriately. The therapist as the farmer can go to another character and say, "Mrs. Jones! I need some help! My sheep has run away. Could you help me find him?" The therapist then can play the part of Mrs. Jones, and be willing to help the farmer; the farmer can be comforted and grateful for the help, regardless of the success of the outcome.

Suppose, instead, that the highest-priority skill for this child is that of tolerating separation, of overcoming the fear that attachment figures will be harmed when he is away from them. The farmer in that case may attempt to get the sheep to come back, and when he is unsuccessful, may talk to himself along these lines: "Gosh, I wonder what's going to happen to the sheep while he's away. I wonder if he'll be all right." The therapist might then hand another character to the child and ask that character, "Do you think my sheep will be all right if I just go back to the barn and wait for him to come back?" If the farmer does go to the barn and wait, he may deliver a soliloquy in which he thinks about the separation: "I hope nothing happens to my sheep. But I can't be with him all the time. He's big enough to take care of himself. He's been away lots of other times, and he's always made it so far."

Now suppose, instead, that the highest-priority skill for the child is that of being able to give in or to back down, or the related skill of being able to tolerate a wide range of behavior in the other person. The farmer may then say, "Well, OK, I'll let you have your way. I wanted you to come back and be with us, but I guess I can't have my way all the time." Then another character may say to the farmer, "Mr. Farmer, I think you're awfully smart to let that sheep have his own way! I bet he likes that!"

If the child needs the most to free up his ability to be silly, the therapist can engage in a slapstick chase of the sheep. If the child most needs to develop language abilities, the farmer may ask the sheep some questions or make comments calculated so as to prompt the child to talk. If the child most needs to develop the ability to be assertive, a friend of the farmer may ask the farmer in a very assertive way to please leave the sheep alone and come back to do some work they have to do. If the child most needs models of the skill of frustration tolerance, the farmer may think out loud to himself as follows: "Well, is this something I want to get upset about? I think I can handle this OK. Nothing terrible is likely to happen. And I've done all I can do, anyway." If the child most needed to improve in generating options for decisions, the farmer may muse about four or five courses of action that he can take at this moment. If the child most needs to get some patient, nurturing behavior into his repertoire, the farmer may say, "I'll let the sheep run and play, and I'll just stay in sight to make sure he's all right. That way he'll have a good time, and I'll be sure he's safe. Yes, I can see him, even though he's a good distance away."

In certain circumstances the therapist needs to take into account the child's position on the hierarchy of the skill in question and the child's mood at the particular moment, so as to estimate the probability that a certain response will spur a rehearsal of a desirable or an undesirable behavior in the child, and to choose the response accordingly. For example, if the child needs to practice compliance, the therapist may think of saying, "Come on, Mr. Sheep! We need to go back. I've got something I want you to help me with back here at the farm." But if the child is in a mood and at a point on the hierarchy where the likely response is to gleefully and defiantly run away, that choice would stimulate practice of disobedience rather than obedience. If the therapist has predicted that this may happen, he or she may choose to issue the request to characters he or she controls rather than characters the child controls. For example, the therapist may have the horse and the dog run out into the vicinity of the sheep, and play with each other and with the sheep, having much fun. Then, after some time of this, the farmer calls for some volunteers to go back to the farm and help him out; the horse and the dog model compliance with this request and get much gratitude from the farmer from their compliance. If the sheep complies, the farmer praises him; if he does not comply, the other characters ignore him and go about their business.

To repeat a point made earlier, the skills-oriented choices should be continually counterbalanced against the goal of keeping the child "hooked" on dramatic play as a medium. Some sequences are to be chosen simply because they delight the child, rather than because they are positive models or positive practice. For example, suppose a child is in the early stages of learning to enjoy dramatic play. The therapist is the driver of the car, and the child repeatedly announces, "It's out of gas!" and fills the car up again. The therapist responds to such announcements with surprise ("Out of gas *again?!*"), and the child laughs delightedly at this display of emotion. The therapist may indulge the child in as many repetitions of this drama as the child wants, and progressively "ham up" the display of emotion as the car runs out of gas—not to model or practice high-priority skills, but to model and practice taking pleasure from dramatic play itself. The therapist should not get so involved in using the tool that he or she forgets to sharpen and oil it.

Sometimes the therapist becomes aware that the child is recreating, through the dramatic play, a specific real-life event. (For example, a child who had experienced the mugging of her grandmother by thugs set up this situation repeatedly in dramatic play.) The fact that the situation is a real event modifies the prescriptions given above very little. The therapist will want to encourage the child's recreation of the scene so that the child can get a cognitive handle on it; the therapist will not want to encourage and reinforce the child's identification with the aggressor in the situation. The therapist, knowing which character in the drama is the child, should strive particularly to model the various options for adaptive handling of the situation by that particular character or one of his peers. The therapist will want to think in terms of the skills necessary for the handling of this particular event, giving secondary importance to the overall skill deficiencies that are the more general focus of the therapy.

Sometimes the process by which the plot of dramatic play is negotiated becomes an arena wherein practice and reinforcement may be provided for the child's emerging skills of joint decision making, letting the other have his way, or asserting his own wishes. For example, some children will wish to determine the direction of the plot all by themselves, and will wish either to exclude the therapist from the plot or to direct the specific actions and words of the characters the therapist plays. Or when the therapist specifies a dramatic convention, the child will contradict it: For example, the therapist says, "Pretend this piece of paper is a lake." The child, however, says, "No, that's not a lake, that's a football field," or the child crumples up the piece of paper and says, "No, it's a ball." Or the therapist has a character get on the tractor, and the child takes her off and says, "No, she doesn't ride the tractor; she's not old enough to climb on." The therapist may experience some frustration at the violation of some of the unwritten conventions of improvisation, and other children who play with such children are likely to be put off by their controlling actions.

When a child is in the early stages of getting "hooked" on dramatic play, I think it is best for the therapist to make concessions to the child's reduced flexibility, and to note the types of interactions and settings the child seems pressured to set up. Only the least skilled adults make the mistake of getting into a power struggle with the child that leads to a "Yes, it is—No, it isn't" interaction. The therapist conceives of the child as low on the hierarchy of the skill of letting the other have his way, and begins to provide opportunities for the child to practice steps upward on that hierarchy; when the therapist sees such positive examples, he or she reinforces them. The therapist may simply act more enthusiastic and positive than before in such circumstances, or may explicitly say to the child, "Hey, I liked it that you let my man do what I wanted him to do. It's a lot more fun to play with you when you do that."

If such comments do not seem to produce progress, it has been useful to invoke formal monitoring and self-monitoring, even with preschool children. With one child, the therapist stopped every 10 minutes or so and asked the child to rate whether he had been "not bossy," "sort of bossy," or "very bossy" during the previous few minutes; the therapist also rated the child's behavior. The child was to aim for the lowest "bossy" scores possible and the most accurate ratings possible. This procedure was also carried out in free play in the child's preschool. This child improved greatly in his interpersonal relations, possibly partly in response to this procedure.

ENDING THE DRAMATIC PLAY

At what point should the therapist end the dramatic play? Should the therapist wait for the child to end it? My impression is that in both dramatic play and story reading, it is far better for the therapist to end the activity, and to err on the side of stopping too soon rather than waiting for the child to become bored with it. If the therapist pays careful attention to the nonverbal signals the child sends out, he or she can usually discern an appropriate moment fairly readily. Some children, however, become so involved with the medium that they are sorry to end it even after an hour or more. In such a case, the ending of the activity becomes a chance for the child to practice compliance and frustration tolerance.

The activity of putting the toys away as the session ends is the first step toward the creation of a happy ending of the session. I have found it best for the adult to say, "Now it's time for us to put the toys back in the box," and to begin doing this. If the child helps put the toys in the box, the adult is appreciative and attentive; if the child does not help put the toys away, the adult may make *one* suggestion, but does not command the child to help. The power struggle that such a command would set up would only reinforce the child for noncooperation by prolonging the interaction. Rather, if the child does not help put the toys away, the adult puts them away quickly and ignores the child while doing so.

When it is time to leave the room, the adult says, "Now it's time for us to go." Turning out the lights in the room is often a good stimulus situation to help the child leave the room. If the child still will not leave, the adult gives the child a choice: "Would you like to come with me, or would you rather I take you by the arm and lead you out?" Usually children need to be dragged from the room only a couple of times before realizing that there is no future in resisting. The therapist, in dealing with the issues of putting the toys away and leaving the room, gets a chance to model two very different strategies: a suggestion to a child followed by differential attention, and a command to the child followed by physically moving the child's body if necessary to enforce the command.

## CAN SYMBOLIC MODELING ELIMINATE THE UPWARD "BLIP" OF THE EXTINCTION CURVE?

It is frequent in clinical work that a child has previously been rewarded for undesirable behavior, and the clinical intervention involves ceasing such rewards. Frequently an *increase* in the behavior is observed as extinction begins, as if the child is seeing whether escalating the rate of the behavior brings on the reward; this has been discussed to some extent in Chapter 5. I believe that it is possible at times to eliminate this upward "blip" of the extinction curve by using dramatic play to demonstrate for the child what the new reward contingency will be. Perhaps the clear communication of such information eliminates the need for the child to confirm it by escalating misbehavior.

For example, the parents of a 2-year-old boy I saw had been letting him sleep with them when he became scared at night. They wished to help him get over his fears; accordingly, we planned that he might be comforted when frightened, but that he would sleep in his own bed. When he was able to sleep in his own bed without getting out, there would be great celebration and much praise the following morning. After making such plans with the parents, I engaged the child in dramatic play with toy people. Soon it became time for all the characters to go to sleep, and the child character wanted to sleep with the mother character. But the mother character insisted that things were going to be different now, and that the child character would sleep in his own bed tonight. The (real-life) child became quite distressed, and ran momentarily to his (real-life) mother for comfort. After a few seconds of that, we began the dramatic play again. It quickly became morning, and now all the other characters congratulated the child character for his bravery in staying in his own bed; there was a great parade. Then we created other plots together for several minutes. After a while, it became evening again, and it was again time for the characters to go to bed. This time the child was somewhat withdrawn, but tolerated the new sleeping arrangement, and once again in the (quickly ensuing) morning there was great celebration of the child character's bravery. On the way home from the session, the child talked about these incidents, not with fear, but with much curiosity. When his parents explained to him that they would be doing the same thing at home that had occurred in the dramatic play, he was able to tolerate this new arrangement with very little protest. Observations like these lead one to wonder what sort of differences might be observed if a controlled study were carred out; I would hypothesize that altered reinforcement contingencies would be much more readily accepted by the young child who has had them communicated in a medium that is sufficiently concrete for him to understand (i.e., dramatic play).

The art of skills-oriented dramatic play with a child involves a complex series of decisions: The adult must constantly seize opportunities to model, provide practice for, and reinforce the high-priority skills for the child, both in the fantasy interaction and in the real-life interaction. These decisions must be made with a view toward the point the child has reached on the hierarchies of each of the skills, as well as in the skill of enjoying dramatic play and of allowing the mutual give-and-take for the joint creation of plots. It is a subtle art indeed; it is a microcosm of human relations, the "finest of the fine arts."

### Models, Practice, and Reinforcement in Spontaneous Conversation with the Child

I began this listing of therapeutic techniques with a reference to using a positive tone in informal conversation with the child as the simplest of techniques; I end the listing by calling the optimal use of informal conversation the most complex. Spontaneous, informal conversation with a child can be, and often is, filled with stories, self-talk, fantasy rehearsals, and emotional responses that constitute vicarious approval and disapproval for hypothetical actions. When a child says to an adult, "Guess what my classmate Johnny Doe did today," the child is getting ready to recount a story, true or otherwise. Because anyone, adult or child, abstracts from real events what he or she chooses to attend to and focus upon, even the recounting of a real-life event is very much an act of the imagination.) If the adult hears what Johnny

Doe did, laughs, and repeats the story to another adult, the message is quite different than if the adult says in a somber-faced manner, "Johnny acted very foolishly, and he should be ashamed of himself. I feel sorry for somebody who doesn't know any better than that." These responses obviously present to the child information about what the adult's approval or disapproval would be for a similar act carried out by the child himself, not just the classmate. Less obvious might be the slight smile or the disapproving shake of the head that the adult shows in hearing of such an action, without even making a verbal response at all. Similarly, when the child is present with two adults and one of them is recounting to the other what a neighbor did, the child is hearing a story. The approval or disapproval in the adult's tone of voice communicates information on the act being recounted. A discussion of a given political act in a child's presence can provide commentary on a variety of psychological skills. A discussion of a package for aid to farmers can potentially involve commentary upon specific patterns concerning conflict resolution, nurturing, asserting one's own rights, accepting help without shame, being independent, planning ahead, and almost all the other skills on the axis.

Reactions to recounted events give information to the child not only with respect to whether the pattern reported is approved or disapproved, but also with respect to how high the stakes are. When the child says to the parent, "I did $X$ today," and the parent says casually, "That's nice," the child gets information much different from that conveyed if the adults says with great relief, "Oh, thank God!"

Since people tend to talk about their own actions and intentions and other people's actions and intentions, the accumulation of thousands of microevents of such conversation should communicate much information to the child. Such communication is probably important far out of proportion to how much it has been studied. How is it that a child becomes phobic of a situation from which he has experienced no direct harm? How is it that a child develops a very punitive conscience, in the absence of much punitive behavior from any adults? How is it that very strong values become internalized that are sometimes quite different from those that are explicitly taught? We might hypothesize that the cumulative influence of the above-mentioned microevents accounts for much that is otherwise unexplained in human behavior and personality development.

The ideally thorough therapist or parent will pay attention to the microevents of spontaneous conversation with the child or with others in the child's presence. At the very least, the models and the vicarious reinforcement of spontaneous conversation should not oppose the development of the child's target skills; ideally, they should optimally promote such development.

There is danger in this technique, as in all techniques. If the therapist or the parent communicates great reverence and admiration for those who possess just the skills the child lacks the most, and gives the child much vicarious disapproval by disapproving of those with deficiencies in such skills, the child may get the message that "people like me are no good." The adult should be careful to value the skills that are sufficient in the child, as well as those that are deficient. Another danger is that the adult, in going too far toward trying to exert vicarious influence, will provoke rebellion by the child, and the influence will be in exactly the opposite direction from that desired. Thus, this "technique" must be used with delicacy and not with a heavy hand.

Thus ends the listing of some of the ways in which fantasy and imagination can be harnessed in the service of skill promotion in therapy sessions. Since I have put such an emphasis upon fantasy play and story reading, it may be useful to take a look at some of the empirical literature that suggests just how valuable these activities are for children.

## LITERATURE ON THE USEFULNESS OF DRAMATIC PLAY AND STORY READING

The use of storytelling in child psychotherapy has been pioneered by Richard Gardner (1971, 1975, 1979). Gardner's technique involves first eliciting a story from a child. Then the therapist infers the psychodynamic meaning of the child's story. Next the therapist tells a story of his or her own, using the same characters that the child's story used, but modeling more healthy coping mechanisms than the child's story used. Thus Gardner uses symbolic modeling through stories in the therapeutic situation; he reports favorable results in many cases. Although inferring the psychodynamic meaning of a child's fantasy, like the task of making conclusions from projective tests, is more easily said than done (Anastasi, 1976), Gardner seems not to rely totally on the child's fantasy for the choice of models to include in his own story, but to use all the information available. The premise that one can model adaptive coping strategies through fantasy is an idea that Bandura (1973, 1977) has researched thoroughly and that is at least as old as Aesop's fables, but that Gardner has most thoroughly introduced into clinical child psychotherapy.

Some psychoanalytic thinkers have spoken of the value of dramatic play in terms that sound very similar to those of some of the "cognitive" psychologists. The idea is that the child who can symbolize through play the wishes, fears, preoccupations, and other mental phenomena that are troublesome is better able, by using that mental device, to process those mental phenomena in an adaptive way. That is, the use of symbols makes information processing more efficient. In the words of Erikson (1950), "I suppose the theory that the child's play is the infantile form of the human ability to deal with experience by creating model situations and to master reality by experiment and planning" (p. 195). Bettelheim (1976) speaks of fairy tales' allowing a child to embody his "contradictory tendencies" in the various characters of the fairy tales, and thus more easily sort them out, and be less "engulfed by unmanageable chaos" (p. 66). According to these ideas, fantasy play serves something of the same function as language itself: It facilitates the thinking process. Several empirical studies support this idea.

Fein (1979) reports a correlational study that assessed, in 1½- and 2-year-olds, the ability to comprehend language and the capacity for symbolic play. High comprehension scores were found to characterize children who engaged in more advanced forms of pretend play. Fein states, "These results are consistent with Vygotsky's position concerning the relation between language and play; the child's comprehension of relationships between words and objects is related to the occurrence of mature symbolic play forms" (p. 11).

The ability to conjure up stories is related to ability in pretend play. Story-making skill seems, according to some data, to be correlated with adjustment. Sutton-Smith (1979) cites a study in which teachers were asked to rate children aged 2 to 14 on a 1–5 scale of "adjustment." The children were asked by the investigators to tell stories. While conditions were unfortunately not conducive to blind ratings, the teachers rated the children with low or no proficiency in storytelling as significantly less well adjusted than the other children. These two studies thus suggest that the ability to create fantasy (disregarding, for the time being, the content of the fantasy) is positively related to adjustment and language ability.

Singer (1973) summarizes a variety of studies in which children were assessed as being "high-fantasy" (i.e., high in the ability to use imagination) or "low-fantasy." High-fantasy children were able to remain seated or standing quietly for significantly longer time periods before giving up than were the low-fantasy subjects. This study suggests that use of imagination as a mediational tool might enable children to defer gratification or suppress impulsivity more readily. Pulaski (1973) found that high-fantasy children became "more deeply absorbed in their play" than low-fantasy children, and gave more evidence of concentration on their play. Yet these high-fantasy children were able to respond more cooperatively when an adult interrupted their play and asked them to tell a story about a new toy. Biblow (1973) also measured fantasy predisposition, and studied the relationship of this characteristic to children's response to frustration. The high-fantasy children showed less overt aggression than their low-fantasy counterparts. Biblow described the low-fantasy children as more "motorically oriented," less creative in their play, and more direct in their approach to play materials and in their expression of aggression than the high-fantasy youngsters.

Several investigators have noted that middle-class subjects are higher in fantasy ability than children of lower socioeconomic status (SES) (Korchin, Mitchell, & Meltzoff, 1950; Rosen, 1974; Smilansky, 1968). This finding raises the question of whether lower-SES children may be helped to be more successful through experimental manipulations involving dramatic play.

A couple of studies have taught dramatic play to lower-SES children. A study by Freyberg (1973) involved manipulation of the fantasy ability variable. The experimenter taught lower-SES 5-year-olds to play more imaginatively. Freyberg's training procedure was one in which groups of four experimental children were taken to a separate room; the children were encouraged to adopt a role and play a character in a story, using pipecleaner people. At first, the investigator used much prompting and modeling; then she gradually excluded herself. A control group put together jigsaw puzzles. The entire intervention consisted of eight 20-minute sessions. The dependent variables were measured by independent raters, observing the children's free play outside the experimental setting. Enhanced fantasy play ability outside the experimental setting did ensue from the procedure; this increase was reported to be associated with greater verbal communication, longer and more complex sentence usage, more sensitive responding to the cues of other children, more apparent spontaneity, increased attention span, and more positive expressions of emotion.

Rosen (1974) carried out a similar experimental intervention with disadvantaged black kindergarten children. After finding that these children engaged in less sociodramatic play in their free-play activities than did advantaged children, the experimenter assigned the disadvantaged children to experimental or control groups. Instruction and guided participation of the experimental group in sociodramatic play extended over forty 1-hour sessions. The intervention was reported to increase the experimental children's productivity in working on tasks, their cooperative behavior in a game to test cooperation–competition, and their capacity to choose appropriate birthday presents for various people (mother, brother, sister, teacher).

Thus there is a fair amount of correlational evidence, and some experimental evidence, that the ability to fantasize is a useful skill for children. Fantasy ability is associated with improved social and cognitive performance, and it appears to be a teachable skill. Now let us look at some of the studies on reading to children.

The skill of comprehending oral language, like other skills, can be expected to improve with practice. And the skill of comprehending oral language, as pointed out in a previous chapter, has much in common with the skill of reading. We would expect, then, that reading to children would improve their language abilities and their reading abilities. In the education literature, we find evidence for that proposition.

Cohen (1968) reported a study in which 20 classes of Harlem second-graders were read to in school for 20 minutes a day for one school year. A control group did not receive this experience. The experimental group was reported to show significantly higher gains in vocabulary and reading comprehension than did the control group.

Durkin (1966) studied 79 "early readers" (children who apparently "taught themselves" to read, and arrived at first grade or kindergarten already knowing how to read). One of the variables studied was whether the child had been read to regularly at home. *All* of the 79 early readers had had this experience.

Harkness (1981) and McCormick (1981) have reviewed other literature on the effects of reading aloud to young children. Both reviews conclude that this activity has positive effects on the child's eventual reading achievements and on language development. Measures positively affected by adults' reading aloud to preschoolers included mean length of the sentences the child used, score on the Peabody Picture Vocabulary Test, frequency of the child's looking at books in an open classrom, score on several reading readiness tests, and scores on reading achievement in first and second grades.

In summary, there is much to lead us to believe that dramatic play and story reading are in general very salutary activities for children.

The central assumption of this chapter is that the therapist does the child good by causing images to go through the child's mind of someone doing positive things, of someone enacting the skills the child needs to learn. Conversely, without causing such images to run through the child's fantasy or behavior somehow or other, it is difficult to do the child good. This principle is obvious in teaching skills such as tennis, dancing, or typing. One would not go far as a tennis teacher if one spent all one's time delving into how the student developed bad habits on his strokes, and never demonstrated how to do the strokes better or gave the student practice in carrying out the strokes properly. Yet, amazingly enough, many psychotherapists try to teach the skill of living well without positive demonstrations and without giving the opportunity for positive practice. The techniques of this chapter should provide ample opportunity for such demonstrations and such practice.

# CHAPTER 7

# Techniques for Sessions with Older Children and Adolescents

## OVERVIEW

For grade-school children, there are many ways to present models and elicit fantasy practice. In one procedure, the therapist may first read a modeling story to the child, then have the child read one to him or her, and then have the child make up a story. Typing out a copy of positive modeling stories the child makes up for the child to take home can multiply the opportunities for rehearsal and reinforcement. Stories for grade-school children not only may give positive models, but also may promote "conceptual sharpening," or learning to name and discriminate alternative ways of thinking, feeling, and behaving. Grade-school children enjoy seeing modeling plays (including plays enacting a child's real-life positive examples) just as preschoolers do, if the props and the stage directions are chosen so as to be developmentally appropriate.

The "scavenger hunt" for positive models is an activity in which the child searches through television shows, other fiction, and real-life experience, looking for positive examples of the high-priority skills. The "shaping" game is one in which the "shaper" helps the other player to carry out a goal behavior; the only permitted clues are positive reinforcers for successive approximations to the goal. This game provides an analogue whereby several crucial skills may be practiced. The "prisoner's dilemma" game provides another analogue for practice of cooperation. In the "situations" game, the therapist and the child pick cards with hypothetical situations designed to elicit practice in the child's high-priority skills. When the therapist responds, the child gets positive models; when the child responds, the child gets practice opportunities. In the "picture–story" game, the therapist and the child draw magazine pictures from a box and make up stories about them; the therapist's stories model the high-priority skills. Spontaneous dramatic play may also proceed with grade-school children, with a few alterations from the methods described in Chapter 6 for younger children.

With adolescents, a new set of techniques becomes available. The adolescent may read developmentally appropriate modeling stories in the session or as homework. Positive modeling stories may be included in ordinary conversation. Hypnosis or guided-imagery exercises may be used to present positive models and provide opportunities for fantasy practice. One imagery exercise consists of revising dreams in waking fantasy; this technique makes no assumptions about the meaning of dreams, but simply assumes that working adaptive skill patterns into fantasies of any sort will provide useful practice. The "inner guide" technique may be used as a versatile vehicle for promoting skills: The adolescent cultivates the fantasy image of a nurturant, loving, wise, and powerful being, and calls upon this image in fantasy practice of high-priority skills. In a less dramatic technique, the therapist may promote a fantasy "walk-through" of a positive rehearsal in imagination, simply by asking questions about real-life events and possible ways of responding to them. Discussing the relationship between the therapist and the adolescent may provide practice in accurately perceiving another person, trusting, disclosing, being assertive, expressing positive feelings, and enough other skills that it too can be classified as a versatile vehicle. Finally, the cognitive abilities of adolescents are conducive to potent use of role play and psychodrama.

---

As the child gets older, as a general rule, there is more and more cognitive processing power to be harnessed, together with more and more potential resistance to be circumvented. Whereas preschool children as a rule enjoy stories of all sorts, no matter how much these are aimed at modeling positive patterns, school-age children—and, even more so, adolescents—can begin to resist people's attempts to influence them in positive directions, sometimes because of disagreement on what the desirable goals are, and sometimes just because of the principle that it is good to declare one's independence.

The techniques to be discussed in this chapter are as follows:

*Techniques for grade-school-age children*
1. Variations on story reading
   a. Adult reads, child reads, child invents
   b. Conceptual sharpening exercises through stories
   c. Stories in the mail to the child
2. Variations on performing modeling plays
3. Celebrating and enacting the child's real-life positive examples
4. The "scavenger hunt" for positive models
5. The "shaping" game

6. The "prisoner's dilemma" game
7. The "situations" game
8. The "picture–story" game
9. Variations on spontaneous dramatic play and role playing

*Techniques for adolescents and older individuals*
1. Variations on story reading and storytelling
   a. Providing positive models for the person to read
   b. Providing models in ordinary conversation
2. Other fantasy practice techniques
   a. Hypnosis and guided imagery
   b. Revision of dreams in waking fantasy
   c. The "inner guide" technique
   d. Walking the person through a positive rehearsal in fantasy
3. Discussion of the relationship with the therapist
4. Variations on role playing and psychodrama

## TECHNIQUES FOR GRADE-SCHOOL-AGE CHILDREN

### Variations on Story Reading

#### ADULT READS, CHILD READS, CHILD INVENTS STORY

As with the story-reading techniques for younger children mentioned in Chapter 6, it is very advantageous if story-reading techniques for older children can be taught to parents and continued at home. One activity that can be fairly easily duplicated is as follows: From the file of modeling stories, stories are chosen that illustrate target skills. The adult reads the child a story; then the child reads the adult a story. The next step that can be added is that the child makes up a story while the adult listens with rapt attention. In this way, the child gets to practice reading, is exposed to a couple of positive models, and has a chance to engage in fantasy practice immediately after being exposed to the influence of the modeling stories.

Like most other seemingly simple techniques, this procedure can be rendered unpleasant or useless in a number of ways. One danger is that the adult will turn the exercise into a poorly taught reading lesson. The adult should remember to read expressively, and to concentrate, when the child is reading, not so much on the quality of the reading as on the content of the story. If the child has trouble with reading (as many behavior-disordered children do), then the therapist should take great care to choose very simple stories, so that the child experiences success in reading the stories. If reading with an adult has become associated with failure and criticism through poor teaching in the past, and if it is thus very aversive for the child, then the therapist may do well to drop to a lower point on the hierarchy and simply read the stories to the child; all the child may be asked to do is to follow the stories with the therapist. That way the child gets to experience comfortable and safe feelings associated with the context of reading, which will prepare the child for more pleasant steps into doing some reading later.

A variation of this technique is that the adult reads the child a story, and then the child retells the same story to the adult before making up his own story. By this means the adult can find out whether the child is comprehending the story, and can also give the child practice in the crucial skill of verbal narration.

When the child makes up a story, the therapist may type it out, keep a copy, and give a copy to the child to keep. The child's repeated reference to his own story may greatly increase the number of rehearsals of the adaptive pattern.

As children grow older, they become more and more capable of making up stories that illustrate a particular psychological skill. I have sometimes said to a child, "We will celebrate if you can make up any story at all, but we will *really* celebrate if you can make up one that illustrates 'enjoying exploring,' " or whatever other skill we are working on. The therapist should keep in mind that making up a story illustrating a certain skill is a fairly difficult task, and that it really does deserve some celebration when the child does it.

It also becomes more appropriate as children grow older to discuss the content of the stories, in order to allow them to be springboards for chatting about issues in the children's lives. A child may be able to identify obstacles that make it difficult to use the skill modeled in the story; the therapist can then in future sessions be aware of the need to address these obstacles. The child may also dismiss certain adaptive patterns out of hand, usually because of overgeneralization from previous experience or from ingrained values of his subculture. Often these are made more concrete when the child's prediction of the likely consequences of the pattern is made explicit. Thus the therapist may find out more about the child's attitude toward certain patterns by asking questions such as "What do you think about what that person did in that story?" "Can you ever imagine yourself doing anything like that? In what circumstances?" "What do you think would be likely to happen if you did do something like that?" Such discussions entail some risk, however: It is possible to thrust children into prematurely crystallized positions that they feel obligated to defend from then on, whereas if they are allowed to be tentative, they may feel less resistance toward adopting adaptive patterns as goals to be aimed for.

CONCEPTUAL SHARPENING EXERCISES THROUGH STORIES

I have mentioned in Chapter 5 that an important means of setting appropriate goals for skill development is what I call "conceptual sharpening," or learning words with which to name alternative strategies of handling situations. It is difficult, for example, for a child to set a goal of responding to frustration less often by blaming himself and others and more often by learning from the experience or by listing options and choosing among them, if none of these concepts are in the child's vocabulary.

Another set of stories that I have constructed gives children practice in identifying both positive and negative cognitive and interpersonal strategies. The plot moves along, and periodically characters say something to themselves or to someone else, giving examples of the strategies to be illustrated in that chapter. The adult reads the story to the child and stops briefly for each example so that the child can identify the strategy the character has used, whether it be positive or negative.

What are the advantages of this technique over that of pure presentation of positive models? The more general question is this: Is it better for the teacher to demonstrate what should be done less often, in addition to what should be done more often? I am not aware of an empirically derived answer to this question. Theoretically, there are advantages in the additional information content of knowing what *not* to do; this advantage has to be counterbalanced with the possible negative effect of giving negative models to the child. My own feeling is that what is appropriate for therapy may not be appropriate for primary prevention: Children who are already frequently using a great preponderance of negative cognitions and utterances have little to lose from seeing and hearing enough more of them to become able to identify them, whereas children who have not become exposed to them may not benefit or may be harmed.

A different light is shed on this question by what seems to be a fairly robust finding that healthy, normal people, when asked to record their thoughts, do record a substantial fraction of negative evaluations of others' behavior, their own behavior, and their circumstances. Interestingly, several studies have reported that the average fraction of positive cognitions tends to be about 0.62, which is the fraction known to ancient Greeks as the "golden mean" (Schwartz & Garamoni, 1986). If 38% of most normal people's evaluative cognitions are negative in nature, it seems unlikely that exposure to a few negative cognitions will do harm.

An example of a chapter from a novella providing conceptual sharpening exercises is provided in Appendix 5 of this book.

STORIES IN THE MAIL TO THE CHILD
When there is an interruption in the therapy and the therapist wants to maintain the continuity of the sessions, or when the therapist wants to keep contact with the child after termination, it may be helpful for the therapist to send stories to the child in the mail. Getting mail may be special and exciting enough for the child that the stories may have an impact beyond what they could have within the sessions themselves.

## Variations on Performing Modeling Plays

Although children outgrow their appreciation of certain types of toys, they need never outgrow their appreciation of dramas enacted for them by adults. The task of the adult is to find those props that are acceptable to a child's need to be grown-up. Sometimes puppets are perfectly acceptable, whereas toy people in a toy house are not. If puppets are used, my own preference is to pick up the characters and not put them on my hand, so that several characters can come in and out of the drama quickly, without my having to stop to take a puppet off and put another on.

With grade-school children, it is possible to demarcate the setting for the drama by whispered verbal stage directions, so that props for the setting are not necessary. For example, the person putting on the play whispers, "This is the woods all over here," and then speaks in a normal voice as the character says, "Hmm, I can't figure out which way to get out of these woods."

## Celebrating and Enacting the Child's Real-Life Positive Examples

As with preschool children, it is usually a treat for grade-school children to see enacted in a drama the positive patterns that the children have performed in real life prior to a session. The parents may report these incidents; with grade-school children, the children themselves may be enlisted to recall and recount such incidents, and then to verify or correct the therapist's enactment of them. Such re-enactments help a child gain experience in translating sequences from one medium to another (i.e., memory to verbal reporting to dramatic enactment); it is hoped that such experience may help the child to make the translation back from the therapist's modeling plays to real-life situations. In addition, when the child is asked to move conceptually down the abstraction ladder from the name of a skill to specific examples of it, the child's full comprehension of the skill is being tested.

If a child of grade-school age tends to exhibit problem patterns (e.g., bossiness, low frustration tolerance, hypersensitivity to criticism) in the interaction with the therapist as well as in real life, one useful option is self-monitoring of the child's skills during the session itself, using a version of the positive behavior scale described in Chapter 4 (see Table 4-1). For example, if persistent bossiness is a problem for the child, the therapist and the child may agree to stop every 5 or 10 minutes during the session and rate how well the child has let the other person have his way. Then they share their results with each other, and they celebrate either positive scores or reliable ratings. If there are positive examples of the skill in question, they can celebrate these specifically.

### The "Scavenger Hunt" for Positive Models

Another technique that is possible with older children is to send the child on a mission, between one session and the next, to look for positive examples of target skills in books, magazines, movies, television shows, and real life. If the adult is working with children in groups, this quest can be made into a competitive game, a "scavenger hunt," in which the child or the team with the most examples wins the game. Each time the child looks for a positive model of a certain sort, or records, recalls, reports, or hears reported one of these positive patterns, one more adaptive rehearsal is taking place. Also, in deciding whether a certain incident is an example of one skill or another, the child gets still more practice at moving along the abstraction ladder.

### The "Shaping" Game

The idea of "shaping" has pervaded a great deal of what has been discussed in this book. Using positive reinforcement with others and using it with oneself are important skills on the skills axis. Two of the methods mentioned previously as promoters of mental health skills are using hierarchies and using reinforcement; the concept of shaping is the combination of these methods. Skinner (1953) defined "shaping" as follows: "By reinforcing a series of successive approximations, we bring a rare response to a very high probability in a short time" (p. 92).

The skills of shaping are not just to be used by the therapist, but are very important skills to be taught to clients. Children who give positive reinforcement to others tend to be liked better, and thus tend to have more adequate social support systems (Hartup, Glazer, & Charlesworth, 1967). Second, people who give rewards and reinforcement to others facilitate cooperation, and thus interpersonal conflict is usually resolved more easily. A third advantage is that when persons begin using reward with other people, they perceive their power to make those people feel good; thus they overcome a feeling of interpersonal helplessness.

Less obvious to external observers is the process of internal shaping—the use of self-statements that reward oneself for movement along a hierarchy. All the skills in Group 5 on the skills axis, which have to do with celebrating good things and feeling pleasure, entail a certain degree of self-reinforcement. These skills are central to the development of healthy self-esteem: We may hypothesize that the concept "I am good" is a corollary of the summation of thousands of internal reward sentences of the "I did something good" nature. Conversely, internal shaping is the opposite kind of pattern from that usually practiced by depressed people, and the learning of cognitive patterns that roughly constitute internal shaping seems to relieve depression in some people (Beck et al., 1979).

Since internal shaping requires giving reinforcing messages to oneself and receiving them from oneself, concentrated rehearsal in both giving and receiving positive reinforcement for movement along a hierarchy is useful. The "shaping" game (Strayhorn & Rhodes, 1985) is designed to afford such rehearsals, both to children and to parents and other adults who work with children. (I have also found it useful for couples.)

The shaping game involves two people, the "shaper" and the "shapee." Here are the rules:

1. The shaper thinks of a desired behavior for the shapee to do, and writes it on paper.

2. The object of the game is for the shaper to give clues that eventually allow the shapee to do that behavior.
3. The object of the game for the shapee is to do that behavior. Thus the two players are in partnership rather than in competition with one another.
4. The shapee begins the game by doing things at random.
5. The shaper gives clues only by complimenting the shapee on things that he has already done. The shaper is permitted to point out very specifically the aspect of what the shapee did that was desirable.
6. It is against the rules for the shaper to give any sort of critical or corrective feedback on actions the shapee does, or suggestions on what the shapee might do; positive reinforcement only is permitted.

Here is an example of how an episode of the shaping game might work. A parent and his 8-year-old daughter are doing the game together. It is the parent's turn to be the shaper. The parent writes down on a piece of paper the words "Turn the lights off and turn them back on." When the parent finishes writing this, the child gets up and starts walking around. When the child moves in the direction of the light switch, the parent says, "Oh, that's a good direction to walk in." When the child walks further in that direction and touches the wall, the parent says, "That's so good that you are touching the wall." The child begins groping around on the wall, and when she moves in the direction of the light switch the parent says, "I am so glad you moved your hands in that direction." The child touches the light switch, and the parent says, "Good for you! You touched the light switch!" The child then turns the lights on and off; the parent applauds, says, "You did it!," and shows the child the piece of paper with the original behavior written on it. The shapee, whether adult or child, usually feels a certain delight or amazement to see the goal behavior in writing, when he or she has been guided to it by no clues other than selective compliments.

When adults play the shaping game with each other, they may start out with very simple goal tasks and work their way up to more challenging and complex ones. I have participated in sessions involving such goal behaviors as "Act out and describe a fantasy vignette in which you make a parachute jump from a plane and your parachute fails to open, but you land safely in a lake." The use of fantasy vignettes as goal behaviors elevates the complexity of the game to a level that can challenge the brightest aficionados of parlor games. If the target behaviors of the shaping game are to act out an example of a given skill on the axis, the game can come to approximate a "versatile vehicle," in which a variety of skills may be practiced and reinforced.

The errors that shapers make in playing the game often prove quite instructive. There are several common sorts of errors. Sometimes players get irresistible urges to criticize or give suggestions and commands. Sometimes they withhold approval too much—waiting for near-perfection, or wanting too large a step along the hierarchy before reinforcement—and thus frustrate the shapee. Other shapers give their approval too indiscriminately, praising behaviors that are digressions or steps down the hierarchy rather than steps upward, thereby confusing the shapee. Some shapers make their compliments too monotonous, without variety; some rely only on dull verbal statements without adding the tones of voice and facial expressions that convey the richness of many degrees of excitement and reinforcement. Some shapers give vague compliments like "That was good," without naming the specific aspect that was good, when a statement such as "I like it that you moved your right hand up and then down" would have conveyed much more useful information. Finally, some shapers seem locked into a competitive mode and delight in stumping the shapee, rather than taking their satisfaction from collaborative work toward the goal.

These are of course very important and frequent errors made in parent–child interactions and other areas of human relations. Accordingly, it is useful to point out to game players (or to challenge them to discover for themselves) the many analogies between the shaping game and the situations in life. The beauty of the shaping game is that when people play it repeatedly, the immediate feedback the shaper gets by seeing the shapee's response to his or her clues tends to "shape the shaper" away from the common errors and toward more proficient use of the art of selective reinforcement. Unlike the feedback of real life, which is often more delayed and ambiguous, that of the analogue situation allows quick learning.

The shaping game is, as it is usually played, not a versatile vehicle; it is meant to teach a particular set of skills. But that set is rather large and of paramount importance. It is perhaps not too gross an oversimplification to say that the two most populated categories of child behavioral problems—acting out and shyness/withdrawal—correspond simply to habits of punishing others and of punishing oneself, respectively, and that if these were replaced by habits of rewarding others and rewarding oneself, the problems would greatly diminish.

## The "Prisoner's Dilemma" Game

The "prisoner's dilemma" game, studied extensively by social psychologists, provides another set of abstract analogues of life situations that can give practice and positive consequences for a particular set of skills—namely, trusting, nurturing another, being honest, and all the skills in the conflict resolution group. In this game, each of two players makes choices in rounds where points or money (real or imaginary) is at stake. The payoffs are arranged in such a way that the pair may maximize their mutual gain by cooperation, but the individual player maximizes his gain on any round by a noncooperative move. For example, in each round, each player simply writes either "A" or "B" on his choice card; after both have chosen, they reveal their choices. If both players choose "A," then both get an imaginary $10. If one chooses "A" and the other chooses "B," the one who chose "B" gets $15 and the one who chose "A" gets nothing. If both choose "B," then both get $5. Thus on any given move, a player maximizes his expected outcome by playing "B"; it is only by *not* maximizing one's short-run expected gain, however, that the two players can jointly maximize their long-run gain. The exact quantities can be manipulated so as to alter the incentives, but the essential element is that the interests of the dyad are in conflict with the short-term interests of either of the individuals. The game gets its name from the situation in which two accused prisoners are held by the authorities, and each is asked to give evidence against the other in exchange for a reduced sentence for himself; mutual trust would yield the greatest payoff to both prisoners, but maximization of individual gains typically results in each giving evidence against the other. The game has also been widely cited as a metaphor for the arms race and many other interpersonal situations.

My experience in using this game with sixth-graders was quite interesting. If the children simply were recruited in pairs and played the game, most tended to choose the uncooperative options most often. On the other hand, if the game was re-explained as a contest in which each pair was conceived of as a team, and the object was to see how high a reward each team could obtain from the bank, the players tended to choose the cooperative option more often. If the children were often reminded that it is within the rules to negotiate with each other, to make agreements, and to tell each other their intentions, they achieved maximum rewards as pairs even more easily. These observations are generally consistent with the results achieved in studies of such games. Deutsch (1958, 1960), for example, used a single trial of a prisoner's dilemma game in experiments. Deutsch reported that when pairs were instructed to maximize the welfare of both players, and were given permission to communicate, the rate of cooperation was 97%; when players were instructed to do as well as possible regardless of the other player and were not given permission to communicate, the rate of cooperation was 36%. Other studies with similar conclusions are reviewed by Steinfatt and Miller (1974).

I see some conduct-disordered or friendless children as trapped into always choosing option "B" in the transactions of everyday life. Because their past experience has led them to expect that failing to exploit others will only result in their being exploited, they adopt the aggressive–defensive posture. Then, when the nature of the contest is such that they need to maximize the gain for the team by cooperating, no one wants them on the team. On the other hand, certain other children let themselves be taken advantage of repeatedly, as if choosing the "A" option in endless rounds when the other person consistently chooses "B." The game can be an arena where skills of sticking up for oneself, sacrificing for mutual gain, making bargains, being honest, and other skills can be practiced.

The prisoner's dilemma game has been used widely as a dependent variable to study the conditions that tend to promote cooperation. I believe that it would also be interesting to use it as a dependent variable in outcome studies of psychotherapy or psychological skills training, particularly those aimed at promoting cooperation and joint decision-making skills. More to the point of the present discussion, it would be very interesting to consider the therapeutic use of the prisoner's dilemma game as an independent variable, and to see how experience with this game might be useful in improving real-life skills of conflict resolution.

The "Situations" Game

The "situations" game is another versatile vehicle, one that can be used for any skill on the axis. In this game, the adult and child examine hypothetical situations and either discuss or act out how they would handle the situation. In carrying out this procedure, it is helpful to have a file of situations relevant to each of the skills on the axis; a subset of such a file is presented in Appendix 4 of this book.

One simple way to play the game is to take the cards with situations corresponding to the high-priority skills for a given child and to put them into a closed box. The two players roll a die to determine who draws out a card without looking at it. Whoever draws out the card gets a point or a chip if he responds to it. A variation on the rules is for the person who draws the card to have the option of letting the other person respond to it if he wants, and for both persons to get a chip, whereas if neither of them can respond to the card, they must both return a chip to the bank. This set-up gives incentives that every card will be responded to by one player or the other.

In order to carry out skill-oriented therapy with this game, the therapist uses cards tailored to the particular skills that should be modeled for and practiced by the child in question. These cards posit a hypothetical situation requiring the particular skill, and ask for a response or for several alternative responses. For example, if making social initiations is a high-priority skill for the child, one card might read, "A bunch of boys are working on building something. Another boy wants to join them. The boy watches them for a while, and then says something. What does he say?" Or if the high-priority skill is handling criticism, a card might read, "Someone watches you playing a sport and says, 'You're not doing it right.' What are two things you could say to yourself, and what are two things you could say to the other person?" Or if the high-priority skill is tolerating separation, a card might read, "A girl is worried that something will happen to her dog while she is away from him. An older girl decides to help this girl not be so worried. How does she help?" If the high-priority skill is tolerating frustration, a card might read, "A girl has just finished her homework, and her little brother accidentally spills orange juice all over it. What could she say to herself and what could she do, so as to stay cool and handle the situation well?" For conflict resolution, a typical card might read, "You want to watch a television show, and your sister wants to watch a different one that comes on at the same time. You only have one television. Act out, with another person, how you would best handle this situation."

With all these cards, the therapist gets to model if he or she draws the card, and the child gets to practice in fantasy or role playing if the child draws the card. At the beginning of the activity the therapist might want to choose situations that draw upon the areas of the child's strengths—the areas where the child may feel most competent while he is getting used to the game. Or the therapist may choose at the beginning the simplest situations to respond to, since some are much more difficult than others. As the game progresses, the therapist may wish to stack the deck toward practicing and modeling the highest-priority skills.

For those cards that direct the players to "act out" a response, the acting may be done with puppets or toy people, or without props, depending upon what works best. For many children puppets make the acting much easier than simply role playing without props.

An example of a specific application of the situations game is using it with family members to promote rational conflict resolution conversations. First, there may be a good deal of instruction and modeling in how to define problems, how to paraphrase and check out the other's point of view, how to redefine the problem if necessary, how to list options without rejecting them immediately, how not to insult the other person's preferences and ideas, and how to come to a choice that seems to maximize joint utility. Then the family members play the situations game, drawing cards with hypothetical conflict situations; for each card, a dyad from the family negotiates the conflict using role playing. If desired, it is possible to score each conflict resolution conversation, giving 0, 1, or 2 points for how well each of the criteria listed above was met. Gradually the therapist can include real conflicts the family has encountered in the past in the situations deck.

A way of playing the situations game that makes it more fun for some children is to use a game board, with each player having a figure that moves along the board according to the results of a die roll; the players choose from certain stacks of cards according to what squares their figures land on as they proceed along the board.

Richard Gardner's "Talking, Feeling, and Doing Game" represents a version of the general strategy described here for the situations game. Gardner uses a game board along which the players advance. In the case of the Talking, Feeling, and Doing Game, reward chips are obtained throughout the game, and the person who accumulates the most chips wins. From examples that Gardner (1983) gives, it is clear that the responses he models are meant to remedy the skill deficiencies he has perceived a particular child as having. Gardner's game has cards that seem aimed at breaking down the inhibitions of oversocialized children or encouraging disclosures about taboo subjects. Examples of cards that a therapist should think twice about including without good reason are "Make believe you're reading a magazine showing pictures of nude men. What do you think about such magazines?" and "Kiss someone in the room." Other cards included in Gardner's set ask the child to practice a negative pattern: Examples are "Make believe you're doing something that would make a person feel sad," "Say something mean to someone," "Scream as loud as you can. How do the people feel who have had to listen to you?" Of course, the intent of such cards is to give the child practice not in the negative pattern, but in the reflection upon it that can follow the task. Sometimes such reflection is discouraged by the pressure to get on with the next move of the game. My own preference, as is obvious from the situations listed, is to have situations that are meant to stimulate a positive response—a response worth repeating in real life.

Since the situations cards given in Appendix 4 present, in most cases, only the situations and not the desired responses, preparing for the situations game forces the therapist to give a great deal of thought to these questions: Which patterns of response to these situations really work best? Which patterns are desirable for children to learn? Such questions obviously deserve a good deal of consideration.

The logistics of shuffling paper cards for the situations game can be cumbersome. A computer program that presents situations for any four or five skills on the axis is available from me.

An empirical trial of something approximating the situations game is reported by Arbuthnot and Gordon (1986). These researchers carried out a group intervention aimed at increasing moral reasoning in aggressive and/or disruptive adolescents; the major activity was discussing possible responses to moral dilemma situations from the authors' files. This activity had positive effects on a number of outcome variables, including academic performance and rate of behavior referrals.

## The "Picture–Story" Game

Another technique useful for grade-school-age children is the game of randomly selecting stimulus objects, words, or pictures, and making up stories about them; this technique was conceived by Richard Gardner (1975). In the "picture–story" game, the therapist cuts from magazines pictures of all sorts of things and characters, and puts them into a box. The therapist and the child then roll a die to determine who gets to select a picture from the box. The person who selects the picture must do so without looking at it. Whoever gets the picture then wins 1 point if he or she can say anything at all about the picture, and another point if he or she can make up a story about the picture. Within the competence-based perspective, the crucial element is that the therapist, through his or her stories, model the important target skills for the child; some prior study of the pictures may be necessary for the therapist to do this optimally. The times when the child selects a picture present an opportunity for the child to practice a skill in fantasy, especially if the child has been influenced by the models heard so far from the therapist. The child's stories can receive differential approval or interest from the therapist in a subtle way, depending upon the skillfulness of the patterns portrayed.

## Variations on Spontaneous Dramatic Play and Role Playing

Like the preschool child, the grade-school child may greatly enjoy and benefit from spontaneous dramatic play with an adult, in which the two jointly create the plot. Like preschoolers, grade-school children are greatly assisted in doing this by first watching the therapist put on plays alone, using puppets or toy people or simply speaking the parts and giving whispered stage directions. The child learns from watching even one such performance the dramatic conventions that facilitate the unfolding of the play.

   The child of 8, 9, or 10 years of age is clearly capable of "processing" dramatic play more extensively than the younger child. By "processing," I mean talking about what sorts of patterns are more desirable than others, talking about how the situations of dramatic play relate to real life, engaging in conscious goal setting, and so forth. The *capability* for such activity does not imply the *motivation* for it, however, and it is good for the therapist still to be able to deliver models, practice opportunities, consequences, and instructions in the context of dramatic play rather than in real-life discussions. In my experience, it is not often productive for the therapist to make direct interpretations (e.g., "Perhaps you'd like to do what the character is doing, but it's scary to you") in the midst of dramatic play. Such interpretations tend to undermine the safety of dramatic play by destroying the basic convention that the actors do not have to shoulder the responsibility for what the characters do. In addition, such interpretations made in the midst of dramatic play interrupt the movement of the play, undermining the dramatic convention that the

actors stay in their roles while advancing the plot and do not frequently bounce back into their real-life roles. If the therapist wants to use
verbal commentary to underline certain facets of the child's actions,
these can almost always be best done by staying in a role: For instance,
one character says to another, "Boy, I think I'd like to do what you
just did, but I'd be scared to do it."


## TECHNIQUES FOR ADOLESCENTS AND OLDER INDIVIDUALS

### Variations on Story Reading and Storytelling

PROVIDING POSITIVE MODELS FOR THE PERSON TO READ
Presenting positive models through stories is such a potent and versatile technique that it should be useful at any age. Adolescents, more
even than adults, need to have such models presented in a way that
lets them feel grown-up rather than childlike. Naturally, it is important that the characters in the stories be imaginable as at least as old as
the adolescents themselves.

One way of presenting modeling stories is meant to challenge
and harness an adolescent's cognitive abilities to move along the
abstraction ladder and to move from the hypothetical to the real.
Suppose the adolescent is having trouble that calls for greater exercise
of a certain target skill—for example, responding to teasing and
criticism. The therapist hands the adolescent a stack of some 10
unillustrated modeling vignettes illustrating ways of responding to
teasing and criticism. One task of the adolescent is to identify the type
of strategy that the main character used in coping with the situation in
the modeling vignette (e.g., "He made other friends and got them to
be on his side, so the teaser would feel isolated"). Such a maneuver is a
move up the abstraction ladder from the specific response to the
more general strategy. The second task of the adolescent is to ponder
and discuss what might constitute an application of that strategy to his
real-life situation, and what the predicted outcome of such an application might be. Such a maneuver represents a move back down the
abstraction ladder to specific circumstances of the adolescent's real
life. This format creates an opportunity for harnessing the skills of
even the most intellectualizing adolescent, and for weaving the modeling stories into discussions laced with insight seeking and goal setting.

The adolescent or older grade-school child may be assigned

"homework" of reading literature that contains models of target skills, or may be sent on a scavenger hunt for such models in literature that is available in libraries. Adolescents who can read large works can of course take advantage of the richness of longer plots and deeper portrayals of character. Naturally, this technique and all others involving homework will be more likely to work with youths whose major problems do not include rebelliousness and defiance, and those whose reading skills are equal to the task.

Let us listen to a description of a couple of modeling stories that had a powerful effect upon a 12-year-old boy. In later life, he wrote,

> Somehow my eyes fell on a book purchased by my father. It was . . . a play about Shravana's devotion to his parents. I read it with intense interest. There came to our place about the same time itinerant showmen. One of the pictures I was shown was of Shravana carrying, by means of slings fitted for his shoulders, his blind parents on a pilgrimage. The book and the picture left an indelible impression on my mind. "Here is an example for you to copy," I said to myself. . . .
>
> There was a similar incident connected with another play. . . . This play—*Harishchandra*—captured my heart. I could never be tired of seeing it. But how often should I be permitted to go? It haunted me and I must have acted *Harishchandra* to myself times without number. "Why should not all be truthful like Harishchandra?" was the question I asked myself day and night. To follow truth and to go through all the ordeals Harishchandra went through was the one ideal it inspired in me. I literally believed in the story of Harishchandra. The thought of it all often made me weep. My commonsense tells me today that Harishchandra could not have been a historical character. Still both Harishchandra and Shravana are living realities for me, and I am sure I should be moved as before if I were to read those plays again today.

This account is from the autobiography of Mohandas Gandhi (1927/1957, p. 7). Have modeling plays and stories also influenced other people who have themselves turned out to be exemplary models? It would be fascinating to undertake a thorough study of this question.

PROVIDING MODELS IN ORDINARY CONVERSATION

Another way in which positive modeling vignettes may be communicated to adolescents is through the medium of anecdotes the therapist relates in ordinary conversation. The general format is as follows: "Someone I knew [or someone I heard of, or I myself] encountered a situation analogous to the situation you face; here is what the person did, and here is the outcome." The anecdote is a metaphor for the patient's experience, and the response option is being presented, but without such opportunities for resistance and rebellion as if direct instruction or suggestion is used.

D. Gordon (1978) gives an example of such a technique with an adult who was having difficulties with his wife. In an insight-oriented conversation, the therapist cast about for various descriptors of how the patient viewed his situation. The therapist tried this: "Perhaps like working on a project together and she wants you to do it all?" The patient replied, "Yeah. That's more like it. She cares what happens all right, but she wants me to do everything." After arriving at an adequate model whereby the problem could be conceptualized, the therapist told the following anecdote:

> You know, Joe, I had a friend in college who was very good at writing lab reports. He had a lovely girlfriend who was also a science major. Consequently they were in many classes together. Naturally, they paired up in order to write their lab reports . . . which he enjoyed—except for one thing. For some reason, his girlfriend felt that she wasn't competent enough to write lab reports. So she kind of sat back and let him write them. . . . He realized that she was missing out on opportunities to broaden her horizons. . . . He got an idea one day that worked really well. While they were working on a lab report, he pretended to be at a loss for words in describing the set-up. He was so completely stopped that she very quickly told him the obvious words needed to complete the sentence. He thanked her for her help and kissed her warmly. Soon, however, he was again "stumped." Again she helped him out, and so it went until he was finally able to turn over to her whole sections of the lab report to do on her own. The next time they did a lab, she actually demanded her fair share of it, and my friend, he was of course very happy to share it with her. (D. Gordon, 1978, p. 19).

This is, of course, a modeling story, and the skill being modeled is on our skills axis—using positive reinforcement, or shaping (along with a somewhat sneaky feigning of incompetence), as a solution to an interpersonal conflict. It is quite fortunate if the therapist can readily produce an interesting story about someone who has demonstrated the sort of skillful response that the patient most needs to learn, in a situation analogous to one encountered by the patient. Such a concrete model may be much more effective than a direct suggestion of the abstract strategy (e.g., "Well, why don't you act like you are stumped on some little thing and then respond very warmly when your wife helps you out, and keep doing that gradually more and more?").

Therapists who use this technique may be tempted to say, "I once knew someone who . . ." illustrated a certain skill pattern, when in fact the therapist is making up the story. I would recommend avoiding this departure from honesty, and clearly identifying the story as fantasy when it is such. The loss of effectiveness of the story will more than be made up for by the gain from maintaining the precedent of honesty.

## Other Fantasy Practice Techniques

### HYPNOSIS AND GUIDED IMAGERY

What is "hypnosis"? At least some current theorists conceive of hypnosis as using social and interpersonal influences to elicit certain cognitive strategies from the subject (Kihlstrom, 1985). Sometimes the cognitions in question may be images of adaptive functioning in high-priority skills areas, and when this is true, the strategy fits nicely into the paradigm of the skills × methods matrix. One of the widely acknowledged masters of hypnosis, Milton Erickson, was also well known for using stories, metaphors, and anecdotes, often within the context of hypnotic sessions. Haley (1973, p. 301) describes a case in which Erickson saw a man who had learned that he had a terminal illness, and as a result became very unhappy and distressed and developed very severe pain. Erickson learned that the man was a grower of flowers, and chose to use the imagery of plants in conversation with him. Below are some excerpts from Erickson's hypnotic monologue:

> Maybe—and this is talking like a child—maybe the tomato plant does feel comfortable and peaceful as it grows. Each day it grows and grows and grows, it's so comfortable, Joe, to watch a plant grow and not see its growth, not feel it, but just know that all is getting better for that little tomato plant that is adding yet another leaf and still another and a branch, and it is growing comfortably in all directions. . . . Would such a plant have nice feelings, a sense of comfort as the tiny little tomatoes begin to form, so tiny, yet so full of promise to give you the desire to eat a luscious tomato, sun-ripened, it's so nice to have food in one's stomach, that wonderful feeling a child, a thirsty child has and can want a drink. Joe, is that the way the tomato plant feels when the rain falls and washes everything so that all feels well? You know, Joe, a tomato plant just flourishes each day just a day at a time. I like to think the tomato plant can know the fullness of comfort each day. (Haley, 1973, p. 302)

This monologue is also a modeling story (although rather long on description and short on plot). The tomato is the main character of the story, and is personified so as to be able to model the skills of feeling pleasure from desirable events and enjoying the blessings of fate, which were just the skills that Erickson wanted the patient to draw upon more effectively when illness had commanded a large portion of his attention.

In therapy, as in all aspects of life, packaging and labeling are important. An adolescent who may be very enthusiastic about participating in hypnosis consisting largely of modeling stories may have been greatly insulted at the suggestion that he go and hear someone tell stories.

Another technique that can be labeled "hypnosis" or that can be called "guided imagery" is one in which the therapist creates parts of the story and asks the patient to create other parts; if the suggestions are given and followed properly, the experience constitutes a fantasy rehearsal of a skillful pattern. For example, suppose the high-priority skill for the patient is that of dealing fearlessly with a nondangerous feared situation. The therapist explains the purpose of guided imagery, gives some suggestions to relax and focus, suggests that images will come of a setting and a character, and asks the imager to describe what comes to mind. Then the therapist suggests that the main character will encounter a situation that presents some difficulty, and asks the person to describe the situation. Next, the therapist suggests that the main character will draw upon resources—from other people, from a major ally, from sources of information, or from objects and materials—to successfully handle the situation. The imager narrates the fantasy. In doing so, the imager has experienced a rehearsal of encountering and mastering a fearful situation. The nonresistant imager may create a situation in the fantasy that is quite analogous to the situation he wishes to handle better in real life.

Fantasy rehearsal does not have to be dressed up in such an exotic package. An alternative is a straightforward exercise in which the person is asked to go into the future and to see and hear himself handling situations in just the ways that embody the attributes or competences the patient wants to attain. The process of imagining these things and reporting upon them constitutes fantasy practice of positive skills—provided, of course, that the person has positive patterns in his memory bank and is able to select them.

A variation on this technique is to keep a list throughout the therapy session, on a blackboard or on a paper, of the situations the adolescent would like to be able to handle better and the ways he would like to handle them. At a routine time toward the end of the session, the adolescent is asked to spend some minutes in fantasy rehearsal, going through those situations and imagining responding to them in just the preferred ways.

Fantasy rehearsal can be carried out with or without simultaneous verbal description. To do it without simultaneous verbal description, the adolescent and therapist simply sit silently while the adolescent rehearses situations in imagination; after the fantasy, they talk about what was imagined. To do it with simultaneous verbal description, the adolescent learns to give a first-person, present-progressive-tense description of the fantasied scene and the action (e.g., "I am walking into the gym, and I'm seeing all the lockers around me, and I can smell sweat, and it's time to change for the swimming meet. I start to feel some anxiety, but I think to myself, '. . .' "). Both methods have their advantages, and the therapist and the adolescent find which is more effective through experimentation.

REVISION OF DREAMS IN WAKING FANTASY

Regardless of whether or what dreams "mean," dreams are fascinating and fun to work with. The strategy mentioned here involves no complex assumptions about the meaning of dream content; the only assumption is that fantasy practice of adaptive, skillful patterns of thought, feeling, and behavior is a useful activity. It is derived from a technique reportedly used by the Senoi, a "primitive" tribe in Malaysia (Garfield, 1974).

Suppose the person remembers a nightmare. The dreamer first simply recounts the dream to the therapist as he remembers it. Then the dreamer, with the help of the therapist's directions and questions, constructs a revised version of the dream that represents a fantasy practice of some skillful coping strategy. This new version provides a "happy ending," at least to the extent that the protagonist may feel good about having carried out the skillful pattern. As always, the therapist chooses questions and suggestions trying to help the person work skill patterns representing the high-priority targets into the reconstruction. When the person first begins to use this technique, the therapist may have to use much modeling to demonstrate how to reconstruct the dream.

For example, suppose a person recounts a nightmare of being pursued by a gorilla-like monster. The person tries to flee, but discovers that he is paralyzed and cannot move; the dream ends in terror. Suppose that a couple of this dreamer's high-priority skills are accepting help from others and resolving conflict rationally. Then he might benefit from reconstructing the dream in waking fantasy in this way: He starts along the same path, and begins to be pursued by the monster. But then he calls upon lots of friends to help him; they come out in force, magically increasing in size and strength if necessary, so as to hold the now outnumbered monster still while the protagonist has a conversation with the monster. In the conversation, the protagonist asks the monster what it wants of him and why it was pursuing him in such a vicious manner. If the monster wants something that is out of the question, such as to devour him, the protagonist asks, "What would you accomplish by doing that?" in order to search for a wish that he can meet. The monster and the protagonist negotiate until they can work out some sort of exchange of services or goods that is satisfactory to each. Or the protagonist convinces the monster to use its power in ways that help make it an ally rather than an enemy.

If, instead, the dreamer's highest-priority target skill is that of recognizing dangerous situations and feeling appropriate fear, the reconstruction in waking fantasy might be one in which he obtains a magic "monster detector" that beeps when a monster is near, and a magic pair of shoes that enable him to run away much faster than the monster. Or if the highest-priority target skill is tolerating his own mistakes and failures without feeling excessive guilt, he might first reach a position of safety, then have a dialogue with the monster in which he finds out what misdeed the monster wishes to punish him for. He then argues his own defense and convinces the monster or an imaginary jury that the misdeed of which he was accused does not deserve the punishment that the monster intended.

These examples obviously exactly parallel the process illustrated in Chapter 6 with spontaneous dramatic play in young children. As with such dramatic play, the therapist is not so much preoccupied with discovering the meaning of the fantasy material as with taking the fantasy material the person presents and turning it into an opportunity for useful fantasy practice.

People have reported to me that through such waking revision of dreams, recurrent nightmares have ended; anecdotal reports of this also exist in the literature (Singer, 1974, p. 115). It would seem reasonable that the practice of adaptive coping mechanisms in fantasy would make them more likely to spill over into dreams. But the major purpose of such activity is usually not so much to change dreams as to help the person function better in real life.

THE "INNER GUIDE" TECHNIQUE

The "inner guide" technique is a way of calling upon and organizing the positive images stored in one's memory bank, and using them in the service of fantasy rehearsal. I first read of this technique in Simonton, Matthews-Simonton, and Creighton (1978); within the psychological skill orientation, this may be modified so as to constitute another "versatile vehicle." In using this technique, one cultivates the image of a being that is loving, nurturant, wise, powerful, and endowed with other positive traits. In imagery exercises, one gradually cultivates the image of this being by searching one's memory bank for positive examples of the trait in question, and then imagines those traits as present in the inner guide. The person with certain high-priority target skills would do well to cultivate the image of the inner guide as strongly possessing those skills. Then after the image is cultivated, the person does other imagery exercises, again corresponding to the high-priority skills. For example, if a target skill is that of feeling good about one's own accomplishments, the person may recall his recent accomplishments and imagine the inner guide giving approval for them. If a target skill is tolerating separation, the person may imagine himself after a separation feeling the presence of the inner guide, and feeling comforted by that presence. If a target skill is relaxation, the person may imagine the nurturing and loving nature of the inner guide, and focus on the feeling of being cared for as he relaxes. If a target skill is forgiveness, the person may imagine the inner guide sending him the power to forgive, and giving approval when forgiveness has been accomplished.

The parallels of this technique to cognitive maneuvers that people have carried out through the ages in the context of prayer and religious meditation are obvious. The technique may be thought of as a theology-free method of tapping into some of the sources of psychological power that religion has offered. For those who wish to integrate such practices into a theological system, the option is of course open. Appendix 6 contains a script for initial practice of exercises with the inner guide.

WALKING THE PERSON THROUGH A POSITIVE REHEARSAL
IN FANTASY

Suppose that a high-priority skill for a given patient is that of problem solving and decision making. The patient comes into the office and tells about a real-life situation. The therapist may reply by asking (1) for more information on the situation, including information the client needs to go out and get in order to make a decision; (2) what the desired outcome of the patient's response is; (3) what options the client can think of for responding to the situation; (4) what the likely outcomes of those options are; (5) what the advantages and disadvantages of the likely outcomes are; and (6) what the best choice is, given the information that is currently available. By asking these questions or others like them, the therapist can prompt the client to go through the steps of decision making in an adaptive manner. After this has been done successfully, the therapist and client can "process" what has just taken place, and the client can think about the problem-solving techniques he or she has just used, in addition to the content of the problem. The cross-age generality of some of these techniques is illustrated by the fact that Spivack and Shure (1974) have examined a very similar technique with preschool children, carried out by preschool teachers.

This "walk-through" by questioning can be applied to any skill, not just problem solving and decision making. For example, the student who is anxious to the point of immobilization about an upcoming test may be asked (1) what the situation causing the distress is; (2) what the feared outcome is; (3) what the thoughts about the situation that induce fear are; (4) what responses the student prefers (i.e., what images, what probability estimates, what internal sentences, and what feelings and behaviors the student wants to enact); and (5) how it may be possible to practice, right now, each of those more preferable responses.

Walking through by questioning is much more effective if the patient already has the desirable patterns firmly entrenched in his or her repertoire, and only needs to be prompted to use them. Thus the technique will be more effective if it has been preceded by adequate modeling or instruction, so that the person has the desirable patterns available.

## Discussion of the Relationship with the Therapist

The notion of "transference" and the great importance accorded to it by analytically oriented therapists was derived from clinical experience, and not simply dreamed up. Deficiencies in almost any of the skills on the axis can lead to difficulties in interpersonal relations, and relations with the therapist are certainly not immune to such difficulties. The person who has great difficulties in trusting, and who has a pattern of starting to trust someone, then getting scared, and finding some reason to reject the other in a very hostile manner, may tend to repeat this pattern with a therapist. The person who defends against the fear of erotic attraction by generating reasons to be hostile may also tend to repeat this pattern with the therapist. Likewise, the adolescent who sees all adults as critical judges constantly finding fault with him may tend to repeat this pattern with the therapist. The person who habitually builds up tremendous fantasies that a given person will be a savior and rescuer from unhappiness, and then is disappointed and angry when the real-life person does not match the fantasy, may do the same with a therapist. Most people in the world, not to mention most therapy clients, are not masters at the skill of accurately assessing the skills and characters of other people without distortions from wish fulfillment, prejudice, or past experiences.

There are two reasons, then, to discuss with the client the nature of the relationship between the therapist and client, and to work on helping the client see the therapist as he or she is rather than through a distorted glass. The first of these is to avoid allowing the client's distortions to build up to a degree that they destroy the working relationship; the second is to help the client improve in crucial skills— among them the crucial skill of accurately appraising others— through goal setting, practice, and the positive consequences that come from an improved relationship. Discussion of the relationship might involve insight-oriented exploration of what the client's fantasies, images, and beliefs about the therapist are; where they have come from; and the extent to which they are based on observable evidence or upon distortions arising from within the client. A desired result of such discussion is that the client will do some goal setting, if necessary, with respect to the skill of accurately assessing the skills and character of another person, and will think about the steps involved in coming to such accurate assessments. At this point, the therapist can provide instruction or modeling with respect to how one really does acquire the information for such assessments. The client may practice, in the context of the relationship with the therapist or in the context of other relationships, and may reward himself for accurate, data-based conclusions.

But the skill of accurately appraising others is not the only skill that can be fostered by a discussion of the relationship between the therapist and the client. The client gets a chance to practice disclosing intimate material; trusting; expressing positive feelings; being assertive; being conciliatory; resolving conflict; reducing jealousy; learning

# CHAPTER 8

# Training Parents and Others to Have Sessions with Children

## OVERVIEW

Many of the techniques discussed in the preceding two chapters can be taught to at least some parents and other lay people to use with children. In fact, such teaching may greatly multiply the benefit of the techniques. The individual session between adult and child is used as the vehicle for training. It is very important that the adult and child develop mutually gratifying activities; reading modeling stories, performing modeling plays, and chatting provide a widely applicable set of activities that can be gratifying if carried out well.

In teaching adults to carry out these sessions well, several tasks are helpful. The therapist may get a baseline picture of how the parent and child interact by watching them together. The therapist may then have sessions with the child, to determine how the adult can best tailor the sessions to the particular child's personality. Next, the therapist shows the adult a checklist of important criteria for successful sessions—items such as using tones of approval, not being too bossy, and so forth—and the therapist explains the meaning of each item. After that, the therapist demonstrates and provides practice in each of these criteria by exercises with hypothetical situations handled in imagination and role playing. The therapist then models sessions with the child while the parent watches and monitors; next, the parent holds sessions while the therapist monitors. Depending upon the parent's performance, the therapist uses modeling and role-played exercises to promote the specific skills the parent most needs. The parent is given adequate practice so that the new patterns become habitual. The therapist adjusts the performance monitoring of the parent so as to be appropriate for the parent's degree of performance anxiety.

Generalization of interaction skills to the home setting can be promoted by several means. Peers and siblings may be included in the sessions; sessions may be held at home and monitored through tape recordings; the parent may rehearse in fantasy generalizing his or her skills to home and community settings; the therapist may ask parents to monitor and report such generalization when it does occur; and the therapist may urge the parent to model the child's high-priority skills in real life.

Sometimes parents need to learn not just specific skills of interacting with children, but more general psychological skills, deficiencies in which interfere with the relationship with the child. For example, the parent with a general deficiency in assertion and in tolerating disapproval from people, including the child, may find it very difficult to keep from giving in when the child complains and protests; the child's frustration tolerance skills suffer accordingly. Sometimes the therapist may benefit the parent through goal-setting discussions in which the therapist permits, encourages, or names the direction of psychological growth in which the parent needs to go. Other alternatives include therapy for the parent; slow movement along the hierarchy of simple to complex techniques; much role playing before putting the child and parent together in sessions; and obtaining some lay person other than the parent to work with the child. In some cases, the therapist must make the sad judgment that the best alternative is to minimize the contact between parent and child, even to the point of promoting changes in the child's living arrangement. The therapist should not be locked into the idealistic view that anyone can be taught to do anything. In general, however, the empirical literature is very positive about the possibilities for teaching lay people to promote psychological strengths in children.

---

We have already dealt with a number of aspects of parent training. Chapter 4 has to do with teaching parents to carry out skills-oriented contingency programs. Teaching parents to regulate consciously the consequences of their children's behavior is an intervention that has had positive results over and over. Patterson and others (e.g., Patterson & Fleischman, 1979) have made important contributions that have focused primarily upon teaching parents to increase the skill of compliance through the manipulation of consequences.

The full range of parent training curricula, however, encompasses many skills in addition to compliance, and many influence methods in addition to manipulation of consequences.

## THE CENTRALITY OF MUTUAL GRATIFICATION IN THE PARENT–CHILD RELATIONSHIP

As I have discussed in Chapter 4, the signals of approval and disapproval the parent sends are among the fundamental tools whereby a parent increases the psychological skills of a child. But sometimes a child dislikes a parent so much that he would rather evoke disapproval than approval from the parent, or is totally indifferent to the parent's opinions. This situation seems most often to occur when the child has received from the parent very little dependable gratification of needs or wishes, let alone pleasant activities. Similarly, sometimes parents are so angry at a child that they find it very difficult to give any but the most wooden and artificial approval. The clinician thus sometimes finds a parent and child in a vicious cycle where each is punishing and rejecting the other for the punishment and rejection he or she is receiving. If either parent or child can start to give some approval and gratification to the other, the feedback loop can sometimes be changed to the opposite sort, in which each member of the dyad feels more like gratifying the other because he or she personally is more gratified. Most often the first step will have to be taken by the parent, but no matter how the process gets started, mutually gratifying activities for parent and child to engage in together are of utmost importance.

There are many mutually gratifying activities possible for parents and children, beginning with the early experiences of holding and feeding. The parents' provision of the child's basic needs for food, clothing, cleanliness, health care, and supervision form the foundation for a mutually gratifying relationship. Once this foundation is in place, the skill-promoting play activities discussed in Chapters 6 and 7 are eminently suitable as mutually gratifying activities; moreover, in addition to being pleasant, they promote skill development by other means. Many parents can learn to use some, if not all, of the "versatile vehicles." This chapter discusses ways of teaching parents and other lay people to use these methods. I limit the discussion in this chapter to those methods appropriate for preschool and grade-school children.

## THE INDIVIDUAL PARENT–CHILD SESSION
## AS A VEHICLE FOR PARENT TRAINING

I have found it useful to train parents toward expertise in holding individual sessions with their children, oriented toward very specific activities. In the sessions, control of the stimulus situation is harnessed to heighten the likelihood of a positive interaction: One-on-one attention from the parent removes for many children the need to seek attention in maladaptive ways; removal from the environment of any

objects but those the child is meant to play with minimizes the need
for parental commands; and the objects that are within reach are
designed to elicit pleasurable responses. In many parent–child dyads
who present clinically, there is little positive interaction; if interaction
in the clinic can at least start under favorable circumstances, it has a
hope of expanding into the natural environment. When the therapist
can see the parent and child together in an interaction, the therapist
gains direct information that cannot be gained by secondhand reports. The therapist can give almost immediate reinforcement to the
parent for progress in skills. The therapist can also insure that the
time together between parent and child is not put off indefinitely. In
short, it is possible for the therapist to be a much more potent
influence when the behavior to be influenced is taking place before
his or her eyes. However, the therapist should continually seek to
promote generalization of skills learned in sessions to the home environment, in ways to be discussed later.


## STEPS IN TRAINING PARENTS TO HOLD SESSIONS
## WITH THEIR CHILDREN

1. *The therapist watches the parent and the child together.* It is useful to
determine where the parent presently is on the hierarchy of skills that
are to be taught. Parents can vary widely in regard to the resources
they bring with them into treatment. The therapist can observe them
informally, or can overtly ask the parent and child to play together
while the therapist observes. When the therapist has the luxury of
having two parents to work with, sometimes each is at different points
on the hierarchy with respect to different skills.

2. *The therapist has sessions with the child.* This step is not absolutely
essential, but it is often very helpful. By having sessions with the child,
the therapist can determine where the child is on the hierarchies of
verbal ability, ability to fantasize, and other relevant abilities, and can
empirically discover activities that seem to work well with this particular child. At least some of those activities should be easy enough that
this particular parent can learn to carry them out (given the therapist's judgment of the parent's skills). The therapist may carry out the
activities often enough with the child that the child gets used to the
routine, and "rough spots" are smoothed over before the parent takes
on the job. If videotaping is available, the therapist may videotape
some or all of these individual sessions with the child, and later may

show them to the parent, stopping the tape at times to explain the rationale for each part of the interaction.

3. *The therapist shows the parent a checklist of important criteria whereby the goals of sessions are obtained, and instructs the parents as to the meaning of each parameter on the checklist.* A sample checklist is shown in Table 8-1; many of the items on this checklist have been explained in Chapter 6. "Tracking and describing," for example, consist of the adult's observing and describing aloud the child's actions, without trying to direct those actions. The "prompt, wait, and hurry" approach is a way of promoting reciprocal interaction between an adult and a reticent child, wherein the adult does something that tempts the child to respond, waits 10 seconds or more for the child to respond, and

---

TABLE 8-1. Checklist for parent sessions

---

0 = None
1 = Only a little
2 = Some
3 = Pretty much
4 = A lot

1. How much did the adult's tone of voice communicate enthusiasm, approval, and a positive attitude, rather than sternness, criticism, and correction? ___
2. About how many times did the adult use positive reinforcement for a desirable behavior of the child? ___ (Tell the approximate actual number; don't use the 0-to-4 scale.)
3. How successful was the adult in not bossing the child around? That is, how much was the adult able to avoid a lot of commands or requests and other directives, but let the child explore and follow his or her own lead? ___ (0 = Lots of orders given; 4 = No unnecessary directives.)
4. How much did the adult give the child chances to have a "chat" with the adult? ___ (Reminders: The adult should ask questions and make restatements if the child talks about his own experience; the adult should model by talking about his or her own experience, especially something about which the adult is glad or proud. The adult should encourage conversation about what happened in the stories and plays.)
5. About how many positive models did the adult present, in stories, plays, or real-life behavior? ___ (Tell the approximate actual number; don't use the 0-to-4 scale.)
6. To what extent did the adult use "tracking and describing" in a way that allowed the child freedom and communicated approval? ___
7. How much was there a "ping-pong" interaction between adult and child? ___ (This means a reciprocal interaction, in which each partner in turn does or says something in response to what the other just said or did. If this fails to happen, often the adult needs to use more of the "prompt, wait, and hurry" approach.)
8. In the times when the child did something undesirable, how well did the adult choose among ignoring, using a reprimand, and applying the consequence of ending the session? ___ (Give 4 points if the child did not do anything undesirable during the entire session.)
9. How much did the child seem to have a good time? ___

hurries to give a reinforcing response in reply if the child does respond. If the child does not respond, the adult chooses between giving another prompt and waiting longer. If another prompt is given, it is important that it not be a nagging, repetitive request for the child to respond to the first prompt.

Most parents will need to have the difference between a positive model and a positive reinforcer defined by several examples. The majority of the positive models should be of the skills that are of the highest priority for this particular child.

The therapist explains how sessions with high scores in all these parameters should be helpful to the child, and in general goes through the persuasion and instruction necessary to help the parent set this goal: that sessions high in these aspects should be carried out regularly.

4. *The therapist uses special exercises with the parent to give concentrated instruction, modeling, and practice in particular aspects of parent–child interaction.* Let us look in detail at several of these exercises.

*"Tones of Approval and Disapproval" Exercise.* This exercise begins with an explanation to parents as to why tones of voice and facial expressions of approval versus disapproval are so crucial in the relationship between parent and child: (a) Tones of approval communicate to the child that he is loved; (b) when the adult's tone of voice communicates enthusiasm and approval during activities with the child, the child will be much more likely to enjoy those activities; (c) giving selective approval for the more desirable actions of the child is an extremely important way to make those actions happen more often; and (d) when the child hears tones of approval for positive actions, he begins to internalize those and turn them into positive self-statements, and thus begins to enhance his self-esteem.

Next, it is emphasized to the parents that tones of voice are even more important in communicating approval to the young child than the particular words chosen. To demonstrate this, the therapist may say, in a very enthusiastic and approving tone, "What you did is fairly good!!!" Then the therapist would say, in a flat and neutral tone, "What you did is just wonderful." Most parents will readily agree that if they were children, they would much prefer to hear the first comment than the second.

Then the therapist introduces the exercise of practicing producing various tones of voice at will, an exercise similar to one that actors and actresses might do. The therapist displays a chart such as the following:

Large approval
Small approval
Neutral
Small disapproval
Large disapproval

Then he or she picks phrases such as "Oh, look," or "Look what you've done," and demonstrates speaking them in each of the five ways. (A little acting practice may be necessary before the therapist can do this accurately.) The parents judge how much approval or disapproval is conveyed in the tone of voice. When the parents' judgments consistently match the therapist's productions, the parents are able to discriminate shades of approval and disapproval in tones of voice.

The next step is for the parents to practice producing the various tones. They are given a list of phrases to use, such as the following:

- "You picked up the table."
- "I see what you've done."
- "There they go."
- "I see you're putting the toys away."
- "Hey, what are you doing?"
- "Does it taste good?"
- "The man's getting in the car."
- "It is blue, isn't it?"

The parents pick one of the phrases and decide upon a degree of approval or disapproval that they wish to convey. They say the phrase, the therapist judges how much approval or disapproval was communicated, and the parent then discloses his or her original intention. The exercise continues until the intentions consistently match the judgments, and the full range of approval and disapproval has been practiced repeatedly.

In promoting generalization of this skill to real-life settings, this exercise may be done with the parents examining the list made for their child of specific examples of the high-priority skills (see Table 4-2). The parents look at the list, imagine the child's doing each behavior on the list, and practice making a comment about the child's activity with a tone of approval.

*"Commands and Suggestions" Exercise.* The therapist defines a "command" as a directive to the child that the child is given no choice

but to carry out. The therapist explains to the parents why it is very important not to give too many commands, perhaps mentioning research findings on the relationship between excessive commands and misbehavior (see G. K. Lobitz & Johnson, 1975; W. C. Lobitz & Johnson, 1975). At the same time, the therapist emphasizes that often it is necessary for the child to follow the adult's directives, and it doesn't do for the parent to be vague or tentative about those directives that the child must follow. The ideal is that only necessary commands are given, and all those are enforced.

By contrast, a "suggestion" is defined as communicating an idea to the child that he can choose to follow or not to follow. A suggestion gives permission to do the action, while also conveying the freedom not to do the action. When the parent decides that a directive is not worth enforcing if the child chooses not to follow it, it should be phrased in the form of a suggestion rather than a command, so that the child does not get into the habit of disobeying commands. The idea is not that suggestions are better than commands, or vice versa, but that the parent should decide how important it is that the child carry out the action, and communicate that accurately. If the child is about to stick a paper clip into a wall socket, it would not do to use a suggestion like "Wouldn't you rather not put that paper clip in there?"

The first part of this exercise involves simply discriminating between commands and suggestions. The therapist presents examples for practice, such as the following:

- "Please come with me and wash your hands." (Command)
- "If you want to, you can wash your hands." (Suggestion)
- "Now we're going to put all the toys away and go home." (Command)
- "When you're ready, we can put the toys away." (Suggestion)

The second part of the exercise involves looking at examples of commands, such as the following, and deciding for each of them whether or not the command is absolutely necessary.

- A 4-year-old boy has found a piece of broken glass. The adult takes it from him, and at the same time says, "No, the broken glass is not something to play with."
- A 7-year-old boy is fidgeting around a lot while the adult is

- reading a story to him, but he is still paying attention. The adult says, "Hold still. Don't fidget so much."
- A 4-year-old boy is playing with some toy people and toy animals. He decides that the lion can fly through the air, and is moving the toy around, saying, "Here goes the flying lion." The adult says, "Lions can't fly. Put it down on the ground."
- An 8-year-old girl is looking at the material in some curtains. She is holding it in her hand and feeling it, and isn't pulling on it or mistreating it in any way. The adult says, "Sally, put that down and leave it alone."
- A 6-year-old is picking up a puppy in a way that is hurting the puppy. The adult says, "Put the puppy down, right now."
- A 4-year-old is playing with toy people and a toy house. The people drive their car up on top of the house, and some of them stand up there. The adult says, "They shouldn't be on top of the house. Get them down from there."
- A 4-year-old is playing with an adult, and reaches up and pulls the adult's hair. The adult says, "That hurt when you did that. Don't ever do that again. If you ever do that again, we'll stop the sesson and go back."
- A 4-year-old boy is playing with crayons and paper. He has drawn a person, and then he starts to scribble all over his own drawing. The adult says, "No, don't scribble on your drawing."
- A 10-year-old boy has come in from outside and still has his coat on, despite the fact that it is warm enough inside. The adult says, "Take your coat off."

After these discrimination exercises are done, the parents can practice further, in the following way. The therapist, or the parent, supplies examples of commands or suggestions, purposely making some of these inappropriate. For each inappropriate command or suggestion, the parent practices translating it into a more appropriate communication.

These exercises may be repeated as often as necessary, with more examples supplied by the therapist or by the parents, until the parents can consistently discriminate between necessary and unnecessary commands, and can make commands and suggestions that clearly communicate the extent to which obedience is expected.

*Exercises on Chatting with the Child.* In introducing this exercise, the therapist emphasizes the importance of pleasant, nondirective conversation between parent and child as a way of promoting a positive relationship with the adult, and feelings of secure attachment; promoting the child's language development; helping the child learn very important skills of social conversation with other people; and helping the adult to know better what the child is experiencing.

The therapist explains that when many adults try to get children to talk, they simply ask the child question after question. This approach is not conducive to a rich conversation. Instead, the following three ways of interacting tend to work much better:

- Telling about your own experience
- Paraphrasing what the child says
- Asking follow-up questions

The therapist explains that the adult's "telling about your own experience" *shows* the child how to tell about his experience. The therapist gives ordinary, everyday examples, such as "Guess what I saw today? I saw a man outside painting his house." After hearing enough examples, the parent practices by thinking of items from his or her own experience that he or she might tell the child.

If the adult tells about his own experience, it will usually not be long before the child starts doing the same thing. One response that enables the child to continue talking about his experience is for the adult to paraphrase the child, or to say back to him what he communicated, so that he knows the adult understood him.

The therapist should give the parents examples of paraphrasing. One can paraphrase even with very young children: If the child finishes a puzzle, and says, "Did it," a paraphrase might be, "You did do it, you finished the puzzle." Or if the child looks out the window and says, "Car outside," a paraphrase might be, "You see a car outside."

As a practice exercise for paraphrasing, the therapist can supply utterances that a child might make, and let the parent practice making up a paraphrase. The following are examples for use with preschool children:

- The child points to a picture of a Mickey Mouse watch and says, "Aunt Susie get this for me." (Sample answer: "Oh, your Aunt Susie might get a Mickey Mouse watch for you?")
- The child points to a picture of a rainbow and says, "Pretty

- colors." (Sample answer: "You like those pretty colors in the rainbow.")
- The child says, "Saw big dog."
- The child points to the play house and says, "Want house."
- The child says, "It was raining."

The therapist then explains that another way to respond when a child says something is to ask a follow-up question—to ask the child to elaborate on what he was just talking about. For example, if the child says, "Saw big dog," the adult might ask, "Was it a nice dog, or was he scary?" or "Whose dog was it?" If the child says, "I got a sticker," the adult might say, "Oh, did you get that for doing something good?" or "What's that on your sticker?"

In group training sessions, a useful way of practicing these three skills is for one person to make up something from his own experience suitable to tell a child; a second person to paraphrase; and a third to use a follow-up question. There are many possible variations on this exercise.

*Practice in "Tracking and Describing."* In this exercise (discussed in Chapter 6), the therapist explains that tracking and describing consist of the adult's observing and describing aloud the child's actions or those of his dramatic characters, without trying to direct those actions. The therapist gives examples, such as the following: If a preschool child is playing with blocks, the adult might comment, "There goes the next block. That tower's getting pretty tall. Will it take one more? Whoops, down it all goes." Or if the young child is having fantasy characters take off in an airplane, the adult might say things like "There you go in your airplane, off into the sky!"

The therapist explains that tracking and describing is a useful skill because it is nondirective, and thus presents no opportunity for the child to argue or oppose the adult, but lets the child follow his own lead; for the young child, it models use of language and helps the child's own language develop; and when done selectively for the positive actions of the child, it may provide attention and approval that tend to reinforce those actions.

The adults may then practice this skill by doing an exercise in which one adult plays the part of the child, and does things with toys or crayons and paper, while another adult tracks and describes. The tracker and describer should not speak constantly, but should allow a period of time for the child to reply if he wishes.

*Practice in Techniques of Reading Stories to Children.* The therapist explains the benefits of reading stories to children: The activity promotes a pleasant interaction between adult and child, as well as promoting the child's language development, and if the stories are chosen so as to exemplify the high-priority skills, they provide positive models to the child. The therapist mentions that although some people may think that reading stories to a child is something so easy as to deserve no discussion, this is not true. The therapist reviews the following suggestions for story reading:

• The adult should put a lot of expression in his or her voice.
• The adult should look at the child sometimes, not just the book; the eye contact reinforces the child for listening.
• An approving tone should be used at the end of the story; this reinforces the child for paying attention.
• If the child's attention wanders, the adult should wait a while, and start reading again when the child's attention returns. If the child keeps attending to something else, the adult should not feel obligated to continue the reading, nor should the child be commanded to listen when he doesn't want to.

The therapist then demonstrates with an imaginary or role-played child the difference between story-reading sessions in which each of these four suggestions is followed and those in which each of them is not followed. The parents may then practice each of the two ways in role playing, and experience the difference in how it feels to be read to.

The therapist might then mention two more suggestions that apply only to parents:

• The child can sit on the parent's lap and should be given a lot of physical affection while he's hearing the story.
• The parent may read stories at bedtime, when the child usually wants to put off saying "good night" and has still another motive for wanting one more story.

*Exercises in Putting on Modeling Plays.* The therapist explains the benefits of the parents' putting on plays with toy people for the young child: (a) The activity is usually pleasant for parent and child to do together: (b) the child gets models of how to do dramatic play; and (c) if the behaviors in the play exemplify the high-priority skills, the child gets important positive models.

The therapist gives the following suggestions about performing the modeling plays:

- The adult should ask the child to sit in a chair out of reach of the toy people.
- The play should be very fast-moving.
- An enthusiastic tone of voice should be used.
- The adult should look at the child occasionally.
- If the child stops paying attention, the adult should stop the play and wait.
- The adult should announce the end of the play with approval to the child.

The therapist distributes to parents copies of modeling plays (see Appendix 3) and demonstrates putting on a play for an imaginary child. The parents may then practice, also with an imaginary child.

*Exercise in "Ping-Pong Interaction" and "Prompt, Wait, and Hurry."* The therapist defines "ping-pong interaction" as one in which the child and adult take turns responding to one another, and defines the "prompt, wait, and hurry" technique as explained in Chapter 6.

In this exercise, someone role-plays the part of a shy and withdrawn child. The other person practices giving prompts, waiting 10 seconds, and giving another prompt. If the child ever responds, the other person practices responding quickly in an approving way.

*Exercises in Responding to the Child's Undesirable Behavior.* The therapist summarizes some undesirable things that a young child could do with an adult in a play and story-reading session, and provides some reasonable consequences to apply to these undesirable behaviors, as follows:

- Child hits adult. . . . Session ends.
- Child throws toys. . . . Session ends.
- Child runs out of area. . . . Session ends.
- Child says insulting things. . . . Adult ignores or reprimands.
- Child plays violently with toy people. . . . Adult ignores, then models helping the victims.
- Child refuses to leave the area at the end. . . . Adult gives clear command, then physically takes child out.

• All undesirable child behaviors. . . . Adult responds in calm, low-arousal way.

After speaking about these consequences, and the importance of having predetermined decisions as to the consequences for each of the child's undesirable behaviors, the therapist models these responses and the parents practice them through role playing.

*The "Shaping" Game.* This activity, described in Chapter 7, is a very useful one for parents as well as for children. The therapist explains the rules of the game and the ways in which it is analogous to real-life experience, and allows the adults to practice it.

Some of these exercises require the parent (or therapist) to risk looking silly or feeling childish while playing the part of a young child. Nevertheless, there is hardly another way that I know to give such concentrated practice to parents in specified skills. For this reason, any salesmanship, persuasion, and sheer artistry that the therapist can muster to help parents feel un-self-conscious doing these exercises (or feel good about doing them though self-conscious) will be amply rewarded.

The role-playing practice exercises are but one step (the fourth on our list) in the total sequence of activities involved in parent training. Let us proceed with the fifth step.

5. *The therapist models these sessions for the parent, while the parent observes, rating the therapist's sessions according to the parameters on the checklist.* These modeling sessions can be carried out either through videotape or through the parent's being present while the therapist has a session with the child. After the session, the therapist spends time with the parent and gets the parent's ratings on the checklist parameters, as well as the parent's justifications for the ratings given. The therapist seeks to corroborate that the parent understands the meaning of each checklist item.

6. *The therapist watches and monitors sessions held by the parent with the child.* After the parent's session, the parent looks at the checklist and gives a self-rating for each parameter; the therapist provides independent corroboration or corrective feedback as necessary. They celebrate reliable ratings, even if the ratings are low.

7. *Depending upon the parent's performance in these practice sessions, the therapist models more sessions and/or does more role-playing exercises with the parent between sessions.* If there is some skill with which the parent has particular difficulty, the therapist might go over the exercise for that

particular skill. For example, if the parent gives too many commands to the child, the therapist might go over the "commands and suggestions" exercise again; if the parent uses overly disapproving tones, the therapist might go over the "tones of approval and disapproval" exercise again. In this manner there is a closed feedback loop, in which any deficiencies observed in the performance are specifically remedied, so that eventually a criterion-level performance can be obtained.

Performance monitoring, in this arena as in others, can be a double-edged sword. If the parent can tolerate it, it is a very powerful tool for improving the interaction. On the other hand, the monitoring can induce so much performance anxiety in some parents that the net effect is counterproductive. The therapist should seek to promote, through the artistry of human interaction, the optimum degree of monitoring for the fastest learning by the parent. For some parents it may be useful for the therapist to give the instruction, "While you're doing the session, forget about the items on the checklist, and just relax and have a good time with your child." One option that is usually more comfortable at the beginning for an anxious parent is for the therapist not to arrive at a numerical score, but simply to observe the session and to point out positive examples of any of the items on the checklist in the feedback afterward. For example, "When you said, 'There goes the garbage collector, oops, he had another wreck,' that was a good example of tracking and describing. When you said, 'Thanks for helping me pick up this garbage,' that was an example of a positive reinforcer." This feedback is best given to the anxious parent in a one-to-one interaction rather than in the child's presence, to prevent the parent's being embarrassed by receiving feedback in the child's presence. If logistics do not permit the child's absence, the therapist may simply hand the parent written notes made during the session about positive examples the parent carried out.

If these measures do not suffice, the therapist may prefer simply to watch the session and ask the parent to monitor himself or herself, without adding any feedback at all. Or the parent may hold the session privately and tape-record it, deciding only after the session whether to allow the therapist to hear it.

Most of the time these measures will be unnecessary, if the therapist can project the attitude that monitoring and rating the parent's sessions are simply ordinary and casual things to do, and that they are approached in a relaxed way with no overblown expectations. The therapist might even resort to a humorous form of paradoxical instruction: "What I want you to do is to have a really bad session this first time, so that we can feel good later on about how much things are improving."

It is probably apparent that the teaching method with parents just described is simply the application of the nine methods of influence described in Chapter 5. The therapist uses goal setting, hierarchy formation, modeling, instruction, control of the stimulus situation, provision of practice opportunities, monitoring, reinforcement, and attribution in teaching the parent to have productive and pleasant sessions with the child.

## PROMOTING GENERALIZATION TO HOME INTERACTION

If the parent learns to have pleasant and skill-promoting interactions with the child in the therapist's office, this in itself is likely to be beneficial. But if what the parent learns can generalize to the home environment, and to activities other than story reading and dramatic play, then the benefits are multiplied many times over. How is such generalization promoted? Stokes and Osnes (1986) and Stokes and Baer (1977) have carefully considered the issue of generalization of behavior; some of the following suggestions are drawn from their ideas.

1. *Siblings or peers can be included in the sessions.* Once the child has learn to cooperate in the sessions and has become "hooked" on stories and dramatic play, it is quite beneficial for the adult to bring a sibling or peer into the sessions and to engage in three-way interaction (or four-way, if both parents are involved). (The other child involved may or may not need to be prepared for the sessions by first having some individual sessions himself.) In the three-way interaction, the parent can sometimes make especially potent use of differential attention: For example, when a child engages in an undesired behavior, it is often very effective for the adult to turn attention to the other child, thus engaging in a form of ignoring. Another advantage of involving peers is that it promotes generalization, for a couple of obvious reasons. First, the parent may have trouble at home isolating one sibling from another to carry out one-on-one interactions. Second, if both siblings can be interested in dramatic play, can learn to play cooperatively, and can be given a repertoire of prosocial themes on

which to make variations in plots, they can have "therapeutic" interactions with each other even in the absence of the parent.

2. *The therapist can promote tape-recorded sessions carried out at home by parents.* Once the parent has learned to carry out the sessions in the office, a next step is to assign as homework that a session be tape-recorded. The parent then brings in the tape to be listened to by the therapist and monitored just as the in-office sessions are. The therapist and the parent can work, if necessary, on the special problems of holding the sessions in a different environment.

Such home sessions require the basic equipment of a set of toys for dramatic play, a tape recorder, and some stories. At the time of this writing, all these can be obtained for about $50. The presence of this equipment in the home constitutes a stimulus that in itself promotes home sessions, especially if the child has enjoyed the past sessions enough to provide assertive reminders to the parent.

3. *The therapist can have fantasy rehearsals, with the parent, of applying the skills learned in sessions to a variety of other circumstances.* For example, the parent is asked to imagine having a chat with the child, telling the child about his or her own experience, paraphrasing the child, and using follow-up questions in a variety of settings: while traveling together, while doing housework, and while at the dinner table. Or the parent is asked to imagine using "tracking and describing" while the child does activities in the house, or avoiding unnecessary commands in hypothetical situations at home.

4. *The therapist can monitor and reinforce the application of skills by parents.* After the parent practices in fantasy the generalization of the skills to various settings, he or she keeps track of the results of such ventures and celebrates them in the next visit with the therapist.

5. *The therapist can encourage real-life modeling by parents.* Through dramatic play, the parent gets concentrated practice at looking for any opportunity to model an imitation-worthy behavior for the child. The therapist may encourage the parent to use positive models in a similar way in real life.

In planning for real-life modeling, the parent can use as a springboard the list of concrete, specific actions of the child that the therapist and the parent have generated (see Chapter 4, Table 4-2), and the specific actions the parent has been trying to model in the dramatic play. The new list involves the same skills, only now the specific examples are of behaviors appropriate for parents to carry out. Thus, again, there is a move down the abstraction ladder to a new set of concrete examples. The parent then monitors his or her performance and celebrates with the therapist the positive examples he or she provided to the child. Obviously, such a venture may turn out to be "therapeutic" for the parent as well as the child.

## INCREASING PSYCHOLOGICAL COMPETENCES IN PARENTS

Sometimes when a child is first assessed for therapy, or sometimes as therapy progresses, it becomes apparent that one or both parents are hampered by psychological skill deficiencies. Sometimes the intervention of choice is to allow the parent to become the identified patient and work on his or her own problems; sometimes, however, fairly brief interventions with parents can be made in the course of counseling them regarding their children. This is especially true when the skill deficiency in question is circumscribed and limited to the parent–child interaction. Sometimes a couple of goal-setting conversations with the therapist may do parents a tremendous amount of good. This section focuses on some of these brief interventions.

### The Skill of Assessing Trustworthiness

Some parents of young children present with a chronic feeling of irritation with their children, which is traceable to an inability to trust an alternative caretaker. That is, the parent feels the need to supervise the child constantly, out of fear that an alternative caretaker will harm or inadequately protect the child. But the task of constant supervision becomes so burdensome that the parent feels the child to be a "ball and chain." The parent's interactions with the child become more and more laced with hostility.

Sometimes, in such cases, parents can greatly benefit from some explicit discussion of how to choose babysitters and preschools. The therapist should celebrate, rather than disparage, the parent's wish to make sure that the child is well protected; the therapist should encourage the parent to harness that protective energy by thoroughly screening the personnel to whom the child will be entrusted. The parent may be taught the two basic techniques of "personnel selection" relevant to the task. First, the parent should watch the prospective caregiver in action with a child or children for long enough to get a sample of how he or she acts and what the environment is like.

Second, the parent should get information from references who have known the person for a long time, and ask specific questions that will attest to dependability and conscientiousness. In other words, if the parent who is hesitant to trust can define the problem as how to discriminate between trustworthy and untrustworthy individuals, and how to gather the information necessary to do so, sometimes this is sufficient to solve the problem.

### The Skill of Nurturing: Accepting the Dependent Status of the Child

Some parents seem to resent the normal attention-seeking and help-seeking actions of their preschool children. In some cases, this resentment is traceable to overly high expectations of how independent and self-reliant a young child "should" be. In such cases, it may be very helpful for the parent to hear that the ability to be appropriately dependent and to seek attention in normal ways are strengths, not weaknesses, for the child, and that they should be enjoyed. Furthermore, the ability to depend is a skill upon which the skills of compliance and delay of gratification may be built; these skills are therefore not to be undermined. If a conversation is cast in such a way that the parent feels that he or she has not been such a bad parent after all by inducing dependent behaviors in the child, the pleasure of such a conversation can furnish the energy needed for a reorganization of thoughts about dependency.

### The Skill of Enjoying Attachment and Commitment

A different situation occurs when the parent resents the child because the parent has never really tolerated a sustained relationship with anyone, and the inability to terminate the relationship with the child when the going gets unpleasant creates great resentment in the parent. This skill deficiency is one that is not so susceptible to brief intervention; nevertheless, it is helpful for the therapist to recognize it when it is present, if for no other reason to temper expectations of the parent to a reasonable level. When this skill deficiency is extreme, finding foster or adoptive placement often becomes an issue.

Social Conversation and Empathic Listening Skills

A parent's inability to chat with the child may contribute to several problems in the child. If the void created by the shortage of pleasant conversation is filled by too many parental commands and suggestions, the result can be rebellious and oppositional behavior on the part of the child. If there is a dearth of conversation with the child, the child's verbal skills will probably suffer, not to mention the child's own social conversation skills.

Specific exercises on chatting with the child, such as those presented earlier in this chapter, are often quite helpful in increasing the parent's skills in social conversation with and empathic listening to the child. If, in addition, such exercises assist the parent in improving relations with other adults, forming a more adequate support network, and feeling happier and more secure, a wide variety of more indirect benefits may accrue.

Skills of Tolerating Separation

Children who are afraid of separating from their parents, who fear that horrible things may happen to their parents or to themselves while separated, will obviously have a much harder time getting over such fears if the parent has the same fears. It is easy for the parent to convey by tone of voice and facial expression catastrophic expectations for separations.

When it becomes clear to the parent that he or she is afraid of separation from the child, simply setting the goal of diminishing this fear in the child's best interest may have a positive effect. It may also be helpful for the therapist to point out that the coping strategies illustrated in modeling stories for the child are the same ones used by adults in overcoming such fears: holding a reality-based image in mind of the absent person's activities, anticipating and imagining the reunion that will occur in time, rationally considering past experience and the probability of catastrophic events, and so forth.

Conflict Resolution Conversations between Parents

When two spouses have conflict resolution conversations characterized by anger or sullenness rather than by rational searching for the best possible solution to the problem, the child often suffers in indirect ways, as well as in a direct way by adopting similar conflict resolution strategies. Sometimes it is beneficial for the spouses to learn to go through a calm process of problem solving focused on listing options and choosing among them, with the intention of sometimes having such conversations in the child's presence to model the skill for the child. If the parents identify the skill as one that is helpful for their own relationship as well as for the child's behavior, the practice can be seen as accomplishing two goals at once.


## Assertion Skills with the Child

Frequently children with low frustration tolerance, noncompliance, maladaptive fears, or tyrannical intolerance of other people's behavior have parents who are afraid of saying "No" to the children and facing the resulting protest. This pattern may be especially common among parents who feel quilty about something perceived as suboptimal in the child's environment (e.g., a divorce or the need for day care). Because the parent gives in to the child when the child whines, protests, or gets scared, the child learns to engage in such patterns persistently.

Sometimes the most powerful antidote to such a pattern is to have an educational goal-setting discussion with the parent, appealing to the same overactive conscience that has originally contributed to the problem. The therapist explains to the parent the crucial importance of frustration tolerance skills or whatever other skills the child is failing to develop. The therapist then points out that by not being assertive with the child, the parent is trying to be kind to the child, but in the long run will actually be doing something very unkind if the pattern is continued. The kindest and most loving thing in the long run is to frustrate the child enough that the child can learn frustration tolerance. When parents can reorganize their cognitions so that they no longer feel guilty over setting limits, but feel as though they are doing a loving act, the same motives that caused the problem can sometimes very quickly solve it.

Once such a cognitive reorganization has come about, the "commands and suggestions" exercise will give the parent practice at deciding when to be more assertive with the child and when not to. The use of time out (see Chapter 4) is often helpful as a technique whereby parents can enforce limits without resorting to punishment methods that induce guilt in the parents.

Tolerating a Wide Enough Range of a Child's Behavior:
The Special Case of Exploring

A parental pattern opposite to the one just described is as follows:
The young child has overly rigid boundaries placed on his behavior—
too many commands to "quit doing that and leave that alone," when
the child's exploratory behavior is actually safe and appropriate. Such
a parent is deficient in the skill of tolerating a wide enough range of
the child's behavior, especially the child's exploratory behavior. Possible results include the child's getting rebellious and oppositional, or
the child's exploratory drive's being suppressed by too much hand
slapping and reprimanding.

Here the cognitive reorganization the therapist aims for in goal-
setting conversations is that the skill of enjoying exploration is a very
important one for the child to develop, and that the therapist would
be quite worried about the child if the exploratory drive were *not*
present. If the child did not tend to explore objects in his environment, the therapist might go on to say, there would be reason to
wonder whether the child were mentally retarded. The child's exploratory drive is what makes the older child want to read a book and find
out about how things work, and what gives an adult the ability to
make a scientific discovery. If the parent can start seeing the young
child's manipulation of harmless objects as "My child, the young
scientist," rather than "My child, who can't keep his hands to himself,"
a great deal of inappropriate negative interaction can be precluded.

Once such a cognitive reorganization has occurred, the "necessary and unnecessary commands" exercise will give the parent practice in making the fine discriminations of when exploration is appropriate and when it is to be stopped.

Recognizing and Praising the Portion of the
Other's Behavior That Is Positive

Using positive reinforcement to increase the acceptable behavior of
the other person, and thereby to resolve conflict and reduce hostility,
is a technique that has been repeatedly emphasized throughout this
book. The "shaping" game and the "tones of approval and disapproval" exercise are designed to increase the parent's ability in this
area; the specific plans described in Chapter 4 give the parent much
practice in using positive reinforcement.

Sometimes, however, some goal setting through insight is useful with parents in overcoming barriers to using positive reinforcement. One such barrier is the hostility that the parent has already accumulated toward the child, which may make it very difficult to give approval for even the most praiseworthy behavior. In such a case, the parent may need to cultivate the skill of forgiveness as a means toward using positive reinforcement. Alternatively, the parent may simply try a "bootstrapping" operation, in which he or she practices acting pleased with the child's behavior so thoroughly and convincingly that the child feels reinforced, responds positively, and helps the parent let go of accumulated resentment.

A second sort of barrier to positive reinforcement occurs in parents who themselves have experienced harshly critical, emotionally abusive childhoods: The parent is inhibited from providing positive reinforcement by jealousy lest the child get something the parent could never have (i.e., the approval of a parent). Now the parent may adopt the goal of increasing the ability to tolerate someone else's getting what he or she wanted, and to celebrate when he or she is able to take pleasure in the child's pleasure. If the parent can use the mental maneuver that so many parents have used—that is, "I'll make sure my child gets what I never had"—the same unhappy memories of childhood can be harnessed for adaptive motives, replacing the very maladaptive cognition of "Why should my child get what I never had?"

A third barrier to positive reinforcement is this: The parent may feel that the child "should" do the desirable behaviors without needing any external reinforcement at all. Here a useful intervention is to educate the parent as to the notion of hierarchy. The therapist explains that, indeed, a long-term goal is for the child to be able to reinforce himself for many desirable behaviors. But the child needs to move along a series of steps, not simply to jump directly to the desired state. The steps toward being able to reinforce oneself involve being able (1) to trust and depend on a parent enough to care about the parent's approval; (2) to do more often those things that gain the parent's immediate approval; (3) to do more often those things that get more delayed approval from the parent; (4) to actually recruit approval from the parent—to tell about a positive behavior so that the parent can confirm its praiseworthiness; (5) to start to give positive messages to oneself sometimes in the absence of external reinforcement; (6) to give positive messages to oneself often in the absence of external reinforcement. If the parent can see that self-reinforcement is a long-term goal best served by effective use of external approval for the time being some of the resistance from this source can be reduced.


## Increasing Relaxation Skills and Frustration Tolerance with Respect to the Child's Misbehavior

Sometimes the parent intellectually realizes that a certain fraction of the child's undesirable behavior is reinforced by attention and should simply be ignored; nevertheless, the child's behavior touches off an emotional response in the parent that makes it almost impossible for the parent to resist shouting orders or reprimands to the child.

With some such parents, it is helpful to teach them to desensitize themselves to the emotional arousal they feel when their children engage in a certain undesirable behavior. If they can adopt as a goal the ability to maintain calm rationality when the children engage in this behavior, then techniques are readily available to help them practice. It is useful to use progressive relaxation, imagery, or repetition of a mantra to help a parent achieve a relaxed state, and then to have the parent imagine the child doing the maladaptive behavior; the parent then continues the mental movie by seeing himself or herself responding calmly and rationally, while staying relaxed in real life. If catastrophic cognitions, such as "If she keeps this up she'll wind up like her aunt!" arise during such fantasies of the child's misbehavior, these cognitions can be examined.


## Organization and Time Management Skills

Many of the parenting suggestions that are very helpful unfortunately require a modicum of organization and work. Parents with behaviorally disordered children often present as exhausted and overwhelmed with the tasks of life, and the suggestion to take on more tasks with the child is seen as yet another unpleasant burden.

Sometimes in such cases the parent can best start with time management and organization skills that will free up some time and energy for doing everything else. Simple suggestions concerning the use of an appointment book with space for a daily to-do list, the assigning of priorities to tasks to be done, deciding not to do certain time-consuming activities, delegating certain tasks to others, setting

up a filing system, and other tried and true organization skills sometimes greatly facilitate further progress.


## WHEN PARENTS HAVE SEVERE SKILL DEFICITS
## OR LACK MOTIVATION

The techniques in this chapter may seem to presuppose an unusual
degree of skill and motivation among parents. In fact, I have found
that parents whose initial performance in sessions with children was
rated very low could, through concentrated teaching, learn to hold
very positive sessions.

If the parent has fairly ingrained maladaptive interaction patterns, the modifications are fairly obvious: (1) The therapist should
move slowly, or stop moving, along the hierarchy of easy techniques
(such as story reading) to more difficult techniques (such as
spontaneous dramatic play); and (2) the therapist should do a good
deal of role playing or fantasy rehearsal with the child absent before
suggesting direct interaction between parent and child, so that the
child does not have to suffer from the parent's initial mistakes.

A different problem is the parent who is fairly interpersonally
competent, but who has great performance anxiety about engaging in
role playing with the therapist or having the therapist watch parent–
child interactions. Here the use of the tape recorder to monitor
sessions may be helpful, in that the performance-anxious parent can
decide only after the recording has been made whether he or she
wants to allow the therapist to hear it. An alternative is to make
extensive use of modeling for the parent, and then to monitor the
sessions by means of the parent's self-report; much can be lost in
translation, but the result is often better than no sessions at all.

A third problem occurs when the parents' time and energy are so
restricted that they cannot put effort into doing any of these things. I
have found it useful at times to collaborate with the parents in hiring
an interpersonally skilled and dependable high school student or
college student to work with the child frequently. The therapist may
supervise this person, using the same teaching techniques as would be
used with parents. This is another way of greatly multiplying the
therapeutic effect, at a fraction of the expense entailed in having the
therapist deliver many hours of direct contact with the child.

A fourth situation occurs when the parent is so filled with hate
for the child or so otherwise incapable of parenting that the therapist

concludes it will be best for the parent to have minimal contact with the child. In some circumstances the therapist should pursue any feasible situational changes, such as adoptive placement, without being rigidly locked into the idea that all people can be taught anything.


## THE EMPIRICAL LITERATURE ON TEACHING LAY PEOPLE TO WORK WITH CHILDREN

How realistic is the thrust of this chapter? Can we really expect lay people to learn to do "therapeutic" work with children? Let us look at what the empirical literature tells us about this question.

Durlak (1979) reviewed 42 studies comparing the effectiveness of professional and "paraprofessional" therapists or helpers. The review concluded that on the whole (subject to methodological limitations of many of the studies), paraprofessionals have achieved clinical outcomes equal to or significantly better than those obtained by professionals.

Bronfenbrenner (1974) reviewed a number of effective and ineffective programs for early intervention with disadvantaged children. The data from this review led the author to conclude that "the family seems to be the most effective and economical system for fostering and sustaining the child's development. Without family involvement, intervention is likely to be unsuccessful, and what few effects are achieved are likely to disappear once the intervention is discontinued" (p. 300). Bronfenbrenner suggested that the reason parent involvement is so important is that when parents are involved, they can continue the favorable influences upon their children when the program has officially terminated.

Interventions without great parent involvement have also been quite effective, however—namely, high-quality preschool programs for low-income children (Berrueta-Clement, Schweinhart, Barnett, Epstein, & Weikart, 1984). A year-long, high-quality preschool program delivers many hours of positive influence to such children; perhaps the general principle is that if parents are not involved, the program has the greatest chance of effectiveness if the children are exposed to a large dose of high-quality influence by other adults.

In addition, Bronfenbrenner (1974) stated that all the effective parent strategies he examined focused attention on interactions between parent and child centered around a common activity, as contrasted with approaches that simply disseminated information to parents. An example of such parent–child interaction was that fostered in a project by Levenstein (1970). This project employed people called "toy demonstrators" who visited the homes of disadvantaged children aged 23 to 40 months. The task of the toy demonstrator was to enhance the mother–child relationship by fostering communication between the two in regard to common activity. The toy demonstrator was to "treat the mother as a colleague in a joint endeavor in behalf of the child" (p. 429). The mother was encouraged to "play and read with the child between home sessions" (p. 429). After 7 months of this intervention, the experimental group of children demonstrated a mean gain of 17 points on the Cattell or the Stanford–Binet intelligence test, whereas the control groups made gains of only a point or two. (Other examples of specific common activities for parent and child, of course, are the story reading and dramatic play described in this book.)

Within the camp of behavior therapists, the field of parent training has enjoyed some documented success, beginning with a study by Wahler, Winkel, Peterson, and Morrison (1965) on mothers as behavior therapists for their own children. This study used a single-case design to demonstrate that mothers could control relevant behaviors in their children, ranging from dependent behaviors to commanding and uncooperative behavior, by altering contingencies of reward and punishment.

The most difficult question regarding behavioral training procedures is how to maintain treatment effects after the training ceases. To date, some data have accumulated suggesting that parent training produces persistent effects. Patterson and Fleischman (1979) reported a follow-up study on parent training for families of aggressive or stealing children between the ages of 3 and 12. There was a quite significant drop in deviant behavior from baseline to posttreatment; this effect was sustained at 6-month and 12-month follow-ups. At the 12-month follow-up, 84% of the children had a score in the normal range, whereas only 42% had scored in that range at pretest. There was no control group for this study. In an earlier study by Alexander and Parsons (1973), juvenile offenders referred for treatment by the juvenile court were assigned to either a group receiving behaviorally oriented family treatment or one of several comparison groups. Follow-up after 6 to 18 months showed that the behaviorally trained group had one-third to one-half the recidivism rates of the comparison groups. Methodological problems, however, vitiate the impact of this study.

Strain *et al.* (1982) reported a follow-up of 40 children who as 3-, 4-, and 5-year-olds had exhibited severe and prolonged tantrums, continual opposition to adults' requests and commands, and physical aggression toward parents. Each child and mother had participated in a standardized intervention package, the main ingredient of which was teaching the parent to attend to positive behaviors and ignore negative behaviors. The treated children, when studied 3 to 9 years after graduation from the program, were found by direct observational measures to have generally positive relations with parents and a habit of compliance with adult requests. The parents' behavior was consistent with that taught in the program. The children did not differ, either by direct observational measures or by scores on a problem checklist, from randomly selected classmate controls.

Parents are not the only possible lay people who may engage in therapeutic sessions with children; another major area of research has been the use of other children as tutors for their peers. Peer tutoring is not a recent invention. Joseph Lancaster, in the early 19th century, founded a school for working-class children in London. Lancaster set up a "monitorial system" consisting of a hierarchy of children who, under the guidance of a single teacher, managed the learning of hundreds of students. The apparent success of this program has been attributed to behavior management principles and hierarchically arranged skill-building curricula that have been formally described only within the last two decades (Gerber & Kauffman, 1981).

Peers have been used as trainers in areas other than academic tutoring. Strain, Shores, and Timm (1977) trained two 4-year-old peers to engage handicapped children in social play. The target children ranged in IQ from 30 to 58. The peers learned to initiate play by saying things like "Come and play," or "Let's play ball." The peers were taught to initiate play physically as well as verbally (e.g., by rolling a ball to a target child). When the intervention was begun with the target children, their responses to social initiations immediately increased; their own positive initiations of social play also increased. In some ways, peer-mediated interventions proved superior to adult-mediated tactics.

What parameters are important in obtaining success in peer tutoring programs? According to a review by Gerber and Kauffman (1981), the nature of the children being tutored and of the children doing the tutoring has varied exceedingly widely in published accounts of successful programs. Two factors appear to be crucial to success, according to these authors: mutual reward between the tutor and the tutored; and a clear hierarchical and sequential arrangement of the material to be taught, so that the tutor can easily follow it. Regarding this second factor, the responses to be expected from the one being tutored were, in successful programs, consistently simple and unambiguous. This type of structure aided the tutors in discriminating the responses that were to signal them to deliver reinforcement or correction.

College students, high school students, housewives, and other lay helpers have also demonstrated success in improving children's psychological skills. Cowen, in a 1973 review, mentions many studies in which college or high school students or housewives were used as helpers in mental health services; although most such programs have not been rigorously evaluated, many have the ring of success.

In a program carried out by Jason, Clarfield, and Cowen (1973), college students worked three times a week for 5 months with young children (average age 20.8 months). These children were from a disadvantaged neighborhood, and were selected because of slow cognitive or social development. At the beginning of the intervention, it was "striking" how little the adults in the children's homes interacted verbally with the children. The student helpers, during their meetings with children, "continually modeled language use, read to the children, and encouraged them to label toys and objects and to use words . . . to communicate requests" (p. 53). During home sessions, which occurred after each session with the child, "parents were encouraged to interact with their children, and techniques that had proved effective in group sessions were modeled for them" (p. 53). The results were positive: "At the end of the program the children, initially 20% slowed down, were functioning within an average intellectual range and their behavior . . . was judged to be significantly more cooperative, content . . . and less distractible" (p. 58). On the Banham Intelligence Test, the children improved by nearly one standard deviation. The study lacked a control group; still, the results are impressive, and the methods combine much that theoretically should be helpful.

A program pioneered by Cowen and his colleagues has paired maladapting school children with housewives trained as "child aides." The aide engages in "educational, recreational, and conversational" activities with the child. During 7 consecutive years of outcome research on this program, this team (Weissberg, Cowen, Lotyczewski, & Gesten, 1983) found that the program children were rated by school mental health professionals as improving in adjustment from preintervention to immediate postintervention. When the intervention was implemented by school districts, in offshoots from the established program model, similar positive results were reported (Cowen *et al.*, 1983). Cowen, Dorr, Trost, and Izzo (1972) conducted follow-up interviews with parents of the children who participated in one wave of this program; these interviews indicated that the short-term gains of the program were maintained over 2 to 5 years. These program evaluations have lacked control groups. In them, as well as in the Jason *et al.* (1973) study, children were initially selected for low adjustment scores; thus the positive effects could have come partially from regression to the mean. Nevertheless, the services appear to have been delivered by lay people in a way satisfying to consumers, and with some objective evidence of improvement in problems not known for their tendency to remit spontaneously. These facts definitely spur further efforts.

To summarize this section, there is mounting evidence to support the notion that maladapting children can be encouraged to flourish without the benefit of direct exposure to someone with a degree in a mental health discipline. In a cost-effective world, the change agents who teach psychological skills should most often be lay people, trained if necessary by mental health professionals. Whenever parents can be trained to be those change agents, they should be selected.

# CHAPTER 9

# Difficulties in Producing Positive Results: The Two Dilution Effects

## OVERVIEW

In reviews of the literature on improving mental health outcomes in children, the reluctance of reviewers to acknowledge positive effects and workable treatments is striking. Does the theory of the skills × methods matrix predict that it is straightforward and easy to produce positive outcomes, and do the obvious difficulties in remediating many problems tend to invalidate the theory? On the contrary, the matrix points our attention to two reasons for difficulty—two "dilution effects." The first dilution effect may be called "too many skills." The prevention or cure of a given syndrome in a given group of people may require promoting proficiency in not just one skill on the axis, but many. Potential benefits produced by enhancing one skill may be diluted by the lack of progress in others. The second dilution effect may be called "too many influences." None of our nine methods of influence is confined to a therapist's office; agents of persuasion and goal setting, modeling, instruction, and the other methods of influence abound in the child's environment. If the influences delivered by other agents are powerfully negative, even the most positive influences delivered by the therapist may be simply overwhelmed and overpowered.

These dilution effects imply remedies that are logical, but usually expensive. One strategy for combating the first dilution effect relies on careful diagnosis of high-priority skills, so that time can be spent on those few skills that will help the most (rather than, for instance, teaching the same skill to all children with a given syndrome); I call this the "prescriptive approach." This approach, however, fails to solve the problem for individuals with globally deficient skills. The second strategy is to invest the time and energy necessary to promote a broad range of skills; I call this the "multiskills approach." Remedies for the second dilution effect that can be used within traditional therapy include assigning homework, intensifying the therapeutic relationship, choosing high-impact activities, and providing anticipatory rehearsal of resisting negative influences. However, a more complete solution to these dilution effects propels us from the consulting room into the community, in the attempt to provide influences in enough skills and in a large enough dose to have a large effect. The ultimate solution occurs when positive influences become "enculturated"—so absorbed into the self-sustaining culture of the community, so deprofessionalized, and so routinized that they are available without the family's needing to search for them.

---

The preceding three chapters have presented many ways of following the general prescription of competence-oriented promotion of mental health. With such a wealth to choose from, does not our theory dictate that it should be a rather simple matter to remedy almost any symptom that results from maladaptive learning, by using the nine influence methods to promote more adaptive learning in the areas of highest priority? And if it is not easy to do so, does that not undermine the theory? This chapter examines the reasons why, on the contrary, the theory of the skills × methods matrix would predict great difficulties under certain circumstances in producing positive results. Having identified these difficulties, we can move on to the remedies that the theory generates.

## IS IT DIFFICULT TO PRODUCE POSITIVE MENTAL HEALTH OUTCOMES?

In review articles dealing with the treatment of clinical syndromes, the unwillingness of reviewers to claim effectiveness of treatment is overwhelming. Let us survey some reviewers' conclusions about the treatment of various syndromes.

Let us begin with the most serious problems, those involving the possibility of danger to others or to oneself—that is, problems of aggressive conduct and of suicidal impulses. With respect to conduct disorders, Herbert (1982) states, "Not only is the prognosis for the 'natural history' of the more severe conduct disorders a grave one (Robins, 1966; West & Farrington, 1973), but they tend to be resistant to traditional therapeutic interventions whether carried out in residential ([R.V.G.] Clarke & Cornish, 1978) or in clinic settings (Wolff, 1977)" (p. 95). Herbert continues, "A realistic assessment of the overall results of behavioral work with juvenile delinquents must concede their somewhat disappointing nature" (p. 126).

With respect to suicidal behavior, Hawton and Osborn (1984) find it difficult to be definite, let alone optimistic:

> There is a remarkable absence of research into the effectiveness of different forms of after-care following suicide attempts by young people. . . . In terms of prevention of both attempted suicide and completed suicide by children and adolescents, we appear to be only at the stage of conjecturing about possible strategies rather than being able to offer firm guidelines based on research findings. (p. 103)

Let us turn to another area where physical safety is at stake: child abuse. Mrazek and Mrazek (1985) note,

> It is impossible to study the "natural history" of child abuse because of ethical and legal imperatives for intervention. However, despite identification, monitoring, and treatment the reoccurrence of abuse is alarmingly frequent. Cohn (1979) found that abuse reoccurred in one-third of families under treatment. When the initial abuse had been "serious," one-half of the parents abused their child again within one year. (p. 687)

What about an exceedingly common problem with adolescents, that of drug or alcohol abuse? Strang and Connell (1985) make a summary statement that "Methods of treatment and rehabilitation have been much discussed, but data regarding the relationship of a particular treatment regime to outcome are lacking" (p. 510). Baar and O'Connor (1985) make a stronger statement:

> The current treatment of alcoholism has been a massive failure. While the industry boasts of transparently inflated success rates, thousands of alcoholics, who spend millions of dollars per year for treatment, are getting drunk again at an alarming rate. Despite their lack of proven effectiveness, current approaches remain unchanged and for the most part unchallenged (Emrick & Hansen, 1983; Vaillant et al., 1983). (p. 570)

After these discouraging conclusions, surely reviewers have something more encouraging to say with respect to those bread-and-butter problems of anxiety and depression. Or do they? Gittelman (1985) says of desensitization as a treatment for anxiety in children, "The only controlled study of desensitization failed to establish its superiority over psychoanalytic therapy and no-treatment control" (p. 69). She concludes, even more sweepingly, that "At this time, there is no aspect of children's anxiety disorders that is relatively well re-searched and understood" (p. 75). With respect to depression in children, Cantwell (1982) states, "Psychosocial intervention directed toward improving social skills and parent–child interaction would seem to be mandatory in the treatment of depressed children. Unfortunately, evidence for the efficacy of various types of psychosocial interventions with depressed children is lacking" (p. 84).

Even the effects of social skills training on peer acceptance are sometimes impossible to demonstrate. Tiffen and Spence (1986) present a state-of-the-art report of an intervention that trained isolated or rejected children in a set of social skills; no beneficial effects were found with either group when each was compared to corresponding randomly assigned no-treatment controls. The authors conclude with a call for a "search for an effective means of training social skills with rejected children" (p. 353).

Lest these quotations cast us prematurely into the camp of biological intervention only, let us also take a look at some conclusions on drug treatment. With respect to attention deficit disorder, Taylor (1985) declares, "Stimulant drugs are a powerful treatment for the component of restless and inattentive behaviour, but are neither sufficient to improve the long-term course of development, nor necessary to help associated conduct disorder. Hyperactive and inattentive children often have multiple problems and need a combination of treatments guided by individual assessment" (p. 437). With respect to drug treatment of depression in children, the most rigorous study to date (Puig-Antich et al., 1987) found a dose–response relationship between blood levels of an antidepressant and clinical response to it; however, although the drug group had a 56% response rate, the placebo group showed a 68% response rate.

With respect to public health and preventive measures, we may ask whether the knowledge that has accumulated over the last few decades has allowed us to decrease the incidence or prevalence of clinical syndromes. Let us consider those syndromes that by definition involve a certain degree of danger. With respect to suicide, "There has been a striking increase in the United States in the suicide rate among 15- to 19-year-olds (especially in males) over the last decade" (Shaffer, 1985, p. 709). Hawton and Osborn (1984, p. 60) summarize data to the effect that from the early 1950s to the late 1970s, the suicide rate among 15- to 19-year-olds has increased by 250–300%. With respect to suicide attempts, Kreitman and Schreiber (1979) reported a 250% increase in the rate of suicide attempts among 15- to 19-year-old girls in Edinburgh, Scotland, between 1968–1969 and 1974–1975. With respect to juvenile delinquency, the statistics are equally alarming. Between 1960 and 1979, there was a 233% increase in arrests for violent crimes among youths 10–17 years of age in the United States (Empey, 1982); a similar "dramatic increase" occurred in Canada and the United Kingdom (Shamsie, 1981). Self-report data with two birth cohorts confirm this increase (Wolfgang, 1983). Death from homicide among U.S. whites aged 15–19 increased by 231.8% during the years between 1960 and 1980 (Uhlenberg & Eggebeen, 1986). The proportion of white 12- to 17-year-olds in the United States who use alcohol increased by 56.2% between 1972 and 1979 (Uhlenberg & Eggebeen, 1986).

## THE QUESTION FOR THIS CHAPTER
## AND THE NATURE OF THE ANSWER

Why are things so difficult? Why can't we simply do skills axis diagnoses, use the nine methods of influence to promote the high-priority skills, and produce marked improvement in these syndromes? Does the fact that improvement seems so difficult to document invalidate the general theory? This chapter argues that, on the contrary, the matrix helps us understand why achieving and demonstrating treatment effects are often so difficult, and why they are particularly difficult with certain sorts of problems. The implications of these arguments propel us out of the consulting room and into the community.

In examining these difficulties, we consider two "dilution effects." A half-teaspoon of food coloring has a dramatic effect upon a glass of water, but no noticeable effect upon an Olympic-sized swimming pool. Yet it often disappoints us in the mental health professions when a few hours of therapy or a several-hour course in problem-solving skills fails to have a large effect on global measures of adjustment, such as the presence or absence of the problems mentioned above. When seeking to increase psychological competence, it is crucial to be aware of two ways in which skill promotion may be diluted—two vessels into which our work should ideally pour more than one drop.

These two dilution effects are easy to remember, because they spring directly from the notion of the skills axis and the methods-of-influence axis. We may think of them, respectively, as "too many skills," and "too many influences." The first, "too many skills," refers to the situation where a program promotes one or a few skills, but there are many other skills necessary for effective functioning without symptoms. Therefore, if a population has many other skill deficiencies, remedying a few of them may not be sufficient to bring about successful working and loving. The second dilution effect is "too many influences." That is, even though a program may provide a very positive influence in the direction of increasing one or several skills, there are myriad other sources of influence afloat in the environment—some favorable, some unfavorable—that may preclude any visible effect of the influence the mental health professional delivers.

## EXAMPLES AND IMPLICATIONS OF THE FIRST DILUTION EFFECT (TOO MANY SKILLS)

Let us perform a "thought experiment." Suppose one finds that children predisposed to delinquency are less sensitive to the feelings of others, as was mentioned by Rutter (1977). Suppose also that at least a portion of such insensitivity may be operationalized as a deficiency in the skill of becoming aware of what others are feeling. Assume that this skill deficiency is causally related to disordered conduct, and not just a correlate. Suppose then we institute a training program to promote the skill of being aware of what others are feeling, and suppose further that the program is absolutely and thoroughly successful in producing very high levels of this skill in all children who participate. Does the achievement of this goal—quite a worthy one—mean that the training program has a large effect (or even, with decent sample sizes, a statistically significant effect) on the symptoms of conduct disorder?

Even with our very liberal assumptions, such an effect will not necessarily take place, because the target group may still have enough other skill deficiencies (also causally related to conduct symptoms) that the benefit in one skill is diluted by the lack of benefit in the other skills. The previously cited review of conduct disorders by Herbert (1982) mentions a wide variety of skill deficiencies that have been linked by various researchers to conduct disorder symptoms: self-control and delay of gratification (p. 122); dealing with criticism and taunting (p. 123); social skills, meaning social initiations and social conversation (p. 114); sustaining attention and concentrating (pp. 98, 105); reading well (p. 114); feeling appropriate guilt (p. 106); being altruistic (p. 106); and discriminating between internal and external control of events (p. 126). Other researchers (e.g., Yu et al., 1986; see also review by Pellegrini, 1985) have linked skills of generating options and predicting consequences (i.e., problem-solving skills) to improved adjustment with respect to conduct. Bernfeld and Peters (1986) studied a group of impulsive children and found them on the average adequate in the cognitive component of social problem solving, but low in motivation to perform well on academic tasks. Now if, as is eminently consistent with clinical experience, any conduct-disordered child is likely to have several if not all of these skill deficiencies and more, and if the number of skill deficiencies present in a group of conduct-disordered children is even more varied, then we should quickly lose any naive optimism that any training program affecting only one skill will have a large effect size.

This line of reasoning is so important that I will ask the reader to go through it one more time with a different example. Suppose we notice that conduct disorders are more prevalent in families with disharmony between the parents (Herbert, 1982, p. 109). Suppose we argue that the reason why conduct disorders are difficult to cure is that people have focused too much on the child and not enough on the family, and that we will achieve much better results by reducing parental marital disharmony. Suppose, then, we hypothesize that marital disharmony is caused in part by skill deficiencies in negotiation of interpersonal problems, and we arrange a program so powerful that all our participants are able at the end of it to communicate in a rational, straightforward way about nearly any conflict that we can name. Does this imply that marital disharmony has been conquered?

Unfortunately, this will not be the case unless we hypothesize that there is a one-to-one relationship between this one skill of negotiating and marital harmony. With our matrix at hand, let us examine some of the other skills on the axis, and ask whether they too may be related to the outcome of marital harmony. We notice the skill of having romantic or erotic feelings attached to desirable stimulus situations, and consider whether our training program can cure the marital disharmony that results when one partner is sexually aroused only by sadism. Or we notice the skill of trusting and depending, and consider whether negotiation skills alone can set right a marriage in which one or both partners are terrified of closeness and dependency. We notice the skills of delay of gratification, and consider whether our negotiation skills program can set right a marriage in which one of the partners cannot work, cannot refrain from spending, and engages in extramarital affairs whenever given the opportunity. We notice the skill of frustration tolerance, and imagine the state of the marriage when one or both partners are incapacitated by the smallest everyday stresses.

Again, we should quickly lose our naive optimism about our negotiation training therapy, despite the fact that it has been hypothesized to be 100% successful in imparting the skill. We predict that it may be extremely helpful in that subset of couples whose marriages are suffering from the single skill deficiency of negotiation. We predict that it will not be helpful at all for couples who are already quite accomplished in negotiation but whose marriages are impaired by some other skill deficiencies. And for that vast majority of couples whose marriages are impaired by a combination of many skill deficiencies, including negotiation, we predict that our program will have a positive effect, but not an overwhelmingly large one. We have reached the same point in our reasoning about marital disharmony that we have reached earlier with regard to conduct disorder. The same analysis can be applied to suicidal behavior and to alcohol or drug abuse: Almost any skill deficiency can conceivably contribute to such behavior in certain individuals.

Thus, with respect to many of the major categories of mental health problems, we are dealing with multifactorial determination; as a result, we may predict that training program affecting one and only one skill will seldom have large effects on groups selected for global adjustment problems. In other words, outcome studies that take a certain population selected for a certain symptom and treat them with a program oriented toward a single skill will usually not find huge benefits.

## REMEDIES FOR THE FIRST DILUTION EFFECT

How can the dilution effect of "too many skills" be overcome? There are two theoretical remedies, which I refer to as the "prescriptive approach" and the "multiskill approach." The prescriptive approach is to use skills axis diagnosis to tailor a program that will address the highest-priority skills for the individuals or the group in question. The multiskill approach is to design a program that will provide favorable influences toward the acquisition of many or most of the skills on the axis, either in sequence or simultaneously.

Relatively few explicit examples of either of these approaches exist in the literature, and with good reason: Such projects are more difficult to carry out than are projects delivering one standardized treatment focusing on one skill. To have some 62 separate standardized training programs, one for each skill, would present a massive logistical problem. In either the prescriptive approach or the multiskill approach, one needs to be prepared to teach all, or nearly all, the skills on the axis. Are we speaking of the impossible?

If such approaches are to be possible without a huge expenditure of resources, we must rely on what in Chapter 6 I have called "versatile vehicles"—procedures that are suitable for any of the skills on the axis, and that can be shifted from one skill to another by making alterations in content, while maintaining the identical process. Two examples of versatile vehicles are modeling stories and modeling plays, in which the content of the stories and plays may model any skill on the axis. Another example is a skills-oriented contingency system, in which recognition or approval can be directed toward positive examples of any of the skills on the axis.

When is the prescriptive approach best, and when is the multiskill approach best? The answer follows fairly simply from our definitions. We should use the prescriptive approach when our skills axis diagnosis reveals only a few skill deficiencies; we should use the multiskill approach when there are deficiencies in many skills, or when we want to prevent deficiencies in many skills. Furthermore, when time and personnel are very limited, as in a hospital stay or in short-term psychotherapy, we should tend toward the prescriptive approach; when time is not in short supply, we are freer to use the multiskill approach.

When we look at mental health intervention in these terms, two questions have the same likely answer. First, how is it that some programs that focus on a single specific skill produce general gains in adjustment? And, second, why is it that comparisons of different types of therapy so often seem to find no difference? The answer to both questions, I believe, is that the drive to produce interventions that work often leads their designers to make them prescriptive or multiskill, or both. It is natural that an experienced, effective psychotherapist, regardless of theoretical orientation, will determine the high-priority skills and seek to foster them. And training programs that effectively promote one skill may often have unplanned effects on others. Can we teach problem-solving skills without also giving the child practice in skills of using language fluently? Can a therapist promote the skills of recognizing one's own feelings without giving practice in the skill of depending upon another person? Can a therapist get a group of children to practice conflict resolution conversations without also giving them practice in overcoming the social anxiety that interferes with the skill of social initiations? And can a preventive mental health worker teach children any skill without giving them practice in compliance and cooperation? The fact that skill-promoting experiences come in packages that are hard to separate into pure components is good for the positive effect of the therapy; it means, however, that our view of what is going on has to be more complicated than it has often been in the past.

Before leaving this section, I should mention that in one sense, the multideterminate nature of syndromes simplifies things. There is a consolation implicit in the dilution effect of "too many skills." The bad news is that for any given syndrome (e.g., conduct problems, marital disharmony, or suicidal behavior), we must promote many skills rather than only a few, and our measurement and intervention tasks become much larger than initially imagined. The consolation, however, is that when we have done the job fully for one syndrome, we may have done a good portion of the job for the second and third syndromes. For example, if we find ways to promote *all* the skills necessary for marital harmony, we may have already done nearly all the work necessary to prevent conduct disorders and suicide. In other words, for any one given syndrome, we may have to do more work than we initially dreamed; the work may have more generality to other syndromes than we initially dreamed, either.

If this corollary of the theory is true, then it makes sense not to focus our research too specifically upon a given outcome. Perhaps, for example, it is more sensible to deliver a multiskill intervention and look for its effects upon school success, conduct problems, social support, suicidal behavior, and a variety of other outcomes than it is to have a project funded solely for the purpose of preventing one outcome.

## EXAMPLES AND IMPLICATIONS OF THE SECOND DILUTION EFFECT (TOO MANY INFLUENCES)

The second dilution effect is even more basically threatening than the first: The finite amount of influence that the mental health professional delivers even for one given skill may or may not prevail, depending upon the number and potency of opposing influences elsewhere in the environment.

Thinking about this dilution effect forces us to come to a humbling realization. When we review the list of methods of influence, and we consider promotion of goal setting, forming a hierarchy, modeling, practice, reinforcement, and the others, we are forced to admit that *not one* of these influences is unique to the therapist's office. All can be applied in huge doses in the rest of the person's life, and often the influences are in the opposite direction from that of skill promotion.

Let us consider a not-so-encouraging example: A family leaves a therapist's office, where the child has gotten some positive models of prosocial behavior and the parents have received some wise instruction about ways to promote prosocial behavior in the child. As soon as they get home, one parent receives a telephone call from a friend or relative who provides his or her own set of instructions and reflections on the therapist's instructions. The child goes into the neighborhood and meets the powerful set of models and reinforcers delivered by his peers (e.g., being challenged to fights, being greatly respected for winning fights, or being taunted for walking away from fights). Later, the child turns on the television and gets a set of models produced with infinitely greater slickness than the models the therapist has delivered. Throughout the day, the child continues to practice the interaction patterns that he has been practicing daily for months or years. A grandparent arrives the following evening, and various family dynamics result in one parent's getting drunk and the parents' fighting with each other. The whole scene provides negative models and a stimulus situation evoking antisocial behavior from the child. Moreover, all these influences are not simply occurring on this one occasion; they have been occurring repeatedly for years, and habit strength has been building up in various individuals over countless repetitions of maladaptive patterns of thought, feeling, and behavior.

Sometimes these outside influences are much more potent than anything the therapist can ethically deliver. Children have told me of their initial membership in gangs: They were physically threatened into joining the gang, given group acceptance for joining, and introduced in turn to a hierarchical sequence of theft activities, each of which was modeled by older group members and reinforced by group approval. Later these children continued the cycle by coercing others to join.

A good deal of empirical research with delinquents, summarized by R.V.G. Clarke (1985), emphasizes the very important effect of the youths' present environment. As Clarke puts it, "greater improvements in performance and behavior are likely to attend efforts to change environments rather than inner dispositions" (p. 505). I would prefer to word this differently, and rather to say that the methods of influence listed in Chapter 5 exist in the home, the school, the peer culture, and the rest of the community in addition to the therapist's office; mental health specialists should accordingly make more favorable whatever influences they have access to.

The discussion thus far of influences that may dilute those of therapy has not even taken into account biological problems, which are not dealt with in this book. These obviously can dilute the therapist's influence to an even greater extent.

The second dilution effect would predict that brief interventions will probably have brief effects. A. M. Clarke and Clarke (1986) conclude a review of intervention research with children by saying, "To summarize this theme, it seems that intervention to be really effective needs to be intense and prolonged" (p. 750).

Paul (1967), in a widely quoted statement, has said that the design of effective interventions requires us to consider the question of *"what* treatment, by *whom,* is most effective for *this* individual with *that* specific problem, and under *which* set of circumstances (p. 111, italics in original). The examples given above suggest that this question, as global as it is, may even yield in importance to another question: "When we know the right types of influences for the particular problem at hand, how can those influences be delivered in the sheer quantity and power needed to overcome the opposing influences of the past and present?"


## REMEDIES FOR THE SECOND DILUTION EFFECT

What remedies are there for the dilution effect of "too many influences"? First, let us look at the possibilities that can be carried out in the therapist's office. One eminently reasonable one is the assignment of homework. The clients are asked to practice, expose themselves to models, and reinforce each other and themselves for successful examples of skills between sessions. However, it is important to realize that homework is seldom sufficient to overcome the second dilution effect. If, for example, the client's time management skills, delay-of-gratification skills, and economic circumstances are preventing him from completing assignments from work or school, where the consequences of nonperformance may be grave, what is the likelihood that the client will complete the homework assignments for the therapist, whose "course" may be "dropped" without drastic effects and even with some relief (e.g., from the burden of having to travel to sessions and pay the therapist's bills)?

A second possible remedy to the dilution effect of extratherapeutic influences is to attempt to make up for the limited number of hours of interpersonal influence by the quality, the intensity, of the therapeutic relationship. Often the client can project upon the relationship with the therapist a larger-than-life quality, such that the influence the therapist delivers comes to be mentally rehearsed over and over during the time between sessions. The fantasy of the upcoming session, particularly report to the therapist of how situations have been handled, can come to be a background image for almost every situation the client encounters. These events are perhaps intensified when the therapist is a very confident, charismatic individual. When such an intense relationship develops, the quantity of influence delivered per session can indeed be large. Yet this situation, even in the fraction of cases where it occurs, is not without its attendant dangers. The therapist who occupies this larger-than-life role may present an image that ordinary people (e.g., spouses) cannot compete with, and the images of the others may suffer by comparison. In addition, the therapist whom the client imagines to be larger than life can after some minor demonstration of imperfection come crashing down from the pedestal—not just to the ground, but further below, so that the larger-than-life image is now devil rather than angel. Finally, the practice of submission to a revered therapist figure is one that, although perhaps useful in the short run as a means to certain ends, is hardly desirable indefinitely if the individual is to acquire adequate skills of independent decision making and of resisting the influence of confident but wrong individuals. In short, positive transference, like homework, is sometimes helpful, but is not a general answer to the problem of the second dilution effect.

Another means of attacking the second dilution effect within the therapist's office is to spend whatever limited time is available upon high-impact rather than low-impact activities. For example, once the therapist and client know clearly what patterns need to be carried out more often, and once goals have been clearly set, less time may be spent in free association or review of events that have taken place, and more time spent in active rehearsal of the desirable patterns through fantasy practice or role playing.

A final approach to overcoming the second dilution effect within the setting of traditional therapy is one we may label "training to anticipate and resist other influences." For example, the therapist may have conversations with the adolescent who is trying to avoid alcohol abuse, in which the two of them systematically identify the people who will pressure the adolescent to drink, how they will exert their pressure, and how the adolescent would like to resist that pressure. Then they may repetitively practice such resistance of unwanted influence.

Such techniques should certainly provide some help toward overcoming the effect of extratherapeutic influences. But they may not be enough, and solutions for many people may ultimately best be provided outside the traditional consulting room. A more global approach to the problem is to transport skill-enhancing influences from the therapist's office to family and community locations, and to have nonprofessional or paraprofessionals rather than professionals deliver them. In this way the intervention becomes less expensive and can be maintained over a much longer time than is possible with psychotherapy.

A related remedy for the second dilution effect involves delivering the positive influence to more people as well as for a longer time. The program can seek to influence an entire social unit simultaneously, such as a family, a classroom, or a neighborhood unit, so that the influences delivered to one person will be enhanced rather than diluted by the rest of the social unit. For example, if a program aimed at preventing conduct problems is aimed toward every single child in a certain urban housing project, we may predict that the effect of exposure to peers' behavior will be much more favorable for the children. Whereas a small-scale intervention in that housing project may show no effect, the same intervention delivered to the entire social unit may perhaps show large effects.

In order to carry out the dissemination across individuals and over time, the program can adopt technological means of reproducing itself at a low cost per person. Therapists can make use of mass reproduction methods such as videotape, television, audiotape, and radio, or even such "low-tech" methods as the printing press or the lecture hall.

The ultimate means of overcoming the second dilution effect is for the favorable influences to become "enculturated," or absorbed into the self-sustaining influences of the community. We may think of "culture" as those influences that are so deprofessionalized, so widely available in the community, that extraordinary efforts are not needed to find them.

The remedies to both dilution effects have sent us out of the therapist's office and into the community. We explore this arena further in the next chapter.

# CHAPTER 10

# Application of the Matrix to Preventive Mental Health

## OVERVIEW

The considerations of Chapter 9 propel us from the therapist's consulting room into the community, with the goal of carrying out primary prevention. Although it is obviously possible to botch an attempt at primary prevention, it should be possible to avoid the possibilities of doing harm and wasting money. Primary prevention with large groups of children does not necessarily preclude harnessing the power of one-on-one interventions, if the "multiplier effect" comes in the ratio of paraprofessionals (who work directly with children) to their trainers, rather than the ratio of children to those who work with them. The competence orientation espoused in this book is one of the mainstays of the field of prevention; some illustrative projects are presented.

The skills × methods matrix provides the basic cells of positive influence for children. If we also consider the various possibilities for the target group, the organization providing the context for intervention, the direct agents of intervention, the ratio of those agents to the child, the media in which instructions and models can be packaged, and the way in which the dilution effect of "too many skills" is addressed, the possibilities for preventive programs become extremely numerous.

Many of the techniques mentioned in Chapters 4, 6, 7, and 8 may be transferred from the therapist's office to the community. The parent training curricula of Chapters 4 and 8, and the techniques for harnessing imagination described in Chapters 6 and 7, can be delivered in any of a variety of community organizations and settings, and (to the extent that the marketplace demands it) through the mass media.

When we think of models and instructions stored in print, video, or other "hard-copy" media as a repository of information available for learning, and when we use analogies from computing, a new model becomes available for us to think about behavior and the way in which cultures enhance or interfere with competent behavior. The thoughts, feelings, and behaviors that people enact represent selections and recombinations from patterns stored in the memory banks of their brains; these patterns are stored because they have been "downloaded" from patterns observed in other people, viewed from stored media, or otherwise communicated (e.g., by a nonrandom pattern of reinforcers for random behavior). As a corollary, several tasks become imperative for the competence-enhancing culture. These are the organizing of stored data bases of adaptive patterns in each of the skills areas, for various age groups, subcultures, and ability levels; the continual updating of these data bases as more and better information becomes available; and the enculturation of methods for downloading the adaptive patterns from these data bases into the memory banks of individuals in the society. The widespread and routinized availability of positive influences—or, in other words, the competence-enhancing culture—is ultimately the major answer to the dilution effects spoken of in Chapter 9.

## RATIONALES FOR INTERVENTIONS IN COMMUNITY SETTINGS

We have been propelled, by the logical considerations of Chapter 9, from the therapist's office to the community—from reliance on professional treatment of learning-based problems to reliance on nonprofessional or paraprofessional influencers. At least two reasons are frequently advanced for this movement. First, the sheer numbers of psychological problems would stagger any system that attempted to deal with them at the cost entailed by using only professional therapists to attack them. Second, there is some evidence, not without its share of controversy, that "an ounce of prevention is worth a pound of cure"—that dealing with problems early, before problem patterns have intensified themselves through vicious circles and have spun off other problems, is a more effective strategy (Strayhorn & Strain, 1986).

The logical considerations of the preceding chapter are much less often used to justify a community-based preventive approach. But they are quite important in this context, and I restate them here. First, community-based prevention is needed to overcome the dilution effect of "too many skills." When individuals need help in attaining growth in many skills, not just a few, community-based prevention allows the time necessary for the multiskill approach, since people spend far larger amounts of time in their homes, at school, and sometimes at religious organizations or in other community organizations than they can usually spend in a therapist's office. Second, community-based efforts are needed to overcome the dilution effect of "too many influences." When positive influences are delivered successfully to an entire social unit, the mutual influence of people upon each other serves to sustain and reinforce the positive influence, rather than to dilute it.


## POSSIBLE HAZARDS OF GENERALIZING METHODS FROM THERAPY TO PREVENTION

1. *Curative methods may be dangerous.* The concept of prevention in mental health is not without its critics. One cogent criticism often rendered is that it is dangerous to transfer methods blindly from therapy to prevention (Rutter, 1982). Just as an anticancer drug may be life-saving for the cancer patient but toxic for the person without cancer, so, it is argued, we should leave well enough alone the members of society who have not been identified as having mental health problems.

2. *The cost of some primary preventive techniques may be prohibitive.* Even if an ounce of prevention is worth a pound of cure, for some techniques an ounce of prevention may cost more than 16 times as much. Some argue that limited resources allocatable to mental health should be spent on those who unquestionably need services.

3. *One-on-one or small-group interventions may not be effective with larger groups.* It may be argued that many of the techniques and principles set forward in this book require the helper to know the persons being helped very well. How can such an arrangement be compatible with the large numbers of people to be served in any primary prevention program?


## RESPONSES TO POSSIBLE OBJECTIONS

The following considerations convince me that the objections just mentioned should not stand in the way of primary prevention.


### The Problem of Danger

How much potential for harm is there in an extension of the methods described in this book? Short of a large-scale empirical study, one way of approaching this question is to ask how frequently such methods have been used in the normal, healthy population. When I have spoken about reading and eliciting positive modeling stories, chatting in a positive way, using dramatic play, giving attention and approval for positive examples, and so forth, I have frequently heard responses such as the following, sometimes voiced in critical tones: "There is nothing new about this—this is what millions of good parents have been doing throughout the centuries"; "Literature throughout the centuries has tried to do this"; or "Religious organizations have been doing these things before psychology even existed." Many of the methods advocated in this book represent simply more systematized and organized approaches to influence methods that have evolved naturally. If true, this notion would differentiate the methods advocated from the example of an anticancer drug mentioned previously. A more apt analogy is that of a change in dietary habits. All people consume some type of diet, and prevention may be carried out if many people shift to the types of diets already partaken of by the healthiest people. Similarly, all people each day consume some "diet" of influences toward patterns of competence or incompetence in psychological skills; if the influence diets of many come to resemble the diets of the most emotionally healthy people more closely, prevention may be accomplished. This analogy preserves the notion that some people may require special diets because of idiosyncratic needs.

A caution regarding the possible harm of extending therapeutic methods to prevention is a corollary of our notion of hierarchy, discussed in Chapter 5. Mental health specialists working with individuals who are at a low point on the hierarchy of a given psychological health skill may celebrate certain behaviors because they represent a movement up the hierarchy; those same behaviors for many of the general population may represent a movement down the hierarchy, and if held up as models of appropriate behavior may be more harmful than helpful. For example, mental health specialists dealing with people who are consumed with anger but unable even to verbalize what they are angry about may reinforce rather obnoxious tantrums, because they represent a stepping stone toward the final goal of being able to understand and deal with interpersonal conflict in a mature way. For the general population, one would hope that such tantrums would not represent a step up the hierarchy. The conclusion is that the preventive mental health specialist should probably err on the side of presenting models of mature psychological functioning too difficult to obtain, rather than that of holding up for emulation examples that are low on the hierarchy.

The Problem of Cost

In some ways, the response to the issue of cost is like the response to the issue of danger: namely, "Something is being done anyway; in many cases it would cost no more to do it more systematically, if people knew how to or wanted to do so." For example, children are being exposed to fictional models of behavior in large quantities; an exposure to models that represent the best current widsom has to offer may not cost any more.

On the other hand, certain interventions, such as those involving much one-on-one time between an adult and a preschool child, are by nature not cheap. The counterbalancing factor is that the costs of psychological skill deficiencies in the population are enormous. An investment in prevention can represent a favorable investment economically as well as morally if it can reduce by even a little bit the incidence of such outcomes as psychiatric hospitalization, imprisonment, chronic unemployability, homicide, or other criminal behavior. Berrueta-Clement *et al.* (1984) have carried out a cost–benefit analysis of the effects of a preschool experience delivered to low-income children, after following up these children some 14 years after preschool; the results demonstrate that the intervention was a good investment for the taxpayer, in that it reduced the need for tax-supported services later on.

One-on-One or Small-Group Methods
versus Large-Group Methods

Some of the methods of change or influence are more obviously applicable for large groups than are others. Modeling and instruction are two of the mechanisms that are very readily delivered either in an individual setting or with larger groups. Attribution would on first glance appear to be a method that would be difficult to apply in group settings, but in fact the attribution of positive qualities to groups is a very frequently used method of influence (e.g., "Marines are tough," "A Scout is trustworthy, loyal, helpful . . ."). Similarly, reinforcement would seem to be an individually oriented method, until we take into account the notion of communicating consequences as well as actually delivering them to an individual. For example, giving awards and recognition to school students for "citizenship" or achievement has an effect on those who observe the awarding as well as those receiving the award. When large groups of people heap adulation on public figures such as movie stars, the vicarious reinforcement for imitation is obviously enhanced. (Would that as much vicarious reinforcement were given for good decision making or acts of kindness as is given, via television, for skills of shooting, fist-fighting, or reckless driving.) The arranging of environmental stimuli that tend to elicit psychologically competent behavior lends itself to macrosolutions as well as microsolutions: Changes in school-wide environment, for example, may have potent effects (Comer, 1980; Newmark, 1976).

It is important to note that preventive intervention with large numbers of children does not necessarily imply that the children must receive the intervention in a group. It is possible, for example, for a trainer to train a substantial number of paraprofessionals in a group, and to let the paraprofessionals work with children individually. The "multiplier effect" allowing delivery to large numbers of children thus occurs in the ratio of paraprofessionals to trainers, rather than in the ratio of children to paraprofessionals. The Primary Mental Health Project model begun at the University of Rochester is an example of a program delivered to large groups of children, but relying primarily upon individual meetings; data suggest that this program is effective and socially useful (Cowen *et al.*, 1972; Weissberg *et al.*, 1983).

## COMPETENCE-ORIENTED PREVENTION PROGRAMS IN THE LITERATURE

The purpose of this chapter is not to provide a review of research in prevention of mental health problems; such a review is available elsewhere (e.g., Roberts & Peterson, 1984). Rather, I wish to extend the usefulness of the skills × methods matrix as an idea generator, a theory dictating possible methods tried and untried. First, however, let us briefly examine certain already tested programs that obviously fall within the rubric of the matrix.

The competence orientation has been an overt mainstay in many preventive mental health programs. Cowen (1984), for example, classifies preventive mental health programs into two clusters: competence-enhancing programs and risk-reducing, problem-averting programs. Even the second cluster of programs, which consists primarily of interventions aimed at reducing the noxious effects of a particular stressful situation, can often be seen as enhancing the competences needed to deal with the situation.

As Cowen (1984) observes, the program developed at Hahnemann Medical College to teach "interpersonal cognitive problem-solving" skills has been important not only with respect to the skills of decision making and conflict resolution dealt with in the program, but as a model for other research on the teaching of psychological competences. Spivack, Shure, and their colleagues (Spivack et al., 1976; Spivack & Shure, 1974) have followed the general strategy of (1) hypothesizing that general adjustment is related to a given skill; (2) teaching the skill to an experimental group of children; (3) demonstrating that the program has increased the specific skill that it is meant to increase; (4) demonstrating that in addition, the program has increased the general psychological adjustment of the treated group over that of controls; and (5) demonstrating a relationship between the increase in the competence and the increase in adjustment.

Other investigators have used similar strategies with other skills. Research similar in strategy but smaller in volume has been carried out with respect to the teaching of skills in self-reinforcement and goal setting (Stamps, 1975, cited in Cowen, 1984), assertiveness (Rotheram, Armstrong, & Booraem, 1982), forming relationships (Vogelsong, Most, & Yanchko, 1979), and sharing (Jason, Robson, & Lipshutz, 1980). Feshbach and Feshbach (1982) taught third- and fourth-grade students skills of seeing things from another person's point of view; this intervention increased positive behavior and self-esteem for both aggressive and nonaggressive children, and decreased levels of aggressiveness.

Sarason and Sarason (1981) describe an interesting and successful application of the strategies advocated in this book, in their work with a group of students from a high school with high dropout and delinquency rates. There was first an effort toward identification of the high-priority skills for the group of students as a whole; interviews were carried out with teachers, former students, counselors, and employers to determine the most important skill deficiencies in the group. These interviews identified such skills as frustration tolerance, thinking before acting, decision making, asking for help on the job and at school, resisting peer pressure, engaging in social conversation with adult authority figures, and job interview skills. Thus the initial information gathering yielded, in the terminology of this book, a skills axis diagnosis for the group rather than for any one individual, and a prescriptive approach based on those group conclusions. Live or videotaped models demonstrated appropriate exercise of these skills in the situations relevant to this group; cognitions as well as behavior were modeled. Discussion of these situations took place in group settings. After this discussion, volunteers from the class took turns role-playing the adaptive behaviors that had been modeled; the students were instructed to carry out the role plays in the same manner that the models had done. The group leaders "liberally reinforced the students' participation in role playing and pointed out deficiencies in students' enactments in as supportive and noncritical manner as possible" (Sarason & Sarason, 1981, p. 911). The students were also given written homework assignments that posed hypothetical situations and asked the students questions to give them practice in analyzing and thinking about these situations. This intervention produced a number of positive outcomes, including such "hard" measures as amount of tardiness and number of referrals for misbehavior.

At least two studies have used the prescriptive approach with individuals rather than groups, reaching a diagnosis using the abbreviated skills axis rather than the full version. As discussed in Chapter 2, factor-analytic studies of most child checklists have come to group problems into four or fewer main factors—namely, acting out, shyness–withdrawal, attention deficits, and learning problems. The AML scale (Carberry & Handal, 1980; Cowen et al., 1973) contains the following factors: Acting Out, Moody–Withdrawn, and Learning Problems. The factors on this scale have been used to formulate prescriptive approaches to individuals in at least two preventive studies (Durlak, 1977; Rickel & Lampi, 1981; Rickel & Smith, 1979; Rickel, Smith, & Sharp, 1979).

Durlak (1977) reports an intervention that did a rough skills axis diagnosis on individual second-grade children and promoted skills accordingly. In this "secondary prevention" project, children were chosen because they scored in the lowest decile on teacher behavior ratings. Paraprofessional aides (mostly college students) carried out the intervention with the children in groups. Using the results of teacher ratings, conversations with teachers and other school personnel, and their own observations during the program's baseline,

> [aides selected] a target behavior for each child that was directly opposite to one of his typical school problem behaviors. Some children were shy and withdrawn, did not usually participate in group activities or discussions, and appeared timid, anxious, or afraid in social interactions. The target behaviors selected for these children were "talking to others" or "working with others." Several children presented moderate to severe management problems by frequent inappropriate talking out, constant

moving about, fighting, and an inability to work cooperatively with peers. These verbally or physically disruptive children were reinforced for "waiting your turn" or "working on your own." Children with learning difficulties were not only academically behind in one or more subject areas, but they also displayed poor work habits. These children, who could not consistently follow directions or finish projects, or who had very short attention spans, were reinforced for such behaviors as "working on a task" or "following directions." (Durlak, 1977, p. 29)

The investigator used the abbreviated skills axis formed by the major factors of the AML scale to define the general clusters of skills to be increased. The aides in the project then reinforced the specific examples of the desirable skills with tokens and praise; positive results, as measured by teacher ratings, occurred in comparison to a (nonrandomly assigned) control group and persisted for 7 months after invervention. The procedure described in this study is almost identical to that advocated in Chapter 4 of this book.

Another secondary preventive intervention with preschool children, described by Rickel and colleagues (Rickel *et al.,* 1979; Rickel & Lampi, 1981; Rickel & Smith, 1979), also used a rough skills axis diagnosis and prescriptive treatment based on such conclusions. University undergraduate students served as child aides; they worked individually with preschool children for at least two 15-minute sessions per week for 8 months. Children's problems were noted, using behavior checklists and direct reports of teachers' observations. "Behaviorally specific prescription strategies were devised for each individual child in the experimental remediation program" (Rickel *et al.,* 1979, p. 106).

> The aide for a shy, withdrawn child would receive a strategy such as "Read a story while holding the child on your lap—using physical communication to convey warmth and acceptance. After reading the story, ask the child to point to various objects in the book and ask, 'Can you tell me about this?' Reward and reinforce all attempts at friendliness and assertiveness." (Rickel *et al.,* 1979, p. 106)

For aggressive children, the aides were directed to encourage verbal expression of feelings by the child and "redirection of aggression into more acceptable outlets" (Rickel *et al.,* 1979, p. 106). (Regarding this last prescription, see my discussion of catharsis and displacement in Chapter 1.) This study included a randomly assigned "placebo" group; the intervention group did better according to teacher rating scales at posttest and at a 2-year follow-up.

## THE RANGE OF POSSIBLE PREVENTION PROGRAMS

Let us reiterate the implications of the methods axis as applied to prevention, in the form of a "to-do list" for the field. Then, to enlarge this already huge list of possible programs, let us examine the range of possible programs formed by the various combinations of target age groups, types of community organizations, types of direct deliverers of the influences to children, vehicles and media for the delivery of positive influences, common stresses to which target populations may be responding (if any), and ways of overcoming the first dilution effect.

### The General Prescription

The general prescription is as follows:

1. Provide persuasive evidence to developing persons and their caretakers and educators of the value of learning the skills on the axis.
2. Construct for each of those skills some notion of a hierarchy of steps in learning the skills.
3. Provide positive examples of each of the skills on the axis, through fictional or real-life enactments.
4. Furnish instructions, explanations, and concept definitions that enable people to recognize and carry out the skillful patterns more readily.
5. Provide environmental situations that tend to elicit those skillful examples most readily.
6. Provide opportunities for practice of the skillful patterns.
7. Monitor progress toward more skillful patterns.
8. Provide or communicate reinforcing and punishing consequence contingencies that promote skill development.
9. Provide attributions about the character of the person or the group in the most growth-enhancing way consistent with honesty.

This general prescription is readily recognized, of course, as the product of the skills axis and the nine change methods discussed in Chapter 5.

Multiplying the Possibilities

Let us now multiply the possibilities for preventive programs by considering the combinations of various other parameters of the intervention. The target persons may be any of the following:

- Infants or toddlers
- Preschoolers
- Elementary-school-age children
- Preadolescents (middle-school-age)
- Adolescents (high-school-age)
- College students
- Adults
- Children via their parents

We also have a choice as to what sort of organization will provide the context for the intervention:

- The individual
- The nuclear family
- Day care centers and preschools
- Schools
- Religious organizations
- Self-help groups
- Mental health centers
- Medical facilities

We have many possibilities as to who will directly deliver the influences to the children:

- Parents
- Teachers
- Religious teachers
- High school students
- College students
- Older students in the same school
- Same-age peers
- Retired people
- Other lay adults
- Characters on television or in other media

There are various possibilities as to how positive influences will be delivered:

- One-to-one interaction
- Very small groups (e.g., two or three children)
- Small groups (e.g., six or eight children)
- Classrooms
- Large lecture halls
- Mass media (printed matter, videotapes, television, computer software)

There are many media in which instructions and models for children can be packaged:

- Written modeling stories or instructions
- Plays put on by older persons or children, with puppets or toy people
- Recounted real-life examples that people have noticed and remembered (examples carried out by oneself, or by other people)
- Recounted examples from fiction that people have noticed and remembered
- Real-life examples directly carried out in the interaction between preceptors and children
- Plays performed by amateur or professional actors
- Animated plays
- Selections from existing movies and videotapes, shown directly to children

We have a choice as to whether the target population will or will not be selected for a certain common stress its members are currently experiencing, and whether the curriculum of the program will relate directly to handling such a stress. A few of the stresses on which groups may focus include the following:

- Divorce
- Retirement
- Transition to high school
- An illness
- Bereavement
- Pregnancy

Finally, we have a choice about the way in which we seek to overcome the first dilution effect, that of "too many skills":

- A prescriptive approach for the individual
- A prescriptive approach for the group (i.e., working with a group that is homogeneous in that they all need high-priority work on a few skills)
- A prescriptive approach using the abbreviated axis rather than the full axis
- The multiskill approach, in which the skills axis is a long-term curriculum

What is the purpose of going through all these lists? First, the various parameters provide a structure within which to view preventive programs that have so far been tested. Second, when one starts to construct various new combinations of these parameters and to imagine possible programs that could be set up and tried, the possibilities become not simply tedious combinations, but exciting possibilities. The following section mentions several strategies that are direct corollaries of the skills × methods matrix—strategies with which I have enough experience to believe worthy of systematic trial. As in previous chapters, I reduce the number of possibilities by focusing on those that emphasize the use of fantasy and imagination as tools.

## WORK IN PROGRESS, AND WORK
## THAT SHOULD BE IN PROGRESS

The following techniques are described here:

1. Parent training in a variety of settings
2. Modeling stories and plays, delivered by parents to preschoolers
3. Teacher-mediated interventions using modeling stories and plays in preschools and schools
4. Peer-mediated interventions using modeling stories and plays in schools
5. Modeling and instruction presented through the readings children are assigned in school

6. Fantasy practice through story writing in the schools
7. Public recognition of skillful patterns in schools
8. Use of previously listed methods in religious organizations
9. Use of previously listed methods in families
10. Organization and promotion of positive models in the electronic and print media

## Parent Training in a Variety of Settings

The methods of training parents mentioned in Chapters 4 and 8 can obviously be extended to group settings, as well as to transmission in the print media and by the mass media. Much information is currently being dispensed to parents in these ways; Twardosz and Nordquist (1987) review some of the literature on such training.

## Modeling Stories and Plays, Delivered by Parents to Preschoolers

Chapter 6 has outlined strategies of using chatting, modeling stories and plays, and spontaneous dramatic play with young children, and Chapter 8 has outlined ways of teaching parents or other lay people to use such methods effectively with children. Such methods may be transferred almost without alteration from therapy to prevention. As in therapy, the preventive mental health specialist should take into account the relative difficulty of the methods (e.g., story reading and modeling plays are much easier than spontaneous dramatic play).

## Teacher-Mediated Interventions Using Modeling Stories and Plays in Preschools and Schools

The presentation of modeling stories and modeling plays can be carried out by teachers, teachers' aides, or classroom volunteers, with groups of students, as well as by parents or paraprofessionals on a one-on-one basis. The most basic technique is that of simply reading the stories or performing the modeling plays for the group of children. One step higher on the scale of skill requirements for the teacher is reading or performing the modeling story or play, and then asking the children to recall and retell what happened. Still higher on the hierarchy is to read a story or perform a play, and then to allow pairs of children to act out the same story or play before the rest of the group; equally high is holding a discussion on what else the character could have done and what the outcomes of other options might have been.

My own experience has been that when children are asked to act out spontaneously created plots in front of groups of other children, the group reinforcement tends to elicit slapstick violence. However, I have observed that in classrooms children can divide into groups of two and practice spontaneous role playing of situations requiring psychological skill.

Another story technique applicable to groups of grade-school-age children is that of conceptual sharpening through providing practice in identifying the cognitive and interpersonal strategies used by a story's characters. The teacher reads the story to the group and stops after a character has used a given strategy, in order to allow a student to identify it.

A manual and a set of stories providing practice in such conceptual sharpening are available from me; see Appendix 5 for an example of such a story.

## Peer-Mediated Interventions Using Modeling Stories and Plays in Schools

I have seen children who could not cooperate or learn in group settings become amazingly cooperative in one-on-one settings; I suspect that many children who do learn in groups could learn much more efficiently in one-on-one situations. Older children represent a vast resource that could be used to provide such individual attention to younger children; the literature on tutoring (Allen, 1976) suggests that this resource should be used much more than it is currently used. Such techniques as reading modeling stories or performing modeling plays can readily be carried out by older children (e.g., sixth-graders with kindergarten or first-grade children). Chatting with the younger child, tracking and describing the younger child's play, eliciting stories from the younger child, and engaging in spontaneous dramatic play are also techniques that many older children or adolescents can be trained to carry out well.

One of the major obstacles to such one-on-one instruction in schools, interestingly, is architectural: It is very difficult to find places in school buildings where two individuals can interact with each other without being distracted by other people.

## Modeling and Instruction in Assigned Readings

Stories and expository essays in textbooks can be selected with attention to modeling the wide range of psychological skills, at levels of difficulty appropriate for the children's reading level. In this way, positive models and instruction can be presented without taking additional time away from any other activity, within the context of the teaching of reading.

Such an idea seems to have been heartily practiced in the past, perhaps before it became fashionable to believe that children hate moralistic writings. For example, the McGuffey's Readers, first published about the middle of the 19th century, contain unabashedly moralistic stories and didactic essays proclaiming the values of kindness, hard work, abstinence from alcohol, honesty, and resistance to unwanted peer influence. By adding to the delay-of-gratification skills those of relaxation, humor, celebration, and so forth for the entire skills axis, a wider range of psychological skills would be modeled, and the entire set would perhaps meet with less opposition.

## Fantasy Practice through Story Writing in the Schools

There is hardly an activity more basic to education than assigning students practice in writing original compositions. In order to harness the power of fantasy practice in the service of psychological skill development, it is logical that after students have been exposed to stories modeling some or all the psychological skills on the axis, or to expository instructions about a certain skill, students should be assigned to write similar stories or essays themselves. The power of vicarious reinforcement could be harnessed by selecting prize-winning writings and publishing them with recognition to the authors. Such an activity would also add to the total body of positive modeling stories available to be read by others.

## Public Recognition of Skillful Patterns in Schools

Public recognition is quite a potent reinforcer for students of almost all ages. There is, in my experience, wide variation among educational institutions in the extent to which psychologically competent patterns in individuals are given public recognition. Those schools that give certificates in public award ceremonies for the students most strongly embodying certain ideals of character have at their disposal a potent means of delivering positive influences. Recognition conferred upon students by adults (i.e., a vote of the faculty) often brings such students more recognition from their peers, in the form of election to class offices or offices of clubs.

Public recognition of students harnesses the power of imagination if the specific behaviors that are rewarded are narrated to other students by the award givers. In such a way, the reinforcement contingency enacted with one child becomes communicated to the rest of them.

It would be quite interesting to test empirically the effects of systematic public recognition of students in school, and to test what methods seem to influence the other students most effectively.

## Use of Previously Listed Methods in Religious Organizations

Religious organizations are in many ways made to order for preventive mental health. They provide ready responses to the dilution effects described in Chapter 9 by at least potentially focusing on many skills over a long period of time, and constituting a social unit whose members can reinforce each other's positive patterns. One of the main functions of religious organizations throughout history has been the socialization of people—the prevention of what we today call "conduct disorders" or "antisocial personality disorders," but what through more ages has been called "sin" or "evil." The surprising thing is that the preventive mental health function of religious organizations has been so little studied.

Many of the activities of traditional religion can be interpreted within the context of the skills × methods matrix. Teaching the skill of feeling good about one's acts of kindness has for centuries been an important part of religion. Symbolic modeling has been used by these organizations since earliest history; the story of the Good Samaritan is a particularly obvious example of a "modeling story." Giving prayers of thanksgiving provides practice in cognitions associated with the skill of celebrating favorable events. Feeling the approval of a loving God is one way of celebrating one's own acts of kindness or accomplishment. Feeling the disapproval of God is one way in which the skill of feeling appropriate guilt can be exercised. Feeling the constant presence of a protecting deity is one way in which toleration of separation from people can be approached.

The teaching of a particular system of morality, or the provision of specific examples of psychological skills in religious organizations as opposed to public schools, does have the advantage that parents have the opportunity to choose whatever organization most closely conforms to their own preferences and values.

## Use of Previously Listed Methods in Families

Certain customs observed by some families constitute applications of the same techniques mentioned earlier. Reading aloud within the family group stories modeling a psychological competence or expository writing providing instruction in it; regular discussion of what patterns really are best; regular communication and celebration of the positive examples various family members have carried out; even a time for creation of fantasies of the positive patterns one wishes to carry out more often—such practices can be, and have been, incorporated into the suppertime or bedtime rituals of some families. Such rituals serve to continually sharpen the psychological competences of the family members, and represent a major promise for overcoming the two dilution effects. For families to get into such habits is of course much more easily said than done, but the conscious cultivation of such activities might be a major tool in preventive mental health.

## Organization and Promotion of Positive Models in the Mass Media

The effect of television models has been a thoroughly studied phenomenon (Eron, 1980; Liebert et al., 1982; Pearl et al., 1982). The harnessing of the immense power of television for the purpose of positive influence is indeed a seductive idea. The potential of television for the presentation of instructions, models, and vicarious reinforcement for positive examples of skill patterns has not begun to be adequately harnessed. With violence as perhaps the most pressing public health problem resulting from psychological skill deficiencies, movies presented on television during the fall 1985–summer 1986 viewing season set a record for violence, with an average of 31 violent acts per viewing hour. Ten network television shows, including five Saturday morning cartoons, contained over 40 acts of violence per viewing hour (National Coalition on Television Violence News, 1986).

A tremendous number of children's books also provide positive models in dealing with wide varieties of situations. There are, of course, negative models in the print media as well as in the electronic media.

In advocating the art of the possible with respect to the mass media, one eminently useful project would not require any change in the market pressures that seem to cause so much violent and anti-social material to be produced; rather, it would make the most im-itation-worthy material more organized and accessible. This project would be to search through the vast amount of printed and videotaped material; to find vignettes presenting positive, imitation-worthy models; and to categorize these vignettes according to which psychological skill is being demonstrated. A retrieval system that would allow the books or videotapes to be obtained quickly and inexpensively would constitute the second part of the system. If a parent, a teacher, a therapist, or anyone else who searches for positive models of a given skill could locate them readily in the existing literature, both prescriptive approaches and multiskill approaches to skill promotion would be greatly facilitated.

This task is complicated by several factors, not the least of which is the fact that models of negative patterns must be present in litera-ture, if for no other reason than to provide challenges for imitation-worthy protagonists to respond to. In other words, villains are some-times necessary in a work if a protagonist is to demonstrate skills of forgiveness, toleration of frustration at the hands of other people, or being fearless in frightening situations. The price of having villains is that certain children may imitate them and not the imitation-worthy protagonists. This means that modeling literature must take into account the viewer's or reader's position on the hierarchy of being able to identify selectively with the imitation-worthy deeds. For chil-dren at the low end of the hierarchy, such as preschool children, I have found it prudent to minimize the presence of villains and to challenge protagonists with well-meaning mistakes of others, acts of nature, and other situations not involving evil characters. But at some stage the existence of antisocial actions has to be confronted and dealt with; this fact may partially explain the fact that violence pervades much of great literature as well as poor-quality literature.

## DATA BASES AND DOWNLOADING OF
## COMPETENT PATTERNS IN THE INFORMATION AGE

Modeling of patterns of thought, feeling, and behavior; communication of reinforcement contingencies; and instruction on psychological strategies all represent information transfer. The information is encodable into words and pictures, and it may be stored, transferred, and revised. As we proceed through the present "information age," we may find it useful to rely less on concepts such as drives or stimulus–response associations and think more in terms of data bases and transfers of information to and from those data bases. Computer jargon dictates that information may be "uploaded" into a large data base, and "downloaded" from that data base to another repository.

To extend this notion, the human brain is the most important medium where competent or incompetent patterns are present or absent. Through whatever encoding mechanism accounts for memory, the patterns of thought, feeling, and behavior that make for competent or incompetent responses are laid down in the brain's storage. Patterns can be "downloaded" from the storage mechanism of one person's brain to that of another's, with information transfer accomplished by behavior and observation. The parents who are violent with each other and with their child are causing the information patterns stored in their brains to be downloaded into the child's brain, with their behavior as the mediating link.

The brain may be thought of as carrying out its own process of information transfer whenever the organism thinks, feels, or behaves. There is some sort of searching through the stored information on possibilities for thought, feeling, and behavior, and there is a retrieval, often with recombination, of some of those patterns for enactment in the present situation.

The brain, with its immense storage capacities, benefits from supplementation by other storage media. When throughout history people have written down information or represented it in drawings, or when in more recent times they have stored it on audiotapes, videotapes, computer disks, and so forth, they have created auxiliary storage media to supplement what the brain can do. Psychological patterns may be transmitted, not only from person to person, but from a person to one of these storage media and thence to another person. The psychological patterns portrayed in the story of the Good Samaritan or in one of Aesop's fables can be downloaded into the brain storage areas and thence into the behavior of persons who live centuries after those patterns existed in the brains of their authors.

Once we become used to thinking in these terms, certain implications for prevention, and for the competence-enhancing culture, become apparent.

## Creating, Updating, and Downloading from Data Bases in the Competence-Enhancing Culture

If psychologically skillful patterns may be uploaded to data bases, maintained in permanent storage media, and downloaded to the human brain and thence to thought, feeling, and behavior, certain tasks are obviously of paramount importance if the society is to promote psychological competence with maximum efficiency. These include the following:

1. In the competence-promoting society, there should be organized data bases of psychologically competent patterns, stored in media that permit easy retrieval. I have spoken above of the task of organizing printed, videotaped, and otherwise recorded material according to the various skills on the skills axis. The gathering and classification of already existing material, plus the creation of much additional material specifically to provide positive models, should constitute the creation of such a data base; as time goes by, many positive patterns will need to be uploaded to the data base.

The skills axis is meant as an organizing principle for such a data base. However, organization and storage should take into account the age of the intended recipients; their particular circumstances; their degree of verbal facility; whether reading, viewing, or listening is most applicable to them; whether their consciences are sufficiently developed that they can be presented models of how to respond to antisocial acts without the likelihood of identifying with such acts; and so forth.

2. These data bases, for maximum usefulness, should be continually updated to include new situations not faced by previous generations, while retaining the accumulated wisdom of the past. The data bases will also need to be updated as empirical research casts light on just what patterns do produce the best outcomes in given circumstances.

3. The competence-enhancing society should not only upload information into these data bases, but should provide enculturated

mechanisms whereby the information can be downloaded from the data base into the brains of individuals. Story reading and modeling play activities in the preschools, story reading in grade schools, the reading of instructional material within families, and so forth, as discussed earlier in this chapter, constitute examples of such downloading mechanisms.

How well does our present society perform each of these functions? We have not really begun to carry out any of the three tasks just listed in an organized manner. It would be difficult to select quickly from a large body of literature even a set of positive models, much less positive models of a particular psychological skill. The downloading of models from the disorganized data base to the memories of people is in many cases determined by the pressure of the marketplace and a great deal of randomness; it does not follow any plan that is meant to enhance the psychological competence of the society.

But in the information age, our capacity to handle the enormous bodies of information necessary to carry out such tasks in a purposeful and organized way has greatly increased, even in the last couple of decades. The widespread availability of personal computers and of personal videotape recorders and players permits the systematization and dispersal of information in ways that were never before possible. The gap between where society is in these tasks and where it is technologically capable of being represents an opportunity for psychological skill promotion and preventive mental health that is quite exciting.

Whether it is organized or scattered throughout society, I would argue that the data base of positive, psychologically competent patterns of thought, feeling, and behavior that resides both in human brains and in storage media represents the most important resource of a society. It is what makes the difference between civilized and barbaric culture; it is what could make the difference between civilized culture as we now know it and something far better.

## "Enculturation" of the Process of Downloading, and the Place of the Preventive Mental Health Specialist

There will always be a need for a certain specialized sort of individual in society, one who examines the tough questions involved in competence promotion: what competences people need, what patterns really work the best, how they may best be encoded and transmitted, what methods of influence work best in what circumstances, and so forth. Recently developed technologies make the information storage, retrieval, and dispersal necessary for the best answers to these questions much more feasible. There will be a need for people at the cutting edge of advances in our information on these questions, and for persons who train the trainers—in other words, preventive mental health specialists.

In an imagined competence-enhancing society, as in present society, most preventive influences would be delivered not by specialists, but through the transmission of competent patterns by means that have been routinized, become enculturated, and moved outside the exclusive province of the specialist. Children would be given competent and incompetent patterns by their families, their schools, their religious organizations, their peer culture, the electronic and print media, and the other influences that pervade the culture. If these influences are adverse, they create the dilution effect of "too many influences" and thereby plague clinical therapists. The converse is that if positive influences can become enculturated, there would then be a salutary "dilution effect"—one in which discrete harmful experiences become diluted and their effects mitigated. The delivery of primary prevention would thus become independent of programs and projects, independent of the whims determining the availability of specialized funds, and, instead, become an integral part of the institutions of the culture.

At first glance, attaining the competence-enhancing culture may seem to be a problem similar to that of the fabled mice who wished to "bell the cat," in that implementation of the solution to the problem requires that the problem already be solved. For families, schools, religious organizations, mass media, and the rest of culture all to be organized in competence-enhancing ways, the society must have already achieved the goals that primary prevention is designed for. It is to avoid this circularity that systematic downloading from data bases of competent patterns becomes necessary, so that the culture of each generation's children may be more enhancing of competence than that of the previous one. Imperfect cultures may improve themselves by systematically selecting, collecting, and dispersing the information most capable of enhancing competence. A movement in this direction is the supreme challenge of the information age.

# CHAPTER 11

# Research Questions

## OVERVIEW

The ideas expressed in this book suggest a large number of empirical studies. Techniques of measuring all the skills on the axis are needed, as are ways of training people to rate multiple skills after observing a large enough sample of behaviors, thoughts, and feelings. Even more basic than research on these techniques is research aimed at discovering which patterns of thought, feeling, and behavior actually are more desirable, by specified criteria, than others. The measurement of environmental exposure to the nine methods of influence with regard to any given skill is also highly desirable, although difficult to achieve. Measurement of the mutually gratifying quality of adult–child interactions and of the extent to which adults do certain things thought to foster the mutually gratifying nature of those interactions poses another challenge to instrument developers.

With reliable and valid instruments, a number of interesting associations can be explored. How do skills relate to one another? How do different skills relate to global measures of mental health, and to symptom clusters? How do skill levels change with age? Do different skills have different curves with respect to malleability as a function of time?

In addition to these correlational studies, numerous experimental studies are suggested. Each of the "versatile vehicles" and other therapeutic methods described in this book can be tested for its effect on skills as well as on more face-valid desirable outcomes; these methods may be tested with community samples as well as with clinical samples. Outcome studies will also indicate whether the predictions implied by the two dilution effects hold up—for example, the predictions that prescriptive or multiskills interventions will work better than those that teach one skill to a sample as defined by a given syndrome, or that interventions with entire social units will work better than those with isolated individuals within social units.

The concept of data bases of thought, feeling, and behavior patterns suggests various ways of examining the data bases to which children actually are exposed; characterizing their contents; and assembling and using in outcome studies data bases selected so as to exemplify the most desirable patterns of skills.

The methodological difficulties in the fields of psychotherapy and prevention should not prevent investigators from carrying out the most useful applied study: combining elements to form a package that is the most useful and effective one the investigators can devise, and testing that package to see how much good it can do for children.

---

One of the tests of any theory or model is that it should generate empirically testable questions. The number of researchable questions generated by the overall theses of this book is in fact too large for any one investigator or any one research team to tackle in a lifetime. Let us examine some of the possible studies generated by the skills × methods matrix.

First, let us summarize the major building blocks of this book's argument. It is possible to list a set of psychological skills whose deficiencies account for a large proportion of learning-based psychological symptoms. It is possible, for each of the areas listed on the axis, to validate certain patterns of thought, feeling, and behavior as more skillful than others, and for such conclusions to be generalizable at least to the culture or subculture being studied. For each of these skills, it is possible to develop measures of how much the person displays the more competent patterns versus the less competent patterns over a given period of time. Various of these skills are important, in various degrees, to acquire at various ages. Skill deficiencies are related to psychological symptoms and syndromes in a complex and fairly nonspecific way: That is, it is possible to predict the presence and severity of symptoms from the severity of overall skill deficiencies; however, it is difficult to predict specific symptoms from specific skill deficiencies. Clinicians can through systematic steps decide which skill deficiencies are of highest priority for remediation in any given individual. Learning-based treatment programs are more logically based on skills axis diagnosis than on symptom cluster diagnosis.

Nine general methods of influence, of which there are many subtypes, account in large part for the extent to which these skills are learned in the general population as well as in a clinical population. If some or all of these nine methods are adroitly applied to the highest-priority skills, the skills can be increased, and often improvement of symptoms can be brought about. Skills-based contingency systems, modeling through stories, modeling through dramatic play, fantasy practice through imagination or through role playing, and exercises of responding to hypothetical situations are "versatile vehicles" through which any of the skills on the axis can be promoted, thus obviating the need for a totally new program for each skill. Not only professionals, but also lay people, can be selected and/or taught to use the skill-promoting methods effectively.

Two dilution effects make it difficult at times to demonstrate large treatment effects. The first dilution effect consists of the fact that many skills are required to preclude a given syndrome, and training in one skill may be diluted by deficiencies in the untrained skills. The second dilution effect refers to the fact that the nine influence methods are widely applied (often in very negative ways) outside the therapist's office over long periods of time, and small doses of positive influence are often diluted by such extraneous influences. There are several possible remedies for these dilution effects; one is the exposure over long periods of time to promotion of multiple skills, which is most feasible only when the promotion methods are carried out by lay people in community institutions. The optimum conditions for the advancement of the general public's mental health exist when the favorable influences become "enculturated"—that is, widely available in the prevailing culture. Among the conditions present when favorable influences are "enculturated" are that data bases of positive models for each of the skills on the axis will abound; that they will be continually updated; and that there will be convenient means for "downloading" them into the memory banks of individuals in the culture.

Now let us proceed through these ideas step by step, and imagine useful research that could test them. In doing so, we consider several different types of studies: those developing measurement instruments and methods, which are the forerunners to quantitative research of any sort; those counting the incidence or prevalence of those measurable phenomena within a specified sample; those noting the naturally occurring association between two or more measured variables in a given sample; and those manipulating one or more variables and measuring the effects on one or more other variables.

## THE SKILLS AXIS:
## MEASUREMENT AND ASSESSMENT TECHNIQUES

How can we best quantify a person's characteristic way of responding to situations in which trust is a possibility, or in which the person

could use some help, or in which there is the opportunity for attachment and closeness, or any of the other situations alluded to in the
skills axis? The development of instruments that classify different
ways of responding to such situations and measure the extent to
which a person responds in a certain way is a continuing challenge for
behavioral science. There are a variety of approaches to measuring
what people actually do, think, and feel in certain situations. One may
observe the person in real life and count his or her responses to
situations; this method was used by Putallaz and Gottman (1983). A
somewhat less expensive approach is to give the person a set of
hypothetical situations and ask the person to describe or role-play
what his response would be. One may also interview the person
regarding his responses to real-life situations. One may ask other
observers to make generalizations upon the person's response patterns, or one may give the person an instrument that asks for his own
generalizations.

### Determining Which Patterns Are Most Skillful

As soon as it is possible to measure different responses to situations,
the next task is to make a necessarily reductionistic decision as to
which patterns are more skillful than others. For many of the skills on
the axis, influential therapists differ greatly in their definitions of
skillful and adaptive patterns; such ideas also swing back and forth as
times change. For example, Lazarus and Fay (1975) advised repudiat-
ing the idea that it is better to give than to receive; Dyer (1976)
implied that the concepts of right and wrong, the words "should" and
"ought," and the emotion of guilt are worse than useless. Other
therapists (perhaps those who address themselves to an undersocial-
ized rather than an oversocialized population) would advocate opposite ideas.

For each of the skills on the axis, there is a need for research
aimed at determining what patterns of thought, feeling, and overt
behavior are actually more desirable than others. Such research involves looking at individuals and families of different levels of mental
health (happiness, success, freedom from symptoms, etc.) and determining which patterns of thought, feeling, or behavior are more
associated with desirable outcomes. Thus there is a need for two
measures: One is a measure of how much the person uses a certain
pattern of thought, feeling, or behavior in a certain type of situation,
and the second is a measure of psychologically healthy functioning.

By looking at the associations between what patterns people choose and the so-called "face-valid" indicators of mental health, we can get at least some suggestive evidence on what patterns work better than others.

Such methods were used, for example, by Raush, Barry, Hertel, and Swain (1974), who gave a set of married couples hypothetical conflicts to negotiate in role plays. The couples, on the basis of other information they gave, were classified as having "harmonious" or "discordant" relationships; the types of communications used in the improvisations were studied as a function of the harmony of the relationship. (The findings of this study, incidentally, constitute another set of data that tend not to confirm the "catharsis" hypothesis.)

The use of fictitious vignettes as a method of exploring what patterns of behavior are most desirable has been, in my estimation, greatly underused. The researcher who hypothesizes that certain patterns are more adaptive than others can construct story vignettes of all the patterns in question (enough of them to permit generalization), and can ask subjects of varying levels of success in functioning to rate the vignettes. Such ratings might quantify both how adaptive the subjects think the patterns are, and how likely they would be to use such a pattern. Relatives and observers of such successful and unsuccessful individuals could be asked to rate how typical or atypical each vignette is of the subjects in question.

Perhaps the most stringent test of whether on pattern really does work better than an alternative one is to carry out an experimental manipulation, in which a group of people who habitually carry out pattern $A$ are taught to carry out pattern $B$. Resulting gains in face-valid mental health indicators would provide good evidence that pattern $B$ works better. In order to have full generality, though, such findings should be demonstrated not just in psychologically distressed individuals, but also in reasonably well-functioning ones.

The answers to the question of what patterns work best will not be simple. They may to some extent be specific to age, subculture, and other variables. In fact, the study of what patterns are appropriate at what age is one of the key questions of developmental psychology; the study of how such patterns vary among social groups is one of the key questions of cultural anthropology.

Determining what patterns actually work best is an important task for the mental health disciplines. However well we refine our means of promoting certain thoughts, feelings, and behaviors, we may only be making ourselves more capable of doing harm or wasting energy if the patterns we promote are harmful or not truly useful.

## Determining the Extent to Which People Use Skillful Patterns

Once an empirical data base suggests that certain patterns are more skillful than others, a somewhat less cumbersome set of measures can be developed that asks to what extent a person tends to use more of the skillful patterns.

The Psychological Skills Inventory presented in Chapter 3 (see Table 3-1) asks raters this question, while leaving undefined exactly what the more skillful and less skillful patterns are. It would be interesting to see how much the validity of such a multiple-skills measuring instrument might be improved by having raters study, before rating, some careful descriptions (low on the abstraction ladder) of patterns defined as more skillful.

Another approach to the measurement of skills involves giving the subject tasks very similar to those presented in the "situations" game (see Chapter 7), to which he or she is supposed to devise hypothetical responses. Such responses may correlate highly enough with real-life responses to be meaningful, although work so far has not shown such correlations to be overwhelmingly high (Kendall, 1985).

## Prevalence and Correlates of Skill Profiles

Measures that give a reliable and valid profile of many skills on the axis would enable many basic studies to be carried out. Such studies might answer such questions as these: What are the average levels of various skills in various parts of the population? What is the differential contribution of the skills to global measures of mental health? It would be interesting, for example, if in some populations the ability to organize time and money contributes more to global mental health than ability to express feelings. Similarly, it would be interesting if at a given age the ability to give in is more important than the ability to assert oneself, whereas at another age the reverse holds true. This research might also ask about the relationship among the skills over time: Is it correct to hypothesize that children skilled at depending when measured at time 1 will be more skilled at compliance when measured at time 2, and that those same children will be more skilled at delaying gratification when measured at time 3?

## Relation of Skills to Symptom Clusters

One would certainly predict that a higher general level of skill deficiencies will be correlated with a higher level of symptoms, and this supposition may be tested in a straightforward manner. What would be predicted with respect to the relation between specific skill deficiencies and specific symptom clusters? As noted in Chapter 2, it is commonly observed that a given symptom cluster will be seen in individuals with widely varying skill deficiencies; conversely, individuals with similar patterns of skill deficiencies may exhibit widely varying symptom clusters. Thus the relationship between skills and symptoms is not a specific one.

However, clinical experience would predict that the relationship is not entirely nonspecific, either. It is difficult to imagine a "borderline" patient with high skills in trusting, depending, handling rejection, and tolerating being alone. It is difficult to imagine a conduct-disordered child with high skills of taking pleasure from acts of kindness, feeling appropriate guilt, resisting the influence of peers when appropriate, thinking before acting, decision making, and conflict resolution. Statements like these give rise to testable hypotheses: Are there patterns of skill *sufficiencies* that essentially rule out a certain symptom cluster? Multiskill measurement methods would enable such a question to be approached in a straightforward manner. An approximation to this sort of research strategy is exemplified by a study of Labouvie and McGee (1986, p. 289), who found that a "net surplus" of "two or more safe attributes" in what could be conceived of as a multiskills inventory predicted lack of heavy drug and alcohol use among a group of adolescents. The inventory used in this study measured attributes such as "harmavoidance" (cf. the skill of appropriately fearing dangerous situations) and "impulsivity" (cf. the skill of thinking before acting).

## Developmental Study of the Skills

The skills axis represents an organizing framework for the study of child development. With respect to normal development, what is the average normal child capable of, with respect to any of the skills on the axis, at a given age? What are the periods of "growth spurts" for the various skills, if it is possible to find such periods?

The question of "malleability" of the organism over the life span is probably best approached not globally, but on a skill-by-skill basis. That is, it may be possible that if people have not learned the skill of feeling appropriate guilt by adolescence, it is very difficult for them to acquire it; on the other hand, it could be that skills of standing up for one's own rights are much easier to enhance even in adulthood.

## The Completeness versus Redundancy of the Skills Axis

Should the skills axis, as I have listed it in this book, be revised so as to have more or fewer items? If multiskill measuring devices are available that cover each of the skills on the axis, it would be interesting to do a study with clinicians and clients in which each is asked to consider the target skills most helpful in the particular course of therapy, and to classify them as falling within or without those on the skills axis. The relative frequency with which the skills are judged important by the clinicians and clients could be tabulated. This frequency tabulation would provide useful epidemiological information, as well as reason to modify or confirm the choice of items for the skills axis. This procedure represents a quantitative version of the more informal process by which the skills axis has been put together. However, in such a study it is important not to confuse "is" with "ought": Because clinicians or clients are not focusing upon a given skill with any frequency does not mean that they should not be.

Another important point with respect to validating the skills axis through empirical data is that factor analysis and other techniques relying on correlations do not allow us to collapse two skills into one concept. For example, it could be that in a certain sample the skills of sustaining attention to tasks and of being honest are highly correlated with each other. This would not imply, however, that one could not find individuals very high in one and very low in the other; more importantly, it would not imply that the content of a curriculum meant to increase one would automatically increase the other. Given the complexity of empirically validating the skills axis, it is likely that judgment and intuition will play a large role in the near future.

Skills Axis Diagnosis versus Symptom Cluster Diagnosis
as a Basis for Treatment

Is learning-based treatment more reasonably based upon skills axis diagnosis than upon symptom cluster diagnosis? The most straightforward way to answer this question would be to attempt a study in which patients are assigned to one of two groups. In the first, therapy would be tailored to specific skill deficiencies; in the second, therapy would be somehow strictly delivered in a set manner for each symptom cluster, regardless of skill deficiency. Such a study would seem to have a very high ratio of difficulty and cumbersomeness to return, however, and I would not urge anyone to do it.

If one did wish to approach this question empirically, I believe the use of fictitious vignettes might be a much more efficient method of determining how clinicians already are approaching their psychotherapy clients. Suppose that clinicians were given vignettes in which both the symptom cluster and the skill deficiencies were obvious from the case material; suppose that the symptom clusters and the skill deficiencies were systematically varied in the vignettes, so that the influence of each upon strategy could be separated; suppose that the clinicians were then asked to choose hypothetical therapeutic goals and strategy. Would their answers be determined more by the symptoms or by the information on skill deficiencies? I would predict the second.

The Skills Axis for Groups and Organizations

The same questions that I have just mentioned with respect to the skills axis can also be raised in regard to using the axis with groups and organizations. For example, is it possible to develop reliable and valid measures of the way in which a group of people handles conflict, and to determine how this may be different from the way any given individual handles conflict?

Training Parents to Use Skill-Oriented Contingency Programs

The matrix raises a variety of testable questions about how to train parents to use consequences most effectively. Is it more effective for parents to reinforce examples of high-priority skills than to reinforce examples of randomly chosen positive behavior? In other words, how much does skills axis diagnosis add to the efficiency of contingency programs? Do the parents provide more appropriate reinforcement when they know concrete examples of what they are looking for? How helpful is it for the child to know the concrete examples of the desirable behavior? How useful is having the parent engage in fantasy practice of the reinforcement, punishment, or ignoring strategies that the parent and therapist have decided to be useful? Can we develop a hypothetical-situations measure of the extent to which a parent gives unnecessary commands or too few commands? Can we develop a self-report instrument, a "parental exhaustion index," that might help us predict how much new work the parent is able to take on in working with his or her child?

## THE METHODS AXIS:
## MEASUREMENT AND ASSESSMENT TECHNIQUES

In the child's household, in the school classroom, or in a therapy session, how would we rate the exposure to positive versus negative models of conflict resolution? Are the consequences for behavior loaded so as to reward positive socialization with peers, or to extinguish or punish it? How much total exposure does the child get to practice in the skill of celebrating accomplishments? To what extent are traits of kindness versus meanness attributed to the child? These are the sorts of questions answerable with the reliable and valid measures of the cells of the skills $\times$ methods matrix. With such measures, we can study the relationship between the environmental exposures a person receives and the degree of skill development he or she achieves—the relationship that is postulated by the general theory of this book.

Such measures could take a variety of forms. One environmental measure would simply ask observers, after they have spent a good amount of time observing the child in a given environment, to rate the average degree of positive or negative influence for each cell in question. Alternatively, the number of models, attributions, or reinforcers could be counted. The obvious question, once such influences are measured, is the way in which they combine to predict mental health outcomes. Can we explain variation in the outcomes of clients of various therapists, or of children with various preschool teachers or with different parents, by quantifying the type and degree of influences delivered?

With goal setting, it would probably be much easier to measure the extent to which a person has set a goal to increase a certain skill than to measure the influences delivered to persuade the person to do so. It would be quite interesting, however, to include such a measure in therapy outcome studies; one would certainly predict, for example, that people who strongly wish to make their cognitions less blaming of others will be more successful in an anger control study than those who feel no desire to do so. Measures of motivation might be a highly useful covariate in psychotherapy outcome research. More importantly, they might be useful in helping a therapist decide when to precede "behaviorally" oriented training with more "insight"-oriented goal setting.

It would also be interesting to discover the effects of conceptual sharpening as a means to goal setting. When, for example, children are exposed to stories giving examples of many cognitive and behavioral patterns that they learn to identify in words, do those children set different goals for which strategies they wish to favor than do children without such training?

## Effectiveness of "Versatile Vehicles" in Promoting Skills

I have described "versatile vehicles," or processes capable of delivering influence in any skill content area, so that a separate program does not need to be devised for each skill. Such versatile vehicles include modeling through stories, modeling through dramatic play, real-life modeling, skills-oriented contingency systems, celebrating real-life positive examples, the "scavenger hunt" for positive models, the "situations" game, informal chatting, and practice through fantasy and role playing (including toy play, guided imagery, hypnosis, revision of dreams in waking fantasy, and the "inner guide" technique).

These intervention techniques are of course best tested by outcome studies. To what extent does the packaging of specific skill content in the various versatile vehicles tend to result in increases in those skills?

Some of these versatile vehicles (e.g., modeling stories) depend upon a route of entry wherein the adaptive pattern first enters the child's fantasy repertoire, and thence is chosen to be enacted in behavior. In such outcome studies, it would seem useful to measure the content of the child's fantasy as well as that of the child's behavior: Do the child's stories become more prosocial, for example, before his or her behavior follows suit? If fantasy is affected by fantasy models, are dreams also similarly affected? Does the waking-fantasy revision of dreams influence subsequent dream content?

What would interviews with successful and unsuccessful people tell us about the effects of fictional models in childhood and adolescence? Is the positive effect of modeling plays mentioned by Gandhi in his autobiography (quoted in Chapter 7) not an isolated example?

Effects of Some Specific Techniques

A variety of specific techniques should also be tested. What are the effects of the "shaping" game and the "prisoner's dilemma" game as practice methods; how useful are they as measurement methods and outcome variables? How useful is the "inner guide" technique? Can modeling of frustration tolerance by play characters for preschool children eliminate the upward "blip" of the extinction curve when parents stop reinforcing the children for negative behavior (e.g., protests over separations from the parent at bedtime or other times)?

With the increasing presence of videotape recorders in households, it becomes more feasible to carry out manipulations of video models and to study the effects of these upon behavioral outcomes. An experimenter, for example, could randomly assign families to two groups. Both would pledge to eliminate regular television viewing or limit it to certain programs, and to substitute for the eliminated programs videotaped programs furnished by the experimenters. One group would receive tapes of programs furnishing positive models, vicariously presented consequences for positive patterns, and other positive cells on the skills × methods matrix; the other group would receive a video diet more typical of the average viewer. If the incentives to the participants were sufficient, such an arrangement could be continued for several months, and the effects of the large quantities of exposures could thus be studied.

Training Parents to Have Sessions with Their Own Children

One of the premises for training parents to have sessions with their children is that mutually gratifying experiences between parent and child are important for the child's development of a variety of skills. A measure (relying on either self-report or observation) of the degree of mutual enjoyment between parent and child would be a worthwhile addition to the armamentarium. Such a measure would be useful in testing the predictive value of this variable with respect to the child's adjustment, and then (if these findings are positive) as an outcome measure in parent training interventions.

Are the criteria for positive sessions between parents and children that I have listed in Chapter 8 (see Table 8-1) predictive of positive outcomes for children? In other words, if these parameters are measured in a large number of parent–child dyads, do they predict important outcomes?

To what extent does training parents to have sessions with their children generalize to the home environment and to everyday interactions?

What is the relation between the skills profile of the parent and that of the child? One simple prediction, based on modeling, would be that the profiles will be similar. A more complex prediction would be that certain skill deficiencies in the parent elicit others in the child. For example, the parent who is unable to be assertive with the child may promote deficiencies in frustration tolerance in the child; the parent who is deficient in nurturing may tend to make the child deficient in accepting help; and so forth.


Effectiveness of Nonprofessionals versus
Professionals in Providing Influences


In what circumstances can nonprofessionals provide favorable influences as well as professionals? One rather simple-minded approach to this question is simply to have both professionals and nonprofessionals apply a procedure, and then to compare the results. A better strategy is to specify the cells on the skills × methods matrix that are thought to be really important in producing positive results in the child; to look at the differences between professionals and nonprofessionals in the extent to which they deliver these cells; and to search for whatever selection and/or training procedures are necessary for professionals or nonprofessionals to deliver the influences in the ways thought to be useful. The separate question as to whether the types of behaviors that are thought desirable really do have positive effects on the adjustment of the child can then be studied in addition.

Another way of getting at this issue is simply to attempt to produce the desired results with nonprofessional workers, through some specified procedures of selection and/or training. If the desirable result is produced, one can conclude that it is possible to do it with nonprofessional people, which is really what is in question.

## STUDIES CONNECTED WITH DILUTION EFFECTS

The first dilution effect, as discussed in Chapter 9, postulates that many skills are required to prevent a given syndrome, and that training in one skill may be diluted by deficiencies in untrained skills. One way of testing this hypothesis is to measure the skills profiles in groups of children with a given syndrome, and to test the hypothesis that a wide variety of skill deficiencies are present in the group, or even in any one individual. For example, in a group of conduct-disordered children, are we not likely to find examples of deficiencies in nearly all the skills on the axis?

A second way of approaching the first dilution effect empirically is to train a group with a certain syndrome (or at risk for that syndrome) in all the skills thought necessary to preclude the syndrome, and to compare this group with control groups that get very thorough training in only one of the skills.

A meta-analytic approach to this question is to examine very carefully the treatment manuals used in studies, to look at the number of skills that are trained, and also to note the effect size produced by the intervention. The hypothesis would be that larger effect sizes will be produced by programs that promote more of the skills necessary to preclude the syndrome.

The second dilution effect is the notion that the influences delivered by any program are only some of several that act and have acted upon the person; the influences in the rest of the environment may run counter to those of the intervention. If there are suitable means of measuring and studying the influences of the rest of the environment, one can directly test whether the subjects who do the best after an intervention are those with fewer influences in the rest of the environment tending to counteract those of the intervention, and more influences tending to reinforce it.

A more specific way of carrying out this study would be to look at an intervention with children whose behavior problems are not accepted by their peer group, as contrasted with the same intervention with children whose behavior problems are normative for their peer group. One would predict more behavior change for the first group, assuming comparability in other variables.

A second approach to the second dilution effect would be to contrast treatment delivered to an entire social unit, such as a classroom or neighborhood group, to the same treatment delivered only to an isolated individual in that group. One would predict greater effects when the peer group has also been influenced by the intervention.

## OUTCOME STUDIES OF PREVENTIVE INTERVENTION

In Chapter 10, I have mentioned a variety of preventive intervention methods, any of which could be subjected to empirical test. How much good is done by exposing children of various ages to stories and plays modeling a wide variety of skills? How much good is done by using parents, paraprofessionals, teachers, or peers as the agents of such an intervention? How much good is done by assigning practice in writing modeling stories? How much good is done by public recognition and communication of the positive models embodied by real-life children or fantasy characters they create?

## STUDIES RELEVANT TO THE
## COMPETENCE-PROMOTING CULTURE

The question of what is best to do is somewhat separate from how to insure that people will do it. What are the conditions that make the delivery of favorable influences easiest to carry out? Into what sort of packages can influences be placed so as to attract participants most readily? We can imagine a set of studies in which the dependent variable is the amount of exposure to influence that is delivered, and not the effect that the influence has on the participants. For example, given a set of high-risk parents, which of these variables determine either initial or continued participation: ease of transportation, financial reward, attractiveness of the activities presented, appropriateness of the curriculum for the verbal level of the participants, interpersonal warmth of the trainer, or the chance for individual attention?

A separate but related question is this: What sorts of interventions tend to develop a "life of their own" most readily? Which sorts, for example, are easiest to keep going when grant funding ceases? Which ones are volunteers most capable of running? The Alcoholics Anonymous-type groups, for example, obviously possess a high degree of staying power. Many ingenious and effective interventions have not had such staying power, such spreading power, such a tendency to become enculturated. An interesting topic for research would be to compare those helping mechanisms that tend to last with those that do not, and to identify the critical elements necessary for enculturation. One would hypothesize that the following have a greater chance for enculturation: very inexpensive programs; programs with a very simple format; programs that require very little departure from one's daily schedule and ordinary life style; programs that require the least amount of habit change with respect to travel and time allocation; and programs that are fun, that provide rewards (such as socializing or being entertained) in addition to whatever the rewards of the favorable influences are.

Another ambitious project relevant to the competence-promoting culture is to devise ways of measuring the content of a given segment of a culture's "data bases"—stored records of thought, feeling, and behavior patterns. For example, how would we rate the average content of prime-time television for one season with respect to which skillful and unskillful patterns are rewarded, modeled, instructed, and so forth? How would we rate the skill patterns modeled in the protagonists of the fiction assigned to students in a year-long high school literature class? How would we rate the skill levels of the cognitions modeled in the top 40 popular songs at a given point in time? How would we measure the average exposure in the peer culture of one high school as contrasted to another? Developing means of measuring variations in the content of our culture's data bases would be an important preliminary step toward moving in the direction of a more competence-enhancing set of exposures.

Each of these questions could, of course, be asked separately for any given skill. It would, for example, be a very interesting project to study films with respect to the single area of sexual association learning. To what extent is sexual arousal associated with aggression, novelty of a relationship, and/or antisocial behavior, as opposed to being associated with love, commitment, and a stable relationship with a mate? It would be quite interesting, but difficult, to study trends in the stored data bases of a society as they relate to trends in divorce, marital fidelty, crimes of sexual aggression, and so forth. It would also be interesting to contrast the psychological patterns modeled in the stored data banks in the homes of successful children as contrasted to those of unsuccessful children.

## THE MOST USEFUL APPLIED STUDY

Some of the studies mentioned so far would not be difficult to carry out; others would be quite expensive. The development of measuring instruments in itself is a laborious and time-consuming process. Deciding empirically, for each skill area, what patterns work better than others is a tremendous task. It is possible, when thinking of all the work that could be done, to be discouraged by the sheer methodological tedium of such work.

I believe, however, that the experimenter can and should use his or her intuition in putting together a package that, given all we know at present, has the highest chance of being helpful. The most useful applied study, then, would be carried out as follows: Many skills are promoted using versatile vehicles with community-wide groups of children, over a long period of time and with much exposure, in conditions judged reasonably conducive to enculturation. Outcome measures consist of multiple skills measures, such as they are, and multiple face-valid outcome measures (e.g., school success, freedom from symptoms, etc.). The results of this intervention are compared to the results with a control group.

Such ambitious projects are dictated by the principles discussed earlier. The multiskills approach is dictated by the first dilution effect discussed in Chapter 9; the large-dose, community-wide approach is dictated by the second dilution effect. The use of multiple outcome measures is dictated by the nonspecific relationship between skills and symptoms. Such principles would imply, then, that although high-dose, multiskill, multiple-measure studies are more expensive, they may provide a high enough return in favorable outcomes that they would provide great economies of scale. It could be, for example, that by doing a large-dose, multiskill, community-wide intervention aimed at the prevention of conduct problems and alcohol abuse, we might also have major effects on suicide, teenage pregnancy, and depression.

# *Appendices*

## APPENDIX 1. SUMMARY SUGGESTIONS FOR PARENTS

What follows is a condensed version of suggestions parents have found most helpful in increasing psychological skills in their children.

1. Keep in mind the important psychological skills you want your child to learn: skills such as being cooperative, kind, and friendly; being enthusiastically interested in people and things; having self-discipline and frustration tolerance; paying attention to tasks for a long enough time; and using language well. Keep in mind very specific, concrete examples of these skills.

2. Expose your child to as many positive examples of these skills as you can—in your own real-life behavior, in the behavior of others that you talk about with admiration, and in stories you read to your child.

3. Let your child have opportunities to practice each of the skills; put him or her in situations where the skills get rehearsed.

4. Watch to see whether you can catch the child in the act of being cooperative or friendly, taking interest in people and things, paying attention to a task for longer than usual, tolerating frustration, or using longer or better sentences than usual. If you do, then give the child some attention and approval as soon as possible. This attention does not have to be praise, but can simply be talking with the child about what he is doing, using an approving tone of voice.

5. If the child is doing something you don't like, especially if the child is doing it to get attention, try ignoring it. Ignoring means not talking to the child, not giving him eye contact, and turning your attention to something else. For example, during a temper tantrum, you remain calm and go about your business. Don't give in in order to get the child to stop a loud, screaming tantrum; in the short run it may stop the tantrum, but it teaches the child that tantrums are a way of getting what he or she wants.

---

Throughout this book I have spoken of a "data base" of instructions and models of psychologically skillful patterns. These appendices are samples of material that is part of a much larger data base I have accumulated. The full set of materials includes illustrated stories for preschool children, a set of nonillustrated stories and plays for each psychological skill, a set of hypothetical situations for each skill, a manual for adults who wish to use stories and plays with preschoolers, several other sets of instructions for adults, a computer program presenting hypothetical situations for the situations game, and a computer program presenting "conceptual sharpening" exercises in cognitive strategies. Those who are interested in these may write to me at Western Psychiatric Institute, 3811 O'Hara Street, Pittsburgh, PA 15213.

6. Give commands only when necessary. Too many commands lead to less obedience and more hostility. Try to influence your child more by models, by paying attention to the positive, and by ignoring the negative, and less by commanding the child to do things. One way to reduce commands is as follows: if there is something you don't want the child to touch or play with, get it out of reach if at all possible.

7. Once you give a necessary command, however, be sure to enforce it. Don't let the child practice ignoring your commands. For a small child you can physically enforce a command, such as by leading the child where you want him to go. When the child learns that there is no future in protesting your commands, he will tend to cooperate with them.

9. If you need to use punishment to enforce a command, be aware that physical punishment of the child gives him models for physical aggression. A different option is time out. This means that the child must spend 2–5 minutes in an uninteresting place with no one paying attention to him.

10. Another option for punishment is a reprimand. When you give a reprimand, do it with disappointment and low emotional arousal, rather than anger and high emotional arousal. That way, the emotional exchange is not nearly so likely to escalate. Give the child the message that you expect better behavior than this and that he knows better than this, rather than the message that he is bad. Reprimands are most useful when the child has previously gotten a lot of positive attention and not much negative attention.

11. Don't punish a child for crying, wetting, exploring objects in a harmless way, or asking lots of questions.

12. Read stories to your child as often as you can, but make this activity something that the child asks for and has fun with. Read with a very expressive tone, and respond to the child's comments on the stories. Don't nag at the child to hear more than he wants to hear. Keep on reading to your child long after the child has learned to read for himself.

13. Consider the behaviors of characters on television shows to be models that will go into your child's memory bank. Consider yourself as having a responsibility to regulate your child's "diet" of models. If you don't want your child imitating a character on TV or in the movies, strongly consider not letting your child watch the show in question. This rule will reduce TV watching quite a bit, and will give your child time for more active pursuits.

14. Have enjoyable conversations with your child as often as you can. When you do so, tell your child about your own experience, so as to model how to put into words what's happened to you and what you've been thinking about. Listen attentively when the child tells about his own experience. Use paraphrases and follow-up questions to make sure you understand what your child is telling you, and don't be too quick to give advice. Chatting like this will help the child talk better, and this in turn will help him read and write better. Even more importantly, it will improve the relationship between you and your child.

## APPENDIX 2. STORIES THAT MODEL
## PSYCHOLOGICAL SKILLS

The following is a small sample of the "data base" of modeling stories I have composed to date. These are for grade-school-age children; illustrated stories are available for preschoolers and young grade-school-age children.

### Trusting and Depending

JANET AND THE DIVING TRIP

Once there was a girl named Janet who was taking a scuba diving class. She learned to swim underwater and breathe air that she carried in tanks on her back. The air came from the tanks into her mask through a rubber hose.

The instructor of the class was named Mr. Timm. Mr. Timm was a very good teacher, and he was very, very careful.

One time Janet and her friends went out in a boat to a place Mr. Timm knew. He said, "There are some very pretty rocks underneath this place. You will enjoy swimming around them and looking at them."

Mr. Timm said, "I want to take you down only one person at a time so that I can watch you very closely. The others will wait while I go with one person."

Janet's turn came, and soon she found herself swimming deep below the surface, on the ocean floor.

The rocks were even more beautiful than Janet had expected. There were huge boulders and big caves going into the rock. There were fish swimming around, and Janet wondered if they thought she was another fish.

Janet was having a wonderful time. She decided to look very closely at something she saw on a coral reef. All of a sudden, she noticed that she could not breathe. She noticed that her air hose was caught between two rocks and squeezed shut so that the air could not get through to her.

At first, her impulse was to panic. For a minute, she tugged at the air hose and frantically wanted to zoom toward the surface of the ocean as fast as she could. But then she saw Mr. Timm, and she saw that he had noticed what had happened. The thought went quickly through her mind, "I can trust him." And that thought helped her not to panic, even though she was running out of breath very quickly.

Mr. Timm took his air hose out of his mouth and gave it to Janet. The students had practiced doing this in class, and Janet knew just what he was doing. She put it in her mouth and gasped for breath. It felt great to be able to breathe again. She then gave the hose back to Mr. Timm so that he could take a breath.

Meanwhile, Mr. Timm was looking at the place where Janet's air hose was caught. He signaled to her that he would pull the rocks apart, while she pulled her air hose out of the crack. Janet understood, and signaled back to him, "OK." Of course they could not talk, because they were underwater.

Mr. Timm pulled very hard to get the rocks apart. When he did, Janet pulled on her air hose, and it slid out from between the rocks very nicely. She looked at it, and it wasn't even torn. Mr. Timm looked at it too, and she could see him nod and smile at her.

They came back up to the surface of the ocean, but they did it slowly because it isn't good to come up a great distance very fast.

When they got to the surface and poked their heads out of water, Mr. Timm said, "Janet, I'm proud of the way you didn't panic, but kept your head when that happened. Good job."

Janet said, "Thank you for helping me out, Mr. Timm."

Janet's friends said, "What happened?"

And Janet said, "Oh, my hose got caught in some rocks for a minute or two, but we got it loose."

Later Janet thought to herself, "I'm glad that I was able to trust Mr. Timm! If I had been afraid to let him help me, things would not have turned out so well!" And she felt good about that.

Nurturing Someone Else: Being Kind and Helpful

MARILYN IS A FRIEND TO CHARLOTTE

One time there was a girl named Marilyn. She had lots of friends and liked to do things with her friends. But every once in a while she liked to take a couple of sandwiches with her and go for a long walk by herself, and sit down in a park and eat her sandwiches.

There was a younger girl whose name was Charlotte living in the neighborhood. Charlotte was not at all pretty, and she also seemed to give people unfriendly looks. Marilyn knew that Charlotte didn't have many friends and was left out of groups a lot.

One day when Marilyn was going out for a walk, she saw Charlotte standing by herself, looking lonesome. Marilyn looked at Charlotte and wished she were happier.

Marilyn said, "Hey, Charlotte, I'm going for a walk. Do you want to come with me?"

Charlotte was so surprised that anyone would ask her to do something that she acted suspicious, rather than friendly. She said, "Well, I don't know . . ." and she looked at Marilyn as if she were thinking, "You must be teasing me."

Marilyn did not let that bother her, and she kept on acting friendly. She said, "Do you ever go over to the park? It's nice on days like today."

Charlotte went along with Marilyn, and when they got to the park, Marilyn gave Charlotte one of her sandwiches to eat. After a while, Charlotte didn't look suspicious any more.

After that, Marilyn invited Charlotte to go for walks with her every now and then. Charlotte told about some sad things that happened to her at home and at school. One time Charlotte cried, and Marilyn put her arm around Charlotte's shoulder and comforted her while she cried. At other times, Charlotte would tell Marilyn about good things that had happened, and Marilyn would be happy with Charlotte about them. Charlotte started acting friendlier and friendlier.

Marilyn was out walking one day when she saw from a long way off, a new girl who had just moved into the neighborhood. She thought to herself, "If I had just moved in, I'd want someone to come up to me and be friendly." But just at that moment the girl turned around a corner, and a few seconds later, Marilyn heard another girl's voice.

This other voice was saying, "Would you like for me to show you some of the good places to go to in the neighborhood? We can take a walk together if you'd like to."

The new girl said, "Sure, that would be nice."

Marilyn listened and peeked around the corner to see two girls walking away. The girl who had been so friendly to the new girl had been Charlotte. When Marilyn saw that, she felt great.

After that, Marilyn saw Charlotte and this new girl together a lot, and sometimes would join them on walks. Whenever she saw them, she felt proud that her friend was starting to get some friends of her own.


Social Conversation

SEAN INTERVIEWS THE LEPRECHAUN

One time there was a boy named Sean, who lived in Ireland. He was walking through the woods one day, when all of a sudden he saw a leprechaun. The leprechaun had grey hair and a grey beard, was about 2 feet tall, and was dressed somewhat like an elf.

The leprechaun had a gold club and a golf ball, and was going through the woods knocking the ball into various holes. Sean watched him as he knocked the ball into a groundhog's hole, and the groundhog came out and spit the golf ball back at him.

Sean remembered that he had been assigned to talk to someone, and write down the results of the talk for his school newspaper. Sean started to walk alongside the leprechaun. Sean said, "Hi."

The leprechaun looked at him, and said "Hi" back, and then went on playing golf.

Sean said, "Is it all right if I ask you some questions for our school newspaper? I'm supposed to write an article."

The leprechaun nodded, and Sean said, "My name's Sean. What's your name?"

The leprechaun said, "I'm Mr. Fooddle O'Fiddle."

After this Mr. O'Fiddle didn't say anything, and Sean said to himself, "This isn't a very talkative fellow. What am I going to find out about him?"

Then Sean thought of his school paper, and the letters in the word "paper." He remembered that someone had told him that each letter stood for something he should find out when he was interviewing someone for the paper. "P" stood for "places," "a" stood for "activities," "p" stood for "people," "e" stood for "events," and "r" stood for "reactions."

The first one was "places." Sean decided to ask him about the place he lived in. Sean said, "I'm glad to meet you, Mr. O'Fiddle. Do you live here in these woods?"

Mr. O'Fiddle said, "Yes, I live in a big cave that you get into by going into a big hollow tree. No human being knows where it is, and no one will find out, because it's invisible. You can walk right through it."

Sean said, "Oh, you mean I could go right through it and not see it or feel it?"

"That's right," said Mr. O'Fiddle.

Sean didn't want to frighten Mr. O'Fiddle away by being too nosey about the secret cave. So Sean thought about the "a," for "activities," and decided to ask Mr. O'Fiddle about the activity he was doing right now.

Sean said, "Tell me about the game you're playing, Mr. O'Fiddle. It looks like golf."

Mr. O'Fiddle said, "It is a little like the golf you play, only different. What you do is to see how many times you can hit the ball without making it go into a hole."

Sean said, "That doesn't sound like it would be too hard."

Mr. O'Fiddle said, "That's just because most of the holes are invisible to you. Why just then, my ball flew right through a hole, that was sitting right up in the air by itself. I tried to miss it, but it went through anyway."

Sean asked Mr. O'Fiddle some more questions about this activity. Then he thought of the second "p," which stood for "people." Sean asked, "Mr. O'Fiddle, do you have some brothers or sisters? Or a wife or some children? Who's in your family?"

Mr. O'Fiddle said, "Yes, I have a wife; her name is Ms. Befuddle O'Fiddle. We have about 42 children."

Sean said, "Wow! That's a lot!"

Mr. O'Fiddle said, "Not so many, seeing that we've been married for 2,000 years."

After Sean found out some more about the people in Mr. O'Fiddle's life, he thought of the "e," which stood for "events." Sean asked, "Mr. O'Fiddle, what sorts of things have been happening with you lately?"

Mr. O'Fiddle said, "Well, it depends on what you think of as 'lately.' About 500 years ago I made a very important discovery. There is one great enemy that we leprechauns have, which is called a Blamboomer. Blamboomers like to eat up leprechauns. You can't see them, because they are usually invisible, just like we are. Anyway, I discovered that they are allergic to human beings. Whenever there's a human around, they start sneezing and coughing so badly they can't stand it. So since I discovered that, we've been able to escape the Blamboomers by running off to where humans are nearby, whenever they chase us."

Sean said, "You made a great discovery. I'll bet the other leprechauns were grateful to you."

Mr. O'Fiddle smiled and looked proud. Then Sean thought of the last letter, "r," which was for the person's reaction to something. He said, "Mr. O'Fiddle, what's your reaction to my asking you all these questions? Have you minded it?"

Mr. O'Fiddle said, "Well, my boy, usually we leprechauns stay away from humans. But it so happened that I and about 50 of my invisible friends were out playing golf, when a Blamboomer came around. You've kept the Blamboomer away by walking with us back to where our cave is. So my reaction is that I'm more than happy to have answered your questions, and I hope you write a good article about us. Goodbye."

And with that, Mr. O'Fiddle disappeared as if into thin air.

Sean wrote up his newspaper story. He felt good that he had gotten to know a leprechaun, and had been able to keep the leprechauns safe from the Blamboomer.


Dealing with Disapproval, Teasing, and Criticism


MARY HEARS SOME CRITICISM FROM JENNY

Once a girl named Mary had just gotten back from a vacation, and she just couldn't wait to tell her friends all about what she had seen and done. So she went next door, where her friends Jenny and Donna were sitting on the porch. She ran up to them and said in a very loud voice, "Guess what happened to me! We went on a vacation and I went down to the ocean, and . . ."

Jenny looked irritated, and she said to Mary, "Mary, you don't have to yell. We're sitting right in front of you. I could hear you if you talked only half as loud as you talk."

Mary thought to herself, "Is she right in giving me this criticism, or is she just trying to be mean?" The more she thought, the more she decided that Jenny was right. Mary could remember other times when she had yelled at people so loudly that they seemed bothered by it. So Mary said, "I guess you've got a point, Jenny. Thanks for telling me."

Jenny smiled, and then Mary began again talking about what had happened on her trip, only much more softly than before.

For the next month or two, Mary watched herself. Every now and then she caught herself yelling at people. But when she did, she would stop herself. She said to herself, "I'm glad that when Jenny told me about that yelling, I listened. It helped me learn something useful."

## Conflict Resolution, Joint Decision Making

### RANDY AND BUTCH DECIDE WHO FLIES FIRST

One time there was an amazing person who was a good friend of Randy and Butch. This amazing person said, "I have two little gadgets that we can strap onto our backs, that will let us fly through the air. And they don't even make a loud noise. But I have to take you one at a time. I'll take first one of you, then the other. I want you to decide together who gets to go first, and I'd like you to decide in a sensible way, without fighting with each other. If you fight, then neither of you gets to go."

Randy and Butch knew the amazing person well enough to know that anything he did with them would be safe. And they both could hardly wait to try flying like Superman.

Randy said, "Well, we need to decide who will go first and who will go second."

Butch said, "Yes. One option is that we could flip a coin, and whoever calls the flip right gets to go first."

Randy said, "Another option is that I could just let you go first. Or another option is that you could let me go first."

Butch said, "Or, we could ask the amazing person to pick a number between 1 and 10, and whoever guesses the closer gets to take his choice."

Randy said, "I think the option I'd like the best is to let you go first. That way I get to look forward to my turn, and my turn isn't over so quickly. Plus I get to see what it's like before I try it out."

Butch said, "Oh, we're lucky, then, because I would like to go first. It's fun for me to do something for the first time, before I've seen someone else do it."

Randy said, "OK, so we've decided that you get to go first."

And they shook hands, and turned to the amazing person, and said, "We've made our decision."

He smiled at them, and said, "You did a very good job of deciding together on that."

So Butch and the amazing person strapped on the flying gadget, one for each of them, and they flew, just like Superman, all around the sky. They landed on top of buildings and mountains and finally swooped down to where Randy was waiting.

Butch said, "You're going to love this, Randy. It was great."

And Randy took his turn, and he did love it.

Being Assertive

### RICKY TELLS WHAT MOVIE HE DOESN'T WANT

One time there was a boy named Ricky. He and some of his friends were planning to see a movie together. One of Ricky's friends said, "Hey, there's this movie called *Bath of Blood*. Let's go see that one."

Ricky had heard about that movie and had heard that it was full of gory scenes of people getting killed. So he said, "Are you kidding? That's one of those sicko movies of people getting sliced up and bleeding all over everywhere. No way would I pay money to see that sort of stuff."

Ricky's friend said, "Oh, you're just chicken."

Ricky said back to him, "You can call it chicken if you want to. The way I see it, people have to be a little warped to actually enjoy seeing other people get mutilated. At any rate, I don't want to see it."

One of Ricky's other friends said, "Well, what else is on?"

And they looked and found another one that Ricky thought he would like. They went, and had a good time.

Afterwards Ricky thought to himself, "Boy, I'm glad I spoke up when we were deciding on the movie, and didn't just go along with everyone. I kept myself from wasting my time and money and having a bad time." And he felt good about himself.


Letting the Other Person Have His Way

### HENRY LETS FRANK LEAD THE WAY

One time there was a boy named Henry. Henry played a lot with his friend Frank, and most of the time they did what Henry wanted to do. One day, Henry said to himself, "I think I'll be less bossy with Frank." So that day, when Frank came over to Henry's house, Henry said, "Frank, what would you like to do today? I'll do anything that you would like to do."

Frank said, "Well, that sounds good. I'd like for us to take a walk."

Henry said, "OK," and they started out.

Whenever they came to a crossroad, Henry would get the urge to say, "Let's go this way," because he was in the habit of being the leader. But today he said, "Let's go whichever way you want to go, Frank." So Frank decided which direction they would walk.

Finally, they came to a woods and walked along a path for a while. There was a river running through the woods. Henry followed Frank to a beautiful waterfall. They stood and watched the water pouring over a cliff. Henry said, "Wow! This is beautiful! I never knew this was here, so close to home. Did you?"

Frank answered, "Yes, I've been here lots of times."

Henry was glad that he had let Frank decide what they would do, since otherwise he never would have seen the waterfall. He was also happy because he could tell that Frank liked to be the leader some of the time.

Tolerating Frustration

THE BOY AT THE AMAZING PEOPLE'S PARTY

Once upon a time, a boy got invited to a party that was to be given by some very amazing people in his neighborhood. He asked his mother if he could go. His mother said, "Well, I see that the party lasts from 3:00 to 6:00 in the afternoon, and our family has to catch a plane at 5:30. If you go, you will have to leave before the party is over. You will get to go to the first 2 hours of the party, but then you will have to leave no matter how good a time you are having. Do you think you can do that?"

"Oh, yes," said the boy. He felt good that he could go to the party even for only part of the time.

So the time came, and he went to the party. The amazing people first had some tame lions and tigers and elephants that the boy and his friends could take a ride on. And then they had a machine that would let everybody fly around in the air like Superman. Then they let everybody play on a tightrope and a trapeze with a special net to catch you if you fell off, just like in a circus. The boy was having the best time he had ever had. Then the amazing people said, "Everything so far has just been very dull compared to what we're going to do next!" The boy was very excited to hear that, but just at that moment his mother came and said, "It's time to go."

He had the urge to whine and gripe and complain, but he remembered he had promised his mother that he would leave right away. So he told the amazing people, "Thank you so much for inviting me. I wish I could stay, but as I told you earlier, I promised my mother."

The amazing people told him good-bye, and one of them told his mother, "Your son has quite a lot of self-control. Not many boys could leave a place where they are having so much fun without griping and complaining and whining. I think we should invite him back again soon to do some more amazing and fun things."

When the boy heard this, he felt wonderful and was glad he had been able to keep his promise.

Handling One's Own Mistakes and Failures

JOE AND THE LIFESAVING COURSE

Once there was a boy named Joe. He went to Boy Scout camp for a week and signed up for a course in saving people who are drowning. The time came to start the course, and he went down to the lake. The lifesaving teacher was a big man who could talk in a very mean tone of voice. The first day, the lifesaving teacher made all the boys swim back and forth between two docks on the lake many, many times. Then he had them fold their hands over their heads and tread water. Then he had them practice some lifesaving methods, and then swim some more laps. If they didn't swim as fast as he wanted them to swim, the instructor would yell at them in a mean tone of voice and say, "Come on, get going! What do you think this is, a picnic?"

Joe had a terrible time. He got very, very tired, and he had to slow down. He felt bad when the instructor yelled at him. That day, he stayed until they finished, but then he said to himself, "I don't want to have 5 more days of this. I'm going to quit." So Joe dropped out of the class.

For a while Joe felt bad that he had failed to finish the class. But then he said to himself, "Well, what can I do about this? I can take the course somewhere else with an instructor who is nicer. Or, I can swim and exercise so much that I'm in really good shape. I can also try to work on not minding when someone yells at me. Then I can come back and take it here next summer. Whatever I do, I don't want to get too angry at myself; I just want to figure out the best thing to do and do it. I want to learn as much from this as I can."

When the next summer came around, Joe made plans to go back to Boy Scout camp. But, 2 months before he went back, he started training. He went to a swimming pool and swam laps, more and more each day. He practiced treading water with his hands folded over his head until he could do it for 15 minutes straight. And he also prepared himself for putting up with being yelled at. He did this by imagining a very kind instructor who would say to him, "That's good, Joe, you're doing a good job." Or, "That's not quite right, Joe, but try again. You'll get it right before long." Joe practiced imagining this instructor. He decided that at camp he would imagine this instructor on the dock being nice to him whenever the other instructor was mean.

Finally the time came to go to camp. Joe signed up for lifesaving, and sure enough, the same man was the instructor. He didn't remember Joe from the year before. The first day, he made people swim a long way and tread water a lot, just as before, but this time it was easy for Joe. The instructor still yelled at them, but Joe imagined the nice instructor saying nice things to him. He even imagined the nice instructor standing right on top of the real instructor's head, and he laughed when he thought of this. He imagined the nice instructor giving him a wink and smiling back at him. Joe felt strong, and said to one of the other boys who was having a harder time, "You're doing OK. I'm on your side. Don't worry about what that teacher says." That seemed to make the other boy feel better.

It turned out that the first day was the hardest. Joe did a great job in the course. The final test was to pretend that the instructor was drowning and to swim out and bring him back to the shore. It you did not have a tight hold, the instructor would get loose from you and push you down under the water. Joe held him very tightly, and when they got back to the dock, the instructor said, "That's the best hold that anybody has had on me yet!"

Joe thought to himself, "That's the first time I ever heard him say anything nice to anybody!" And then Joe thought proudly, "I failed the first time at this, but then I figured out what I needed to learn and learned it! Hooray!"

## Enjoying One's Own Acts of Kindness

### MACK HELPS THE LITTLE GIRL

Once there was a boy named Mack who was in a grocery store. All of a sudden a little girl, a lot younger than Mack, came up to him. She looked like she was about to cry. "What's the matter? Can I help you?" Mack said.

"I can't find my mother," said the little girl. So Mack took her by the hand and said, "Don't worry, we'll find her." So Mack took the little girl to the back of the store, where they could look down the first aisle. Mack said. "Do you see her from here?" The little girl shook her head. Then they walked to the second aisle. Mack said. "Now do you see her?" The little girl shook her head. Then they walked to the third aisle. Before Mack could even say anything, the little girl ran to her mother. Her mother looked happy to see her, because she had been worried and looking for her daughter too. They were so happy to see each other that they forgot to say thank you to Mack. But he felt good just to see them happy and to realize that if it hadn't been for him the little girl would have been scared and crying.

## Compliance

### TINA OBEYS HER SKI INSTRUCTOR

One time there was a girl named Tina who was a very good skier. She was a friend of the ski instructor, and one day she got a special invitation. The ski instructor said, "Tina, would you like to go with me and scout around on one of the trails that isn't being used now? I want to look and see if we should open it up for people to ski on."

"You bet!" Tina said. "That really sounds like fun."

The instructor said, "But, Tina, these trails might be dangerous. If you come with me you have to agree to do everything I tell you to. Is that a deal?"

Tina said, "Sure, I'll do whatever you say."

So they rode the ski lift up to the top of the mountain, and they saw a beautiful view from the top. There was nobody else up there, so they had the trail all to themselves. They started skiing down, and Tina was having a great time. She loved whizzing past the trees and feeling the breeze on her face as she flew downward on her skis. They came to a place where the trail divided into two. Tina said, "Oh, let's go down that way. That looks so beautiful." And she started off in that direction.

But the ski instructor stopped her and said, "No, Tina."

Tina didn't want to stop, but she remembered her promise to do what the instructor told her to. So she stopped and skiied back.

The instructor explained to her, "I can tell from the way the snow looks that the trail is not safe down there. Do you see all that snow farther up the mountain above the trail? Sooner or later it's going to slide down on that trail, and anybody who is there could get hurt or killed."

Then the instructor said, "I wonder if I can make it fall now, while I can see that there's no one there." The instructor picked up a piece of ice and threw it in the direction they were looking. The ice knocked loose some other snow that then knocked loose more snow, and pretty soon there were tons of snow sliding down the mountain below them, right across the trail that they were looking at. The instructor said to Tina, "That's what you call an avalanche."

Tina was really glad she had listened to what the instructor said, because she knew now that if she had kept on skiing, the snow probably would have fallen on her.

They skied down the other trail, and Tina continued to have a great time.

## Being Honest When It Is Difficult to Be So

### CATHLEEN AND THE TELEVISION COMMERCIAL

One time there was a girl named Cathleen. One day Cathleen's mother said to Cathleen, "Would you like to go downtown and try out to be an actress in a commercial? There's an advertisement saying they need a girl your age."

Cathleen thought that sounded like fun. She had always liked to act, and often daydreamed about being a star in a movie. So she and her mother went together. There were lots of other girls trying out. Cathleen went into a room with a woman she didn't know, and the woman asked her to look at the camera and say some words just like she said them. Cathleen thought this was a fun game, and she was able to imitate the woman very well.

They went home and the next day there was a phone call. Cathleen's mother answered the telephone, and Cathleen heard her say, "Hey, that's good news!" Then she gave Cathleen the telephone.

It was the woman from the advertising agency, who said, "Guess what, Cathleen, we've chosen you! You get to be on television! All you have to do is to tell people how much fun it is to own a Gruesome Twosome set of monster soldiers, and act like you're having a great time with another child, having them have a war with each other. I'm sure you'll do a great job, and congratulations to you! May I talk to your mother again now?"

Cathleen gave her mother the telephone, and her mother wrote down the time and place that the woman told them the filming would be made. But Cathleen did not feel happy. She thought about what she would do, and she made her decision. When she had decided, she felt better, even though she knew that what she was going to do would be hard.

Cathleen's mother gave Cathleen a big smile and hugged her, and said, "Hooray for you!" But Cathleen did not smile. Her mother looked at her and said, "What's the matter, aren't you excited? They picked you out of all those other girls!"

Cathleen said, "Mother, I'd really like to be on television, but it wouldn't be honest for me to do this commercial. I can't stand Gruesome Twosome monster soldiers—-I think they're disgusting. I know that I could act like I liked them, but I would be lying if I did. I can't do it."

Cathleen's mother sat quietly and thought for a few minutes. Cathleen could see that her mother was disappointed, because she was excited about Cathleen's being on television. But she finally said, "You're right, Cathleen. I'm very proud of you, even though I'm disappointed, too. Well, do you want to call the woman back up, or shall I?"

Cathleen decided to let her mother call up. Her mother called, and asked the woman, "Couldn't there be something other than Gruesome Two-some monster soldiers? My daughter doesn't like them and can't be honest in advertising them."

Then after a few more seconds, she hung up the phone. Cathleen asked, "What did she say?"

Cathleen's mother said, "She sounded irritated and said that if you want to be an actress you can't be so picky, and said good-bye. So that's the end of that. But you still did the right thing, Cathleen."

Cathleen went out for a walk by herself. Things had happened quickly. But the more she thought about it, the better she felt about what she had decided. She said to herself, "I want to keep on refusing to lie, no matter how much I would get rewarded for lying." And she felt glad.

Relaxing; Letting the Mind Drift

NANCY USES THE INNER GUIDE

Once there was a girl named Nancy who was old enough to get a summer job. The job that she really wanted to get was as a lifeguard. But before she could get the job, she had to have a talk with the head person who hired all the lifeguards. If this person liked her, she might get the job, but if the person didn't like her, she probably wouldn't get the job.

She got to the head person's office a few minutes early. She could feel herself starting to get very tense. But then she did some things that always seemed to help her get less tense, or at least act as if she was less tense. First, she took a deep breath, using her stomach muscles to pull the air in and push it out. Then she imagined someone whom she called her "inner guide," who was a very old and wise woman. She imagined the inner guide saying to her, "I'll help you think of what to say. I'll be on your side, even if the person you're talking to doesn't like you. I'll even help you to have a good time."

Nancy saw the face of the inner guide looking very kind and calm. Even though she knew it was all her imagination, she felt really relaxed and confident as she thought of the inner guide being beside her.

In a few minutes, she had her talk with the head person, and she enjoyed the talk. They talked about what she had done before and what she thought it would be like to be a lifeguard, and all sorts of other things. When Nancy walked out of the head person's office, she had a big smile on her face. She knew that whether she got the job or not, she had had a good talk with the head person. She looked at her imaginary inner guide, who said to her, "You did a good job!"

And Nancy said to her guide, "Thanks for helping me."

Thinking before Acting

HAL THINKS BEFORE GOING DOWN THE TRAP DOOR

One time a boy named Hal was visiting an amazing person who had all sorts of magic things in his house. The amazing person told Hal, "There are amazing things in my house, but some of them are dangerous. So always think and remember to ask me before you do anything."

The amazing person left the room for a few minutes, and Hal was there by himself. Then he noticed something he had not noticed before. There was a trap door in the floor of the room. Hal loved to explore, and his first impulse was to open the trap door and see what was inside it. But he remembered what the amazing person had said. "Before I open that trap door," Hal thought to himself, "I should check and see that it's all right."

When the amazing person came back into the room, Hal said, "I noticed a trap door. May I look and see what is inside it?"

The amazing person said, "Sure, I'll take you inside it, but first you'll have to put on a fireproof space suit. Otherwise, you'll get burned up."

At this, Hal said to himself, "Boy, I'm glad I thought before I acted." They both put on their fireproof space suits and opened the trap door and walked down some steps. In a minute the amazing person said, "Hal, I want you to meet Pretzel, my pet dragon." When Pretzel, the dragon, heard this, she turned around and said, "HELLO!" and as she spoke great flames came out of her mouth and went all around Hal and the amazing person. The flames would have burned them up if they had not had on their suits.

The amazing person said, "You see, Hal, Pretzel never has learned to talk without breathing fire at the same time. I'm trying to teach her, but I think it will take her a while to learn."

After that, Hal had a great time playing with Pretzel. She loved to talk, and they had a long talk about all sorts of subjects, such as baseball and pig farming and who should be President. Hal thought it was wonderful being able to talk to a dragon and not worry about the flames because he was safe in a space suit.

## APPENDIX 3. MODELING PLAYS FOR PRESCHOOLERS OR YOUNG GRADE-SCHOOL CHILDREN

These plays are to be acted out by the adult who works with the child, with the adult playing all the characters in the play. Toy people, toy animals, and props such as a house, farm, or airport (with accompanying people) are used. When the adult has a character speak, he or she picks up that character and makes it move up and down and face the character being spoken to. (Characters are kept nameless in the plays as given here so that the adult and child can supply names themselves.)

The plays are also meant to suggest plots that the older person can introduce when the older person and the child are doing spontaneous dramatic play together. In this situation, however, the adult must be more flexible and must allow the child to modify the plot; the adult can insert the positive models when an appropriate chance arises, but should not steamroll over the child's imaginative production. To engage in joyous and spontaneous dramatic play that promotes psychological skill development is one of the finest of the fine arts.

The therapist will wish to introduce plots into the dramatic play that model the skills of highest priority for the child to acquire. For a more complete set of plays, contact me.

Enjoying One's Acts of Kindness; Nurturing Another; Accepting Help without Shame; Expressing Positive Feelings

HELPING MOVE THE BED

FIRST PERSON: I've got to move this big bed over there. Boy! This is heavy.

SECOND PERSON: Do you need some help?

FIRST PERSON: I sure do. If you could get the other end of this bed, we could move it over there together.

SECOND PERSON: OK, I'll get this end, and let you get the other end.

*(They get on either end of the bed, pick it up, and carry it to where it is supposed to go.)*

FIRST PERSON: This is where it's supposed to go! Thank you for helping me!

SECOND PERSON: It was my pleasure!

NARRATOR: And that's the end of this play.

THE VISITOR GETS SOME LEMONADE

*(One person, the host, is in the house. Another person, the visitor, is outside the front door. The visitor rings the doorbell.)*

HOST: I wonder who that is. I hope it's not somebody mean. *(The host, sounding a little scared, walks across the living room floor to the door.)* Who is it?

VISITOR: It's me, it's _____.

HOST: Oh, good, my friend _____ has come to visit. *(Opens the door.)* Hi, _____! Welcome! Come in!

VISITOR: Thank you! I'm glad to see you!

HOST: Would you like some lemonade?

VISITOR: Yes, that would be really nice!

HOST: *(Goes and gets lemonade in other room. Comes back and says:)* Here's your lemonade.

VISITOR: Thanks! This is really good.

HOST: You're welcome. Sit down. *(They sit down.)*

NARRATOR: That's the end of the show.

LENDING A COLD PERSON A BLANKET

*(The prop for this play is a piece of paper about 3 inches by 5 inches.)*

FIRST PERSON *(in house)*: It's cold out there! I'm going to wear a heavy coat. I think I'll fold up this blanket and take it along with me, too. *(When this person talks about the blanket, he gets the piece of paper, folds it up, and walks out of the house with it.)*

SECOND PERSON *(who is outside, some distance away)*: Brrr! I'm cold! I wish I could get warm somehow!

FIRST PERSON *(coming up to the second person)*: Hi! You look cold!

SECOND PERSON: I sure am cold! I'm about to freeze!

FIRST PERSON: Would you like to borrow my blanket, and put it around you?

SECOND PERSON: Yes! Thank you! That's really nice of you. *(They put the blanket around the second person.)*

SECOND PERSON: Now I'm not cold any more! You really helped me!

FIRST PERSON: You're welcome! *(To himself:)* I'm really glad I could help!

HELPING TO FIND THE CART

FIRST PERSON *(pulling the cart behind him)*: Let's see, where should I leave this cart? Here's a good place. *(Leaves cart in back of barn and exits.)*

SECOND PERSON: Well, it's time for me to take the pig to the doctor to get a checkup. I'll drive the tractor, and the pig will go in the cart. Come on, Pig.

PIG: OK. I like the doctor that I go to. I'm looking forward to our trip.

SECOND PERSON: Here's the tractor. Now where is that cart? Last time I saw it, it was right here, but I don't see it here any more. Hmm. Where can it be? *(The person looks around.)*

PIG: I'll help you look. We can probably find it quicker if we both look. *(Looks behind the barn, and finds it.)* Here it is, I found it!

SECOND PERSON: You sure did! There it is! Thank you for finding it for us. Now we're ready to go.

*(The second person hooks the cart to the tractor, and the pig gets in the cart, and off they go.)*

NARRATOR: And that's the end of the show.

LETTING THE TRAVELER COME INTO THE BARN
FROM THE RAIN

PEOPLE AND ANIMALS: Hey, it's starting to thunder. It looks like it's going to rain. We'd better go into the barn.

*(They go into the barn.)*

SOUND EFFECTS: Boom! Boom! *(thunder)* Pssshhh! *(with finger motions representing rain)*

PEOPLE AND ANIMALS: Listen to that thunder, and look at that lightning! It's really raining hard now!

TRAVELER: Boy, I wish I'd brought my umbrella. I've gotten caught in the rain.

ONE PERSON IN BARN: Hey, look at that person; he doesn't have any place to go to. Let's let him come in here, to get out of the rain.

ANOTHER PERSON: Yes, we can help him out that way. I'll yell to him. HEY! Come on in here, if you want to get out of the rain!

TRAVELER: Thank you! *(He runs to the barn, and the people inside open the door and let him in.)* You really helped me! If it hadn't been for you, I would have gotten really wet, and I might even have been hit by lightning!

FIRST PERSON: We're glad to be of service. Would you like some hot apple cider, to warm you up?

TRAVELER: Yes, please! You are really nice! *(The people bring the traveler hot apple cider.)* This feels really good, to drink this. Let me know if I can do something for you in return.

NARRATOR: And that's the end of this show.

Tolerating Separation

THE BOY STAYS IN HIS OWN BED

FATHER *(to mother):* I think our son is getting to be such a big boy. It's time for him to learn to stay in his own bed all night, and not to sleep in our bedroom, don't you think?

MOTHER: Yes, I think that's a good idea. It might be a little hard for him at first, but I think once he gets used to it, he'll not be scared any more, and he'll enjoy sleeping lots more than he used to.

SON: Hi, Mom! Hi, Dad!

FATHER: Hi, son! Your mom and I were just talking about how it's time for you to start staying in your own bed all night. We think you're big enough to handle that.

SON: What if I get scared during the night?

FATHER: You can still come in to our room, but you'll just go back to your own room to go back to bed. We won't talk with you very much when you get up. But you can always check and make sure we're here, if you want.

MOTHER: If you're able to stay in your own room all night long, without coming into our room once, we will really celebrate in the morning. We'll clap and cheer that you were able to be so brave.

SON: This might be scary, but I bet I can do it.

NARRATOR: Now it's getting close to bedtime. Let's see what the boy does.

SON: Well, it's time to go to bed. Let's see if I can stay in my own bed tonight. *(Gets in his bed.)*

MOTHER AND FATHER: Good night, son! Good luck!

SON: Well, this is a little scary, being in here by myself. But it helps if I think about all sorts of nice people who are on my side and are my friend, and make up a story to myself about them. . . .

NARRATOR: Now it's morning again.

SON: Yawn! Well, I guess it's morning. Hey, I did it! I slept in my own bed all night long! *(Runs down to mother and father.)*

MOTHER AND FATHER: Hooray! You did it! You slept in your own room all night long, without even getting out once! Congratulations!

SON: Thank you!

*(They parade around, marching to a tune such as "The Stars and Stripes Forever" or "The Triumphal March" from* Aida.)

NARRATOR: And that's the end of the play.


Handling Interpersonal Conflict

THE BROTHER AND SISTER TAKE TURNS WITH THE BOOK
*(The mother and father come home with a book.)*

CHILDREN: Hi, Mommy! Hi, Daddy!

MOTHER AND FATHER: Hi! We brought you a present!

CHILDREN: Oh, look! It's a new book! *(The mother and father exit.)*

BROTHER: I want to read it, right now!

SISTER: Hey, but I want to read it right now, too!

BROTHER: Hmm, what can we do about this? We could read it together, but that wouldn't work out well, because I like to read so much faster than you do.

SISTER: Well, we could take turns, and I could let you go first.

BROTHER: That's awfully nice of you to offer that. Why don't I let you go first, and I'll go jogging while you're reading the book? I was just ready to go jogging anyway.

SISTER: OK, that sounds really nice of you.

*(Sister reads the book, and brother goes out jogging. As sister reads book, she giggles and laughs.)*

*(Brother comes back from his run.)*

SISTER: Boy, are you going to enjoy this book. It's funny!

BROTHER: Oh, good. Are you through with it now? Is it my turn?

SISTER: Yes.

*(Brother reads book, and giggles and laughs also.)*

SISTER *(thinking out loud):* I sure am glad that we were able to take turns with this book!


Tolerating Winning and Losing in a Competition

HAVING A RACE

FIRST PERSON: Want to race?

SECOND PERSON: Yes! Let's race to that thing over there. *(They designate something as the finish line for their race. The first person and the second person line up.)*

FIRST PERSON: On your mark, get set, go!

*(They race to the finish. One of them wins.)*

WINNER: Hooray, I won!

LOSER: Good for you. You ran really well.

WINNER: You ran a good race too. Do you want to race again?

LOSER: Yes.

*(They line up. One of them says:)* On your mark, get set, go!

*(They race again. This time the other one wins.)*

LOSER: Hey, this time you won! Congratulations!

WINNER: Thank you! I'm glad I won! You ran fast too.

*(They continue racing, and tie sometimes, if the child stays interested.)*

NARRATOR: That's the end of that play,


APPENDIX 4. SAMPLE SITUATIONS FOR FANTASY PRACTICE

If skill is to be developed, it must be repetitively practiced. The situations listed in this section provide practice opportunities for each skill on the axis.

One method of carrying out such practice is the "situations" game, as described in Chapter 7. The helping person, when he or she draws cards, models desirable responses for the child; when the child draws cards, he gets to practice responses that are (one hopes) worth rehearsing. The responses to the situations may be carried out by fantasy and verbal report on the fantasy, or by role playing. For a more complete set of situations, or for a computer program that presents situations for any selected set of skills, contact me.

Accurately Assessing the Trustworthiness of Another Person,
and Trusting When Appropriate

A boy got to know two boys in his neighborhood who were not nice to him: They hit him and took some things that belong to him. So the boy stays away from these other two boys. There is a third boy in the neighborhood, who seems to be nicer. But the boy is afraid to get to know this third boy, because he feels as if he can't trust anybody in the neighborhood. What advice would you give him?

Accepting Help, Being Dependent without Shame,
Asking for Help Appropriately

Suppose you are in school, and your teacher has given you an assignment for some seat work. You don't understand the teacher's directions very well, and you are not sure exactly what you are supposed to do. Act out how you would ask the teacher for some help in understanding what to do.

Tolerating and Enjoying Sustained Closeness, Attachment,
and Commitment to Another

A boy has wanted a dog more than anything else in the world. When he first gets the dog, he is overjoyed. But then he discovers that it takes a lot of work to feed the dog, to take it for walks, and to figure out something to do with it when the family goes on vacations. The dog is very nice and lots of fun, but the dog tends to chew things up; it chews up the boy's baseball glove. The boy starts to have second thoughts about what he has gotten himself into. Pretend that you are the boy, and talk to yourself out loud. What would you like to say to yourself?

Nurturing Someone Else: Being Kind and Helpful

Suppose that there is someone at school who is on your team in a baseball game. Suppose this person has just struck out. Everybody is mad at him, and he feels really bad. What could you say to him that would make him feel better?

## Nurturing Oneself: Delivering Assuring or Caretaking Cognitions to Oneself, and Feeling Comforted by Such Cognitions

A girl in a basketball game has just shot for the basket for the third time and missed. She is the type who tends to feel very bad about things like that. What could she say to herself to comfort herself and not feel so bad?

## Expressing Gratitude, Admiration, and Other Positive Feelings toward Others

Pretend that someone has just finished helping you with some schoolwork. The person has really helped you understand some new things, and has done it in a nice way. Act out how you would let the person know that you appreciate this.

## Initiating Social Contacts Appropriately; Getting Attention from Others in Appropriate Ways

Suppose that somebody you know is trying to fix a bicycle. You want to start talking to this person. What are the first things that you would say?

Suppose that you are at a party, and you know everyone but one person. You decide to introduce yourself to that person. Act out how you would do this.

## Engaging in Social Conversation

Think of something interesting or funny or unusual that happened— something that somebody would enjoy hearing about—and tell about it.

## Listening, Empathizing, Encouraging the Other to Disclose

A friend is talking with you about something on his mind. He says, "I'm thinking of trying out for a play. But I'm not sure I'm good enough at acting. I don't want to look foolish." Suppose that you don't know enough about the person's situation to give him any advice, but you want to encourage him to keep talking about the situation. What would you say back to him?

### Making Decisions Independently; Carrying Out Actions Independently

Suppose that you have seen a movie, and you don't like it at all. You are with four other people, and they are all talking about the movie. All four of them are saying, "I really loved it!" "I thought it was the greatest movie I ever saw!" and things like that. Someone says to you, "What did you think of it?" Act out what you would say.

### Tolerating Separation from Close Others

A girl is going for the first day of school. She is afraid to say good-bye to her mother when it is time for school to start. What would you advise her to say to herself, to help her feel better?

### Handling Rejection

A boy makes very good grades in school. He starts to play with a couple of other boys, but they say to him, "Go play with someone else. We don't want you bookworm types around. You're just the teacher's pet." If you were this boy who makes good grades, what would you say to yourself, and what would you say to them?

### Dealing with Disapproval and Criticism

A boy is with some teenage boys who are drinking beer; this boy, however, does not drink. The other boys say to him, "What's the matter, are you chicken? What's the matter, won't your mother let you drink? Oh, you poor little baby." If you were this boy, what would you do, or say, or say to yourself?

### Having a Good Time by Oneself, Tolerating Aloneness, Tolerating Not Getting Someone's Attention

A girl has the afternoon to spend at home by herself. There is no one at home, and there is not even a telephone working in the house. Think of four different things that she might do by herself that would be fun.

### Dealing with Someone's Doing or Wanting Something That Conflicts with One's Own Preferences

You like to play music fairly loudly, but your sister likes to have things very quiet. Your sister says to you, "The music is a real problem for me. I want it much quieter." What would you do, or say, or think to yourself?

Generating Creative Options for Solutions to Interpersonal Problems

Pat and Lee live together. Pat likes to cook a certain type of fish, but the fish is very smelly and Lee really dislikes the smell. Think of at least four options for what they could do to solve their problem.

Recognizing and Choosing Reasonable Solutions
to Interpersonal Problems

Suppose that you are a parent, and you have two children who argue with each other and get mad a lot over the issue of who gets to use the telephone. Both of them like to talk on the phone a lot. Of these four solutions, which is your first choice, second choice, third choice, and fourth choice? (A) Not to let either of them talk on the phone at all, until they can settle their disagreement nicely. (B) To stay out of it, let them fight with each other all they want, and let it be their problem. (C) To get a new phone line for the house, if both of them are willing to work to pay for it. (D) To set up a schedule, so that each of them uses the phone at certain times only.

Negotiation: Talking Out Conflicts and Reaching Joint Decisions

Sue and Nick are brother and sister. There is one bicycle owned by the family, and Sue and Nick have to share it. Sue wants it tomorrow afternoon to go on a bike trip with some friends. Nick wants it tomorrow afternoon to ride over to a baseball game. Play the part of Sue, and let your partner play the part of Nick, and negotiate this problem.

Assertion and Dominance Skills

There is a dog chained up in a yard. Some boys are shooting a water gun at the dog. The dog is very frightened by this and is running around dodging the water, looking very agitated. You walk by and see this happening. Act out what you would say or do.

Conciliation and Submission Skills

There is a boy named Mike who tells his friend John that sound travels just as fast as light; John argues that light is much faster. That night, Mike goes home and looks it up in a book and finds out that John was right. Pretend that you are Mike, and let your partner be John, and say whatever you would say to him the next day, if you would say anything at all.

Recognizing and Praising the Portion of Another's Behavior
That Is Positive

Sandra has a little brother. The brother sometimes wants to play with Sandra when Sandra has homework to do. He knocks on her door and asks her to play with him, and when she says no he usually (but not always) has a tantrum, screaming and crying. Suppose that Sandra wants to help him learn not to do this. How can she use praise and reward to help him?


## APPENDIX 5. CONCEPTUAL SHARPENING EXERCISES:
## A STORY ILLUSTRATING COGNITIVE RESPONSES

Conceptual sharpening is mentioned in Chapter 5 as one of the tools by which goal setting is sometimes best promoted. Exercises such as the following provide practice in conceptualizing the cognitions people have in desirable and undesirable situations.

Below are some ways that people think when responding to undesirable situations.

| | |
|---|---|
| • "Awfulizing" | • Not "awfulizing" |
| • Getting down on themselves | • Not getting down on themselves |
| • Blaming someone else | • Not blaming someone else |
| | • Listing options and choosing among them |
| | • Learning from the experience |

Below are some ways that people think when responding to desirable events:

| | |
|---|---|
| • Not celebrating | • Celebrating something they did |
| | • Celebrating something somebody else did |
| | • Celebrating something that just happened to happen |

The following is the first chapter of a novella that provides conceptual sharpening practice in recognizing the responses to undesirable situations listed above. After each cognition in the chapter, there is a question in brackets as to what sort of cognition it is; answers to the questions are provided at the end.


The Saga of Dilly, Lilly, and Bo-Billy Willy

EPISODE 1. THE TRAVEL BOX
One day a boy named Bo-Billy Willy was sitting at the table eating breakfast, and he knocked over a glass of milk. His sister had asked him to pass the

butter, so he said to her, "I wouldn't have knocked that over if it hadn't been for you! See what you made me do?!" [1. What is he doing?]

At this his sister, whose name was Lilly, reached over to put a napkin in the puddle of milk, and she knocked over a whole pitcher of orange juice! At this she felt really bad, and said to herself, "Oh, I'm such a nitwit! I've really done it now. I'm so stupid, I can't do anything right!" [2. What is she doing?]

When Bo-Billy Willy and Lilly's father, whose name was Dilly, saw all this, he said to himself, "Hmm, those glasses and pitchers that I bought seem to knock over very easily. I bet that's because they're so tall and skinny. I learned something from this, which is that the next time I buy glasses, I'm going to buy short fat ones, so they won't knock over so easily." [3. What is he doing?]

At this point there was a knock at the door. "Hark," said Lilly.

"There's a knock," said Dilly.

"It's at the door," said Bo-Billy Willy.

So they answered the door, and who should it be but a salesman whose name was Jabbermore Smif, who said: "I'm selling glasses that are specially made so as to be hard to knock over." And with this Jabbermore kept right on talking in a very loud voice and wouldn't shut up. Finally Dilly got so sick of hearing him talk so loudly that he said to him, "When you talk so long and so loudly, it really gets on my nerves, so would you leave please, right now?" and Dilly closed the door, leaving Jabbermore standing outside.

When Jabbermore had just gotten kicked out of the house, he said to himself, "Hmm, the reason he kicked me out was that I talked too long and too loudly. I learned something that I can use next time; now the next house that I go to I won't talk so long and so loudly, but I'll shut up a little more." [4. What is he doing?]

Just after Dilly had kicked out Jabbermore, he said to himself, "I wish I hadn't done that. I needed some glasses that don't knock over so much, and I just passed up the opportunity to get some at a good price. Oh well, I won't get down on myself about it, though; nobody's perfect, including me." [5. What is he doing now?]

So then Dilly said to himself, "Now let's see, what can I do about this? I can just forget it. Or I can go out to the store and get some more glasses while I'm still thinking about it. Or I can go back and run after Jabbermore Smif, and buy the glasses from him anyway. I think I'll do that, right now, before he gets too far away." [6. What is he doing now?]

So Dilly went out and caught up with Jabbermore Smif, and bought the glasses. And while he was at it, Jabbermore Smif sold him an amazing little box that would enable you to go anywhere you wanted to if you stood inside it—you could go wherever you chose in an instant.

Only there was one problem, and that was that it didn't work very well. Sometimes it took you where you didn't want to go rather than where you did want to go. Jabbermore Smif might have remembered that he hadn't told Dilly this, and might have decided that he'd made a mistake by not telling him, but he didn't. He was just happy to have sold the amazing little box, and he didn't give it another thought.

So Dilly went back to Lilly and Bo-Billy Willy with his short fat glasses and his new travel box, and he said, "Let's take a trip!"

"Yes, let's do it," said Lilly and Bo-Billy Willy. So they all got into the box, and Bo-Billy Willy set the dial on the inside of the box for Miami Beach, Florida. But to their great surprise they wound up instead in Beirut, Lebanon, where there was a war going on, and they just barely missed being hit by a bullet that whizzed right past them. "Oh my gracious," said Dilly, "we're not in Miami Beach, we're in Beirut Lebanon, right in the middle of two sides shooting at each other!"

When Lilly heard this, she said to Bo-Billy Willy, "It's your fault! You must not have set the dial on the box right. You got us all into this mess!" [7. What is she doing?]

Then when Bo-Billy Willy heard this, he said to himself, "Oh, I'm so stupid, I just can't do anything right. I don't deserve ever to feel good after making such a horrible mistake!" [8. What is he doing?]

But Dilly said, "Well, we've got some options. We can stand here and maybe catch a passing bullet, or we can run for cover, or we can get back into our box and go somewhere else, anywhere but where we are now. I think I like the last one best." [9. What is he doing?]

So they all got back in the box and set the dial for Hawaii, and where should they end up but Toronto, Canada. "What are our options?" said Lilly. "Well, we could try the box again, and see if we get any closer to home," said Bo-Billy Willy.

"Or we could throw the box away and take a plane home," said Lilly.

"Or, since I don't have enough money for a plane, we could take the Greyhound bus back home to the United States and carry this magic box home with us," said Dilly. [10. What are they doing there?]

"Let's do the last thing you said—take the bus home," said Lilly and Bo-Billy Willy, and so they boarded a bus.

As they were riding the bus, Dilly said to himself, "Well, I learned something from that. Next time I buy something like that from a salesman, I'm going to have the salesman demonstrate that it works before I buy it!" [11. What is he doing now?]

All of them thought that the bus would take them straight home, and that their adventure would end. Soon, however, they would find that it had just begun.

EPISODE 1. THE TRAVEL BOX—ANSWERS

1. Blaming somebody else
2. Getting down on herself
3. Learning from the experience
4. Learning from the experience

  5. Not getting down on himself
  6. Listing options
  7. Blaming somebody else
  8. Getting down on himself
  9. Listing options (and choosing among them)
 10. Listing options
 11. Learning from the experience

## APPENDIX 6. EXERCISES USING THE INNER GUIDE

The "inner guide" technique is discussed in Chapter 7; it can be a versatile vehicle for practice of psychological skills. The first exercise presented below is a general exercise in cultivating the ability to use the inner guide. The second is an illustration of how it may be used with specific skills—namely, relaxation, self-nurture, celebration of positive events, frustration tolerance, celebration of one's accomplishments and acts of kindness, decision making, tolerating aloneness and separation, and forgiveness.

### Exercise 1: Empowering the Inner Guide

This exercise has to do with an imagery method, the use of the inner guide. When using it, you may or may not wish to get into a comfortable posture; you may let your eyes close or not close, as you choose; you may at times wish to experiment with writing notes that capture your thoughts during the experience. The only important thing is to be ready to use your imagination to access certain very important functions and parts of your mind. Let yourself feel relaxed and peaceful as this process begins.

In a moment you will let take shape in your mind an image of a person—a very wise, very loving, very strong person. You may choose to form a visual image of the person in great detail, or you may choose to have an image that gives only an indirect indication of the person's presence. If you do visualize the person, the image may take whatever form you wish to give it. When you communicate with this person, you may do so by inner speech, or there may be voiceless transmission of ideas and images. The person you call to your mind is to be your "inner guide"—a being that dwells within you, one whom you have invested with the power to be of great service to you—in fact, an ever-available source of help and strength. Comfort yourself with the knowledge that the ability to use this resource is gradually cultivated over time, and that your ability to use it to fullest advantage will gradually increase with practice.

Allow to come into your mind some image that will for now represent for you the inner guide. Let this image reside peacefully in your mind.

One of the ways that the power of the inner guide can be cultivated is to imbue it with the power derived from other powerful images. Please search your memory for images associated with love, with good will between people, with kindness. Especially look for images of loving parents, of parents who care very deeply about their children, who are nurturing and watchful and protective. Let the feelings, the aura produced by these positive images be duplicated so as to reside within your image of the inner guide.

Now search your memory for images associated with benign potency, with the power to get desirable goals accomplished, with a sense of efficacy. Think of people or events that embody this aspect, and let the idea of benign power be duplicated and projected onto your image of the inner guide. The inner guide will gradually acquire more and more power to help you influence the workings of your own inner life—your own thoughts, feelings, choices, and behavior.

Now let your mind focus upon the majesty of the universe, the beauties of nature, the miracle that the universe was somehow created, the miracle that complex living things exist, the miracle of human beings, and the miracle of your own existence. Let your mind range over these things for some time, and from time to time duplicate some of the aura associated with these images and project them onto your inner guide, empowering the inner guide with the awe associated with the wonders of the universe.

Now bring the mind images of permanence, eternity, and infinity, and experience the way in which these concepts stretch your consciousness. Project upon the inner guide some of the power gained from these concepts, and associate with these concepts the comforting thought that the inner guide is with you and available to you at any moment you choose, no matter where you are, so that you need never feel totally alone or abandoned.

Bring to mind images of wisdom: wise decisions, intelligent actions, carefully reasoned solutions to questions about living, the power of being fully open to the entire truth. Recall concretely specific wise actions or thoughts that you have encountered in others or have carried out yourself. Picture the inner guide absorbing such wisdom, gradually becoming wiser and wiser, becoming a source of serene and calm thoughts about handling any given situation.

Now let your mind range for some time among the images of kindness, of benign power, of the majesty of the universe, of permanence and unlimited availability, and of wisdom, and let these aspects pervade your image of the inner guide.

Exercise 2: Using the Inner Guide's Power

Now, as you let yourself feel relaxed and peaceful, let the image of the inner guide come into your mind. As you do so, feel comfort and warmth being transmitted to you by the love that emanates from the inner guide. Take some time to do this.

The nature of the inner guide is not to influence external events, to cause things to happen in the physical world outside you. But the inner guide may have great power, as if magical power, in influencing the internal world, the life of the mind. One of the powers of the inner guide is to give you the ability to rise above whatever stresses you may now be encountering, and to feel joy and gratitude and happiness over those blessings that you do have. Let your inner guide assist you in recognizing the ways in which you have been blessed, and in fully appreciating these fortunate aspects of your life and your situation. Take some time to let your mind range over these things.

Now, if you wish, let come into your imagination some of the stresses and frustrating events that you would like to handle well. See yourself handling them with the help of your inner guide, in the way most pleasing to the wisest part of yourself. Take some time to let this happen.

The inner guide may also be a source of approval, of celebration of the good, kind, wise, or brave things you have done. This source of approval can be much more reliable, and much deeper, more ethical, and wiser, than the approval that is given or not given by the external world. Let your mind roam over the acts, thoughts, and feelings you have done or had that are worthy of any praise, any pride, any celebration—even very small examples. Feel the approval that comes from your inner guide for these good, wise, and brave things, and let this approval make you feel good. Take some time to experience this.

Another way in which your inner guide may be of help to you is in making wise decisions about the situations you face or will face in the future. Call upon the wisdom of the inner guide to let there come into your mind a decision worthy of some thought. Allow your inner guide to help you see the situation in new ways, from new perspectives. Ask the inner guide to give you the creativity to consider options that you may not have considered before. Ask the inner guide for the wisdom to predict the likely effects of options. And call upon your inner guide's love and ethical sense to evaluate which outcomes, which effects the deepest part of you wishes to see happening. Feel yourself strengthened and more ready for the decision-making process, whether you engage in it now or later.

Another way in which your inner guide may be of help to you is by being a loving, supportive companion to you, no matter what situation you encounter. So that you may not forget to take advantage of this companion, let your imagination take you to situations—whether difficult or pleasant or tedious or commonplace or crucial—that you may encounter in the future. See yourself encountering situations, acting in the way you've decided you want to act, being the way you want to be, with the knowledge in the back of your mind that your inner guide is with you, giving peace and love and support to you in your dealings with life.

The nature of the inner guide is to be loving and forgiving, both of yourself and of others. This forgiveness is of the sort that is wholly compatible with the strongest efforts to keep the undesirable deeds from being repeated. This sort of forgiveness of yourself relieves you of the defensiveness that would stand in your way of making improvements in your own actions; this sort of forgiveness of another person relieves you of the anger that would interfere with your making the most rational decision about whether, or how, to improve the other person's behavior. Let your mind roam over the things that you have done that you wish you had not, and let the inner guide help you forgive yourself. Let your mind go to the actions of someone else that would tend to cause you anger, and call upon the power of your inner guide to help you extend forgiveness to this person. Take some time for this activity.

Finally, you may wish to celebrate within yourself the fact that you have been able to spend time seeking the resources that the inner guide can give. Or you may wish to carry out any of a vast number of other mental activities in the time that remains available to you for this meditation.

## APPENDIX 7. WRITTEN EXERCISES FOR PSYCHOLOGICAL SKILL BUILDING

In Chapter 10 I have spoken of written assignments for school children and adolescents that provide practice in psychological skills. One obvious exercise is the assignment to compose a story that illustrates any one of the skills on the axis. The following are some more exercises that can give practice in goal setting, celebrating positive events, decision making, tolerating frustration (referred to here as building fortitude), and nurturing oneself.

### Goal-Setting Exercise

Writing your goals is a surprisingly powerful technique for improving your life. This exercise asks you to write goals for various time frames.

In writing your goals, think of (1) what you'd like to accomplish in work and school; (2) what you'd like to have happen with family relationships; (3) what you want with respect to leisure and fun experiences; (4) what you want to happen with respect to personal growth and psychological development.

Once you have written your goals, you can revise this same file over and over again, adding or subtracting goals from the lists, without having to write all of them all over again.

1. Please think forward to the time when your life is complete. What are your lifetime goals? List them below, and revise them as you wish. Think of work and school, family, leisure, and personal growth. You may also wish to give them priority scores—a rating of 0 to 10 that indicates how important each of them is.

2. Now please list and prioritize your goals for the next 5 years of your life. Think of work and school, family leisure, and personal growth.

3. Now please list and prioritize your goals for the next 6 months of your life. Think of work and school, family, leisure, and personal growth.

4. Now please list and prioritize your goals for the next month of your life. Think of work and school, family, leisure, and personal growth.

5. Finally, please list and prioritize what you want to accomplish in the next day of your life, with respect to work and school, family, leisure, and personal growth.

Celebration Exercise

The purpose of this exercise is to focus attention on the things you have to celebrate. Sometimes doing this helps you make more of such things happen in the future.

1. Please think about the things that other people have done that you are grateful for or proud of, and write at least two of them.

2. Please think about the things that you have done (or thought or felt) that you are glad you did (or thought or felt), and write at least two of them. Think of accomplishments, kind acts, wise choices, or fun things you've done.

3. Please think about the blessings of fate that are present in your life—the lucky things that have happened to happen to you—and write at least two of them.

4. Please think of some things that you could do or that could happen in the future that would be worth celebrating, and write down at least two of them.

Decision-Making Exercise

1. Please identify and describe a situation in which you want to make a decision. Go into as much or little detail as you wish in telling about the situation.

2. Please estimate how high the stakes are in dealing with this situation. A scale from 0 to 10 might be helpful, where 0 is a decision of absolutely no consequence (such as whether to start walking with your left foot or right foot on the way to lunch) and where 10 is a decision that has the hugest possible consequences in your life.

3. Please define your goals in dealing with this situation. What factor, or what combination of factors, are you trying to maximize or minimize?

4. Please list several options for responding to this situation. You might wish to include options of things to think and things to try to feel, as well as things to do.

5. Please think about the costs, risks, benefits, and consequences of each option that is a serious contender. Write the advantages and disadvantages of each of those options.

6. For the sake of this exercise, please come to a decision about what option or set of options you wish to adopt. Definitely decide something; you can always decide to gather more information or to think or talk more about the situation in preparation for the final decision, but that too is a decision. Or you can pretend to decide, and adopt an option or set of options hypothetically, just to try it out.

7. Please do some planning about the details of how you intend to put this option into effect: what exactly you will do, when you'll do it, how long it will take, what you will need, and so forth.

8. How well do you think you did in this decision-making exercise? Is that better than your previous level?

Fortitude-Building Exercise

1. Please think of and describe a situation that is hard to handle. You may go into as much or as little detail as you wish about the situation and what makes it hard to handle.

2. Sometimes in thinking about difficult situations, other difficult situations come to mind—situations that might be consequences of the present difficult situation, things the present difficult situation might portend, and so forth. Please list any of these, for future reference. (You can then go back and do this exercise with them later.)

3. Please return to the first difficult situation, the one you listed in question 1. Please write a scenario in which you describe yourself handling that situation in the best way that you can imagine, in a way that demonstrates fortitude. Include your thoughts as well as your actions.

Self-Nurture Exercise

A very helpful ability is that of aiding oneself, comforting oneself, and giving reassuring messages to oneself. This ability requires two component skills: that of giving help and comfort, just as one would give it to somebody else; and that of receiving help and comfort, just as one would receive it from someone else. Accessing memories of times when nurture has been given to and received from another person will provide models useful in nurturing yourself.

1. Please imagine or remember a scenario in which you give nurture to someone else: where you are comforting someone, helping, being kind, being understanding, being forgiving, giving support, being patient, giving approv-

al, or being a wise teacher. Write a description of that scenario. Include the thoughts and feelings as well as the visible behaviors.

2. Now please imagine or remember a scenario in which you are accepting nurture from someone else: where someone is comforting you, helping you, being kind, being understanding, being forgiving, giving support to you, being patient with you, giving approval, or being a wise teacher to you. Write a description of that scenario. Include the thoughts and feelings as well as the visible behaviors.

3. Now please imagine a scenario in which you nurture yourself: where you comfort yourself, help yourself, are kind and understanding with yourself, forgive yourself, support yourself, are patient with yourself, give approval to yourself, or function as a wise teacher to yourself. Include thoughts and feelings as before.

4. How vividly did you experience this exercise? How does that compare with how you did it in the past?

# References

Achenbach, T. M. (1982). Assessment and taxonomy of children's behavior disorders. In B. B. Lahey & A. E. Kazdin (Eds.), *Advances in clinical child psychology* (Vol. 5). New York: Plenum Press.

Achenbach, T. M., & Edelbrock, C. S. (1978). The classification of child psychopathology: A review and analysis of empirical efforts. *Psychological Bulletin, 85,* 1275–1301.

Alexander, J. R., & Parsons, B. V. (1973). Short-term behavioral intervention with delinquent families: Impact on family process and recidivism. *Journal of Abnormal Psychology, 81,* 219–225.

Allen, V. L. (Ed.). (1976). *Children as teachers: Theory and research on tutoring.* New York: Academic Press.

Alvord, M. K., & O'Leary, K. D. (1985). Teaching children to share through stories. *Psychology in the Schools, 22,* 323–330.

American Psychiatric Association. (1980). *Diagnostic and statistical manual of mental disorders* (3rd ed.). Washington, DC: Author.

American Psychiatric Association. (1987). *Diagnostic and statistical manual of mental disorders* (3rd ed.—Revised). Washington, DC: Author.

Anastasi, A. (1976). *Psychological testing* (3rd ed.). New York: Macmillan.

Arbuthnot, J., & Gordon, D.A. (1986). Behavioral and cognitive effects of a moral reasoning development intervention for high-risk behavior disordered adolescents. *Journal of Consulting and Clinical Psychology, 54,* 208–216.

Arnold, L. E. (1977). Prevention by specific perceptual remediation for vulnerable first-graders: Controlled study and follow-up of lasting effects. *Archives of General Psychiatry, 34,* 1279–1294.

Asch, S. E. (1955). Opinions and social pressure. In S. Coopersmith (Ed.), *Frontiers of psychological research.* San Francisco: Freeman.

August, G. J., & Stewart, M. A. (1983). Familial subtypes of childhood hyperactivity. *Journal of Nervous and Mental Disease, 171,* 362–368.

Axline, V. M. (1947). *Play therapy.* Boston: Houghton Mifflin.

Baar, M., & O'Connor, S. (1985). Relapse in alcoholism: New perspectives. *American Journal of Orthopsychiatry, 55,* 570–576.

Baer, D. M. & Wolf, M. M. (1970). The entry into natural communities of reinforcement. In R. Ulrich, T. Stachnik, & J. Mabry (Eds.), *Control of human behavior: From cure to prevention* (Vol. 2). Glenview, IL: Scott, Foresman.

Bandura, A. (1973). *Aggression: A social learning analysis.* Englewood Cliffs, NJ: Prentice-Hall.

Bandura, A. (1977). *Social learning theory.* Englewood Cliffs, NJ: Prentice-Hall.

Bandura, A., Grusec, J. E., & Menlove, F. L. (1966). Observational learning as a function of symbolization and incentive set. *Child Development, 37,* 499–506.

Bandura, A., & Menlove, F. L. (1968). Factors determining vicarious extinction of avoidance behavior through symbolic modeling. *Journal of Personality and Social Psychology, 8,* 99–108.

Barton, E. J. (1981). Developing sharing: An analysis of modeling and other behavioral techniques. *Behavior Modification, 5,* 386–398.

Beck, A. T. (1976). *Cognitive therapy and the emotional disorders.* New York: International University Press.

Beck, A. T., Rush, A. J., Shaw, B. F., & Emery, G. (1979). *Cognitive therapy of depression.* New York: Guilford Press.

Becker, W. C. (1971). *Parents are teachers: A child management program.* Champaign, IL: Research Press.

Behar, L., & Stringfield, S. (1974). A behavior rating scale for the preschool child. *Developmental Psychology, 10,* 601–610.

Benjamin, R., Mazzarins, H., & Kupfersmid, J. (1983). The effect of timeout (TO) duration on assaultiveness in psychiatrically hospitalized children. *Aggressive Behavior, 9,* 21–27.

Bellack, A. S., & Hersen, M. (1979). *Research and practice in social skills training.* New York: Plenum Press.

Berkowitz, L. (1970). Experimental investigations of hostility catharsis. *Journal of Consulting and Clinical Psychology, 35,* 1–7.

Berne, E. (1961). *Transactional analysis in psychotherapy.* New York: Grove Press.

Bernfeld, G. A., & Peters, R. D. (1986). Social reasoning and social behavior in reflective and impulsive children. *Journal of Clinical Child Psychology, 15,* 221–227.

Berrueta-Clement, J. R., Schweinhart, L. J., Barnett, W. S., Epstein, A. S., & Weikart, D. P. (1984). *Changed lives: The effects of the Perry Preschool Program on youths through age 19.* Ypsilanti, MI: High Scope Press.

Bettelheim, B. (1976). *The uses of enchantment: The meaning and importance of fairy tales.* New York: Knopf.

Biaggio, M. L. (1980). Anger arousal and personality characteristics. *Journal of Personality and Social Psychology, 39,* 352–356.

Biblow, E. (1973). Imaginative play and control of aggressive behavior. In J. L. Singer (Ed.), *The child's world of make-believe: Experimental studies of imaginative play.* New York: Academic Press.

Biglan, A., & Campbell, D. R. (1981). Depression. In J. L. Shelton & R. O. Levy (Eds.), *Behavioral assignments and treatment compliance: A handbook of clinical strategies.* Champaign, IL: Research Press.

Bijou, S. W., & Baer, D. M. (1961). *Child development: Vol. 1. A systematic and empirical theory.* New York: Appleton-Century-Crofts.

Bower, E. M. (1966). The achievement of competency. In *Learning and mental health in the school.* Alexandria, VA: Association for Supervision and Curriculum Development.

Bowlby, J. (1969–1980). *Attachment and loss* (3 vols.). London: Hogarth Press.

Brenner, C. (1955). *An elementary textbook of psychoanalysis.* Garden City, NY: Doubleday.

Bridgman, P. W. (1927). *The logic of modern physics.* New York: Macmillan.

Bronfenbrenner, U. (1974). Is early intervention effective? *Teachers College Record, 76,* 279–303.

Brown, J. L. (1960). Prognosis from presenting symptoms of preschool children with atypical development. *American Journal of Orthopsychiatry, 30,* 382–390.

Camp, B. W. (1977). Verbal mediation in young aggressive boys. *Journal of Abnormal Psychology, 86,* 145–153.

Camp, B. W., & Bash, M. A. S. (1981). *Think aloud: Increasing social and cognitive skills—a problem-solving program for children.* Champaign, IL: Research Press.

Camp, B. W., & Zimet, S. G. (1975). Classroom behavior during reading instruction. *Exceptional Children, 42,* 109–110.

Cantwell, D. (1977). Hyperkinetic syndrome. In M. Rutter & L. Hersov (Eds.), *Child psychiatry: Modern approaches.* Oxford: Blackwell Scientific.

Cantwell, D. P. (1982). Childhood depression: A review of current research. In B. B. Lahey & A. E. Kazdin (Eds.), *Advances in clinical child psychology*. (Vol. 5.). New York: Plenum Press.

Carberry, A. T., & Handal, P. J. (1980). The use of the AML scale with a Headstart population: Normative and validation studies. *American Journal of Community Psychology, 8*, 353–363.

Carter, J. L., & Russell, H. L. (1985). Use of EMG biofeedback procedures with learning disabled children in a clinical and an educational setting. *Journal of Learning Disabilities, 18*, 213–216.

Cautela, J., Flannery, R., & Hanley, E. (1974). Covert modeling: An experimental test. *Behavior Therapy, 5*, 494–502.

Chittenden, G. E. (1942). An experimental study in measuring and modifying assertive behavior in young children. *Monographs of the Society for Research in Child Development, 7*(1, Serial No. 31).

Christie, D. J., Hiss, M., & Lozanoff, B. (1984). Modification of inattentive classroom behavior: Hyperactive children's use of self-recording with teacher guidance. *Behavior Modification, 8*, 391–406.

Clarke, A. M., & Clarke, A. D. B. (1986). Thirty years of child psychology: A selective review. *Journal of Child Psychology and Psychiatry, 27*, 719–759.

Clarke, R. V. G. (1985). Jack Tizard Memorial Lecture: Delinquency, environment and intervention. *Journal of Child Psychology and Psychiatry, 26*, 505–523.

Clarke, R. V. G., & Cornish, D. R. (1978). The effectiveness of residential treatment for delinquents. In L. A. Hersov & M. Berger (Eds.), *Aggression and anti-social behavior in childhood and adolescence*. Oxford: Pergamon Press.

Coates, B., Pusser, H. E., & Goodman, I. (1976). The influence of "Sesame Street" and "Mister Rogers' Neighborhood" on children's social behavior in the preschool. *Child Development, 47*, 138–144.

Cohen, D. (1968). The effect of literature on vocabulary and reading achievement. *Elementary English, 45*, 209–217.

Cohn, A. H. (1979). Essential elements of successful child abuse and neglect treatment. *Child Abuse and Neglect, 3*, 491–496.

Comer, J. P. (1980). *School power: Implications of an intervention project*. New York: Free Press.

Conger, J. J., & Miller, W. C. (1966). *Personality, social class, and delinquency*. New York: Wiley.

Cowen, E. L. (1973). Social and community intervention. *Annual Review of Psychology, 24*, 423–472.

Cowen, E. L. (1984). Research on primary prevention interventions: A sampler of action programs. In S. E. Goldston & M. F. Shore (Eds.), *Primary prevention: An idea whose time is now*. Washington, DC: U.S. Government Printing Office.

Cowen, E. L., Dorr, D., Clarfield, S., Dreling, B., McWilliams, S. A., Pokracki, R., Pratt, D. M., Terrell, D., & Wilson, A. (1973). The AML: A quick screening device for early identification of school maladaptation. *American Journal of Community Psychology, 1*, 12–35.

Cowen, E. L., Dorr, D. A., Trost, M. A., & Izzo, L. D. (1972). Follow-up of maladapting school children seen by nonprofessionals. *Journal of Consulting and Clinical Psychology, 39*, 235–238.

Cowen, E. L., Weissberg, R. P., Lotyczewski, B. S., Bromley, M. L., Gilliland-Mallo, G., DeMeis, J. L., Farago, J. P., Grassi, R. J., Haffey, W. G., Weiner, M. J., & Woods, A. (1983). Validity generalization of a school-based preventive mental health program. *Professional Psychology: Research and Practice, 14*, 613–623.

Deluty, R. H. (1979). Children's Action Tendency Scale: A self-report measure of aggressiveness, assertiveness, and submissiveness in children. *Journal of Consulting and Clinical Psychology, 47*, 1061–1071.

Denkowski, K. I. M., & Denkowski, G. C. (1984). Is group progressive relaxation training as effective with hyperactive children as individual EMG biofeedback treatment? *Biofeedback and Self-Regulation, 9,* 353–364.

Deutsch, M. (1958). Trust and suspicion. *Journal of Conflict Resolution, 2,* 265–279.

Deutsch, M. (1960). The effect of motivational orientation upon trust and suspicion. *Human Relations, 13,* 123–139.

Dolliver, P., Lewis, A. F., & McLaughlin, T. F. (1985). Effects of a daily report card on academic performance and classroom behavior. *Remedial and Special Education, 6,* 51–52.

Durkin, D. (1966). *Children who read early.* New York: Teachers College Press.

Durlak, J. A. (1977). Description and evaluation of a behaviorally oriented school-based preventive mental health program. *Journal of consulting and Clinical Psychology, 45,* 27–33.

Durlak, J. A. (1979). Comparative effectiveness of paraprofessional and professional helpers. *Psychological Bulletin, 86,* 80–92.

Dyer, W. W. (1976). *Your erroneous zones.* New York: Funk & Wagnalls.

Ebbesen, E., Duncan, B., & Konecni, V. (1975). Effects of content of verbal aggression on future verbal aggression: A field experiment. *Journal of Experimental Social Psychology, 11,* 192–204.

Eisenberg, L., Landowne, J., Wilmer, M., & Iamber, D. (1962). The use of teacher ratings in a mental health study: A method for measuring the effectiveness of a therapeutic nursery program. *American Journal of Public Health, 62,* 18–28.

Ellis, A. (1977). The basic clinical theory of rational–emotive therapy. In A. Ellis & R. Grieger (Eds.), *Handbook of rational–emotive therapy.* New York: Springer.

Empey, L. T. (1982). *American delinquency: Its meaning and construction.* Homewood, IL: Dorsey Press.

Emrick, C., & Hansen, J. (1983). Assertions regarding effectiveness of treatment for alcoholism: Fact or fantasy? *American Psychologist, 38,* 1078–1088.

Erikson, E. H. (1950). *Childhood and society.* New York: Norton.

Eron, L. D. (1980). Prescription for reduction of aggression. *American Psychologist, 35,* 244–252.

Evers, W. L., & Schwarz, J. C. (1973). Modifying social withdrawal in preschoolers: The effects of filmed modeling and teacher praise. *Journal of Abnormal Child Psychology, 1,* 248–256.

Fein, G. G. (1979). Echoes for the nursery: Piaget, Vygotsky, and the relationship between language and play. In E. Winner & H. Gardner (Eds.), *New directions for child development* (Number 6). San Francisco: Jossey-Bass.

Feshbach, S. (1956). The catharsis hypothesis and some consequences of interaction with aggression and neutral play objects. *Journal of Personality, 24,* 449–462.

Feshbach, N. D., & Feshbach, S. (1982). Empathy training and the regulation of aggression: Potentialities and limitations. *Academic Psychology Bulletin, 4,* 399–413.

Fraiberg, S. (1967). The analysis of an eight-year-old girl with epilepsy. In E. R. Geleerd (Ed.), *The child analyst at work.* New York: International Universities Press.

Frankl, V. (1963). *Man's search for meaning.* Boston: Beacon Press.

Franklin, B. (1950). *The autobiography of Benjamin Franklin.* New York: Modern Library. (Quoted section written in 1784)

Freedman, J. L. (1984). Effect of television violence on aggressiveness. *Psychological Bulletin, 96,* 227–246.

Freedman, J. L. (1986). Television violence and aggression: A rejoinder. *Psychological Bulletin, 100,* 372–378.

Freud, A. (1946). *The psycho-analytical treatment of children: Technical lectures and essays.* London: Imago.

Freud, A. (1965). *Normality and pathology in childhood.* New York: International Universities Press.

Freud, S. (1953). Three essays on the theory of sexuality. In J. Strachey (Ed. and Trans.), *Standard edition of the complete psychological works of Sigmund Freud* (Vol. 7). London: Hogarth Press. (Original work published 1905)

Freud, S. (1958). Formulations regarding the two principles in mental functioning. In J. Strachey (Ed. and Trans.), *Standard edition of the complete psychological works of Sigmund Freud* (Vol. 12). London: Hogarth Press. (Original work published 1911)

Freyberg, J. T. (1973). Increasing the imaginative play of urban disadvantaged kindergarten children through systematic training. In J. L. Singer (Ed.), *The child's world of make-believe: Experimental studies of imaginative play.* New York: Academic Press.

Friedrich-Cofer, L., & Huston, A. C. (1986). Television violence and aggression: The debate continues. *Psychological Bulletin, 100,* 364–371.

Galef, B. G., Kennett, D. J., & Wigmore, S. W. (1984). Transfer of information concerning distant foods in rats: A robust phenomenon. *Animal Learning & Behavior, 12,* 292–296.

Gandhi, M. K. (1957). *An autobiography: The story of my experiments with truth.* Boston: Beacon Press. (Original work published 1927)

Gard, G. C., & Berry, K. K. (1986). Oppositional children: Taming tyrants. *Journal of Clinical Child Psychology, 15,* 148–158.

Gardner, R. A. (1971). *Therapeutic communication with children: A mutual storytelling technique.* New York: Science House.

Gardner, R. A. (1975). *Psychotherapeutic approaches to the resistant child.* New York: Jason Aronson.

Gardner, R. A. (1979). Helping children cooperate in therapy. In S. I. Harrison (Ed.). *Basic handbook of child psychiatry: Vol. 3. Therapeutic interventions.* New York: Basic Books.

Gardner, R. A. (1983). The talking, feeling, and doing game. In C. E. Schaefer & K. J. O'Connor (Eds.), *Handbook of play therapy.* New York: Wiley.

Garfield, P. L. (1974). *Creative dreaming.* New York: Ballantine Books.

Garmezy, N. (1984). Stress-resistant children: The search for protective factors. In J. E. Stevenson (Ed.), *Recent research in developmental psychopathology (Journal of Child Psychology and Psychiatry,* Book Supplement No. 4). Oxford: Pergamon Press.

Gelfand, D. M. (1962). The influence of self-esteem on rate of verbal conditioning and social matching behavior. *Journal of Abnormal and Social Psychology, 65,* 259–265.

Gerber, M., & Kauffman, J. M. (1981). Peer tutoring in academic settings. In P. S. Strain (Ed.), *The utilization of classroom peers as behavior change agents.* New York: Plenum Press.

Ginott, H. G. (1965). *Between parent and child: New solutions to old problems.* New York: Macmillan.

Gittelman, R. (1985). Anxiety disorders in children. In B. B. Lahey & A. E. Kazdin (Eds.), *Advances in clinical child psychology* (Vol. 8). New York: Plenum Press.

Goldstein, A. P. (1973). *Structured learning therapy: Toward a psychotherapy for the poor.* New York: Academic Press.

Goldstein, A. P. (1981). *Psychological skill training.* New York: Pergamon Press.

Goldstein, A. P., & Pentz, M. A. (1984). Psychological skill training and the aggressive adolescent. *School Psychology Review, 13,* 311–323.

Gordon, D. (1978). *Therapeutic metaphors: Helping others through the looking glass.* Cupertino, CA: META.

Gordon, T. (1970). *Parent effectiveness training: The tested new way to raise responsible children.* New York: Wyden.

Guerney, B. G. (1977). *Relationship enhancement: Skill-training programs for therapy, problem prevention, and enrichment.* San Francisco: Jossey-Bass.

Guerney, L. F. (1980). *Parenting: A skills training manual* (2nd ed.). State College, PA: Institute for the Development of Emotional and Life Skills.

Haley, J. (1973). *Uncommon therapy: The psychiatric techniques of Milton H. Erickson, M.D.* New York: Norton.

Harkness, F. (1981). Reading to children as a reading readiness activity. *Viewpoints in Teaching and Learning, 57,* 39–48.

Harris, F. R., Wolf, M. M., & Baer, D. M. (1967). Effects of adult social reinforcement on child behavior. In S. W. Bijou & D. M. Baer (Eds.), *Child development: Readings in experimental analysis.* New York: Appleton-Century-Crofts.

Hartley, R. (1986). Imagine you're clever. *Journal of Child Psychology and Psychiatry, 27,* 383–398.

Hartup, W. W. (1979). Peer relations and the growth of social competence. In M. W. Kent & J. E. Rolf (Eds.), *Primary prevention of psychopathology: Social competence in children.* Hanover, NH: University Press of New England.

Hartup, W. W., Glazer, J. A., & Charlesworth, R. (1967). Peer reinforcement and sociometric status. *Child Development, 38,* 1017–1024.

Harvey, J. H., & Weary, G. (1984). Current issues in attribution theory and research. *Annual Review of Psychology, 35,* 427–459.

Hawton, K., & Osborn, M. (1984). Suicide and attempted suicide in children and adolescents. In B. B. Lahey & A. E. Kazdin (Eds.), *Advances in clinical child psychology* (Vol. 7). New York: Plenum Press.

Hayakawa, S. I. (1978). *Language in thought and action* (4th ed.). New York: Harcourt Brace Jovanovich.

Hazaleus, S. L., & Deffenbacher, L. (1986). Relaxation and cognitive treatments of anger. *Journal of Consulting and Clinical Psychology, 54,* 222–226.

Henderson, M., & Furnham, A. (1983). Dimensions of assertiveness: Factor analysis of five assertion inventories. *Journal of Behavior Therapy and Experimental Psychiatry, 14,* 223–231.

Herbert, M. (1982). Conduct disorders. In B. B. Lahey & A. E. Kazdin (Eds.), *Advances in clinical child psychology* (Vol. 5). New York: Plenum Press.

Hersen, M., & Barlow, D. (1976). *Single-case experimental designs: Strategies for studying behavior change.* New York: Pergamon Press.

Hine, F. (1971). *Introduction to psychodynamics: A conflict-adaptational approach.* Durham, NC: Duke University Press.

Jason, L. A., Clarfield, S., & Cowen, E. L. (1973). Preventive intervention with young disadvantaged children. *American Journal of Community Psychology, 1,* 50–61.

Jason, L. A., Robson, S. D., & Lipshutz, S. A. (1980). Enhancing sharing behaviors through the use of naturalistic contingencies. *Journal of Community Psychology, 8,* 237–244.

Johnston, W. A., & Dark, V. J. (1986). Selective attention. *Annual Review of Psychology, 37,* 43–75.

Jorm, A. F., Share, D. L., Matthews, R., & Maclean, R. (1986). Behaviour problems in specific reading retarded and general reading backward children: A longitudinal study. *Journal of Child Psychology and Psychiatry, 27,* 33–43.

Kahn, M. (1966). The physiology of catharsis. *Journal of Personality and Social Psychology, 3,* 278–286.

Kanareff, V. T., & Lanzetta, J. T. (1960). Effects of success–failure experiences and probability of reinforcement upon the acquisition and extinction of an imitative response. *Psychological Reports, 7,* 151–166.

Kazdin, A. E. (1974a). Comparative effects of some variations of covert modeling. *Journal of Behavior Therapy and Experimental Psychiatry, 5,* 225–231.

Kazdin, A. E. (1974b). Covert modeling, model similarity, and reduction of avoidance behavior. *Behavior Therapy, 5*, 325–340.

Kazdin, A. E. (1974c). Effects of covert modeling and model reinforcement on assertive behavior. *Journal of Abnormal Psychology, 83*, 240–252.

Kazdin, A. E. (1974d). The effects of model identity and fear-relevant similarity on covert modeling. *Behavior Therapy, 5*, 624–635.

Kazdin, A. E. (1976). Effects of covert modeling, multiple models, and model reinforcement on assertive behavior. *Behavior Therapy, 7*, 211–222.

Kazdin, A. E. (1980). *Research design in clinical psychology.* New York: Harper & Row.

Keller, M. F., & Carlson, P. M. (1974). The use of symbolic modeling to promote social skills in preschool children with low levels of social responsiveness. *Child Development, 45*, 912–919.

Kendall, P. C. (1985). Behavioral assessment and methodology. In C. M. Franks, G. T. Wilson, P. C. Kendall, & K. D. Brownell, *Annual review of behavior therapy* (Vol. 10). New York: Guilford Press.

Kendall, P. C., & Braswell, L. (1985). *Cognitive–behavioral therapy for impulsive children.* New York: Guilford Press.

Kihlstrom, J. F. (1985). Hypnosis. *Annual Review of Psychology, 36*, 385–418.

Kirkland, K. D., & Thelen, M. H. (1977). Uses of modeling in child treatment. In B. B. Lahey & A. E. Kazdin (Eds.), *Advances in clinical child psychology* (Vol. 1). New York: Plenum Press.

Kohn, M. (1977). *Social competence, symptoms, and underachievement in childhood: A longitudinal perspective.* Washington, DC: Winston.

Korchin, S. J., Mitchell, H. E., & Meltzoff, J. (1950). A critical evaluation of the Thompson Thematic Apperception Test. *Journal of Projective Techniques, 14*, 445–452.

Korzybski, A. (1933). *Science and sanity: An introduction to non-Aristotelian systems and general semantics.* Lancaster, PA: Science Press.

Kreitman, N., & Schreiber, M. (1979). Parasuicide in young Edinburgh women, 1968–75. *Psychological Medicine, 9*, 469–479.

Labouvie, E. W., & McGee, C. R. (1986). Relation of personality to alcohol and drug use in adolescence. *Journal of Consulting and Clinical Psychology, 54*, 289–293.

Lakein, A. (1973). *How to get control of your time and your life.* New York: McKay. (Paperback: New American Library, Signet edition, 1974)

Lazarus, A. (1977). *In the mind's eye: The power of imagery for personal enrichment.* New York: Rawson Associations.

Lazarus, A., & Fay, A. (1975). *I can if I want to.* New York: Warner Books.

Lefcourt, H. (1982), *Locus of control: Current trends in theory and research* (2nd ed.). Hillsdale, NJ: Erlbaum.

Lee, D. Y., Hallberg, E. T., Slemon, A. G., & Haase, R. F. (1985). An assertiveness scale for adolescents. *Journal of Clinical Psychology, 41*, 51–57.

Levenstein, P. (1970). Cognitive growth in preschoolers through verbal interaction with mothers. *American Journal of Orthopsychiatry, 40*, 426–432.

Lewis, S. (1974). A comparison of behavior therapy techniques in the reduction of fearful avoidance behavior. *Behavior Therapy, 5*, 648–655.

Liebert, R. M., Sprafkin, J. N., & Davidson, E. S. (1982). *The early window: Effects of television on children and youth.* (2nd ed.). New York: Pergamon Press.

Linehan, M. M., & Egan, K. J. (1979). Assertion training for women. In A. S. Bellack & M. Hersen (Eds.), *Research and practice in social skills training.* New York: Plenum Press.

Loban, W. (1963). *The language of elementary school children.* Urbana, IL: National Council of Teachers of English.

Lobitz, G. K., & Johnson, S. M. (1975). Normal versus deviant children: A multimethod comparison. *Journal of Abnormal Child Psychology, 3,* 353–374.

Lobitz, W. C., & Johnson, S. M. (1975). Parental manipulation of the behavior of normal and deviant children. *Child Development, 46,* 719–726.

Luborsky, L., Singer, B., & Luborsky, L. (1975). Comparative studies of psychotherapies. *Archives of General Psychiatry, 32,* 995–1008.

Madsen, C. H., Becker, W. C., Thomas, D. R., Koser, L., & Plager, E. (1968). An analysis of the reinforcing function of "sit-down" commands. In R. K. Parker (Ed.), *Readings in educational psychology.* Boston: Allyn & Bacon.

Mahler, M., Pine, F., & Bergman, A. (1975). *The psychological birth of the human infant.* New York: Basic Books.

Mallick, S. K., & McCandless, B. R. (1966). A study of catharsis aggression. *Journal of Personality and Social Psychology, 4,* 591–596.

Marburg, C. C., Houston, B. K., & Holmes, D. S. (1976). Influence of multiple models on the behavior of institutionalized retarded children: Increased generalization to other models and other behaviors. *Journal of Consulting and Clinical Psychology, 44,* 514–519.

McCormick, S. (1981). Reading aloud to preschoolers age 3–6: A review of the research. *Research in Education.* (On microfiche; Accession Number ED199657)

McFall, R. M., & Twentyman, C. T. (1973). Four experiments on the relative contributions of rehearsal, modeling, and coaching to assertion training. *Journal of Abnormal Psychology, 81,* 199–218

Meichenbaum, D. H. (1971). Examination of model characteristics in reducing avoidance behavior. *Journal of Personality and Social Psychology, 17,* 298–307.

Meichenbaum, D. H. (1972). *Clinical implications of modifying what clients say to themselves* (Research Report No. 42). Waterloo, Ontario, Canada: University of Waterloo.

Meichenbaum, D. H. (1977). *Cognitive-behavior modification: An integrative approach.* New York: Plenum Press.

Meichenbaum, D. H., & Goodman, J. (1969). Reflection–impulsivity and verbal control of motor behavior. *Child Development, 40,* 785–797.

Meichenbaum, D. H., & Goodman, J. (1971). Training impulsive children to talk to themselves: A means for developing self-control. *Journal of Abnormal Psychology, 77,* 115–126.

Michelson, L., & Mannarino, A. (1986). Social skills training with children: Research and clinical application. In P. S. Strain, M. J. Guralnick, & H. M. Walker (Eds.), *Children's social behavior: Development, assessment, and modification.* New York: Academic Press.

Midlarsky, E., & Bryan, J. H. (1972). Affect expressions and children's imitative altruism. *Journal of Experimental Research in Personality, 6,* 195–203.

Miller, D. T., & Turnbull, W. (1986). Expectancies and interpersonal processes. *Annual Review of Psychology, 37,* 233–56.

Mineka, S., & Cook, M. (1986). Immunization against the observational conditioning of snake fear in rhesus monkeys. *Journal of Abnormal Psychology, 95,* 307–318.

Minuchin, S. (1974). *Families and family therapy.* Cambridge, MA: Harvard University Press.

Moustakas, C. E. (1959). *Psychotherapy with children: The living relationship.* New York: Harper & Row.

Mrazek, D., & Mrazek, P. (1985). Child maltreatment. In M. Rutter & L. Hersov (Eds.), *Child and adolescent psychiatry: Modern approaches* (2nd ed.). Oxford: Blackwell Scientific.

*National Coalition on Television Violence News.* (1986). Vol. 7, pp. 1–12. (Available from P.O. Box 2157, Champaign, IL 61820)

Newmark, G. (1976). *This school belongs to you and me.* New York: Hart.

Norman-Jackson, J. (1982). Family interactions, language development, and primary reading achievement of black children in families of low income. *Child Development, 53,* 349–358.

Novaco, R. W. (1975). *Anger control.* Lexington, MA: Heath.

O'Connor, R. D. (1969). Modification of social withdrawal through symbolic modeling. *Journal of Applied Behavior Analysis, 2* 15–22.

O'Connor, R. D. (1972). Relative efficacy of modeling, shaping, and the combined procedures for modification of social withdrawal. *Journal of Abnormal Psychology, 79,* 327–334.

Oden, S., & Asher, S. R. (1977). Coaching children in social skills for friendship making. *Child Development, 48,* 495–506.

O'Leary, K. D., Poulos, R. W., & Devine, V. T. (1972). Tangible reinforcers: Bonuses or bribes? *Journal of Consulting and Clinical Psychology, 38,* 1–8.

Patterson, G. R. (Producer). (1982). *Time out* [Videotape]. Eugene, OR: Northwest Family and School Corporation.

Patterson, G. R., & Fleischman, M. J. (1979). Maintenance of treatment effects: Some considerations concerning family systems and follow-up data. *Behavior Therapy, 10,* 168–185.

Patterson, G. R., & Forgatch, M. (Producers). (1975). *Family living series* [Audiotapes]. Champaign, IL: Research Press.

Patterson, G. R., Littman, R. A., & Bricker, W. (1967). Assertive behavior in children: A step toward a theory of aggression. *Monographs of the Society for Research in Child Development, 32* (5, Serial No. 113).

Paul, G. L. (1967). Strategies of outcome research in psychotherapy. *Journal of Consulting Psychology, 31,* 109–118.

Pearl, D., Bouthilety, L., & Lazar, J. (1982). *Television and behavior: Ten years of scientific progress and implications for the eighties.* Rockville, MD: National Institute of Mental Health.

Pellegrini, D. S. (1985). Training in social problem-solving. In M. Rutter & L. Hersov (Eds.), *Child and adolescent psychiatry: Modern approaches.* Oxford: Blackwell Scientific.

Phares, E. (1976). *Locus of control in personality.* Morristown, NJ: General Learning Press.

Puig-Antich, J., Perel, J. M., Lupatkin, W., Chambers, W. J., Tabrizi, M. A., King, J., Goetz, R., Davies, M., & Stiller, R. L.. (1987). Imipramine in prepubertal major depressive disorders. *Archives of General Psychiatry, 44,* 81–89.

Pulaski, M. A. (1973). Toys and imaginative play. In J. L. Singer (Ed.), *The child's world of make-believe: Experimental studies of imaginative play.* New York: Academic Press.

Putallaz, M., & Gottman, J. (1983). Social relationship problems in children: An approach to intervention. In B. B. Lahey & A. E. Kazdin (Ed.), *Advances in clinical child psychology* (Vol. 6). New York: Plenum Press.

Rapport, M. D. (1987). Attention deficit disorder with hyperactivity. In M. Hersen & V. B. Van Hasselt (Ed.), *Behavior therapy with children and adolescents: A clinical approach.* New York: Wiley

Rausch, H. L., Barry, W. A., Hertel, R. K., & Swain, M. A. (1974). *Communication, conflict, and marriage.* San Francisco: Jossey-Bass.

Reiter, S. M., Mabee, W. S., & McLaughlin, T. F. (1985). Self-monitoring: Effects for on-task and time to complete assignments. *Remedial and Special Education, 6,* 50–51.

Rennie, D. L., & Thelen, M. H. (1976). Generalized imitation as a function of instructional set and social reinforcement. *JSAS Catalog of Selected Documents in Psychology, 6,* 107–108. (Ms. No. 1360)

Research Press. (Producer). (1983). *Parents and children: A positive approach to child management* [Videotape]. Champaign, IL: Producer.

Rickel, A. U., & Lampi, L. (1981). A two-year follow-up study of a preventive mental health program for preschoolers. *Journal of Abnormal Child Psychology, 9,* 455–464.

Rickel, A. U., & Smith, R. L. (1979). Maladapting preschool children: Identification, diagnosis, and remediation. *American Journal of Community Psychology, 7,* 197–208.

Rickel, A. U., Smith, R. L., & Sharp, K. C. (1979). Description and evaluation of a preventive mental health program for preschoolers. *Journal of Abnormal Child Psychology, 7,* 101–112.

Roberts, M. C., & Peterson, L. (1984). *Prevention of problems in childhood: Psychological research and applications.* New York: Wiley.

Robins, L. N. (1966). *Deviant children grown up.* Baltimore: Williams & Wilkins.

Robins, L. N., & Helzer, J. E. (1986). Diagnosis and clinical assessment: The current state of psychiatric diagnosis. *Annual Review of Psychology, 37,* 409–432.

Rosen, C. E. (1974). The effects of sociodramatic play on problem-solving behavior among culturally disadvantaged preschool children. *Child Development, 45,* 920–927.

Rosenthal, R., & Jacobson, L. (1968). *Pygmalion in the classroom.* New York: Holt, Rinehart & Winston.

Rosenthal, R., & Rubin, D. B. (1978). Interpersonal expectancy effects: The first 345 studies. *Behavioral and Brain Sciences, 3,* 377–415.

Ross, L. (1977) The intuitive psychologist and his shortcomings: Distortions in the attribution process. In L. Berkowitz (Ed.), *Advances in experimental social psychology* (Vol. 10). New York: Academic Press.

Rotheram, M. J., Armstrong, M., & Booraem, C. (1982). Assertiveness training in fourth- and fifth-grade children. *American Journal of Community Psychology, 10,* 567–582.

Rushton, J. P. (1975). Generosity in children: Immediate and long-term effects of modeling, preaching, and moral judgment. *Journal of Personality and Social Psychology, 31,* 459–466.

Rutter, M. (1967). Classification and categorization in child psychology. *International Journal of Psychiatry, 3,* 161–172.

Rutter, M. (1977). Individual differences. In M. Rutter & L. Hersov (Eds.), *Child psychiatry: Modern approaches.* Oxford: Blackwell Scientfic.

Rutter, M. (1982). Prevention of children's psychosocial disorders: Myth and substance. *Pediatrics, 70,* 883–894.

Rutter, M., Tizard, J., Yule, W., Graham, P., & Whitmore, K. (1976). Research report: Isle of Wight studies 1964–1974. *Psychological Medicine, 6,* 313–332.

Rutter, M., & Yule, W. (1977). Reading difficulties. In M. Rutter & L. Hersov (Eds.), *Child psychiatry: Modern approaches.* Oxford: Blackwell Scientific.

Sacco, W. P., & Graves, D. J. (1984). Childhood depression, interpersonal problem-solving, and self-ratings of performance. *Journal of Clinical Child Psychology, 13,* 10–15.

Sarason, I. G., & Sarason, B. R. (1981). Teaching cognitive and social skills to high school students. *Journal of Consulting and Clinical Psychology, 49,* 908–918.

Schwartz, R. M., & Garamoni, G. L. (1986). A structural model of positive and negative states of mind: Asymmetry in the internal dialogue. In P. C. Kendall (Ed.), *Advances in cognitive behavioral research and therapy.* New York: Academic Press.

Selman, R. L. (1980). *The growth of interpersonal understanding: Developmental and clinical analyses.* New York: Academic Press.

Selman, R. L., & Byrne, D. (1974). A structural–developmental analysis of levels of role-taking in middle childhood. *Child Development, 45,* 803–806.

Selman, R. L., Jaquette, D., & Lavin, R. (1977). Interpersonal awareness in children: Toward an integration of developmental and clinical child psychology. *American Journal of Orthopsychiatry, 47,* 264–274.

Shaffer, D. (1985). Depression, mania, and suicidal acts. In M. Rutter & L. Hersov (Eds.), *Child and adolescent psychiatry: Modern approaches.* Oxford: Blackwell Scientific.

Shamsie, S. J. (1981). Antisocial adolescents: Our treatments do not work—Where do we go from here? *Canadian Journal of Psychiatry, 26,* 357–364.

Simonton, O. C., Matthews-Simonton, S., & Creighton, J. (1978). *Getting well again.* Los Angeles: Tarcher.

Singer, J. L. (Ed.). (1973). *The child's world of make-believe: Experimental studies of imaginative play.* New York: Academic Press.

Singer, J. L. (1974). *Imagery and daydream methods in psychotherapy and behavior modification.* New York: Academic Press.

Singer, J. L., & Singer, D. G. (1983). Psychologists look at television: Cognitive, developmental, personality, and social policy implications. *American Psychologist, 38,* 826–834.

Singer, J. L., & Singer, D. G. (1985). Television-viewing and family communication style as predictors of children's emotional behavior. *Journal of Children in Contemporary Society, 17*(4), 75–91.

Skinner, B. F. (1953). *Science and human behavior.* New York: Free Press.

Smilansky, S. (1968). *The effects of sociodramatic play on disadvantaged preschool children.* New York: Wiley.

Smith, H. (1958). *The religions of man.* New York: Harper & Row.

Snyder, W. U. (1947). *Casebook of non-directive counseling.* Boston: Houghton Mifflin.

Spivack, G., Platt, J., & Shure, M. (1976). *The problem-solving approach to adjustment.* San Francisco: Jossey-Bass.

Spivack, G., & Shure, M. (1974). *Social adjustment of young children: A cognitive approach to solving real-life problems.* San Francisco: Jossey-Bass.

Staub, E. (1971). The use of role playing and induction in children's learning of helping and sharing behavior. *Child Development, 42,* 805–816.

Staub, E. (1978). *Positive social behavior and morality: Vol. 1. Social and personal influences.* New York: Academic Press.

Staub, E. (1979). *Positive social behavior and morality: Vol. 2. Socialization and development.* New York: Academic Press.

Steinfatt, T. M., & Miller, G. R. (1974). Communication in game theoretic models of conflict. In G. R. Miller & H. W. Simons (Eds.), *Perspectives on communication in social conflict.* Englewood Cliffs, NJ: Prentice-Hall.

Stokes, T. F., & Baer, D. M. (1977). An implicit technology of generalization. *Journal of Applied Behavior Analysis, 10,* 349–367.

Stokes, T. F., & Osnes, P. G. (1986). Programming the generalization of children's social behavior. In P. S. Strain, M. J. Guralnick, & H. M. Walker (Eds.), *Children's social behavior: Development, and modification.* New York: Academic Press.

Strain, P. S., Shores, R. E., & Timm, M. A. (1977). Effects of peer initiations on the social behavior of withdrawn preschool children. *Journal of Applied Behavior Analysis, 10,* 289–298.

Strain, P. S., Steele, P., Ellis, T., & Timm, M. A. (1982). Long-term effects of oppositional child treatment with mothers as therapists and therapist trainers. *Journal of Applied Behavior Analysis, 15,* 163–169.

Strang, J., & Connell, P. (1985). Clinical aspects of drug and alcohol abuse. In M. Rutter & L. Hersov (Eds.), *Child and adolescent psychiatry: Modern approaches* (2nd. ed.). Oxford: Blackwell Scientific.

Straus, M. (1974). Leveling, civility, and violence in the family. *Journal of Marriage and the Family, 36,* 13–29.

Strauss, C. C. (1987). Anxiety. In M. Hersen & V. B. Van Hasselt (Eds.), *Behavior therapy with children and adolescents: A clinical approach.* New York: Wiley.

Strayhorn, J. M. (1982). *Foundations of clinical psychiatry*. Chicago: Year Book Medical.

Strayhorn, J. M. (1983). A diagnostic axis relevant to psychotherapy and preventive mental health. *American Journal of Orthopsychiatry, 53,* 677–696.

Strayhorn, J. M. (Producer). (1984). *Building psychological skills in preschoolers through stories and dramatic play* [videotape]. Pittsburgh: Western Psychiatric Institute and Clinic.

Strayhorn, J. M., & Rhodes, L. A. (1985). The shaping game: A teaching tool. *The Pointer, 29,* 8–11.

Strayhorn, J. M., & Strain, P. S. (1986). Social and language skills for preventive mental health: What, how, who, and when. In P. S. Strain, M. J. Guralnick, & H. M. Walker (Eds.), *Children's social behavior: Development, assessment, and modification.* New York: Academic Press.

Suinn, R. M. (1972). Behavior rehearsal training for ski racers. *Behavior Therapy, 3,* 519–520.

Sutton-Smith, B. (1979). Presentation and representation in fictional narrative. In E. Winner & H. Gardner (Eds.), *Fact, fiction, and fantasy in childhood.* San Francisco: Jossey-Bass.

Tavris, C. (1982). *Anger: The misunderstood emotion.* New York: Simon & Schuster.

Taylor, E. (1985). Drug treatment. In M. Rutter & L. Hersov (Eds.), *Child and adolescent psychiatry: Modern approaches.* Oxford: Blackwell Scientific.

Thomas, D. R., Becker, W. C., & Armstrong, M. (1968). Production and elimination of disruptive classroom behavior by systematically varying teacher's behavior. *Journal of Applied Behavior Analysis, 1,* 35–45.

Thomas, G. M. (1974). Using videotaped modeling to increase attending behavior. *Elementary School Guidance and Counseling, 9,* 35–40.

Tiffen, K., & Spence, S. H. (1986). Responsiveness of isolated versus rejected children to social skills training. *Journal of Child Psychology and Psychiatry, 27,* 343–355.

Turner, C. W., & Goldsmith, D. (1976). Effects of toy guns and airplanes on children's antisocial free play behavior. *Journal of Experimental Child Psychology, 21,* 303–315.

Twardosz, S. & Nordquist, V. M. (1983). The development and importance of affection. In B. B. Lahey & A. E. Kazdin (Eds.), *Advances in clinical child psychology* (Vol. 6). New York: Plenum Press.

Twardosz, S., & Nordquist, V. M. (1987). Parent training. In M. Hersen & V. B. Van Hasselt (Eds.), *Behavior therapy with children and adolescents: A clinical approach.* New York: Wiley.

Uhlenberg, P., & Eggebeen, D. (1986). The declining well-being of American adolescents. *The Public Interest, 82,* 25–38.

Urbain, E. & Kendall, P. (1980). Review of social-cognitive problem-solving interventions with children. *Psychological Bulletin, 88,* 109–143.

Vaillant, G., Clark, W., Cyrus, C., Milofsky, E. S., Kopp, J., Wulsin, V. W., & Mogielnicki, N. P. (1983). Prospective study of alcoholism treatment: Eight year follow-up. *American Journal of Medicine, 75,* 455–463.

Vogelsong, E. L., Most, R. K., & Yanchko, A. (1979). Relationship enhancement training for preadolescents in public schools. *Journal of Clinical Child Psychology, 8,* 97–100.

Vygotsky, L. (1962). *Thought and language.* New York: Wiley.

Wahler, R. G., Winkel, G. H., Peterson, R. T., & Morrison, D. C. (1965). Mothers as behaviour therapists for their own children. *Behaviour Research and Therapy, 3,* 113–134.

Webster–Stratton, C. (Producer). (1984). *Parents and children: III. The art of effective praising* [Videotape]. Chapel Hill, NC: Health Sciences Consortium.

Weissberg, R. P., Gesten, E. L., Rapkin, B. D., Cowen, E. L., Davidson, E., Flores De

Apodaca, R., & McKim, B. (1981). Evaluation of a social problem-solving training program for suburban and inner-city third-grade children. *Journal of Consulting and Clinical Psychology, 49,* 251–261.

Weissberg, R. P., Cowen, E. L., Lotyczewski, B. S., & Gesten, E. L. (1983). The Primary Mental Health Project: Seven consecutive years of program outcome research. *Journal of Consulting and Clinical Psychology, 51,* 100–107.

West, D. J., & Farrington, D. P. (1973). *Who becomes delinquent?* London: Heinemann.

White, B. L. (1975). *The first three years of life.* Englewood Cliffs, NJ: Prentice-Hall.

Williamson, D. A., McKenzie, S. J., Goreczny, A. J. & Faulstich, M. (1987). Psychophysiological disorders. In M. Hersen & V. B. Van Hasselt (Eds.), *Behavior therapy with children and adolescents: A clinical approach.* New York: Wiley.

Winston, S. (1978). *Getting organized: The easy way to put your life in order.* New York: Warner Books.

Wolff, S. (1977). Nondelinquent disturbances of conduct. In M. L. Rutter & L. A. Hersov (Eds.), *Child psychiatry: Modern approaches.* Oxford: Blackwell Scientific.

Wolfgang, M. E. (1983). Delinquency in two birth cohorts. *American Behavioral Scientist, 27,* 75–86.

Yarrow, M. R., & Scott, P. M. (1972). Imitation of nurturant and nonnurturant models. *Journal of Personality and Social Psychology, 8,* 240–261.

Yu, P., Harris, G. E., Solovitz, B. L., & Franklin, J. L. (1986). A social problem-solving intervention for children at high risk for later psychopathology. *Journal of Clinical Child Psychology, 15,* 30–40.

# Index

Ability versus motivation, skills axis in diagnosis, 49, 50
Absence seizures, epilepsy, 7
Abstraction ladder, 24–26, 48
  skills-oriented contingency programs, 62–65
  with young children, 108, 109
Acting out
  aggression, 88–90
  situations game, 154
Adjunctive instructions, 91
Admiration, expressing, fantasy practice, 274
Adolescents. *See* Techniques for adolescents and older individuals
Aggression, acting out, 88–90
Aggressive conduct, 200, 203
Aloneness, fantasy practice, 275
AML scale, 220
Anger, 31–33
Animal studies of modeling, 87
Antidepressants, 202
Assertion skills, 32
  fantasy practice, samples, 276
  increasing parents' psychological competences, 189
  skills axis in diagnosis, 54
  stories, sample, 261
Attachment, 27, 28, 30, 31
  fantasy practice, sample situations, 273
  increasing parents' psychological competences, 187
Attention-deficit disorder, 37
Attention, reinforcing power, methods axis, 98–100
Attributions, methods axis, 103, 104
Attribution theory, 104
Audiotapes, 67, 92, 183, 185
Awfulizing (Ellis), 33, 34, 84, 277

Baar, M., 201
Banham Test, 197

Beck, A., 36
Behavioral parent training, 195
Behavior rehearsal, 94
Bettelheim, Bruno, 137
Biblow, E., 138
Biological theories, 13, 14, 106
Bossiness
  older children, 147
  stories, sample, 261, 262
Bronfenbrenner, U., 194

Case illustrations, skills × methods matrix, 3–10
Catharsis, 16–19, 39, 240
Cattell Intelligence Test, 195
Celebration, 29, 35, 36
  and adult sexuality, 36
  exercises, 284
  techniques for older children, 142, 146, 147
Change, identification of, 57
Chatting, 227
  exercises, 177–179, 188
  techniques for young children, 111–114
Child abuse, 201
Child-proofing and emotional environment, 96
Clarke, R. V. G., 209
Commands and Suggestions Exercise, 175–177, 189
Commitment skills, 27, 28, 30, 31
  fantasy practice, sample situations, 273
  increasing parents' psychological competences, 187
Competence-based approach, 2, 3
Competence-enhancing culture, 233, 234
  research questions, 250–252
Competence orientations, alternatives, 14–19

Competent patterns, data bases and downloading, preventive mental health, 232–235, 251, 252

Compliance, sample stories, 264, 265

Conceptual sharpening exercises, 84
 availability, 253n
 older children, 145, 146
 samples, 277–280

Conciliation, fantasy practice, sample situations, 276

Conflict resolution skills, 28, 31–33
 fantasy practice, sample situations, 275
 increasing parents' psychological competences, 188, 189
 modeling plays, sample, 271, 272
 stories, sample, 260

Connell, P., 201

Contaminating child's fantasies, techniques for young children, 110

Contingency. See Skills-oriented contingency programs

Contracted version, skills axis, 42, 43

Conversation
 increasing parents' psychological competences, 188
 techniques for adolescents and older individuals, 158–160

Cost of preventive programs, 215, 217

Covert modeling, 94

Covert rehearsal, 94

Criticism
 fantasy practice, sample situations, 275
 sample stories, 259, 260


Danger of preventive programs, 215, 216

Data bases, 232–235, 251, 253n

Decision-making, psychological skill building, exercises, 284, 285

Delayed gratification skills, 29, 36–38

Delinquency, 37, 204, 219

Dependence skills, 22, 28, 30, 31
 fantasy practice, sample situations, 273
 increasing parents' psychological competences, 187

Depressed children, 201, 202

Deutsch, M., 152

Development
 research questions, 242, 243

and skills axis, 27

and skills × methods matrix, 12

Diagnostic advantages over DSM-III, 23–26; see also Skills axis in diagnosis

Diet, changes in, compare with preventive mental health, 216

Dilution effects, 235, 238
 positive outcomes, difficulty of achieving, 203, 204
 research questions, 249, 250, 252

Direction and purpose skills, 29, 41
 role models, 41

Disapproval
 fantasy practice, sample situations, 275
 stories, sample, 259, 260

Displacement of painful feelings, alternative to competence orientation, 16–19

Dramatic play, jointly created, 111, 124–134
 ending, 132, 133
 fun/productivity balance, 127
 involving child in, 124, 125, 131
 monitoring and self-monitoring, 132
 plot creation by therapist, 125
  skills-oriented choices, 128–132, 134
 undesirable behavior/violence, 126, 127, 133, 134

Dramatic play, older children, 143, 156, 157

Dreams, revision in waking fantasy, adolescents and older individuals, 162, 163

Dropouts, 219

Drug/alcohol abuse, 201, 203

DSM-III, 21–23, 37, 47
 Revised, 22

Durlak, J. A., 194, 220, 221


Effectiveness, modeling, 90–92

Empathy, 39
 fantasy practice, sample situations, 274
 in listening, increasing parents' psychological competences, 188

Enculturation, 234, 238

Epilepsy, absence seizures, 7

Erickson, Milton, 160, 161

Erikson, Erik, 31, 137

Extinction curve, upward blip, 133, 134, 247
Extratherapeutic influences, 204, 208–212, 215

Fading versus continuing skills-oriented contingency programs, 80, 81
Failure, sample stories, 262–264
Family
    preventive mental health, 226, 230
    situations game, 154
    skills axis in diagnosis, 54–56
    see also Parent(s); Training parents and others; Skills-oriented contingency programs, parents
Fantasy, 34, 35, 40
    methods axis, 93–95
    practice, preventive mental health, 226, 228
        abstraction ladder, 108, 109
    rehearsal, adolescents and older individuals, 161, 162
    repertoire, skills axis in diagnosis, 50, 51
    young children, 111, 134–136
        contaminating, 110
        orientation of child, 138
Fantasy practice, sample situations, 272–277
Fear reduction, modeling, 87
Feedback and review, skills-oriented contingency programs, 69, 70
Fein, G. G., 137
Fiction, 4, 5, 9
Film, social skills training, 87, 88
Flight or fight response, 97
Following-up young children, 112, 113
Fortitude-building exercises, 285
Fraiberg, Selma, 6, 7
Franklin, Benjamin, 69, 70
Freud, Anna, 5, 6, 12
Freud, Sigmund, 31
Freyberg, J. T., 138
Frustration tolerance, 28, 29, 33–35
    increasing parents' psychological competence, 192
    stories, sample, 262
Fun/productivity balance, dramatic play, 127

Gandhi, Mohandas, 158
Gardner, Richard, 8, 20, 122, 136, 137, 154, 155

Gathering information, skills axis in diagnosis, 47–49
Gittelman, R., 201
Global ratings versus frequency counts, skills-oriented contingency programs, 72
Goal rehearsal, 94
Goal setting, 6, 83–86
    persuasion, 84, 85
    psychological skill building, exercises, 283, 284
Gordon, D., 159
Grade-school children. See Techniques for older (grade-school age) children
Gratitude, expressing, fantasy practice, sample, 274
Group approval, methods axis, 101, 102
Group methods, preventive programs, 215, 217, 218
Guided imagery, adolescents and older individuals, 160, 162

Hahnemann Medical College, 219
Harris, F. R., 75
Hawten, K., 201
Hayakawa, S. I., 24, 25
Helping, centrality of, skills axis, 43, 44
Herbert, M., 200
Hierarchy, forming, methods axis, 86, 87
Home versus school problems, skills-oriented contingency programs, 81
Honesty, sample stories, 265, 266
Hostility to child, parents, 191, 193, 194
How-to-think versus what-to-do, 58
Hypnosis and guided imagery, adolescents, 160–162

Ignoring undesirable behaviors, 77, 99, 100
Imaginal rehearsal, techniques for young children, 111, 134–136
Independence, fantasy practice, sample situations, 275
Information transfer, methods axis, 97, 102, 103
Inner guide technique, 164, 247, 280–283
Insight-oriented therapy, 6, 83, 166

Instructions
  adjunctive, 91
  providing, methods axis, 92, 93
Interactions, reciprocal, young children,
  113, 114
Interpersonal conflict skills, 28, 31–33
  fantasy practice, sample situations,
    276
  modeling plays, sample, 271, 272
Intervention
  in community settings, 214, 215
  peer-mediated, 225, 227
  teacher-mediated, 225–227
Interviewing techniques, 48, 49

Juvenile delinquents, 37, 204, 219

Kindness
  sample plays, 268–270
  sample stories, 264

Lancasta, Joseph, 196
Learning-based problems/treatment, 2,
  13, 14, 106
Listening, empathic, increasing parents'
  psychological competences, 188
Losing, sample modeling plays, 272
Low-income children, 138, 139, 194,
  217

Malaysia, Senoi tribe, 162
Mastery (Beck), 36
Masturbation, 7, 8
Matrix, skills × methods, 1–20
  case illustrations, 3–10
  competence-based approach, 2, 3
  competence orientations, alternatives,
    14–19
  developmental theory and, 12
  as emerging method in mental health
    field, 19, 20
  as general framework for mental
    health promotion, 104–106
  learning-based problems/treatment, 2,
    13, 14, 106
  methods of inference, defined, 1
  preventive intervention. See Pre-
    ventive mental health
  psychological skills, defined, 1
  psychopathology, hypotheses about,
    11, 12
  psychotherapy strategies and, 10, 11
  theory structure, 2, 3
  see also Methods axis; Skills axis entries

McGuffey's Readers, 228
Media, preventive mental health, 226,
  230, 231
Mental rehearsal, skills axis, diagnostic
  advantages over DSM-III, 23, 24
Methods axis, 3, 10, 82–104, 184
  attributions, 103, 104
    dishonest, 104
  consequences, controlling or com-
    municating, 98–103
    attention, reinforcing power, 98–
      100
    ignoring as nonreward, 99, 100
    reinforcement contingencies,
      effectiveness, 100–102
  fantasy and role-playing, 93–95
  goal setting, 83–86
    persuasion, 84, 85
  hierarchy, forming, 86, 87
  information transfer, 97, 102, 103
  instruction, providing, 92, 93
  modeling, 87–92; see also Modeling
    entries
  practice opportunities, providing, 93–95
  progress, monitoring, 97, 98
  research questions, 245–252
  stimulus situations, controlling, 95–97
  see also Techniques entries
Mistakes/failures, stories, sample, 262–
  264
Mister Rogers' Neighborhood, 89
Modeling, 87–92
  adolescents/older individuals
    conversation, 158–160
    stories, 157, 158
  animal studies of, 87
  effectiveness, 90–92
  literature on, 87–90
Modeling plays
  older children, 142, 146
  parent training, 180, 181
  preventive mental health, 225, 226
  young children, 111
    creating, 111, 120
    performing, 118–120, 124–134
Modeling plays, sample, 268–272
  conflict, 271, 272
  kindness/nurturing, 268–270
  separation, 270, 271
  winning/losing, 272
Modeling, real-life, generalizing parent
  training to home interaction, 185
Modeling stories. See Stories entries

Monitoring
    dramatic play, jointly created, 132
    skills-oriented contingency programs,
        70
Motivation
    versus ability, 49, 50
    lacking of, in parents, 193, 194
Mrazek, D., 201
Mrazek, P., 201
Multiskills approach
    positive outcomes, difficulty of
        achieving, 206, 207, 214
    research questions, 252
Mutual storytelling, 8


Negative cognitions, older children,
    145, 146
Negotiation, fantasy practice, sample
    situations, 276
Negotiation skills, 205, 206; see also
    Conflict resolution skills
Nondirective play therapy, 122
Nonpejorativeness, skills axis, diagnostic
    advantages over DSM-III, 23, 24
Nurturing skills
    fantasy practice, sample situations,
        273, 274
    increasing parents' psychological com-
        petences, 187
    modeling plays, sample, 268–270
    stories, sample, 256, 257
    see also Self-nurturing skills


Objections and responses, preventive
    mental health, 215–218
O'Connor, S., 201
Oedipal conflicts, 34
Organization skills, 40
    increasing parents' psychological com-
        petence, 192, 193
Osborn, M., 201
Outcome. See Positive outcomes,
    difficulty of achieving


Painful feelings, displacement of,
    alternative to competence
    orientation, 16–19
Paraphrasing, 112, 113, 178
Parent(s)
    helping recognize trigger situations,
        67, 68

hostility to child, 191, 193, 194
level of demands on, 70, 71
modeling plays, older children, 120
performance anxiety, 193
preparing for reinforcement, 66, 67
    tapes, 67, 92
reinforcement, 78, 80
    telephone, 80
story reading practice, 180
summary suggestions, 253, 254
see also Skills-oriented contingency
    programs; Training parents and
    others
Parent–child relationship, centrality of
    mutual gratification, 170, 171
Parent training. See Training parents
    and others
Peabody Picture Vocabulary Test, 140
Peer(s)
    and generalizing parent training to
        home interaction, 184, 185
    -mediated interventions, preventive
        mental health, 225, 227
    pressure, 167, 168
    tutoring, 196
Performance anxiety, parents, 193
Performance monitoring, training par-
    ents and others, 182–184
Piaget, Jean, 12
Picture–story game, techniques for old-
    er children, 143, 155, 156
Play
    dramatic. See Dramatic play entries
    therapy, nondirective, 122
    tracking and describing, 227
Plays, modeling. See Modeling plays
    entries
Pleasure principle, 36, 38
Plot creation by therapist, dramatic
    play, jointly created, 125
    skills-oriented choices, 128–132, 134
Positive behavior, recognizing and
    praising, increasing parents' psy-
    chological competences, 190–192
Positive model, compare with positive
    reinforcer, explaining to parents,
    174
Positive outcomes, difficulty of achiev-
    ing, 199–212
    dilution effects, 203, 204, 235, 238
    multiskill approaches, 206, 207, 214
    remedies for, 206–208, 210–212
    research questions, 249, 250, 252

Positive outcomes (continued)
    too many extratherapeutic in-
        fluences, 204, 208–212, 215
    too many skills, 203–208, 214, 225
    frequency, 200–203
Practice opportunities, providing,
    methods axis, 93–95
Praise
    avoiding, methods axis, 101
    fantasy practice, sample situations,
        277
    increasing parents' psychological com-
        petences, 190–192
Prevalence and correlates of skill pro-
    files, research questions, 241, 242
Preventive mental health, 12, 13, 213–
    235
    compare with changes in diet, 216
    competent patterns, data bases and
        downloading, 232–235
    hazards, 215
    intervention in community settings,
        214, 215
    literature, 218–221
    objections, responses to, 215–218
    programs, 222–225
    research questions, 250
    target groups, 223, 224
    work in progress, 225–231
Primary Mental Health Project, Univer-
    sity of Rochester, 218
Prisoner's dilemma game, 143, 151,
    152, 247
Procrastination, 40
Professional, compare with non-
    professional influence provision,
    research questions, 248, 249
Progress, monitoring, methods axis, 97,
    98
"Prompt, wait, and hurry," 113, 114,
    125, 173, 181
Props, 118, 119, 124, 128–130
Psychodrama, adolescents and older in-
    dividuals, 167, 168
Psychological competence, increasing
    skills in parents, 186–193
Psychological skill building exercises,
    283–286
    celebration, 284
    decision-making, 284, 285
    fortitude-building, 285
    goal-setting, 283, 284
    self-nurture, 285, 286

Psychological skills, defined, 1
Psychological Skills Inventory, 51–53,
    241
Psychopathology, hypotheses about, 11,
    12
Punishment
    methods axis, compare with instruc-
        tion, 93
    time-out, skills-oriented contingency
        programs, 77
Puppets, older children, 146
Pygmalion effect, 104

Reading
    older children, 143
    young children, 116, 117
        promoting child's retelling, 118
    see also Stories entries
Reality principle, 36, 38
Real-life modeling, generalizing parent
    training to home interaction, 185
Reciprocal interactions, young children,
    113, 114
Recordkeeping, skills-oriented contin-
    gency programs, 62
    positive behavior scale, example, 63
Reframing, 6
Reinforcement, 71, 72, 100–102
    tangible versus social, 72–76
Rejection, fantasy practice, sample situa-
    tions, 275
Relaxation skills, 29, 38
    increasing parents' psychological com-
        petence, 192
    stories, sample, 266, 267
Religious organizations, 226, 229, 230
Reprimands, skills-oriented contingency
    programs, 77, 78
Research questions, 236–252
    competence-promoting culture, 250–
        252
    dilution effects, 249, 250, 252
    matrix summarized, 237, 238
    methods axis, 245–252
    multiskills, 252
    preventive intervention, outcome
        studies, 250
    skills axis, 238–245
Rewarding procedure, skills-oriented
    contingency programs, 70
Rickel, A. U., 221
Risk preference, 168
Role models, importance of, 41

Role playing
  adolescents and older individuals,
      167, 168
  older grade-school children, 143, 156,
      157
  parent training, 182

Sarason, B. R., 219, 220
Sarason, I. G., 219, 220
Scavenger hunt, 142, 147, 246
School
  assignments, preventive mental
      health, 225, 228
  versus home problems, skills-oriented
      contingency programs, 81
Scientific manner, skills axis in di-
      agnosis, 46, 47
Self-assertion, 8, 9
Self-esteem, 174
Self-motivation as skill, 49, 50
Self-nurturing skills, 30
  exercises, 285, 286
Senoi Tribe, Malaysia, 162
Separation skills, 28, 31, 188
  fantasy practice, sample situations,
      275
  modeling plays, sample, 270, 271
Sex experiences, telling about, young
      children, 112, 113
Sexuality, 7, 8, 36
Shaping game, 142, 147–151, 182, 190,
      247
Siblings, generalizing parent training to
      home interaction, 184, 185
Single-task psychotherapy, alternative to
      competence orientation, 14–16
Situational theories/approaches, 13, 14,
      106
Situations game, 143, 152–155, 246
Skill deficits in parents, training, 193,
      194
Skillfulness of pattern, research ques-
      tions, 239–241
Skill patterns use extent, research ques-
      tions, 241
Skill profiles, prevalence and correlates
      of, research questions, 241, 242
Skills axis, 3, 9, 10, 26–44
  contracted version, 42, 43
  as guide for differential action, 106
  helping, centrality of, 43, 44
  length, 41, 42

major goups, 26–41
  and development, 27
  listed, 28, 29
  research questions, 238–245
    completeness versus redundancy,
        243
    groups and organizations, 244
  see also Matrix, skills × methods
Skills axis in diagnosis, 21–26, 45–59
  ability versus motivation, 49, 50
  advantages over DSM-III, 23, 26
  assertiveness, 54
  defining skillful response, 56–58
  families, 54–56
  fantasy repertoire, 50, 51
  gathering information, 47–49
    interviewing techniques, 48, 49
  questionnaire information, psycholog-
      ical skills, 51–54
  scientific manner, 46, 47
  skills sufficiencies, 54, 55
  symptoms, relation to skill deficienc-
      ies, 58, 59
  verbal ability, 53
Skills-oriented contingency programs,
      60–81
  abstraction ladder, positive examples
      from, 62–64
    sample, 65
  baseline observations, 64, 66
  checklist, 78, 79
  fading versus continuing, 80, 81
  feedback and review, 69, 70
  monitoring and rewarding pro-
      cedures, 70
  nontraditional aspects, 71–76
    global ratings versus frequency
        counts, 72
    reinforcement priorities, 71, 72
    reinforcement, tangible versus so-
        cial, 72–76
  parents
    helping recognizing trigger situa-
        tions, 67, 68
    level of demands on, 70, 71
    preparing for reinforcement, 66,
        67, 92
  parents, reinforcement, 78, 80
    telephone, 80
  recordkeeping, 62
    positive behavior scale, example, 63
  school versus home problems, 81
  target skills, choosing, 61, 62

Skills-oriented contingency programs
(continued)
undesirable behavior, dealing with,
76–78
Skills, recognition in schools, preventive
mental health, 226, 228, 229
Skills × methods matrix. See Matrix,
skills × method
Skinner, B. F., 148
Social contact, initiating, fantasy practice, sample situations, 274
Social conversation
fantasy practice, sample situations,
274
increasing parents' psychological competences, 188
stories, sample, 257–259
Social skills training, 95, 202
film, 87, 88
Socioeconomic status, 138, 139, 194
preventive programs, 217
Spontaneous conversation, reinforcement in, young children, 111,
134–136
Stanford–Binet Test, 195
Stimulus situations, controlling,
methods axis, 95–97
Stories, 4, 5, 9
mutual, 8
older children
invention, 143
mailing, 146
preventive mental health, 225, 226
writing, 226, 228
reading/telling
adolescents and older individuals,
157–160
older children, 142–146
practice for parents, 180
for young children
constructing, 111, 123, 124
eliciting, 111, 122, 123
master file, 114–116
reading, 111, 114–118
Stories, sample, 255–268
assertiveness, 261
bossiness, 261, 262
compliance, 264, 265
conflict resolution, 260
disapproval, teasing, criticism, 259,
260
frustration tolerance, 262
honesty, 265, 266

kindness, 264
mistakes/failures, 262–264
nurturing, 256, 257
relaxation, 266, 267
social conversation, 257–259
thinking before acting, 267, 268
trusting and depending, 255, 256
Strang, J., 201
Stress management, 40
Submission, fantasy practice, sample
situations, 276
Suicidal impulses, 200–202
Summary suggestions, parents, 253, 254
Symptom-cluster-based diagnoses, 21,
22, 242, 244
Symptoms, relation to skill deficiencies,
58, 59

Talking, Feeling, and Doing Game
(Gardner), 154
Target groups, preventive mental
health, 223, 224
Target skills, choosing, skills-oriented
contingency programs, 61, 62
Taylor, E., 202
Teacher-mediated interventions, preventive mental health, 225–227
Teasing and criticism, sample stories,
259, 260
Techniques. See Methods axis
Techniques for adolescents and older
individuals, 141–143, 157–168
conversation, models in, 158–160
dreams, revision in waking fantasy,
162, 163
hypnosis and guided imagery, 160–
162
inner guide, 164, 247, 280–283
role playing and psychodrama, 167,
168
storyreading/storytelling, 157–160
abstraction ladder, 157
positive models, 157, 158
therapist, relationship with, discussion, 165–167
walking person through positive rehearsal in fantasy, 164, 165
Techniques for older (grade-school age)
children, 141–157
celebrating/enacting real-life positive
examples, 142, 146, 147
dramatic play and role-playing, 143,
156, 157

modeling plays, 142, 146
picture–story game, 143, 155, 156
prisoner's dilemma game, 143, 151,
152
scavenger hunt, 142, 147
shaping game, 142, 147–151
fantasy vignette, 149, 150
situations game, 143, 152–155
acting out, 154
use by family members, 154
story reading, 142–146
Techniques for young children, 107–
140
abstraction ladder, moving down, using fantasy, 108, 109
chatting, positive, 111–114
contaminating child's fantasies, 110
fantasy models, 111, 134–136
imaginal rehearsal, 111, 134–136
literature on dramatic play and story
reading, 136–140
fantasy orientation, 138
socioeconomic status, 138, 139
modeling plays, performing, 111,
118–120
modeling stories, reading, 111, 114–
118
plays, 111
creating, 111, 120
performing, 118–120, 124–134
spontaneous conversation, reinforcement in, 111, 134–136
stories
constructing for child, 111, 123,
124
eliciting, 111, 122, 123
therapist sessions as ground for parent sessions, 109
tracking and describing, 111, 121,
122
versatile vehicle concept, 110, 111
Telephone reinforcement for parents,
80
Television violence, 230, 231
Therapist
relationship with, discussion, adolescents and older individuals, 165–
167
sessions as ground for parent sessions, young children, 109
Therapy, insight-oriented, 6, 83, 166
Thinking before acting, stories, sample,
267, 268

Time management, increasing parents'
psychological competence, 192,
193
Time-out punishment, skills-oriented
contingency programs, 77
Timing and reinforcement contingencies, methods axis, 100
Tolerance skills, 33
Toleration of child's behavior, increasing parents' psychological competences, 190
Tones of Approval and Disapproval Exercises, 113, 174, 175, 183, 190
Tracking and describing, 111, 121, 122,
173, 179
Training parents and others, 169–198
checklist, 173
individual parent–child session as
vehicle, 171, 172
literature, 194–198
performance monitoring, 182–184
preventive mental health, 225, 226
promoting generalization to home interaction, 184–186
psychological competence, increasing
in parents, 186–193
research questions, 244, 245, 247,
248
skill deficits in parents, 193, 194
steps/exercises, 172–184
see also Parent(s) entries
Transference, 165
Trigger situations, helping parents recognize, 67, 68
Trusting and relationship-building
skills, 27, 28, 30, 31
Trustworthiness
assessing, increasing parents' psychological competences, 186, 187
fantasy practice, sample situations,
273
stories, sample, 255, 256

Undesirable behavior
parent training, 181, 182
responding to, dramatic play, jointly
created, 126, 127
skills-oriented contingency programs,
76–78
upward blip in extinction curve, 133,
134, 247
University of Rochester, Primary Mental Health Project, 218

Use extent skill patterns, research questions, 241

Verbal skills, 29, 38–40, 53
Versatile vehicles, 164, 167, 171, 207
  research questions, 246
  techniques for young children, 110, 111
Videotapes, 172, 173
  generalizing parent training to home interaction, 183, 185
  methods axis, instruction on, 92
  skills-oriented contingency programs, 67, 92

Violence
  responding to, dramatic play, 126, 127
  television, 230, 231

Walking person through positive rehearsal in fantasy, techniques for adolescents and older individuals, 164, 165
What-to-do, compare with how-to-think, 58
Winning/losing, modeling plays, sample, 272
Work in progress, preventive mental health, 225–231